D1739315

Sustainable Development in Crisis Conditions

Sustainable Development in Crisis Conditions

Challenges of War, Terrorism, and Civil Disorder

Phillip J. Cooper and Claudia María Vargas

ROWMAN & LITTLEFIELD PUBLISHERS, INC.
Lanham • Boulder • New York • Toronto • Plymouth, UK

ROWMAN & LITTLEFIELD PUBLISHERS, INC.

Published in the United States of America
by Rowman & Littlefield Publishers, Inc.
A wholly owned subsidiary of The Rowman & Littlefield Publishing Group, Inc.
4501 Forbes Boulevard, Suite 200, Lanham, Maryland 20706
www.rowmanlittlefield.com

Estover Road, Plymouth PL6 7PY, United Kingdom

British Library Cataloguing in Publication Information Available

Library of Congress Cataloging-in-Publication Data
Cooper, Phillip J.
  Sustainable development in crisis conditions : challenges of war, terrorism, and
civil disorder / Phillip J. Cooper and Claudia María Vargas.
      p. cm.
  Includes bibliographical references and index.
  ISBN-13: 978-0-7425-3132-1 (cloth : alk. paper)
  ISBN-10: 0-7425-3132-5 (cloth : alk. paper)
  ISBN-13: 978-0-7425-3133-8 (pbk. : alk. paper)
  ISBN-10: 0-7425-3133-3 (pbk. : alk. paper)
  1. Sustainable development. 2. War—Environmental aspects. I. Vargas, Claudia
María. II. Title.
  HC79.E5C6548 2008
  338.9'27—dc22

                                                                      2007025396

Printed in the United States of America

♾™ The paper used in this publication meets the minimum requirements of
American National Standard for Information Sciences—Permanence of Paper
for Printed Library Materials, ANSI/NISO Z39.48-1992.

For Rosen. May you and your generation dedicate yourselves to a life in a world in which there will be no need for knowledge of the subject matter of this book.

Contents

Preface

In times of great crisis, in which thousands die and many more lose their families and financial support, it is difficult to contemplate a future. In the midst of war, when survival is a full-time job, it seems absurd to speak of what is to happen after the battle. Yet, for many countries around the world, including the United States after September 11, 2001, it is necessary to think about the challenges of implementing sustainable development in the wake of war, terrorist attack, or civil disorder. That challenge is the focus, though September 11 is not the origin, of this book.

While, for many Americans, the questions of how to respond and what kind of future to imagine may seem a relatively recent dilemma, it has, unfortunately, been an ongoing challenge for millions of people in many countries in recent decades. This book began long before the recent events in the United States, Iraq, Afghanistan, or the Balkans. Indeed it can be traced to a research project more than twenty-five years ago, concerning the postwar redevelopment of Japan after World War II. The more proximate cause was a UN project on the implementation of the Rio Earth Summit commitments in Asia and the Pacific Rim. In selecting six nations for the study, we chose Sri Lanka precisely to learn how a country that had been engaged in a civil war for well over a decade contemplated its future.

Interviews with various Sri Lankan ministers indicated that, while virtually everyone agreed that the question of how to undertake sustainable development after hostilities was critical, there had not even been any discussions on the subject. We found the lack of attention to this subject surprising in light of the fact that the country's environment had been savaged, its economy was in shambles, and its people were living in unsafe and unhealthy conditions, even in the capital city some distance from the fighting centered in the Jaffna Peninsula and in the eastern part of the country. The nation's budget was largely dependent upon various kinds of international assistance. Important watershed areas had been cut and blocked in various ways by roads built by the security forces. In some areas, the water situation was so bad that elephants were beginning to confront local residents at water tanks, since they could not travel their usual routes to find water. Palmyra trees and other vegetation had been cut down, either to carve out military access roads or to build fortifications. The government had been so consumed with its battle with the Tamil Tigers that it had been unable to address the fact that much of the country had little or no sewage treatment. Even in the capital city, so much raw sewage entered the waterways that a lake in the center of Colombo was essentially a cesspool that reeked in the hot sun. It became apparent that Sri Lankans had a variety of ideas about sustainable development, but there had been little effort to link those ideas to the conflict, its resolution, and what would come next.

After that, we began to pay attention. We learned two important lessons. First, there had been little serious study of sustainable development following war, terrorism, and civil disorder. The discussions in Sri Lanka came after the 1991 Gulf War, in which the term *environmental warfare* gained notoriety, largely in the aftermath of the Iraqi decision to blow up oil fields. Even so, the focus remained mostly on the warfare rather than what was to come next. The good news is that the United Nations Environment Programme (UNEP) and UN Habitat published a report on the environmental consequences of the Kosovo conflict prepared by the Balkans Task Force (BTF). The Kosovo report considered some impacts on human settlements, particularly with respect to housing issues. Another report was prepared by the BTF with respect to Albania. While important contributions, these reports were relatively narrowly focused and technical in character. Such work was essential and welcome, but a wider lens was also needed.

Second, there is an ongoing need to undertake such studies from a broad-based and integrative perspective. While destruction of the environment has been a factor in warfare for a long time, it has become more important as general pressures on the environment have intensified in the contemporary era. In addition, it has become increasingly common to target civilians and even international aid workers, as in Afghanistan. Rape and genocide, euphemistically known as ethnic cleansing, have become common in such places as Bosnia, Kosovo, Rwanda, and Darfur. These behaviors have driven large numbers of refugees into flight.

Hence, the three part living triangle that is the core of sustainable development is critical to nations and communities seeking to move forward after these traumatic events. Environmental concerns, economic development, and social development are critical factors. The events in New York and Washington are among the exemplars of this kind of challenge closer to home.

This book is a preliminary exploration of this complex subject. It focuses on the types of challenges that arise for those contemplating a way forward in the wake of war, terrorism, or civil disorder. The critical message that emerges from this study is that the tendency to view post-conflict action from post-World War II driven conceptions of reconstruction or redevelopment, or from the more recent nation-building perspective, is inadequate and inappropriate to most of the contemporary post-conflict situations that really require a sustainable development approach.

Acknowledgments

This book, along with the *Implementing Sustainable Development* volume that preceded it, has developed over such a lengthy period that it is impossible to thank everyone who has contributed in one way or another. The research in this two-volume project has involved work in many countries, with officials from so many more at conferences and workshops, and with international institutions and NGOs. That is in addition to the research in the United States in a range of states and cities where so many other people have provided their experiences.

Then there were the researchers, often members of the international civil service and government agencies, who have labored diligently over many years to produce the truly significant work that appears in the form of institutional reports, both international and domestic, that too often goes unread by academic researchers, but that sometimes is not only seen, but felt in public policy. What we said in the earlier volume bears repeating here. Whether it is the reports of the United Nations conferences or those generated by the U.S. General Accounting Office, these documents represent excellent data sources, careful research, creative syntheses, and effective explanations.

We also noted in the previous book that a number of people and groups have been particularly helpful and we are grateful to them for their good efforts and from the lessons that we learned in working with them. Among these are the units of the United Nations Department of Economic and Social Affairs, including the Division for Sustainable Development, the Division for Social Development, and the Division of Public Administration and Development Management. It has been our privilege to interact with members of these organizations and the work they have produced over the years.

We have taught the sustainable development implementation course at Portland State University together and have for the past three years presented that seminar with a post-conflict emphasis. We are grateful for the thoughtful discussions our students provided as we worked through the development of this book.

We owe a particular debt to a number of people who have made important contributions to the previous volume, but to this one in particular. They include Frances McQueen, Mahshid Esfandiari, and the survivors of torture attended at and the staff of the Vancouver Association for Survivors of Torture. We are very grateful to Lucila Spigelblatt, Afarin Beglari, Shukria Samantar, and Huong Thai. We are indebted to Dr. Carol Locust for enlightening us on the subject of post-colonialization trauma. Our continued appreciation goes to Mary DeFeo for her lucid mind and loving heart. You continue to inspire with your youthful heart and grand spirit even at this age.

Brian Romer and his colleagues at Rowman & Littlefield have been helpful and patient along the way. In the time since this project began more conflicts have evolved than anyone would have anticipated, including the dramatic changes that have been wrought by the attacks of September 11, 2001. These developments, and the increasingly complex state of the world in recent years meant that this volume took much longer to complete than we had anticipated. Thanks, too, to Erica Nikolaidis for her good efforts as production editor on the project.

Of course, none of the fine people or organizations acknowledged above bear any responsibility for any errors in the book.

Phillip J. Cooper and Claudia María Vargas
Portland, Oregon

1

War, Terror, and Civil Disorder in Today's World

War, violent civil disorder, and terrorism are the antithesis of sustainable development.[1] If by sustainable development we mean attention to environmental protection, social development, and economic development such that choices made to meet the needs of society today will not "compromis[e] the ability of future generations to meet their own needs,"[2] then these three sad, violent, and all too common facts of modern life are clearly challenges to the many commitments that have been made over the past quarter century as part of the international common commitments and programs of action. Indeed, Principle 24 of the Rio Declaration, issued at the United Nations Conference on Environment and Development (better known as the Rio Earth Summit), asserted that "Warfare is inherently destructive of sustainable development."[3] It takes countless lives, ravages the environment, and destroys economies. Yet, the plague of war has been with humankind throughout history and shows no signs of ending. In fact, some estimates indicate that more than fifty countries were involved in armed conflict of some sort in 2002 (though more recent estimates discussed later in the chapter suggest that the number has declined sharply since then).[4]

Of course, wars are generally and formally understood as conflicts among sovereign states. And while there continue to be nation-state conflicts, there are many more civil wars as well as regional or ethnic clashes within nations that are not technically recognized as wars.[5] Then there is the rise of international terrorism that respects no borders and operates in otherwise peaceful societies. Many of these forms of conflict observe no rules of war and target civilians and natural resources as readily as they do enemy combatants. However conducted, they leave in their wake conditions that can only be described as sustainable development nightmares. "Civil wars are not temporary glitches in an otherwise smooth development path—the direct and indirect costs during the conflict are typically so high that even when post-conflict progress is dramatic and sustained, it will take countries a generation or more just to return to prewar conditions."[6]

This book is about the effort to respond to war, terrorism, and civil disorder with a sustainable development approach that addresses all three elements of the living triangle, including environmental protection, social development, and economic development. It concerns the application of the international common commitments for sustainable development to the aftermath of war, civil disorder, and terrorism. This is not a normative argument about theories of terrorism, just war, or Lockean arguments about the legitimacy of rebellion by oppressed people against tyrannical regimes.[7] Rather, it is a study in public policy and public administration that seeks to understand the challenges faced by those who seek to move conflict-ridden communities toward sustainable development.

Iraq is not the first arena in which this challenge has been presented. Neither were Afghanistan, or, for that matter, Vietnam. There have been many nations, regions within nations, and even individual cities within developed countries that have faced the challenges of life after conflict, usually without the kind of international attention and assistance provided in international conflicts.

While, for some readers, this challenge of national or even regional response to violent conflict of all types may seem a recent development, it certainly did not begin with the attack on the World Trade Center in New York on September 11, 2001, the attack in Afghanistan that came in response to it, or the 2003 invasion of Iraq. Neither is it only a matter for developing countries. One need not reach far back in time to recall the riots in Los Angeles and the politicians who flocked to the scene in the aftermath of those events, promising action to address the damage and the stresses that may have been important causal factors. Well before that, there were the urban riots of the 1960s and 1970s in places like Watts, Newark, Detroit, and Chicago. A century before those events, of course, there was the massive destruction and loss of life left in the aftermath of the Civil War. All of this is to say nothing of the devastation that came from repeated attacks over decades, not only on Native Americans themselves but also on the environments in which they lived, conducted in an effort to make it impossible for tribal peoples to exist in ecosystems that had supported their lives and cultures for centuries.[8]

What was once referred to simply as postwar recovery has become far more complex in a world in which there are so many types of violence and disorder with such dramatic scope and intensity. Indeed, it is the thesis of this volume that it is no longer enough to speak in terms of recovery, reconstruction, redevelopment, or nation building, but it is critical to think seriously and carefully about sustainable development in the wake of war, terrorism, or civil disorder.

Before plunging into the special challenges posed by conflict situations, it is important to note that this book is a companion volume to a book entitled *Implementing Sustainable Development: From Global Policy to Local Action* and takes as a foundation a number of the key premises established in that book.[9] Specifically, it draws on the principles of sustainable development articulated in the international common commitments and utilizes the "feasibility framework," a conceptual map presented in chapter 1 of that volume. A brief introduction to these foundations is essential and is provided in the next section.

THE FOUNDATIONS FOR POST-CONFLICT SUSTAINABLE DEVELOPMENT

In 1987, the World Commission on Environment and Development produced its seminal report entitled *Our Common Future*. Commonly known as the Brundtland Commission after its chairperson, Dr. Gro Harlem Brundtland, the report defined the challenge in clear and direct terms: "Humanity has the ability to make development sustainable—to ensure that it meets the needs of the present without compromising the ability of future generations to meet their own needs."[10] The commission went beyond the contemporary debate about issues of the environment and economic development to emphasize that sustainable development could only exist if the focus of effort was the living triangle, a balance among environmental protection, social development, and economic development. Environmental protection is critical and necessary, but not sufficient to ensure future generations the options required for meeting their own needs central to sustainable development. That said, the global community would not be able to rely upon economic growth alone to reach a sustainable world either. Indeed, economic development to this point in history, as the Brundtland Commission explained, has brought large scale environmental destruction along with its more positive contributions. At the same time, the majority of the world's population living in developing nations desperately needs and has demanded the right to develop and produce for their families the kinds of lifestyles that residents in the most developed countries have taken for granted. The piece that had largely been missing from debates at all levels about environment and development, the Brundtland Commission insisted, was the social dimension. Unless issues of illiteracy, grinding poverty, widespread preventable diseases, growing inequality, and a host of other considerations were addressed, there would be neither acceptable levels of economic development nor environmental protection and conservation. Even the World Bank, an international institution committed to economic growth as the engine of progress, has recognized that reality.[11] The effort to move toward sustainable development is a continuing attempt to balance the three elements of the living triangle and remains a critical ongoing challenge.

In the years since the Brundtland report, the global community has undertaken a series of actions to articulate critical principles of sustainable development, establish common commitments and action plans to advance those principles, and set goals against which to evaluate progress.

Principles of Sustainable Development

Throughout the decade of the 1990s, from the Rio Earth Summit through the Johannesburg conference of 2002, most of the nations of the world assembled in a set of conferences to translate the broad concept of sustainable development into a full agenda of commitments and programs of action. Unlike many international meetings, these sessions employed a common language and developed a consistent set of principles that flowed throughout the discussions explored at some length in the *Implementing Sustainable Development* volume.[12] It is important to understand the basic principles and the guiding questions developed to apply them.

The Change Principle is based on the clear evidence that contemporary patterns of development and even of day-to-day living are not sustainable along any of the three dimensions, particularly for groups who have historically been vulnerable to discrimination and mistreatment. One of the key factors that renders current patterns of life unsustainable is the continuing pestilence of war and other forms of armed conflict.[13] There are two questions to be asked with respect to this principle. First, is the community addressing existing unsustainable conditions? Second, is a proposed action a change in the direction of a more sustainable future?

The Environmental Protection Principle asserts that sustainable development requires serious attention to the conservation and management of natural resources (the so-called Green Agenda) and a dedicated effort with respect to pollution control and cleanup (often known as the Brown Agenda). Despite decades of political rhetoric and some progress, the global environmental situation continues to deteriorate. Therefore, it is essential to ask in any given situation whether a proposed action will preserve environmental quality and resources to the greatest extent possible. Second, do plans and decision processes restore environmentally damaged areas to an ecologically viable condition and render them useful places in terms of economic and social development?

The Principle of Balance and Integration insists that one of the keys to a sustainable future is to ensure that all three elements of the living triangle are considered in decision making and that efforts are made to avoid a medium-by-medium, sector-by-sector, and group-by-group approach to problem solving and planning. This is one of the most difficult challenges in sustainable development, since economic interests, sociopolitical interest groups, and scientific and technical experts have vested interests in maintaining their limited perspectives and demands for attention and resources. Few are readily amenable to the need to address the kinds of trade-offs essential to sustainable development without careful mediation or, in some cases, the judicious application of political power to encourage balanced and integrated action. The two questions presented by this principle are: Is a planned action based upon consideration of environmental protection, social development, and economic development as compared to only one or two of these dimensions? Second, were trade-offs among these competing priorities consciously and carefully balanced?

The controversial Principle of Human-Centered Development holds that sustainable development must focus on people, both because those who suffer in poverty and unsafe and unhealthy conditions have a right to development and because humans pose both the greatest threat to the ecosystem and the hope for improvement. Armed conflict is the antithesis of sustainable development in large part because it destroys the environment, threatens human life and health, and deprives countless people of a decent standard of living. It is an ongoing demonstration of the reality that humankind has the ability not only to destroy itself as a species but also to destroy the environment and the ecosystems it supports. Thus, while many critics challenge this principle as the ultimate conceit of human beings by which we set ourselves up over all other creatures and species in the world, the nations of the world have answered that this principle merely recognizes a set of fundamental realities, however harsh they may be. The question presented by this principle is whether the specific impacts of a planned action on the affected community have been considered.

The Principle of a Right to Development, but with an Obligation of Mutual Respect—sometimes known as the transboundary obligation—obliges nations and communities not to confuse the human-centered development principle with the arrogant and egocentric idea that communities need focus only on their own interests without regard for others. While the Rio Declaration repeated the principle from Stockholm that nations have a right "to exploit their own resources pursuant to their own environmental and developmental policies," it added the requirement that they have a "responsibility to ensure that activities within their jurisdiction or control do not cause damage to the environment or other States or areas beyond the

limits of national jurisdiction."[14] This principle requires decision makers to
ask: To what degree are contemplated actions likely to interfere with the
right of another jurisdiction to social and economic development? In implementing development policies, have the potential impacts on other jurisdictions been fully considered? If there are likely transboundary issues,
have the other jurisdictions been notified and consulted?

The Intergenerational and Intragenerational Equity Principle demands
that current decision makers meet "the needs of the present without compromising the ability of future generations to meet their own needs"[15] (the
intergenerational equity dimension) and also consider the distribution of
costs among different groups within the current generation, particularly
vulnerable groups who have faced discrimination or particular burdens in
the past (the intragenerational dimension). There are three critical questions with respect to this principle. First, has the decision calculus for a
pending action seriously considered the costs to future generations in terms
of limited choices? Has the decision process contemplated whether the
pending decision will impose increased liabilities on future generations? Finally, does a pending action threaten to fall with unfair weight upon disad-
vantaged groups such as women, ethnocultural minorities, indigenous persons, or those with disabilities?

The Equality Principle is separate from the intergenerational and intragenerational equity principle and requires that all persons are to be valued
without regard to their race, gender, religion, cultural heritage, physical condition, or age. It demands that decision makers remove barriers to personal
and social development (the nondiscrimination principle) and requires
regimes to ensure opportunities for full participation of all groups in the society, the economy, and the political process (the participation principle). Is
the contemplated action truly nondiscriminatory? Second, does it provide
meaningful opportunities for participation and does it seek to build capacity for participation by those previously excluded?

The Decentralization Principle calls for ensuring a focus on the local
level, the point of action and impact, in decision making that engages the
communities and governing units at that level. It presents two obvious concerns. First, does the planned action actually involve the local jurisdiction
affected? Second, are the local governments afforded serious opportunities
for involvement in the decision process, including funding?

The Partnership Principle calls upon decision makers to make certain that
sustainable development efforts make use of partnerships among governmental and nongovernmental nonprofit and for-profit organizations, with
an appreciation for the importance of partnerships, but also with an awareness of what they entail and what is required to make them successful. No
one sector or level of society can achieve sustainable development alone. As
the Johannesburg conference put it, "[S]uch partnerships are key to pursuing

sustainable development in a globalizing world."[16] Here again there are two guiding questions. Does a planned action contemplate the development and utilization of collaborative relationships as opposed to single-unit responsibility for action? If partnerships are considered, has serious attention been paid to the actual design and management of the relationships in question?

The Transparency and Accountability Principle holds that "democracy and transparent and accountable governance and administration in all sectors of society are indispensable foundations for the realization of social and people-centred sustainable development."[17] There is no small irony in the fact that transparency has become a far more complex subject than it was before. Similarly, in times of war or other conflict, it is more difficult to ensure accountability, since the nature of the situation tends to encourage an ends-justify-the-means mentality. This principle presents two questions. What mechanisms are included in a planned action to ensure transparency? What forms of accountability, political, legal, or fiscal, have been built into the planned action?

The Family Principle requires that sustainable development policies "[r]ecognize the family as the basic unit of society, and acknowledge that it plays a key role in social development and as such should be strengthened, with attention to the rights, capabilities and responsibilities of its members."[18] That said, in an era of culture wars and civil conflict, it is essential to note that the international accords recognize that: "In different cultural, political and social systems various forms of family exist. It is entitled to receive comprehensive protection and support."[19] With that in mind, the family principle presents two basic questions. Has the proposed action been considered in terms of its impact on families? Is any such consideration of the family sensitive to different cultural conceptions of the family unit and its lifestyle?

The Livable Community Principle requires a commitment to foster "those spatial, social and environmental characteristics and qualities that uniquely contribute to people's sense of personal and collective well-being and to their sense of satisfaction in being the residents of that particular settlement."[20] These extend from the need for a decent dwelling place to concern with the special needs of communities such as those that result from rural or urban contexts, and a recognition of the interconnectedness of different types of communities. It consists of both the objective component, including such obvious qualities as environmental quality, health care, education, and economic development, as well as the subjective elements, including such matters as cultural factors, ways of life, or linguistic elements. First, is the planned action likely to improve the livability of the community as judged by the people who live there? Second, what is the objective evidence as to the impact of a proposal or a comprehensive plan on the quality of life in the community?

The Education Principle requires a commitment to the requirement that: "Everyone has the right to education, which shall be directed to the full development of human resources, and human dignity and potential, with particular attention to women and the girl-child."[21] It is also grounded in the judgment that a society will not be equipped to ensure a sustainable future if its members lack the opportunity to meet the full range of their education needs throughout their lives. Education in this sense is not limited to formal classroom instruction or to elementary, secondary, or postsecondary schooling. It also requires that generations of indigenous knowledge not only be preserved, but that they be passed on, given the evidence that many indigenous societies have demonstrated their abilities to live sustainably. This principle presents three important questions. Is the educational infrastructure sufficient to provide the foundation in the affected community for understanding of, participation in, and evaluation of the proposed actions? Second, is there educational support associated with the effort not merely for primary and secondary education for children but for the full range of lifelong learning experiences required for sustainable development? Finally, for any given policy, have the specific educational requirements been assessed and the services provided?

The Health and Wellness Principle assumes that people will not be able to pursue sustainable development unless the society is committed to "promoting and attaining . . . the highest attainable standard of physical and mental health, and the access of all to primary health care. . . ."[22] The lack of assurance of health undermines the ability to pursue a "productive life, in harmony with nature."[23] At the same time, a polluted environment and unsustainable economic development often lead to serious health problems, often afflicting the most vulnerable in the society.[24] For these reasons, the Johannesburg agreements obligate the signatory states to: "Deliver basic health services for all and reduce environmental health threats, taking into account the special needs of children and the linkages between poverty, health and environment, with provision of financial resources, technical assistance and knowledge transfer to developing countries and countries with economies in transition."[25] As a result, the health and wellness principle calls for decision makers to consider two questions. First, does the proposed course of action have health care impacts? Second, do inequalities in health care access or quality of care affect the ability of community members to participate in or benefit from the planned action?

The Poverty Eradication Principle requires that conditions of poverty be addressed because they often lead to disease or injury, undermine economic development, and may exacerbate environmental damage.[26] Thus it is important to ask to what extent and in what way does a planned action affect the poorest members of the community?

The Culture Sensitivity Principle acknowledges that cultural factors play a critical—in some cases even a predominant—role in the way that policies and plans are developed and implemented. They therefore should be considered by decision makers as significant elements in proposed actions. This principle poses two questions. Are proposed actions culturally appropriate for the context in which they are implemented and can they be revised to make them more appropriate and consistent with the common commitments? Can developed countries, in implementing their own policies, learn lessons from indigenous cultures or others who have lived with a better long-term balance, in sustainable development terms?

The Scope, Scale, and Wealth Principle requires that wealthy nations have a special obligation to help less-developed nations, in no small part because the developed countries have often behaved in extremely unsustainable ways in the past with resulting damage to what are now less-developed countries. The historic operation of extractive industries often left a great deal of environmental damage, as well as removing valuable natural resources with little or no meaningful compensation to the country involved. Additionally, the conduct of business and sometimes official and at other times de facto colonial dominion, as well as more contemporary globalized business practices, have often taken a human toll. Indeed, the Rio Declaration requires in Principle 7 that: "In view of the different contributions to global environmental degradation, States have common but differential responsibilities. The developed countries acknowledge the responsibility that they bear. . . ."[27] As a result, the developed countries accepted a special obligation for assisting developing countries. While few have followed through with the promised financial assistance, the principle still requires that the differential obligations for sustainable development are to be considered in any given decision-making process. In the case of warfare, the belligerents incur particular obligations under existing treaties.

From the vantage point of the group planning the effort under consideration, are there sufficient resources available within the jurisdiction or will outside assistance be required? To funding organizations, in addition to the merits of the proposal, the inquiry is whether the jurisdiction involved has a special claim on resources because (a) of the obligation to assist those less well off or because (b) the community has suffered from damaging behavior from others in the past.

The Market Principle is another of the controversial precepts of sustainable development, since it accepted that free trade, deregulation, and other market-based policy tools were essential to the effort. Trade liberalization and other obligations pressed by donor nations and international institutions like the World Bank and the International Monetary Fund (IMF) have also brought serious problems for many countries. Therefore, the Johannesburg

Declaration warned that: "The rapid integration of markets, mobility of capital and significant increases in investment flows around the world have opened new challenges and opportunities for the pursuit of sustainable development. But the benefits and costs of globalization are unevenly distributed, with developing countries facing special difficulties in meeting this challenge."[28] Even so, the principle recognizes the need to harness the power of the marketplace in the search of sustainable development. This principle presents two questions. The first question is whether market forces offer tools useful to the goals of a particular policy in a particular cultural context. Second, how can those devices fit together with the other principles and with the social and environmental aspects of sustainable development?

The Rule of Law Principle insists that sustainable development is not possible without stable, just, and equitable systems of law, as well as equitable systems of liability and compensation for legal violations. Central to the purposes of the current study are the recognition by the nations involved in the commitments that war and civil disorder are in many respects the antithesis of sustainable development, and the agreement therefore to work toward more effective and frequent use of the rule of law to resolve disputes among and within countries.[29] When evaluating a program or project proposed for sustainable development, it is important to consider whether it provides adequate mechanisms for dispute resolution and, if necessary, legal accountability in a credible forum according to legitimate principles.

There is, then, a body of principles with criteria for application that help to define and operationalize the concept of sustainable development. As with any complex concept or framework, there are multiple challenges in its use in any given situation. To assist decision makers in such settings, the previous volume explained the use of a feasibility framework, drawn from research involving a wide range of countries and contexts.

The Feasibility Framework

The *Implementing Sustainable Development* volume employed the feasibility framework to assist in understanding the challenges of policy implementation in particular, but it serves a wider use in assisting decision makers and scholars in assessing their decision environment in any given situation. It is based on a series of questions developed out of a research process presented in the earlier volume.

First, is the effort in question technically feasible? That is, do we have the technical knowledge and skills to address it and, if not, can we acquire them in a timely manner in order to address the challenge at hand? The technology must be appropriate, which means that it must be consistent with sustainable development principles and culturally appropriate.[30]

Second, is a planned course of action legally feasible? That is, do we have the authority to do what we need to do to implement the policy? Furthermore, how do we fashion our implementation efforts such that they do not violate legal constraints, from constitutional rights and liberties to constraints posed by other existing legislation or regulations? In contexts where the rule of law is either not adequately developed, or authority is fundamentally illegitimate or has broken down, as may very well be the situation in the aftermath of war, civil disorder, or terrorism, it is often necessary to build the required law and legal institutions and processes needed to operate it in order to meet sustainable development principles.

Third, is there fiscal feasibility for the proposed course of action? It is necessary to determine just how and how much fiscal wherewithal can be brought to bear in any given effort. This may involve a variety of creative financing techniques, involving the public, private nonprofit, for-profit, or international organizations.[31]

Next, is there administrative feasibility? That is, are the necessary organizations, trained people, and management capacity available to implement proposed policies? Sustainable development efforts require organizations that have the infrastructure and people to get the job done.[32] Indeed, as more policy implementation is carried out through networks of governmental, nonprofit, and for-profit organizations, the coordination and governance of networks becomes an increasingly significant challenge.

The next question is whether the planned action is politically feasible. Technical experts may be certain of the right solution to a problem and may even have the fiscal and administrative capacity to implement it, but the action may be unacceptable for political reasons. The opposite problem also arises, in which experts may not agree that any particular effort is needed, but political demands may be such that some action must be taken. If they wish to succeed, decision makers must respond to constraints of political feasibility pressures or take steps to build the political support required to move ahead.[33]

Then there is the question of whether the effort is ethically feasible. In some settings, of course, this question calls for attention to the obvious and destructive problem of corruption. Because normal systems for providing essential goods and services often break down in war, civil conflict, or in the aftermath of terrorism, corruption is a particular challenge in these settings. However, ethical feasibility must often be assessed against a range of standards, from what are termed regime values,[34] to organizational standards, to professional norms, to individual ethical commitments.[35] In some settings, there are cultural dimensions that are involved in understanding what is thought to be corrupt or that stand in the way of eliminating what are more broadly understood to be corrupt practices.[36] Here again post-conflict situations may present special problems, as when a country has operated for years, even decades, under a corrupt regime and the people have incorporated that corruption into their lifestyles in order to survive and provide for their families.

It is also necessary to ask whether a proposed action is culturally feasible, where culture is understood both in its anthropological sense and in terms of organizational culture. Cultural feasibility requires attention to patterns of social relationships, sets of acquired values, dominant religious beliefs, and commonly accepted concepts of authority and legitimacy. Conflict may present special problems with respect to culture, especially where there are contending cultural groups within a given society, such as in Rwanda and Sri Lanka.

Sustainable Development Goals

Of course, commitments and modes of analysis are fine, but action may be quite another matter. Contrary to the picture that has occasionally been presented, the advocates of sustainable development have not been simply a group of idealistic—even utopian—social critics who had the naive belief that all of their expectations would somehow be met in a complex world full of competing demands. In fact, the Brundtland Commission and the Rio Earth Summit were born out of a realization that, notwithstanding all of the grand rhetoric and celebration of the first major global conference on the environment of the contemporary era in Stockholm in 1972, there had been a lack of follow-through and considerable political backsliding, even among nations like the United States that had been in the forefront of the Stockholm effort.[37] As a result, efforts were made in the 1990s to ensure that there would be standards and a way to keep them before the global community in the years ahead.

Thus it was that the Rio Earth Summit produced not merely the Rio Declaration but also Agenda 21. That document developed the sets of commitments and a plan of action for implementation that set the pattern for the other conferences to come in the decade ahead. Each would provide not merely broad principles, but also more specific sets of expectations for action. Indeed, by the time of the Copenhagen social summit in 1995, the standard-setting had become quite specific in setting goals for, among other things, health care and education.[38] *Implementing Sustainable Development* considered those goals in detail. For the present, however, the important point was to create commitments to action plans and goals of which the signatories could be reminded in later years.

In order to ensure that the progress toward the goals was tracked and shortcomings reported, the conferences established agencies or tasked existing international organizations with responsibility for monitoring and analyzing movement toward achievement of the standards. For example, the United Nations Environmental Programme (UNEP) was required to produce state of the environment reports every three years; the United Nations Development Programme (UNDP) was tasked with developing and expanding annual human development reports; and individual divisions of the United Nations Secretariat were created or reorganized to provide research and staff support for the Economic and Social Council (ECOSOC), which would ensure formal attention to the commitments. Interestingly, there were also changes in progress at the World Bank that would conclude that its long-standing focus almost exclusively on markets had not proven adequate to the challenges of sustainable development. The result was a much expanded set of annual human development reports and the undertaking of several related projects such as the Voices of the Poor program and efforts to study the causes and consequences of civil war.[39] Later, the World Bank, UNEP, and UNDP would cooperate along with the World Resources Institute to project a pilot ecosystem assessment, a quite different approach to provide an integrated evaluation of progress and challenges that would later be part of the basis for the Millennium Ecosystem Assessment.

The conferences also set five-year follow-on meetings at which progress or the lack of it would be addressed in a high-level and very visible forum. The fact that Rio Plus-5 and Copenhagen Plus-5 conferences reported serious shortfalls against the action commitments and goals set earlier may have been disappointing, but the process demonstrated that the utility of setting goals, assigning evaluation responsibilities, and ensuring follow-up consideration was far more effective than the usual run of conferences that produced nothing and were promptly ignored in the future.[40]

On the other hand, with the new millennium and the ten-year anniversary of the Rio Earth Summit approaching, efforts were made to update the goals and recommit the global community to attaining them. The Millennium Declaration, issued in 2000, and the Johannesburg commitments and plan of action, in 2002, were the result.[41] These goals sought to remind the developed countries of their earlier commitments, press for more intensive efforts to meet them, and recalibrate the goals in an attempt to provide a basis for ongoing evaluation.

But even as the global community accepted these challenges and moved toward the Johannesburg meeting, the situation had become far more complex. The attack on the United States on September 11, 2001, set in motion a course of action that meant an invasion of Afghanistan. Then the United States determined to invade Iraq as well. The situation in many parts of Africa was seriously troubled, with renewed violence in several quarters, of which the multiple conflicts in the Great Lakes region are perhaps best known. Even as the tenth anniversary of the genocide in Rwanda approached, another genocide was in progress in the Darfur region of the Sudan. Terrorist attacks in several parts of the world drew attention away from sustainable development and placed a variety of countries on a war footing, with resources and policy making far more devoted to arms and security than to the three elements of the living triangle.

A WORLD OF CHALLENGES: THE CONCEPTS AND CHARACTERISTICS OF CONFLICT

There is nothing new about violence in the world. Scholars and policy makers have studied conflict in a host of ways for different purposes, from the Peloponnesian wars to Clausewitz to the latest tracts on the Middle East wars, insurgency, and terrorism. However, not only has the sustainable development literature not adequately addressed the question of what to do after the conflict has ended, but it has not even considered, in a serious way at least, how to think about conflict and its significance for sustainable development beyond the rather broad observation that the two are in opposition. More generally, there is a tendency to fall back on old and outdated models of post-conflict action from the post-World War II era.

As to the first problem, progress toward a sustainable future requires that we consider how better to conceptualize conflict in order to understand its challenges, respond, and move beyond them. To demonstrate just how complex a problem this is, there continues to be considerable disagreement as to just how many wars, civil wars, or terrorist incidents are ongoing at any given moment in time in part because there are so many different ways to conceptualize conflict. For purposes of sustainable development analysis, there are several factors essential to understanding the challenges of conflict. They include: (1) types of conflict; (2) geographic distribution and geopolitical character and consequences of conflict; (3) domestic versus international perspectives; (4) ethnocultural understandings; and (5) temporal and historical views of conflict and its impacts.

Types of Conflict

While the most common ways of referring to conflict break down into war, civil war, insurgency, or terrorism, the picture is more complex than that and the differences can matter in terms of how we understand not only the causes, but the consequences of conflict. Even classic wars—formal conflicts among nations—vary dramatically, from conflicts involving two belligerents to world wars that engulf virtually the entire globe.

It may come as a surprise to those not familiar with the academic literature on international conflict that there continues to be debate as to just how to classify such conflicts and how to count them.[42] "Despite the best efforts by scholars in the field, the empirically based knowledge on the causes, courses, and consequences of interstate conflict is still far from complete. The literature on interstate conflict is both extensive and fragmentary, at the same time."[43] The widely respected Correlates of War (COW 2) project classifies conflicts as Interstate conflicts (which are generally understood to be wars with casualties of at least one thousand people), Intrastate conflicts, and Extrastate conflicts.

To that list is added what are known as Militarized Interstate Disputes (MIDs), defined as "sub-war interstate conflicts that are serious enough to become militarized but which do not produce the requisite numbers of casualties to qualify as a war."[44] Even here, there are difficulties because there are various kinds of behavior counted as MID short of actual armed conflict, such as positioning of forces near volatile borders. Other actions are not counted as MIDs even if they do involve conflict and produce casualties because they do not meet a set of technical criteria about the presence of a system of command and control.[45]

In an era of so-called low-intensity conflicts, where small numbers of special operations forces may be introduced with limited casualties but with significant political or psychological effect, the question of just what we mean by conflict becomes even more elusive. In part this difficulty stems from the fact that the data on conflict are largely classified, collected, and analyzed by international relations scholars who are most often interested in interstate behavior and in the causes of war rather than the kinds of issues that are important to those interested in sustainable development after conflict.

Into this mix, analysts have added an additional type, which is conflict associated with peacekeeping interventions. Michael Bhatia, in fact, speaks of three variations on this theme, which include "peacekeeping, second-generation operations, and peace enforcement."[46]

> A peacekeeping operation's purpose is to facilitate direct contact and cooperation between military officers, particularly on the front lines, to provide a buffer between the combatants, and to monitor this zone and report cease-fire violations. . . . [S]econd-generation operations includes preventive deployment, internal conflict resolution measures, assistance to (interim) civil authority, the protection of humanitarian relief operations, and the guaranteeing and denial of movement. . . . Enforcement and high-intensity operations, sanctions, and embargoes are all envisaged under Chapter VII of the UN Charter. . . . [and] typically [permit] the use of "all necessary means" in order to achieve the given objective.[47]

These operations have been at the heart of some of the most controversial issues about post-conflict action in recent years. Bhatia even goes so far as to argue that, in some instances, peacekeeping operations have been used "as a tool of conflict."[48]

Until 2002, the National Defense Council Foundation published an annual list of international conflicts, at that point showing some fifty-three such conflicts.[49] However, the organization ceased its counting effort late in 2003 because the role of international terrorism had made the process so complex. The COW 2 project reports that there have been twenty-three interstate conflicts from the end of WWII to 1991, and 128 intrastate conflicts from 1946 to 1997.[50] The PRIOS database of the International Peace Research Institute at Upsalla University in Oslo counts 567 armed conflicts of all types and durations between 1946 and 2002, including such clashes as between the United States and al Qaeda.[51] The Stockholm International Peace Institute (SIPRI) has indicated that there were fifty-nine major armed conflicts between 1990 and 2003, and just four of those were considered interstate wars of the classic variety.[52] The SIPRI reports found seventeen major armed conflicts in progress in 2005.[53] As one scholar who sought to make sense of the complex picture put it:

> The use of violence to effect political change is a generalized phenomenon around the world. Singer and Small (1994) put at 137 the number of civil wars that killed at least 1,000 during the period from 1820 to 1990. The death toll from civil wars fought after World War Two has been estimated at a minimum of 16.2 million deaths (Fearon and Laitin 2003). According to the data gathered by Banks (1997), between 1919 and 1997 there were over 500 spells of guerrilla warfare around the world. In the same period of time, close to 1,500 politically-motivated assassinations or attempted assassinations of high government officials or politicians were committed—at a rate of one every three weeks. Banks codes a similar number of revolutionary or rebellious acts against the central government and about 4,000 political riots—or almost one per week.[54]

There appears to be a tendency among policy makers and media reporters to assume incorrectly that words like civil war, insurgency, and terrorism are well-understood. For example, Bard E. O'Neill, widely considered to be a leading expert on the subject, defines an insurgency as "a struggle between a nonruling group and the ruling authorities in which the nonruling group consciously uses *political resources* (e.g., organizational expertise, propaganda, and demonstrations) and *violence* to destroy, reformulate, or sustain the basis of legitimacy of one or more aspects of politics"[55] (emphasis in original). He then defines terrorism as a form of warfare, specifically one of three forms of waging an insurgency, which include: "terrorism, guerilla war, and conventional warfare."[56] For some observers, insurgency may be understood to be an effort to take over from a ruling party, while terrorism may be either narrower or more general than that in its purposes. Examples would include ecoterrorism activities aimed at efforts to block seal or whale hunts, for example.

Of course, terrorism has become a far more widely recognized problem in the world after the September 11, 2001, attack on the United States, but terrorism has long been with us. Indeed, many of those who live in developing countries felt the brunt of terrorism long before it was a matter of serious concern to others. Even so, the exact contours of the concept continue to be far from clear. According to the U.S. State Department, an international terrorism incident is "judged significant if it results in loss of life or serious injury to persons, major property damage (more than $10,000), and/or is an act or attempt that could reasonably be expected to create the conditions noted."[57] The State Department's revised numbers show that in 2003 there were significant terrorist incidents in thirty countries.[58] The 2005 report concluded that: "11,000 terrorist attacks occurred in 2005 and resulted in over 14,600 deaths," of which nearly one-third of the incidents and more than half of the deaths were in Iraq.[59]

Notwithstanding the 9/11 attack, there is still a tendency to perceive terrorism and civil disorder as international rather than intrastate phenomena, and not to acknowledge that domestic terrorism happens in the United States. However, the Federal Bureau of Investigation (FBI), which tracked terrorism over time, and the Memorial Institute for the Prevention of Terrorism's (MIPT) Terrorism Knowledge Base provide reminders of a variety of incidents in the United States.[60] They include anthrax attacks, the Unabomber's blasts, the bombing of Atlanta's Olympic park, the first attack on the World Trade Center, bombing of family planning clinics linked to abortion services, murder of a Buffalo, New York, physician who performed abortions, the Oklahoma City federal building bombing, a variety of attacks by animal rights activists, and a continuing string of attacks by ecoterrorists on everything from new home construction to automotive dealerships. Long before these incidents, there were a number of other well-known examples, including the Simbianese Liberation Army (SLA) kidnapping of Patricia Hurst and bombings of university research facilities and other locations by the Weathermen faction of the group calling itself "Students for a Democratic Society." And there is a long, sad history of racist terrorism, such as lynching of African Americans from the Reconstruction era to modern attacks by so-called skinheads in the United States and elsewhere against minorities, immigrants, foreign visitors, or members of targeted religious groups.

One type of terrorism that has come to be widely discussed is generally termed state-sponsored terrorism. This term is usually applied to instances in which a regime supports terrorist groups or activities in another country or region. However, tyrannical regimes may also engage in state-sponsored terrorism within their own borders, as in the case of politically supported death squads that attack perceived opponents of the regime, as has been seen in some Latin American contexts. A contemporary example is the support by the government of Sudan for the Janjaweed in Darfur. The goal of such governmentally sanctioned terrorism may vary from the attempt to instill fear in the populace to outright genocide, as in the case of the Holocaust in Hitler's Germany.

Despite its obvious importance and significance, terrorism is not the only type of intrastate conflict. In addition to terrorism and civil war, there is another class of conflict perhaps best described as civil disorder. Civil disorder may be planned and may be related to terrorism or efforts to foment civil war or to advance an insurgency, or it may be very different. It may be the result of discrete circumstances in a particular place at a moment in time, or even such a random event as large-scale violence or destruction following sports events. It may have multiple facets, as was true in the case of the Seattle demonstrations against the World Trade Organization, in which there were certainly peaceful protesters, but there were also others, ranging from anarchists to violent provocateurs, who fit most descriptions of terrorists. Apart from such planned events, there have been any number of examples of civil disorder that were neither planned nor organized. Although they drew national attention at the time, the Los Angeles riots faded quickly from public attention, as did the promises made by the parade of politicians who traveled to the city, vowing to reinvigorate efforts to develop effective urban policies. Other cities, from Miami to Chicago to Philadelphia to Detroit, have experienced serious riots. In several countries, civil disorder has been driven by religion or ethnic conflict and may or may not have been clearly related to a political movement.

The discussions about the numbers and nature of conflict and the status of belligerents may seem unhelpful or even trivial issues to be left to international lawyers or scholars of international relations, but they are in truth important matters with very practical significance for sustainable development. Thus, for example, one of the issues for the United States in Iraq related to the question of when sovereignty would be transferred to the interim Iraqi government. Under international law, an occupying power—and until it returned sovereignty to the Iraqi people, the United States was formally an occupying power—is obligated to ensure that a system of rule of law and protection of rights of civilians and combatants is in place and operating effectively.[61] In a different setting, when Secretary of State Colin Powell announced that the situation in Darfur, Sudan, was a genocide, that triggered an obligation to act under international law.[62] The status of and participants in a conflict matter.

Additionally, in the case of true multinational forces, it is critical to understand just who has what command and control authority, a particularly complex matter where there may be a rotating command authority. Those commanders must also have mission definitions and rules of engagement appropriate to that conflict. Thus, General Roméo Dallaire found himself in a situation described in one way in terms of the UN mandate he was given, but he was dealing with conditions that were dramatically different from that formal description on the ground.[63] Also, the question of who has a role and what kind of role is bounded in both political and legal respects by the nature of the conflict. Finally, the international law of conflict that is intended to influence how commanders behave during the battle as well as who may be held accountable is based on the type of conflict. Thus, what few provisions of international law exist to address destruction of the environment in war apply to formal international conflicts and not in any meaningful way to the much larger number of other types of conflict.[64]

The Geographic Context and Geopolitical Character and Consequences of Conflict

The geographic setting and geopolitical perception also condition the way in which we understand and respond to conflict. That perception, in turn, influences whether donor countries and international institutions are willing to make a conflict a priority for resolution and post-conflict action, as well as influencing the level of resources they are prepared to invest.

Geographical region or eco-region is an important factor that conditions the nature and perception of conflict.[65] The *Implementing Sustainable Development* volume discussed the contextual factors that constrain or support sustainable development efforts. In the case of the development work following conflict, these factors can be even more important. Thus, for example, extended conflict in a relatively small island country such as Sri Lanka can have devastating impacts on the environment, the economy, and the people, leaving limited resources for development after the violence ends. There are also likely to be difficulties where the complexity of the context within which conflict is waged is underestimated or misperceived. Thus, the George W. Bush administration clearly overestimated the resources available and underestimated the problematic contextual factors for development in Iraq. While the Future of Iraq Project had been moving toward a more complete picture and plan of action, executive branch politics cut off that effort and focused the work largely in the Department of Defense. There is an irony in this situation, given the fact that international organizations like UNEP, the World Bank, and various health care nongovernmental organizations (NGOs) had all prepared pre-invasion studies on the conditions in Iraq with suggestions as to the challenges that the international community would face if and when it invaded, based in part at least on information from the more limited conflict in 1991.[66]

The other dimension of this problem is that the evaluation of conflict and response to it are most often driven by geopolitical perspectives. Thus, the United States twice perceived Iraq as strategically important enough to its national interests that it was prepared to go to war. Similarly, Kosovo met the test of geopolitical importance sufficient to engage armed forces, though that was a hotly debated point in the United States in particular, largely because of the location of the conflict. However, numerous serious situations in Africa and Latin America have not been regarded as significant enough to draw serious attention, let alone action. Thus, despite its strategic importance in terms of its role of oil production, there has been little interest in addressing the violence and related issues in Nigeria. When the United States has historically engaged in Latin America, it clearly has done so in its perceived geopolitical interests, with little regard for the interests, needs, or well-being of the inhabitants of the countries involved. Chile and Guatemala are only two of many obvious examples of this kind of behavior. This is not a criticism of the United States alone, but a common problem around the world, including for a number of the European countries. Consider, for example, the difference in the level of concern and serious commitment shown in East Timor as compared to Rwanda and Burundi. Similarly, terrorism and civil disorder in India has received relatively little attention compared, for example, to incidents in Spain. This is not a new problem. An example is the fact that the UN Convention on Refugees was almost two decades old before it was modified in 1967 to include refugees from countries outside Europe.[67]

A typical formulation of this problem is presented in the report entitled *Play to Win: The Commission on Post-Conflict Reconstruction* prepared by the bi-partisan Commission on Post-Conflict Reconstruction and published in 2003 under the auspices of the Association of the United States Army and the Center for Strategic and International Studies. The report presents the post-conflict challenge as one of post-conflict reconstruction and indicates that the problem is to prompt the United States to reevaluate "its approach to dealing with failed states," a term that carries considerable problematic meaning in its own right. The report quickly adds: "However, not all failed states are created equal. Not all will be equally important to the United States and the international community. Each stable country must gauge its involvement in failed or failing states according to its own interests."[68]

Viewed from the traditional perspective of international relations, there is nothing surprising about that perspective or the defining role of perceived national interest. Indeed, much of contemporary international relations thought and policy focuses on the view of nation-state actors and assumes as a guiding principle that those states will act or refuse to act based upon their leaders' perceptions as to what is in their national interest. Too often, however, that perspective has meant a short-term and narrow approach to decisions taken by many of the world's most powerful nations, not only as to the nature of a given conflict, but also to what happens afterward.

Guided by such a perspective, too many nations have ignored the obligations of international agreements to which they committed themselves, including a decade of common commitments for sustainable development signed by more than 120 nations over more than a decade. Too often, it has meant an eighteenth- or nineteenth-century approach to life in the twentieth and now the twenty-first century; an approach that assumes that there is a modest number of nations that act and many more which are acted upon that matter little. The calculations of national interest and strategic importance are often idiosyncratic, transitory, and seriously flawed, but they operate in ways that affect not only how much damage is done, but what conditions are perceived as tolerable to key international players during and after conflict.

The problem of geopolitical interest is not only an issue in understanding the nature of a conflict and the willingness of powerful nations to engage. It is also a critical factor in the willingness of those powers to pay attention to the impacts of conflict and make commitments to sustainable development after conflict ends. Hence, there has been an ongoing unwillingness to engage in what has been derisively termed "nation building" in settings where there has been significant conflict. Often, traditional policy logic simply suggests that another challenge is more important elsewhere in the world. The damage that such an approach can cause is well illustrated by the situation in Afghanistan. When the USSR became embroiled in conflict in Afghanistan, like other powers before it, the United States perceived support for Afghan insurgents as something that was in America's Cold War interests. Once the USSR pulled out, the United States no longer regarded the country as important and worthy of careful attention and development assistance, which, in turn, contributed to the rise of the brutal Taliban government and support for Osama bin Laden and al Qaeda.

Intrastate versus International Facets of the Problem

The problem of geopolitical perception points to a larger concern. It is the fact that international and intrastate perspectives can be dramatically different, and both significantly affect the nature and understanding of conflict. Those varied perceptions may have important consequences for efforts at sustainable development when the conflict ends. Apart from perceptions, however, conflicts do differ depending upon whether they are intrastate in nature or international.

International conflict is governed, to some extent at least, by a formal set of conventions that have sought to mitigate some of the worst effects of war on nonbelligerents, vulnerable populations, and even some aspects of a country's heritage sites and resources.[69] Those same conventions impose a set of obligations on warring parties.

Intrastate conflicts, whether they are civil wars, acts of terrorism, or civil disorder, by contrast, often represent a breakdown of law and are not subject to anything like the rules of war. Indeed, insurgent groups often use to their advantage the fact that governments are expected to operate according to law and ethical norms while others are not. Neither is there any set of obligations for what is to happen when intrastate conflict has presumably ended. Much of our perception of conflict has been shaped by wars among nations, but in recent decades, intrastate or hybrid conflicts, in which there are both international and local combatants directly or indirectly involved, are far more common. Terrorism, of course, may be either intrastate or international in character. The intrastate variety may be government-sponsored or direct actions by government itself, as is evident not only in cases of genocide, but also in targeted violence or torture.

There are also cases in which conflict may have begun as an intrastate matter, but then drew intervention by the international community or other nations. Alternatively, countries may invite the involvement of outside forces in an internal conflict, as in current efforts by countries to fight what has been termed the global war on terrorism. Hence, U.S. Special Forces became involved in the Philippines against terrorist operations in a country that has long faced an insurgency, and involved in Colombia's efforts to address narco-terrorism.

Whatever the facts on the ground, the problem of the intrastate versus international perceptions of conflict has real consequences. Those in the target country may view what international interests consider an insurgency to be a legitimate revolution. Thus, there was a failure to distinguish between such movements in Asia in the 1950s and 1960s that led Western governments to choose stability over dramatic change regardless of the nature of the forces involved, as was true in Vietnam. A governmental entity may take power and conclude that the conflict is over, but other countries may refuse recognition and continue the conflict from the outside. For example, the United States rejected the Sandinista regime's claim to govern Nicaragua and pressed the fight to bring down that government through the Contra rebels.

From a sustainable development perspective, this difference between local reality and international perspectives can be extremely important. Following a change of government, the international community may conclude that the problems within a particular country have been resolved and no longer perceive an urgent need, for example, to address refugee problems or to address the difficulties that flowed from the conflict. The breakup of the former Soviet Union provided examples. In some of what were at that time termed "newly independent states," there was widespread disorder with rampant crime and considerable violence, some of which flowed from ethnic clashes, while other violence could be traced to criminal activity. In that context, vulnerable groups sometimes found themselves under attack and fled, seeking asylum in other countries. However, since those other nations had recognized the new government, there was a tendency to perceive that the claimants no longer had the kind of "well-founded fear" of persecution required by the international convention on refugees.[70] Too often the tendency has been to substitute political perception for evidence of real conditions on the ground.

A similar problem arose in Guatemala, where a civilian government was elected after decades of military rule. Nevertheless, Guatemala was the scene of considerable continuing violence. In a case involving a labor activist seeking asylum in 1989, and after this new government had come to power, U.S. authorities concluded that the asylum seeker was merely involved in an economic dispute and therefore did not have a well-founded fear of persecution. A U.S. court rejected that position, concluding that: "The overall picture reveals a pattern of persecution that is horrific, and rivaled in this hemisphere perhaps only by the pattern of persecution in El Salvador."[71] (See chapter 4 for a case study on Guatemala.)

Quite apart from this narrower perspective related to individual or group impacts, the international perception can revise the reality in another way, and shape donor nation or institutional contributions to post-conflict sustainable development efforts accordingly. Thus, there is a considerable international commitment to success in the post-Taliban government of Afghanistan. However, much of the focus was on the removal of the Taliban regime and installation of a stable and acceptable regime to replace it. Even as many nations lauded the success of the new government, the fact was that only limited commitments had initially been made to help the new government provide security, much less development, outside the Kabul-to-Kandahar corridor. And, in fact, most of the country remained under the control of the warlords and others who had been in charge earlier. Once the international community decides to declare victory and leave, the country may very well be left with conditions that fall far short of security and safety.

The other side of this situation is that the internal perceptions may also be at variance with reality. Hence, international institutions or countries that have sought to provide assistance may be perceived locally by the receiving population as unjust intervenors and even as enemies. Hence, UN peacekeepers and international NGOs have increasingly been targeted while they are engaged in what they understand to be humanitarian efforts. Prejudices, a lack of education, or years of life under abusive regimes that inculcated false pictures of other countries can all exacerbate this problem. If one has only known violence, corruption, or crime, it is not difficult to perceive the actions of others in those terms.

Ethnocultural Character and Perceptions of Conflict

Ethnocultural perspectives may also mean that conflict looks different and may have different kinds of consequences in different places. Fiji provides an example. Fortunately, the last coup d'état in Fiji produced limited violent activity, but it profoundly shook this subregional capital of the South Pacific. (It remains to be seen whether yet another coup, which is in progress at the time of this writing—the fourth coup in recent history—will remain peaceful.) Such actions as a decision to hold tourists hostage for a time had an immediate and dramatic impact on one of the country's most important economic sectors. The fact that the coup came after the election of the first Indo-Fijian president under the new constitution, following a peaceful but nevertheless a military government imposed in a previous coup, brought international condemnation and a precipitous decline in what had been a growing commercial and light industrial sector. Indeed, what was surprising was that the president who was removed in the coup was a person who had a long record of working well with both major ethnocultural groups in the country. But even beyond the international dimension, this is not a country with a traditionally violent culture. Indeed, this level of disorder was highly disruptive from a cultural perspective, and it was not at all clear how it would be handled or just what the long-term effects of this conflict might be.

Apart from the actual differences in any given location there is also a serious question whether donor nations and international institutions perceive and respond to conflict situations differently in different parts of the world, in part perhaps because of a lack of understanding of the cultural dimensions of conflict.

Temporal and Historical Views of Conflict and Its Impacts

Another key lens with which to understand and differentiate among conflicts is through their temporal dimensions. Conflict is a dynamic phenomenon that takes place over time, often for long periods. It both shapes and is shaped by the times in which it occurs. It is therefore somewhat surprising that those who consider sustainable development after conflict are only recently coming to address the temporal dimensions of the challenge.

At the time that conflict emerges, analysts often do not anticipate or recognize just how significant an impact it is likely to have on the future of a nation and its people for generations to come. It is unlikely that any serious student of American politics would, for example, suggest that the Civil War does not continue to shape Southern politics in significant ways. Similarly, modern Europe continues to be affected by the devastation of World War II and the horrors that attended it, and to see, in such places as the Balkans, the shadows even of World War I. The Holocaust has influenced a great many people, including large numbers who have never been to Germany or had a relative murdered in Hitler's terrible genocide. And in the United States, the lives of Native Americans continue to be shaped by more than a century of efforts to eliminate them; first physically in the period in which it was perceived that "the only good Indian is a dead Indian," and then later through political efforts to destroy tribal connections to the land and to break up the tribes themselves through the Dawes Act and later through derecognition.

Much of the contemporary era has been understood as the "postwar" period, the years since World War II. In the Middle East, much of the current period is defined in terms of the Six-Day War. At the time of this writing, life is defined in the United States and some other parts of the world in terms of the abbreviated date 9/11, referring of course to the September 11, 2001, terrorist attack on the World Trade Center in New York and the Pentagon just across the river from Washington, D.C. In fact, many people of the world continue to be taught their history in terms of the conflicts that have shaped it.

One of the reasons that wars have such an impact is that many have gone on for extended periods such that entire generations may come of age knowing only conflict. Certainly Vietnam provides an example, but there are other even more recent cases as well, including Guatemala and Sri Lanka.

> For almost two decades from 1983–2002, Sri Lanka was embroiled in a bitter, "no mercy" civil war that claimed a devastating human toll, and that comprised a number of different phases and even different protagonists. Some 60,000 to 70,000 people are estimated to have died since July 1983, when a simmering insurgency campaign in the north escalated traumatically into war. In the late-1990s, almost a million people, amounting to one-third of the total population of the north-east were living as internally displaced persons (IDP's), while one-quarter of the total Sri Lankan Tamil population had left the country, mostly as a direct or indirect result of the war. A further large number of people estimated as at least 10,000 and sometimes as high as 60,000, are estimated dead or disappeared in a separate, but indirectly related insurgency in the south between 1987–1990.[72]

Rajesh Venugopal pointed out that the period of conflict in Sri Lanka "spans a number of distinct historical phases that straddle important external political, economic and cultural changes, including the end of the cold war, the rise of a global liberal economic order, and the effects of the emerging global war on terrorism—all of which are playing an important role in the dynamics of the conflict."[73] Conflicts, then, not only shape their times, but are shaped by them as well.

Another often ignored reality is the dynamic and changing character of conflict over time. For example, one study of the conflict that raged in Guatemala from 1960 to 1996 found the "temporal texture of the conflict to be far from smooth," even though "[t]he state carried out most of the killing during the conflict in an ongoing campaign of repressive terror involving the military, the police, semi-autonomous 'death squads' and state organized civilian 'civil patrols.'" More particularly,

> In the early parts of the conflict, the violence was typically between middle class people of the non-indigenous Ladino group struggling for control of the government. As the conflict progressed, it moved from an urban conflict focused on Guatemala City to a rural counter-insurgency campaign. The victims of state repression shifted at this point (about 1981) from middle class Ladino dissidents to indigenous Mayan peasants who were suspected of aiding rebel groups in the northwestern highlands. The scale and nature of the conflict changed as well, becoming vastly more deadly and including many acts which have been found to meet the formal definition of genocide.[74]

The dynamic character of conflict over time and the complexity of its impacts suggest the importance of contemplating the consequences for sustainable development before the conflict ends and, if possible, even before it begins. That is, our perception of conflict, as well as the conflict itself, must respond in time, as well as being shaped by temporal considerations. The fact that the U.S. government failed to take that fact into consideration in Iraq was devastating not only to coalition troops, but also to Iraqi civilians.

Interestingly, there has been some movement in the direction of contemplating the future with respect to conflicts. After the conflict in Kosovo, the United Nations Environmental Programme (UNEP) and UN Habitat conducted studies on Kosovo and Albania aimed at understanding the sustainable development challenges that would have to be addressed in the region.[75] While the fight continued against Taliban and al Qaeda forces in Afghanistan, UNEP launched a similar study on sustainable development challenges there.[76] However, even before the United States and its coalition partners launched the spring 2003 assault in Iraq, groups began studying the likely consequences of such a war and what would happen in its aftermath.

The UNEP launched its *Desk Study on the Environment in Iraq* in February of 2003 and completed it only six weeks later with a call for full field studies as soon as possible.[77]

> Timeliness is paramount. Lessons learned from earlier conflicts show that the immediate environmental consequences must be addressed as soon as possible to avoid a further deterioration of humanitarian and environmental conditions. . . . Earlier UNEP post-conflict studies also demonstrate that the envi-

ronment can have major implications for human livelihoods and for sustainable economic development. . . . UNEP is recommending that field research and analysis be carried out in Iraq at the earliest possible time.[78]

The *Iraq Desk Study* reads far more like a sustainable development study since it plainly sought to integrate the social and economic development dimensions in addition to the admitted focus on the environmental leg of the living triangle. That study was then used for comparative purposes when, in October 2003, UNEP published a follow-on study.[79]

The UNEP was not the only organization to mobilize in the run-up to the Iraq invasion. The international NGO MedAct published "Collateral Damage: The Health and Environmental Costs of War on Iraq" in November 2002, warning of some of the likely consequences of an attack in an attempt to support international opinion opposing the then impending U.S. action.[80] Not only did the organization seek to accelerate consideration of sustainable development issues to an earlier point in the decision process, but both UNEP and MedAct used data and materials from the previous Gulf War to support their projections for the impending war. As a result, both reports discussed the likely interactive effects between the ongoing problems from the previous conflict and the likely new difficulties ahead. Although it did not precede the invasion, the World Bank soon launched a joint "needs assessment" for Iraq with the United Nations in June 2003, ultimately published in October.[81]

That effort to relate previous impacts and challenges to likely future concerns demonstrates another temporal aspect of the problem, the cumulative effects of conflict over time. Thus, MedAct observed:

> The Iraqi people's mental and physical health and well-being were seriously harmed by the direct impact of the 1990–1991 war. They were further weakened by the indirect effects of the conflict in a variety of ways that stem from the consequences of economic collapse, and from widespread infrastructural destruction and damage to services and facilities. . . .

> It cannot be emphasized too strongly that even a "best-case" scenario of a limited war of short duration, perhaps comparable to 1991, would have much greater impact on the Iraqi people and would initially kill three times the number who died on September 11. . . . They are now far less able to withstand further assaults on their health, suggesting an exponential growth in the potential harm.[82]

Efforts were also being made at a governmental level to have a more timely and well-thought-out approach to Iraq. The Future of Iraq Project was begun in the fall of 2001 and formally launched in early 2002 by the State Department under the leadership of Executive Director Thomas Warrick, following earlier discussions at the Middle-East Institute at Columbia

University. It involved a variety of government officials and academics. However, as the war began, the Defense Department was given the leadership role for postwar action in Iraq and the Future of Iraq Project was terminated. Its materials were not disseminated to the public.

Clearly, then, there is a range of temporal considerations that are essential to an understanding of conflict and sustainable development efforts afterward. Of course, one of the problems is the manner in which what is to come after conflict is understood and described.

THE TASK IS MORE THAN RECONSTRUCTION, ECONOMIC RECOVERY, OR NATION BUILDING: TOWARD SUSTAINABLE DEVELOPMENT

The way that we understand a problem has a great deal to do with how we address it. For a variety of reasons—some historical, others ideological, and yet others based upon the disciplinary and professional silos that experts and institutions inhabit—the challenges to be faced following conflict are most often approached from inadequate and frequently inaccurate foundations. The dominant approaches to the work to be done after conflict are reconstruction, economic recovery, or nation building. Each of these terms represents an intellectual framework that drives policy. All are inadequate to contemporary post-conflict challenges. Sustainable development provides a far more comprehensive and appropriate foundation for post-conflict action. Consider first just some of the problems with the existing approaches and then a brief survey of the advantages of the sustainable development model.

Reconstruction, Economic Recovery, and Nation Building: Inadequate and Counterproductive Approaches

There are several different factors that lead to the inadequacies of the reconstruction, economic recovery, and nation-building post-conflict models. First, they derive in large part from two historical cases that are not comparable to contemporary challenges, Germany and Japan. Second, the reconstruction, economic recovery, and nation-building approaches are partial and inadequate in their own right. Third, there are troublesome, even pernicious and counterproductive, qualities to these three dominant frameworks.

It should come as no surprise that the Japanese and German experiences would be attractive touchstones for both policy makers and scholars concerned with post-conflict action. To be sure, both nations were devastated by WWII and yet both became powerful global leaders. In an era when it is increasingly difficult to find large-scale success stories, these two countries are strikingly positive exemplars of what can happen even in the face of massive loss of life, devastation of infrastructure, and the destruction of national economies. If so much was possible under those circumstances, it would appear that success should be far more likely and less challenging with respect to smaller countries in a period when the set of international institutions and sophisticated economic tools that were only just being created as World War II came to a close are now well established. The ability to gather and analyze many kinds of data, to deliver a wide variety of materials and supplies, and to move large amounts of capital with incredible—sometimes frightening—speed would seem to suggest that the accomplishments of the German and Japanese experience should be replicable and that it should be possible to meet contemporary post-conflict challenges faster and with less difficulty.

Indeed, both President Bush and National Security Advisor and later Secretary of State Condoleezza Rice have suggested comparisons between the challenges in postwar Iraq and the German example. During hearings on her confirmation as Secretary of State in January 2004, Rice repeatedly described the post-conflict task as "reconstruction and stabilization." In fact, one of the few areas in which Rice admitted Bush administration short-comings in his first term was that the administration had underestimated the task of post-conflict reconstruction. To that end, she noted, the State Department had created in the summer of 2004 the Office of the Coordinator for Reconstruction and Stabilization. It was clear that her view of the task ahead was to improve the process of reconstruction for the purpose of ensuring stability. Stability is a prized Cold War era value in Western foreign policy, but has a great deal more to do with rendering the global context controllable and manageable than in focusing on sustainable development for the people of a war-torn society based upon their needs and goals, rather than those of other countries.

The focus on reconstruction aimed at stability from a Western international relations perspective has not been limited to speeches from the president and secretary of state. The language of the Afghanistan Freedom Support Act of 2002, providing for post-conflict assistance, set forth a declaration of policy and statement of purposes for assistance that makes the point clearly.

Sec. 101. DECLARATION OF POLICY.

Congress makes the following declarations:

(1) The United States and the international community should support efforts that advance the development of democratic civil authorities and institutions in Afghanistan and the establishment of a new broad-based, multi-ethnic, gender-sensitive, and fully representative government in Afghanistan

(2) The United States, in particular, should provide its expertise to meet immediate humanitarian and refugee needs, *fight the production and flow of illicit narcotics, and aid in the reconstruction of Afghanistan.*

(3) *By promoting peace and security in Afghanistan and preventing a return to conflict, the United States and the international community can help ensure that Afghanistan does not again become a source for international terrorism.* . . .

(6) *To foster stability and democratization and to effectively eliminate the causes of terrorism,* the United States and the international community should also support efforts that advance the development of democratic civil authorities and institutions in the broader Central Asia region.

Sec. 102. PURPOSES OF ASSISTANCE.
The purposes of assistance authorized by this title are—

(1) *to help assure the security of the United States and the world by reducing or eliminating the likelihood of violence against United States or allied forces in Afghanistan and to reduce the chance that Afghanistan will again be a source of international terrorism;* . . .

(4) to help achieve a broad-based, multi-ethnic, gender-sensitive, and fully representative government in Afghanistan that is freely chosen by the people of Afghanistan and that respects the human rights of all Afghans, particularly women, *including authorizing assistance for the rehabilitation and reconstruction of Afghanistan* with a particular emphasis on meeting the educational, health, and sustenance needs of women and children to better enable their full participation in Afghan society. . . .[83] (Emphasis added.)

One of the other reasons that may lead many in the West to think in terms of the German and Japanese examples is that it is intuitively satisfying that the effort to address the needs of these two countries were focused and strong—qualities often lacking in later post-conflict efforts around the world. With the leadership of General George C. Marshall and President Harry Truman, it was clear that the United States was prepared to focus energy and resources in Europe after the war. In addition to the humanitarian and foreign policy impulses, the effort also helped fuel and protect the U.S. postwar economy. The occupation under General Douglas MacArthur saw to postwar action in Japan, resulting in a variety of dramatic developments. As the tensions grew in the postwar period between the United States and the Soviet Union, the strategic incentives grew for the United States and its allies to invest in the future of their former adversaries.

Unfortunately, since these countries are so successful and important today, it is easy to underestimate the unique circumstances and also the difficulty of their postwar experience. The ironies of war are manifold, but the scope and scale of World War II and the devastation that it produced left needs of such magnitude and intensity that the task seemed nothing short of reshaping the world. "What they were attempting was, besides, different from what had gone before. They were pioneering, the state of the world being, as Acheson said, 'wholly novel within the experience of those who had to deal with it.'"[84] General Marshall, in his address announcing the challenge to rebuild Europe, made clear the enormity of the task. "Our policy is directed not against any country or doctrine, but against hunger, poverty, desperation and chaos. Its purpose should be the revival of a working economy in the world so as to permit the emergence of political and social conditions in which free institutions can exist."[85] Winston Churchill described Europe at that time as "a rubble heap, a charnel house, a breeding ground of pestilence and hate."[86]

Despite the focus and intensity on postwar efforts, particularly in Europe, the process took considerable time, effort, and resources. The Marshall Plan did not develop until 1947 and implementation efforts continued for years. What became East Germany did not enjoy the benefits of these efforts and lagged even further behind.

That said, Germany and Japan had previously been nations with complex and sophisticated economies and infrastructures, as well as significant levels of ethnocultural cohesion. It was possible to speak of reconstruction and economic recovery in meaningful ways. Their development had been dramatically set back by war, but the use of terms that connoted a return to an acceptable national condition were reasonable descriptions of the challenges that those engaged in the effort faced.

These conditions are dramatically different from most contemporary post-conflict cases. Many of today's situations do not involve the kind of obvious and formal international wars among global powers that provided the setting for the German and Japanese experience. Many have been revolutions against colonial powers or governments put in place or propped up by other nations, civil wars, religious or ethnic conflicts, or clashes among developing countries with problematic regimes. The evidence to date in many situations suggests that the future success of affected nations may not be seen as important enough to mobilize dramatic post-conflict investments. Afghanistan, for example, has too often been wracked by conflict and then largely abandoned by other powers who vied for control or influence in that part of the world, from the British versus the Russians in the eighteenth century, to the United States versus the Russians in the late twentieth century. The failure to follow through with positive action there also affected neighboring countries, most notably, in this case, Pakistan. Similar problems have arisen in Latin American countries like Nicaragua and El Salvador.

Additionally, for many of the nations that had seen violence in the contemporary period, it is seriously inappropriate to use the reconstruction or economic recovery approach, since they had not possessed sufficiently developed infrastructure, governance capability, social policy development, or adequate—much less healthy—economies before the conflict to which they could return afterward. Instead, these terms have often been ways of describing the minimum building of basic infrastructure and fundamental economic conditions sufficient to declare the society stable such that the major powers could move on to their next priorities. Temporary stability as a leading goal and the ready desire to disengage have left country after country, from Afghanistan to Guatemala, ripe for authoritarian governments, the next round of violence, or both.

In many important respects, the encouragement by developed countries of what the Brundtland Commission termed the "arms culture" is one of the most devastating parts of conflict.[87] The demands of armaments and troops take nations that were not on the path to sustainable development before and undermine efforts to move beyond their negative focus to a more positive and sustainable future. We shall return to this theme later, but these circumstances are far different from the postwar experiences of Germany and Japan.

Another significant difference from post-World War II is that many of the societies afflicted by conflict in the contemporary era have been ignored as insignificant to major powers or, worse, have been victims of racism or dislike for their religious or cultural traditions. It is often forgotten that it was nearly two decades after the end of World War II that the world community extended the protections of the convention on refugees to anyone from anywhere else on the globe other than Europe. American policy toward Latin America, European approaches toward Africa, and the general stresses within the Asia/Pacific region are not fully comprehensible without an honest recognition of these destructive underlying attitudes.

In sum, approaches to post-conflict development that rest on an idealized view of the post-World War II German and Japanese reconstruction and economic recovery are inappropriate to most current challenges. There may certainly be lessons to be learned from those experiences, but these two cases are not appropriate models for contemporary situations.

Quite apart from the problematic comparison with other cases, the reconstruction, economic recovery, and nation-building models fail as mechanistic, externally imposed, partial, inadequate, and often arrogant. The reconstruction and economic recovery approach conveys the sense that the task at hand after conflict is to repair or replace the elements of the infrastructure and parts of governmental or market processes that were broken or destroyed in the clash. When the machinery once again has working parts, according to these approaches, it will function properly. That is a backward-looking, closed-system, and mechanistic view that is at best partial and in several important respects inaccurate.

To be sure, critical infrastructure and properly functioning institutions are necessary but not sufficient conditions for a positive future. For example, as evidence of progress the U.S. Agency for International Development (US-AID) listed new schools and repaired roads in Afghanistan, as well as the progress toward restoration of electric power systems and sewage systems in Baghdad. It is as if the construction of schools will solve any educational issues, the creation or restoration of clinics and hospitals will address the country's health issues, and the development of a Western-style market mechanism will take care of poverty. The fact that civilian courts are in operation and improving their operations is helpful. The announcement that rudimentary stock exchanges are developing and markets are once again in operation may also be signs of near-term improvements in the lives of residents of these communities. However, a society is far less a mechanism than an organism and clearly not a closed—but instead an open and dynamic—system. Institutions are critically important, but they are far more than physical entities.[88] They are not simply parts, but organs of the society.[89] Indeed, the community is far more than its built environment.

For one thing, the emphasis on the built environment often means a focus on urban centers and frequently ignores or significantly underestimates the importance and diversity of the rural parts of a country (an interesting contrast with the views often taken by global environmental groups). Thus, discussions of progress in Afghanistan emphasized two of the nation's cities at a time when the new government had little control over other parts of the country, much less was it in a position to manage reconstruction and economic recovery in the rural areas. Similarly, the emphasis is often on development of central economic institutions and market operations in the cities with an emphasis on trade goods. However, what is often ignored is the importance of the informal economy in many developing countries. Government is important, but the creation of institutions and processes alone does not ensure effective governance, particularly if efforts are made, despite a long history of knowing better, to transplant models from other countries and cultures. Of course, governance is not just government, but a far more complex activity that involves a range of participants outside government.[90]

These standard post-conflict models are partial for another reason. The World Bank civil war project and others like it often take as their focus the effort to stop the recurrence of civil war. Having identified the destructive consequences of civil war, the World Bank project identifies clashes over resources as leading causes not only of individual conflicts, but ongoing cycles of civil war over time.[91] The emphasis is then placed on efforts to ameliorate those resource tensions. It is not surprising that the bank's report takes an economic perspective, and it certainly is true that resource scarcity and clashes over who controls them is a critically important issue. However, that is but one piece of a much larger challenge.

The concept of nation building has many of the deficiencies discussed to this point and one additional problem. From a sustainable development perspective, nation building is externally motivated and imposed. Consider the task of nation building as described in a recent report.

Various terms have been used over the past 57 years to describe the activities we are seeking to analyze. The German and Japanese operations were referred to as occupations. The operations in Somalia, Haiti, and Bosnia were generally termed peacekeeping or peace enforcement missions. The current U.S. administration has preferred to use the terms stabilization and reconstruction to refer to its post conflict operations in Afghanistan and in Iraq. In all these cases, the intent was to use military force to underpin a process of democratization. Occupation, peacekeeping, peace enforcement, stabilization, and reconstruction do not fully capture the scope of such operations. Neither does the term nation-building, but we believe it comes closest to suggesting the full range of activities and objectives involved.[92]

The idea that representatives of conquering nations, donor states, or international institutions can come into a country and build a nation—whatever terms of art may be used to soften the fact—is both paternalistic and arrogant. It harkens back to a colonial mentality. The idea of nation building, in some respects at least, goes to the opposite end of the continuum from reconstruction. It suggests that there was nothing before and a new society must be built for a given group of people. It adds to the mechanistic picture of the challenge and suggests little emphasis on important cultural and indigenous strengths often quite clear to those who study the history of the country involved.

There is another set of criticisms of nation building that emphasizes a different but related set of problems. Though there are, to be sure, humanitarian factors, for many leaders these approaches are driven not so much by a concern for the long-term consideration of the lives and well-being of the people in war-torn lands as they are by a desire to avoid what are increasingly termed "failed states" that would disrupt stability and interfere with the maintenance of an international order created by and for developed countries. Thus understood, nation building becomes little more than an instrument of foreign policy to achieve security and stability for reasons of other actors apart from the needs of the people of the target country.

Finally, behind reconstruction, economic recovery, and nation building is the assumption that the activity is a limited and short-term challenge. Once the pieces are in place and processes are operating, the need for assistance and support will presumably end and the developed countries and international institutions can move on to their next priorities. However, post-conflict needs are rarely short-term. There seems to be a collective willingness to forget how long it took the United States to move from the Declaration of Independence in 1776 to the Constitution that took effect in 1789, and then through the first transitions of power toward a positive future. There is a tendency to forget how long European countries, with all of their sophistication and historic foundations, took to develop after World War I, and how complex and lengthy the efforts were to move forward after World War II. The needs are long-term and the process must be ongoing and integrative. That is not to disregard Anthony Downs's well-known warning about the volatility of the "issue-attention cycle."[93] It is to contend that short-term solutions have historically rarely been solutions at all, and certainly not in the context of post-conflict development.

The Case for a Sustainable Development Model

Sustainable development is a very different approach to post-conflict action than the reconstruction, economic recovery, and nation-building models. It starts from today and looks forward to an ongoing effort to encourage a balanced process that integrates economic development, social development, and environmental protection. It is far less mechanical than the standard approaches and recognizes the organic character of the effort to develop a society in which the current generation can make important choices for a better life, while protecting the ability of future generations to do the same. It is about an effort that is holistic, integrated, inclusive, and respectful, and emphasizes culturally appropriate responses to problem-solving. There is no assumption that the mere creation of institutions or market processes will be adequate to meet the needs of a people.

Sustainable development is oriented toward the long-term future and not short-term security or economic interests. It seeks to engage the range of people and institutions necessary to address critical challenges. Sustainable development is also an invitation to the country involved not simply to be acted upon, but to take charge of its future and join the world community in a common effort to achieve not only international but also national and local goals. Moreover, sustainable development rejects the outmoded idea that answers to complex local questions can be met by imposing models from developed Western countries.

Sustainable development does not assume that stability, defined in terms of the security of a political regime, is an end in itself but that human security is a starting point for a better future. The first Afghanistan Human Development Report provided perhaps the best statement of the distinction. "For too long, the security problem in Afghanistan has been interpreted narrowly as the security of the 'state' from internal and external aggression, or as the protection of the interests of fragmented groups claiming political legitimacy, or from the perspective of global and regional interests. Often neglected have been the human security needs of the population at large. Forgotten were the legitimate concerns of ordinary people who sought safety and dignity in their daily lives."[94] Instead, security and stability must be understood in terms of sustainable development.

Security is not just the end of war, but the ability to go about one's business safely, to go to work or home, to travel outside knowing that one's family will not suffer harm. It is the assurance that development gains made today will not be taken away tomorrow. For Afghans, human security is not only the ability to survive, but also the chance to live a life of dignity and have adequate livelihoods. Bringing an end to insecurity should not therefore be sought solely through short-term military solutions, but with a long-term, comprehensive strategy that abides by the promises of development and the promotion of human rights.[95]

In sum, while notions of security and stability are important to sustainable development, it is not at all the same set of concerns as are most often employed in discussions of reconstruction, economic recovery, and nation building. And, lest the critical character of the distinction be missed somehow, the report added: "Centring a discussion about security on all the people of Afghanistan entails the idea that human security is a public good to which everyone is equally entitled. It is not the privilege of those defending their interests through war."[96]

Finally, while a sustainable development approach does not reject out of hand efforts to meet immediate needs by addressing the destruction of infrastructure or the need to assist institutions like hospitals and schools, it insists that such efforts need to be undertaken with care and with the recognition that short-term efforts are just that. They are not steps expected by themselves to end the need for external support and engagement.

In order to move forward with a sustainable development approach to post-conflict action, however, it is necessary to understand the challenges posed by conflict situations for sustainable development and then develop knowledge as to how sustainable development policies can be implemented in any given context. The latter task was addressed in *Implementing Sustainable Development*. The rest of this book seeks to address the former need.

The chapters that follow include first an effort to understand some of the sustainability challenges that arise from contemporary environmental, economic, and social warfare. Chapter 3 turns to issues of the problems of flight with an emphasis on asylum seekers and internally displaced persons, including the social, economic, and environmental aspects of that reality. Chapter 4 examines the trauma that is inflicted by conflict and its significance. Chapter 5 focuses on the demobilization process, which turns out to be a considerably more complex process than is often pictured, with critical social, economic, and environmental dimensions.

NOTES

1. After writing this, we encountered the following very similar description. "First, civil war usually has devastating consequences: it is development in reverse."

Paul Collier, V.L. Elliott, Håvard Hegre, Anke Hoeffler, Marta Reynal-Querol, and Nicholas Sambanis, *Breaking the Conflict Trap: Civil War and Development Policy* (Washington, D.C.: World Bank, 2003), ix.

2. World Commission on Environment and Development, *Our Common Future* (New York: Oxford University Press, 1987), 8.

3. United Nations, *Agenda 21* (New York: United Nations, 1992), 11.

4. Associated Press, "The National Defense Council Foundation's List of 53 Countries Involved in Conflict in 2002," December 30, 2002.

5. See Collier et al., *Breaking the Conflict Trap*.

6. Ian Bannon and Paul Collier, eds., *Natural Resources and Violent Conflict: Options and Actions* (Washington, D.C.: World Bank, 2003), 1.

7. John Locke, *The Second Treatise of Government*, ed. Thomas P. Peardon (New York: Bobbs-Merrill, 1952).

8. See, e.g., Dee Brown, *Bury My Heart at Wounded Knee* (New York: Henry Holt, 1971).

9. Phillip J. Cooper and Claudia María Vargas, *Implementing Sustainable Development: From Global Policy to Local Action* (Lanham, MD: Rowman & Littlefield, 2004).

10. World Commission, *Our Common Future*, 8.

11. See, e.g., World Bank, *Sustainable Development in a Dynamic World: World Development Report 2003* (Washington, D.C.: World Bank, 2003) and World Bank, *Attacking Poverty: World Development Report 2000/2001* (Washington, D.C.: World Bank, 2001).

12. Cooper and Vargas, *Implementing Sustainable Development*.

13. United Nations, *Agenda 21*, 11.

14. United Nations, Rio Declaration, Principle 2, *Agenda 21*, 9.

15. World Commission, *Our Common Future*, 8.

16. United Nations, *Report of the World Summit on Sustainable Development, Johannesburg, South Africa, 26 August–4 September 2002* (New York: United Nations, 2002), 8. (Hereafter *Johannesburg Report*.)

17. United Nations, *Copenhagen Declaration and Program of Action* (New York: United Nations, 1995), 3. (Hereafter *Copenhagen Accords*.)

18. United Nations, *Copenhagen Accords*, 9.

19. United Nations, *Copenhagen Accords*, 9

20. United Nations Habitat, *The Istanbul Declaration*, Paragraph 135, at www .unchs.org/declarations/ch-4c-5.htm.

21. United Nations, *Report of the International Conference on Population and Development, Cairo, 18 October 1994*, Principle 10, at www.un.org/popin/icpd/conference/ offeng/poa.html (accessed May 26, 2003). (Hereafter *Cairo Population Report*.)

22. United Nations, *Cairo Population Report*, 22.

23. United Nations, *Johannesburg Report*, 39.

24. United Nations, *Johannesburg Report*, 39.

25. United Nations, *Johannesburg Report*, 10.

26. World Bank, *Poverty Trends and Voices of the Poor* (Washington, D.C.: World Bank, 1999); Deepa Narayan et al., *Voices of the Poor: Can Anyone Hear Us?* (Washington, D.C.: World Bank, 2000); *Voices of the Poor: Crying Out for Change* (Washington, D.C.: World Bank, 2000); *Voices of the Poor: From Many Lands* (Washington, D.C.: World Bank, 2002).

27. United Nations, *Agenda 21*, 10.

28. United Nations, *Johannesburg Report*, 1.

29. See, e.g., World Bank, *World Development Report 1997: The State in a Changing World* (Washington, D.C.: World Bank, 1997), 7.

30. See Cooper and Vargas, *Implementing Sustainable Development*, Chapter 3.

31. See Cooper and Vargas, *Implementing Sustainable Development*, Chapter 4.

32. See Cooper and Vargas, *Implementing Sustainable Development*, Chapter 5.

33. See Cooper and Vargas, *Implementing Sustainable Development*, Chapter 6.

34. John Rohr, *Ethics for Bureaucrats*, 2nd ed. (Marcel Dekker, 1986).

35. See Cooper and Vargas, *Implementing Sustainable Development*, Chapter 7.

36. See Cooper and Vargas, *Implementing Sustainable Development*, Chapter 8.

37. See Mostafa Kamal Tolba, ed., *Evolving Environmental Perceptions: From Stockholm to Nairobi* (London: Butterworths, 1988).

38. See United Nations, *Copenhagen Accords*.

39. See Collier et al., *Breaking the Conflict Trap*; Bannon and Collier, *Natural Resources and Violent Conflict*; World Bank, *Poverty Trends*; Narayan et al., *Voices of the Poor: Can Anyone Hear Us?*; *Voices of the Poor: Crying Out for Change*; *Voices of the Poor: From Many Lands*.

40. United Nations, "Program for the Further Implementation of Agenda 21, United Nations General Assembly Nineteenth Special Session, June 23–27, 1997, at http://daccessdds.un.org/doc/UNDOC/GEN/N97/857/86/IMG/N9785786.pdf?Open Element (accessed August 7, 2007).

41. United Nations, "Implementation of the Outcome of the World Summit for Social Development and of the Special Session of the General Assembly in This Regard," United Nations General Assembly Fifty-Fifth Special Session, June 26–July 1, 2000, at http://daccessdds.un.org/doc/UNDOC/GEN/N00/629/80/PDF/N0062980 .pdf?OpenElement (accessed August 7, 2007).

42. Kristian Skrede Gleditsch, "A Revised List of Wars between and within Independent States, 1816–2002," *International Interactions* 30, no. 3 (2004): 231–262.

43. Daniel M. Jones, Stuart A. Bremer, and J. David Singer, "Militarized Interstate Disputes, 1816–1992: Rationale, Coding Rules, and Empirical Patterns," *Conflict Management and Peace Science* 15, no. 2 (1996): 164.

44. Jones et al., "Militarized Interstate Disputes," 165.

45. Jones et al., "Militarized Interstate Disputes," 169–170.

46. Michael V. Bhatia, *War and Intervention: Issues for Contemporary Peace Operations* (Bloomfield, CT: Kumarian Press, 2003), 12.

47. Bhatia, *War and Intervention*, 12–14.

48. Bhatia, *War and Intervention*, 4.

49. National Defense Council Foundation, "World Conflict List," at www.ndcf .org (accessed December 25, 2006).

50. Correlates of War Project, "COW Inter-State War Data, 1816–1997 (v3.0)" and "COW Intra-State War Data, 1816–1997 (v3.0)," at http://cow2.la.psu.edu (accessed December 5, 2006).

51. These data sets are continually being updated and may be found at International Peace Research Institute (PRIO), Center for the Study of Civil War, "UCDP/PRIO Armed Conflicts Dataset," at http://new.prio.no/CSCW-Datasets/ Data-on-Armed-Conflict/UppsalaPRIO-Armed-Conflicts-Dataset (accessed December 26, 2006).

52. Stockholm International Peace Research Institute, "Appendix 3A: Patterns of Major Armed Conflicts, 1990–2003," *SIPRI Yearbook 2004* (New York: Oxford University Press, 2004), quoted in UNICEF, *State of the World's Children 2005: Children under Threat—Executive Summary* (New York: UNICEF, 2004), 40.

53. Stockholm International Peace Research Institute, *SIPRI Yearbook 2006*, *Summary Edition*, 3, at www.sipri.org/contents/publications/pocket/pocket_yb.html (accessed December 5, 2006).

54. Charles Boix, "Political Violence," paper prepared for the Yale Conference entitled "Order, Conflict and Violence," April 30–May 1, 2004, 2, at www.princeton .edu/~cboix/political-violence.pdf (accessed August 7, 2007).

55. Bard E. O'Neill, *Insurgency and Terrorism: Inside Modern Revolutionary Warfare* (Dulles, VA: Brassey's, 1990), 13.

56. O'Neill, *Insurgency and Terrorism*, 24.

57. U.S. Department of State, Office of the Coordinator for Counterterrorism, *Patterns of Global Terrorism—2003, Appendix A—Chronology of Significant International Terrorist Incidents*, 2003 (revised June 22, 2004), archived online at www.global security.org/security/library/report/2004/pgt_2003/pgt_2003_33773pf.htm (accessed December 5, 2006). (Hereafter U.S. Department of State, *Patterns, Appendix A*.)

58. U.S. Department of State, *Patterns, Appendix A*.

59. U.S. Department of State, Office of the Coordinator for Counterterrorism, *Country Reports on Terrorism 2005* (Washington, D.C.: Department of State, 2006), Statistical Annex, v.

60. Some of the FBI data that ran up to 2000/2001 was shifted to the Memorial Institute for the Prevention of Terrorism, *Terrorism Knowledge Base*, at www.tkb .org/AnalyticalTools.jsp (accessed December 5, 2006).

61. Amnesty International provided a concise summary of the obligations of an occupying power under the "Hague Convention (IV) respecting the Laws and Customs of War on Land (Hague Convention) and Its Annexed Regulations Respecting the Laws and Customs of War on Land (Hague Regulations) of 18 October 1907; The Fourth Geneva Convention Relative to the Protection of Civilian Persons in Time of War (Fourth Geneva Convention) of 12 August 1949; Article 75 of the 1977 Protocol Additional to the Geneva Conventions of 12 August 1949 and Relating to the Protection of Victims of International Armed Conflicts (Protocol I); and Rules of Customary International Law." Amnesty International, "Iraq: Obligations of the Occupying Powers," at http://web.amnesty.org/library/Index/ENGMDE140892003 (accessed December 26, 2006).

62. Glenn Kessler and Colum Lynch, "U.S. Calls Killings in Sudan Genocide: Khartoum and Arab Militias Are Responsible, Powell Says," *Washington Post*, September 10, 2004, A01, referring to the Convention on the Prevention and Punishment of the Crime of Genocide, 78 U.N.T.S. 277, at www.unhchr.ch/html/menu3/ b/p_genoci.htm (accessed December 26, 2006).

63. Roméo Dallaire, with Brent Beardsley, *Shake Hands with the Devil: The Failure of Humanity in Rwanda* (Toronto: Random House Canada, 2003).

64. Jay E. Austin and Carl E. Bruch, eds., *The Environmental Consequences of War: Legal, Economic, and Scientific Perspectives* (Cambridge, UK: Cambridge University Press, 2000), 43.

65. See, generally, Douglas Lemke, *Regions of War and Peace* (Cambridge, UK: Cambridge University Press, 2002).

66. See, e.g., United Nations Environment Programme, *Desk Study on the Environment in Iraq* (Nairobi, UNEP, 2003); MedAct, *Collateral Damage: The Health and Environmental Costs of War on Iraq* (London: MedAct, 2002).

67. United Nations High Commissioner for Refugees, "Convention and Protocol Relating to the Status of Refugees," at www.unhcr.org/protect/3c0762ea4.html (accessed December 26, 2006), providing documents and information on the Convention Relating to the Status of Refugees, 189 U.N.T.S. 150 (1951) and the Protocol Relating to the Status of Refugees, 606 U.N.T.S. 267 (1967).

68. Commission on Post-Conflict Reconstruction, *Play to Win: Final Report of the Bi-Partisan Commission on Post-Conflict Reconstruction* (Washington, D.C.: Center for Strategic and International Studies and the Association of the U.S. Army, 2003), 2.

69. See Austin and Bruch, *Environmental Consequences of War*, part II. See also Amnesty International, "Iraq: Obligations of the Occupying Powers."

70. See *Gailius v. Immigration and Naturalization Service*, 147 F.3d 34 (1st. Cir. 1998).

71. *Osorio v. Immigration and Naturalization Service*, 18 F.3d 1017 (2nd. Cir. 1994).

72. Rajesh Venugopal, "The Global Dimensions of Conflict in Sri Lanka," *Queen Elizabeth House Working Paper Series—QEHWPS99*, Queen Elizabeth House, University of Oxford, February 2003, 2, at www2.qeh.ox.ac.uk/pdf/qehwp/qehwps99.pdf (accessed November 13, 2004).

73. Venugopal, "Global Dimensions of Conflict in Sri Lanka," 1.

74. Timothy R. Gulden, "Spatial and Temporal Patterns in Civil Violence, Guatemala 1977–1986," Brookings Institution, Center on Social and Economic Dynamics Working Paper No. 26, February 2002, 1–3, at www.refugees.org/uploaded Files/Participate/National_Center/Resource_Library/Guatemala_1977_1986_Spatial_ and_Temporal_Patterns_in_Civil_Violence.pdf (accessed December 23, 2006).

75. United Nations Environmental Programme and United Nations Center for Human Settlements (Habitat), *The Kosovo Conflict: Consequences for the Environment and Human Settlements* (Nairobi: UNEP, 1999); United Nations Environmental Programme, *Post-conflict Environmental Assessment—Albania* (Nairobi: UNEP, 2000).

76. United Nations Environmental Programme, *Afghanistan: Post-conflict Environmental Assessment* (Nairobi: UNEP, 2003).

77. UNEP, *Desk Study on the Environment in Iraq*.

78. UNEP, *Desk Study on the Environment in Iraq*, 6.

79. United Nations Environment Programme, *Environment in Iraq* (Geneva: UNEP, 2003).

80. MedAct, "Collateral Damage: The Health and Environmental Costs of War on Iraq," November 2002, at www.medact.org/content/wmd_and_conflict/Medact_ Iraq_report%20(1).pdf (accessed December 26, 2006).

81. World Bank and United Nations, *United Nations/World Bank Joint Iraq Needs Assessment* (Washington and New York: UN and World Bank, 2003).

82. MedAct, "Collateral Damage," 11.

83. Afghanistan Freedom Support Act of 2002, P.L. 107–327, 116 Stat. 2797, Sections 101–102.

84. David McCullough, *Truman* (New York: Simon & Schuster, 1992), 555.

85. McCullough, *Truman*, 563.

86. McCullough, *Truman*, 562.

87. World Commission, *Our Common Future*, 297–300.

88. James G. March and Johan P. Olsen, *Rediscovering Institutions* (New York: Free Press, 1989); Michael J. Sandel, *Democracy's Discontent* (Cambridge, MA: Harvard University Press, 1996).

89. Sandel, *Democracy's Discontent*, ix.

90. H. George Frederickson, "Whatever Happened to Public Administration: Governance, Governance Everywhere," in Ewan Ferlie, Laurence E. Lynn, and Christopher Pollitt, eds., *The Oxford Handbook of Public Management* (London: Oxford University Press, 2006).

91. Bannon and Collier, *Natural Resources and Violent Conflict*; Collier et al., *Breaking the Conflict Trap*.

92. James Dobbins, John G. McGinn, Keith Crane, Seth G. Jones, Rollie Lal, Andrew Rathmell, Rachel Swanger, and Anga Timilsina, *America's Role in Nation-Building from Germany to Iraq* (Santa Monica, CA: RAND, 2003), 1.

93. See Anthony Downs, "Up and Down with Ecology—The 'Issue-Attention Cycle,'" *Public Interest* 28 (Summer 1972): 38–50; John W. Kingdon, *Agendas, Alternatives, and Public Policies* (Boston: Little, Brown, 1984).

94. UNDP Afghanistan, *Afghanistan Human Development Report: Security with a Human Face 2004* (New York: UNDP, 2004), xxv.

95. UNDP Afghanistan, *Afghanistan Human Development Report*, xxv.

96. UNDP Afghanistan, *Afghanistan Human Development Report*, xxv.

2

Environmental, Social, and Economic Warfare

Deliberate Destruction, Collateral Damage, or Something More Complex?

When dozens of people perish in a fire, hundreds die as the result of a hurricane, or thousands are killed and illness follows in the wake of a tsunami and massive flooding, there is great sadness and much that must be done under difficult conditions to address the damage and console the grieving families. But when death, destruction, famine, and impoverishment are not the result of natural disasters but of intentional human actions, where the consequences of those acts were specifically planned or were the foreseeable consequences of deliberate strategies or policies, the situation is much different and far worse. It is far more than disaster response. What must be done in such circumstances to address the devastation and to move forward is more complex and challenging than the most difficult natural tragedy in significant part because of the nature and intentionality of the damage. The path forward to sustainable development in these cases is affected not merely by the death and destruction but also by its character and design.

Unfortunately, it has become increasingly common in recent conflicts for one or more of the parties involved to deliberately target noncombatants and the environment as well as the economy. At the same time, even those who deny any intention to attack either innocent people or the environment accept the fact that noncombatants are killed or injured in significant numbers and that the environment suffers a variety of serious insults. These unintended consequences are euphemistically referred to in the language of modern conflict as collateral damage.

This chapter explores the ways in which contemporary conflict involves deliberate attacks on the key elements of sustainable development, what might be termed social, economic, and environmental warfare, ranging along a continuum from deliberate targeting to that which is properly regarded as collateral damage. A consideration of this difficult subject provides an important foundation for next steps when the conflict ends. A recognition that the nature of contemporary conflict attacks society, environment, and economy provides particularly strong evidence for the argument that post-conflict action must move beyond reconstruction and nation-building models to sustainable development. In such circumstances rebuilding physical infrastructure and governmental bodies is necessary but not sufficient even to achieve the limited objective of the avoidance of more conflict in that same society.

The discussion proceeds by examining two very important contemporary case studies that explore environmental, social, and economic warfare in action. Second, it considers the concept and the practice of environmental warfare. It then turns to the contemporary practice of social warfare with particular attention to soft-target attack strategies, focused on attacks on civilians and aid workers. The analysis then addresses modern elements of economic warfare.

IRAQ AND NEW YORK CITY:
THE CHARACTER AND THE CONTEXT OF CONFLICT

Previous studies of sustainable development implementation demonstrated that context counts. Case studies can help to frame key issues and explore contextual factors that influence the choice of policy tools and the challenges of sustainable development policy implementation.[1] For these reasons the *Implementing Sustainable Development* book considered case studies at the outset of each chapter and a similar approach is used in this volume. The dramatic conflicts of Iraq and the 9/11 attacks on the World Trade Center in New York City provide useful and revealing case studies to examine post-conflict sustainable development challenges in the face of environmental, economic, and social warfare.

Iraq: A Study in Multifaceted Destruction

Iraq is an ancient land with a rich cultural history. From ancient times, Iraq has benefited from the great resources of the Tigris and Euphrates rivers. In the contemporary era, it has enjoyed a windfall from its abundant oil reserves. Yet, Iraq has long been the scene of conflict and conditions that presented the danger of more and new tensions for the future.

Indeed, in recent years Iraq has been the scene of one conflict after another. These clashes have included a range of violent conflicts conducted by various parties, from the Iraqi government's domestic actions under Saddam Hussein, to the Iran-Iraq War, to the Desert Storm and later Iraqi Freedom coalitions, to the insurgents targeting the Coalition Provisional Authority and the new Iraqi government, to the late-arriving terrorists of al Qaeda and other terrorist groups who came, after the way provided fertile ground, to support the insurgents and wage their own conflict with targets intended to serve the global aims of their organizations. In the course of these events, and particularly after the 1991 war, international institutions, nongovernmental organizations (NGOs), and various governments studied the effects of conflict on the people and environment of Iraq.[2] What they did not realize at the time, of course, was that they were also providing a foundation for understanding the conditions during and after the 2003 war. When it appeared likely that there would be another war in Iraq, some of these organizations used the earlier studies in their attempts to rally international opposition to the impending U.S.-led attack or to move quickly to consider the likely impacts of this new round of conflict with the earlier reports as baseline data.[3] For all these reasons, Iraq is an instructive case study to consider environmental, social, and economic warfare in terms of deliberate destruction, collateral damage, and other steps in between the two.

A Story of Unrelenting Internal and External Tensions

It would be difficult for most Iraqi citizens today to remember a time before life became one story of crisis-level tension after another that flowed from both internal and external causes. Even such seemingly positive attributes as the fact that Iraq is the location of the confluence of the Tigris and Euphrates rivers have presented difficulties. As long ago as 1952, the World Bank pointed out that the need to deal with potential tensions with Syria, Turkey, and Iran would be critical to development in Iraq, since each of these countries controlled the headwaters of the two great rivers and would themselves be seriously affected by Iraq's decisions on the use of that water for irrigation and other purposes.[4] Iraq was at that time developing its oil reserves and these riches would in turn become another source of international conflict. Domestically, Iraq has faced a complex set of religious and ethnocultural divisions that have been at the core of many conflicts, and those conflicts have had dimensions that extended beyond the borders of the country into neighboring states.

Well before the more recent years of stress and outright conflict among these groups, there was the rise of local fiefdoms based in significant part on the abilities of some to acquire large land holdings for virtually nothing, which then served as the basis for a troublesome system of tenant farming. The 1952 World Bank report observed:

> In the past much of the vacant land available for an expansion of crop production which ostensibly belonged to the state has fallen into the hands of big

landowners. The so-called Land Settlement Law of 1932 . . . facilitated this process. . . . [I]t has been possible to obtain title on the presentation of proof that a crop was produced on the land in one year, and the land settlement committees have occasionally accepted even more tenuous proof of cultivation. In this way many sheikhs and other influential persons have managed to obtain title to large tracts of land without any payment whatsoever.[5]

Of course, the debates over who owned which land and controlled what water were critically important to life in Iraq. To these individual disputes were added the broader arguments over which elements of Iraqi society controlled the oil fields, a debate that remains a continuing source of tension even as the first elected Iraqi government under the country's new constitution has taken power. But the contemporary era in Iraqi history has been marked by more than disputes. Iraq has been the scene of several types of armed conflict and precursors to it.

Internal Strife—The Battle for Control of Power by the Baathists

The process that ultimately brought Saddam Hussein to power took many years and proved over time to be an increasingly ruthless campaign. The country had, in fact, endured an ongoing contest for power. The Baathists actually took power in 1963, but could not maintain control. Then in 1968, another coup d'état brought them back into power, but this time as a much stronger organization.

The centerpiece of the emerging Baathist regime came to be a group known as the Tikritis—from their origins as relatives from Tikrit. Ultimately, efforts to undermine Baathist power provided excuses for ruthless actions against their opponents, many of which were led by Saddam Hussein, who was rapidly becoming one of the two most powerful of the Tikritis. By the time he formally assumed control of Iraq and consolidated all authority in himself in 1979, it was clear that he would use any and every means at his disposal to maintain power and achieve his ends.

The Iran-Iraq War 1980–1988: A War Whose Toll May Never Be Known

There had long been tensions between Iran and Iraq and that situation became even more complex following the 1979 Iranian revolution that deposed the Shah and ultimately placed a fundamentalist Islamic government in power under the direction of Ayatollah Khomeini. There had been border issues and traditional tensions among neighboring nations, but there was more at issue in the case of Iran and Iraq. There were both broad questions related to religion, ethnicity, the power position of Saddam Hussein's rule, and a little understood role in the Cold War.

The tension between the majority Shia and the minority—but ruling— Sunnis was a central fact of life in Iraq. The tensions between these two understandings of Islam had been serious matters for generations, since the time when the original battles had been fought over the correct leader to follow the Prophet Muhammad had been fought out in Iraq. The rise of a committed Shia regime in Iran on its eastern border promised to rekindle the long-standing disputes over such matters as control over the Shatt al Arab waterway and other unresolved issues. From Saddam Hussein's perspective, it also threatened to foster Shia fundamentalist opposition within Iraq.

Indeed, the Iraq regime was convinced that a fundamentalist Shia movement in Iraq was becoming more active as the Iranian theocracy took shape. The Iraqi foreign minister, Tariq Aziz, survived an attempted assassination. An assassination attempt against the minister of culture and information also failed. Both were attributed to a group known as Ad Dawah al Islamiyah. The Saddam Hussein regime launched a program of deportations of Shia and had the leader of Ad Dawah and his sister killed.[6] Relations between Iran and Iraq continued to deteriorate and the two countries moved from individual clashes toward full-scale warfare.

The conflict between the two countries was also a central field of conflict of the Cold War. The United States had long supported the Shah of Iran. Indeed it had led the coup d'état known as Operation Ajax in August 1953 that brought down the government of Prime Minister Muhammad Mosaddeq of Iran and restored the Shah to power.[7] During the Cold War, the United States provided American weapons and aircraft to Iran, which became the core of the revolutionary Iranian military arsenal after the revolution of 1979, while the Soviet Union had supplied Iraq with weaponry. Of course, there were other interests at stake as well, not the least of which was oil, and both the Soviets and the French were engaged in a range of enterprises in that area. The French also provided weapons, particularly Mirage jets and Exocet anti-ship missiles, to Iraqis.

The ironies of the foreign intrigues in the Iran-Iraq conflict were considerable. Even as the Iranian Air Force was flying U.S.-built fighters and helicopters against Iraqi targets, Washington was reacting to the hostage crisis and the rise of a regime that was a leading force for anti-American sentiment in the Middle East. With the United States pursuing the Cold War strategy that the "enemies of our enemies are our friends," the White House was quietly moving to support Saddam Hussein against Iran. "On May 28, 1984, President Reagan issued National Security Decision Directive (NSDD) 141 on 'Responding to Escalation in Iran-Iraq War' which authorized intelligence sharing with the Government of Iraq in order to forestall an Iranian victory. . . . In 1986, the scope of intelligence sharing with Iraq was expanded twice, according to a Senate Intelligence Committee report."[8]

Senator Tom Harkin (D-Iowa) later opposed the nomination of Robert Gates for CIA director based upon his role in providing intelligence information to Saddam Hussein in the 1980s that Harkin thought gave the Iraqi leader knowledge that helped him act against American interests later, including in the 1991 war.[9]

On the other hand, the Reagan administration had other interests that it decided could be served by arranging a deal with Tehran. This was the infamous Iran-Contra matter, in which the United States agreed to provide missiles to Iran with the proceeds then to be redirected toward illegal assistance for the Contra rebel operations against the Sandinistas then in power in Nicaragua. In support of this operation, President Reagan issued an intelligence finding that read in part:

> The USG will act to facilitate efforts by third parties and third countries to establish contact with moderate elements within and outside the Government of Iran by providing these elements with arms, equipment and related material in order to enhance the credibility of these elements in their effort to achieve a more pro-U.S. government in Iran by demonstrating their ability to obtain requisite resources to defend their country against Iraq and intervention by the Soviet Union.[10]

There were two other issues that brought the attention of the international community at the time. There was concern that the targeting of vessels might lead to attacks on oil tanker traffic. Though it did not then draw as much attention as it might have, the sinking of vessels posed a variety of environmental risks given the kinds of toxic cargoes on board. What attracted more international attention and concern, however, was the use of chemical weapons by Iraq against Iran in violation of the 1925 Geneva Protocol. While Iraq denied the allegations, the evidence was more than ample to support charges by the UN and others that Iraq had used both blister agents and nerve gas against its adversary. Later studies estimated that more than 21,000 Iranian troops were killed by chemical weapons during the conflict and many more wounded.[11]

> The chemical weapons deployed by Iraq reportedly included mustard gas and the nerve gases sarin, tabun and GF, which have environmental persistence times ranging from thirty minutes, in the case of tabun, to as much as two years in the case of mustard gas. . . . A UN expert team, which conducted investigations between 1984 and 1988, confirmed that chemical weapons had been used by Iraq.[12]

There was some evidence of the use of bacteriological weapons as well, but these allegations were never conclusively confirmed.[13]

Several issues flowed from the chemical warfare that extended well beyond the Iran-Iraq conflict. Those attacks would have a great deal to do with the targeting of air strikes in the 1991 war aimed at reported chemical weapons facilities and other plants labeled "dual-use" plants that were assumed to produce materials that were in themselves normal industrial products but that could be used as part of chemical weapons manufacturing. Then, of course, there were implications drawn from the use of chemical weapons in the Iran-Iraq War for the argument in support of the invasion of Iraq, part of the ill-fated weapons of mass destruction (WMD) case advanced in the United Nations prior to the 2003 attack.[14]

The Iran-Iraq War ended in a cease-fire in August 1988. The formal settlement came as the parties accepted UN Security Council Resolution 598, which was adopted in late 1987.[15]

Saddam Hussein's War against the Kurds 1988–1990

The Iran-Iraq War was not the only time Saddam Hussein employed chemical weapons. There were a number of reports of the use of chemical weapons against Kurdish communities from 1987 to 1988. Indeed, later reports noted that: "Clinical evidence and soil samples confirmed the use of mustard gas and the nerve agent tabun against the Kurdish population in 1987."[16] The specific case that attracted worldwide attention and horror was the attack in March 1988 on Halabja, with some 5,000 dead men, women, and children whose pictures were shared around the world.[17] The regime's willingness to use these weapons against women and children was one of the most devastating indictments of Saddam Hussein's rule.

That said, it is interesting to note that the first indictment issued against Saddam Hussein as he faced the Iraq Special Tribunal concerned a massacre in the largely Shia town of Dujail in July 1982. He was found guilty of ordering the destruction of the village and the deaths of dozens of people following an assassination attempt on his life in that town. This was but one of the earlier documented cases, but there were more to follow among Shia as well as Kurds.[18] The first trial alleging the use of chemical attacks in the so-called Operation Al Anfal campaign from 1988 to 1991 was under way at the time of this writing, though Hussein had already been sentenced to death in the Dujail case and was subsequently executed in December 2006.

The 1991 Gulf War: From the Invasion of Kuwait to the Coalition Response and Cease-Fire

With a million Iranians and Iraqis dead, a million refugees, and billions of dollars in costs and destruction, the events that had taken place by the end of 1988 would have been sufficient to require massive post-conflict development efforts, but only two years after the end of the Iran-Iraq War, in August 1990, Iraq launched an attack on Kuwait. In January 1991, the

United States led a coalition of more than two dozen countries into battle
to drive Iraqi forces out of Kuwait. On January 15, President Bush issued
National Security Directive (NSD) 54, which directed the attack on Iraq,
and Operation Desert Storm was launched the next day.[19]

> Pursuant to my responsibilities and authority under the Constitution as Presi-
> dent and Commander in Chief, and under the laws and treaties of the United
> States, and pursuant to H.J. Res. 77 (1991), and in accordance with the rights
> and obligations of the United States under international law, including UN Se-
> curity Council Resolutions 660, 661, 662, 664, 666, 667, 670, 674, 677, and
> 678, and consistent with the inherent right of the collective self-defense af-
> firmed in Article 51 of the United Nations Charter, I hereby authorize military
> actions designed to bring about Iraq's withdrawal from Kuwait.[20]

While the war ended with a cease-fire on February 28, this brief conflict would have serious consequences for many years to come. First, the
war began with an Iraqi invasion of Kuwait, which was rapidly overrun
by attacking forces. Even so, Kuwait and its people suffered serious damage in the relatively brief period of attack and occupation. With all that
has happened since 1991, there has been a tendency to focus on Iraq itself and not the overall impact of that conflict in the region. Second, the
attack on Iraq targeted a wide range of facilities, the destruction of which
had important environmental consequences in offensives that employed
some 88,500 tons of bombs and missiles.[21] In the process, large quantities of chemicals, some of them toxic, were released into the environment. There was also a dramatic loss of infrastructure in Iraq, from electricity generation to water and sewage treatment plants. Those treatment
plants, in turn, were badly needed to address some of the social, environmental, and economic impacts on the people of Iraq in the years to
come.

Third, the 1991 war brought worldwide attention to the concept of environmental warfare, as Saddam Hussein made deliberate and destructive use
of oil pollution and oil fires that damaged the environment in a variety of
ways.[22] The Iraqi invasion force destroyed some 1,164 oil wells in Kuwait,
sending more than 60 million barrels of oil into the environment. Some of
the oil flowed from the wells and formed more than two hundred oil
lakes.[23] In other cases, the oil wells sprayed an oil mist into the air and blanketed a wide territory. All of that was complicated by the fires from the
burning wells, fires that sent tons of airborne pollutants across a wide area
of land and sea. In fact, estimates found that 953 square kilometers were
polluted in one way or another by the destructions of the wells.[24] As if that
was not damage enough, the Iraqi regime ordered the deliberate release of
an additional 10 million barrels of oil into waterways and the sea, a spill
that spread over a six-hundred-kilometer distance, despoiling the fisheries

and complicating the operation of the desalinization plants necessary to provide fresh water supplies for Gulf nations.[25]

Fourth, the cease-fire left Saddam Hussein and his government in power with the plan that the United Nations Special Commission (UNSCOM) would be in place to monitor compliance with the terms of UN resolutions that required the elimination of chemical, biological, or nuclear weapons potential. Conflicts in this process would lead to UN sanctions and limited military actions to enforce the so-called no-fly zones. The sanctions, the Iraqi response to them, the UN Oil-for-Food program, put in place to address some of the consequences of the sanctions, and Iraqi reactions, all had important consequences for the social conditions of Iraqis, but also for the environment and the economy of the nation.[26] Moreover, they would provide important foundations for the further conflict that was to follow and end in the 2003 war.

Ongoing Strife with Manifold Dimensions: Life under Sanctions, Continuing Aggression toward Kurds and Shia, and the Attack on the Marsh Arabs

Following Desert Storm Saddam Hussein moved quickly to tighten his grip within the country. Kurds in the north were moving as well, but in their case it was to consolidate their self-governing, quasi-independent status. In the south, there was a developing Shia revolt. Hussein responded with his customary ruthlessness. The Kurds in the north received protection in the form of coalition air patrols to block Iraqi attacks. Hussein used his full panoply of powers to punish the rebellious communities where he could.

One of the most dramatic moves by the Iraqi ruler was his effort to destroy what are known as the Marsh Arabs, Shia of southern Iraq living in communities in the marshlands. He launched massive projects to drain the marshlands. "Totaling almost 9,000 square kilometres of permanent wetlands, the Iraqi marshlands dwindled to just 760 square kilometres in 2002."[27] The attack on the Marsh Arabs was an effort to destroy a 5,000-year-old civilization, a form of social and cultural warfare. It was also deliberate environmental warfare that devastated thousands of square kilometers of wetlands that was a world heritage ecosystem supporting a wide range of flora and fauna.

The 2003 Iraq War: A Disaster in the Making

The stresses within Iraq and from the Hussein regime following the 1991 war continued and grew on several fronts. By March 20, 2003, Iraq was again at war, this time facing an invasion led by the United States and Great Britain, backed by a smaller number of coalition partners than in the previous Gulf War. First justified on grounds of threats from weapons of mass destruction (WMD), the defense of the invasion gradually shifted to an argument for regime change in order to remove Saddam Hussein as a threat to the region and a claim that the regime supported international terrorists. Later still, the emphasis was placed, by the George W. Bush administration at least, on claimed intentions to bring democracy to the Middle East.

With the publication of books by a number of those involved, it became clear that almost immediately after the September 11, 2001, attacks that Iraq was targeted by President Bush. He was quoted as telling key staff on September 12 to see if there was any shred of evidence that might link Saddam Hussein to the 9/11 attacks and, even after he was reminded that efforts had been made to determine whether there was a link, Bush insisted that they "Look into Iraq, Saddam."[28] There was no evidence that Iraq was in any way connected to the 9/11 attacks, or that it was an important base for al Qaeda operations. Neither was there strong evidence that Iraq had seriously attempted to reconstitute the weapons-of-mass-destruction programs that had been hit during the 1991 war. Yet in October 2001, a State Department Future of Iraq Project briefing showed, "the State Department began planning on the transition" in Iraq.[29]

Also late in 2001, Lieutenant General Gregory Newbold briefed OPLAN 1003-98, the existing contingency plan for an attack on Iraq to Secretary of Defense Donald Rumsfeld and Chairman of the Joint Chiefs of Staff, General Richard B. Myers, along with other military commanders.[30] This plan had been developed earlier, but a new plan was already in process, with work in progress beginning on September 13.[31] The earlier plan had called for a force approaching half a million troops, but Secretary Rumsfeld reportedly began pressing General Tommy Franks, CENTCOM commander, for a plan that could be put in readiness faster and with fewer troops. On December 28, Franks flew to Texas to brief President Bush.[32] Discussions continued until Franks returned to brief the president on March 3, 2002, by which point it was clear that the Pentagon was not viewing this as a contingency planning exercise.[33] Michael R. Gordon and General Bernard E. Trainor report that shortly thereafter the president ordered administration officials to begin talking with countries that might be allies in such an operation or at least provide corridors of access for attacking forces.[34]

April 9, 2003, marked the fall of the government of Saddam Hussein and, by the beginning of May, the Bush administration asserted that major combat operations were largely complete. It would not be long before it became clear that the combat operations were about to shift from standard warfare to a counterinsurgency effort.

The United States dominated efforts to put in place a new government after the fall of Hussein's Baathist regime with the move to install the Coalition Provisional Authority (CPA). On July 12, 2003, the CPA appointed an Interim Governing Council with a twenty-five-member cabinet and a constitutional commission also consisting of twenty-five members.[35] The

United States formally transferred control from the Coalition Provisional Authority to a sovereign Iraqi interim government on June 28, 2004. The interim government moved to elections at the end of January 2005, which not only appointed a set of officials for a new government but also approved a temporary administrative law to both guide governance and advance a constitution-drafting process. A draft constitution was published and adopted by the voters in an October 2005 referendum. Elections were held to select the first government under the new constitution that is operating presently.

While these formal steps were being taken toward a new governing structure, the lack of planning and implementation of an effective post-conflict process produced serious challenges. Among the many problems posed by the idea of removing Saddam Hussein, the primary issue was not the military ability to drive the Baathist regime from power, but what would take place afterward. Even so, the administration blocked efforts by officials in its own State Department who were alert to many of the dangers ahead. In fact, the U.S. Department of State began preparing for the transition to what was to happen after Saddam Hussein in October of 2001.[36] The Future of Iraq Project was developed and was ultimately funded by Congress in the late spring of 2002. Working group meetings began in early July of that year. The State Department briefing document on the project provides a useful explanation of the project, which was headed by Thomas Warrick.[37]

The working groups, made up of "10–20 Iraqis and 2–5 international experts," were central to the project, with groups created to address "transitional justice, public finance, public outreach development, democratic principles, water, agriculture & environment, public health & humanitarian needs, defense policy, local government, economy & infrastructure, civil-society capacity building, anti-corruption measures, education, refugees & internally displaced persons, building a free media, foreign policy, and oil & energy."[38] These groups then had subgroups of four to eight for detailed work on reports. The meetings were also attended by observers from several executive branch agencies.

Secretary of Defense Rumsfeld Takes Control and
Rejects Serious Efforts to Address Post-Conflict Development

However, Secretary of Defense Donald Rumsfeld and others in the administration successfully blocked serious State Department participation and the Department of Defense (DOD) took control over post-conflict matters in January 2003.[39] Rumsfeld even rejected the effort by the person chosen by DOD to head post-conflict efforts, retired Lt. General Jay Garner, to have Thomas Warrick, formerly the head of the Future of Iraq Project, as a member of his staff as he was preparing to go to Iraq.[40] Although the work product from the Future of Iraq Project was provided to some members of

Congress, the reports were not publicly available (and have not been made available since).

The United States dramatically underestimated the likelihood of violence that would come when the Iraqi regime fell. The number of troops committed beyond the actual invasion force designed to defeat the Iraqi army was totally inadequate to address the multitude of other challenges and needs, most particularly including security, rapid repair of essential infrastructure, and support for community development. Then Army Chief of Staff General Eric K. Shinseki had made clear to Congress the size of the force that would be necessary during a hearing before the Senate Armed Services Committee.

> I would say that what's been mobilized to this point—something on the order of several hundred thousand soldiers are probably, you know, a figure that would be required. We're talking about post-hostilities control over a piece of geography that's fairly significant, with the kinds of ethnic tensions that could lead to other problems. And so it takes a significant ground-force presence to maintain a safe and secure environment, to ensure that people are fed, that water is distributed, all the normal responsibilities that go along with administering a situation like this.[41]

Shinseki's statement was promptly repudiated by the Pentagon and he left his position shortly thereafter to enter retirement.

General Garner went in to lead the initial post-invasion governance efforts with so little support and resources that it was necessary to redesign the approach quickly and in the midst of the turmoil. Excessive reliance had been placed earlier on the use of large-scale contracts to do virtually all of the critical construction and service operations, contracts that were entered only with U.S. firms and most on a sole-source basis with no competition. Moreover, the Coalition Provisional Authority headed by L. Paul Bremer soon displaced Garner. Bremer then undertook actions that would have dire consequences. On May 16, 2003, Bremer issued Coalition Provisional Authority Number 1, entitled "De-Ba`athification of Iraqi Society." The order read in part as follows:

> 2) Full members of the Ba`ath Party holding the ranks of "Udw Qutriyya" (Regional Command Member), "Udw Far" (Branch Member), "Udw Shu'bah" (Section Member), and "Udw Firqah" (Group Member) (together, "Senior Party Members") are hereby removed from their positions and banned from future employment in the public sector. . . .
>
> 3) Individuals holding positions in the top three layers of management in every national government ministry, affiliated corporations and other government institutions (e.g., universities and hospitals) shall be interviewed for possible affiliation with the Ba`ath Party, and subject to investigation for criminal conduct and risk to security. Any such persons detained [*sic*] to be full members of the Ba`ath Party shall be removed from their employment. . . .[42]

Since Baath party membership was a requirement for many administrative positions in Iraq at the time, that order meant that thousands of educated, talented, and experienced administrators who understood the essential organizations, services, and context would be thrown out of work, creating serious economic and social dislocations at a time when the problem was to address post-conflict development.

A week later, Bremer issued Coalition Provisional Authority Order Number 2, which was entitled "Dissoulution [*sic*] of Entities."[43] This order disbanded a variety of Iraqi organizations, but most particularly the military and other security-related organizations. Any officer of the rank of colonel or higher would be presumed to be a senior Baath Party member and therefore excluded from public employment under CPA Order No. 1. This order caught many U.S. officers by surprise, since they expected to be able to use at least elements of the Iraqi military to help maintain order and to convert into a new defense force for the country. Indeed, psychological warfare efforts had for some time sent messages to Iraqi officers that they should not resist the move against the regime and they would have the opportunity for a positive future.[44] The Future of Iraq Project had called for action to: "Organize plans for restructuring the Iraqi armed forces to play a positive role in rebuilding Iraqi society, and to defend Iraq without threatening Iraq's citizens or Iraq's neighbors."[45] Instead, thousands of armed, trained, and seasoned troops and their officer corps found themselves unemployed and under the control of an occupying force that not only took their income, but also their pride. Bremer had been warned by CIA officials that these actions would fuel an insurgency, and they did.

The actions taken by the CPA also ensured that there would be a great deal more work to do to provide security to the Iraqi people and to undertake the many other tasks necessary to deliver essential services. It soon became clear that the security situation was deteriorating. In that setting, foreign fighters determined to increase their efforts and sectarian violence grew.

It is clear that even the most obvious failures by the United States and its coalition partners in preparation for and action following the fall of the regime in Iraq were known ahead of time, were not adequately addressed, and ultimately produced catastrophic consequences. These events affected all three dimensions of sustainable development and were recognized by the major agencies that conducted assessments in Iraq, including the United Nations and the World Bank.

The United Nations Environmental Programme (UNEP) *Desk Study* made clear at the time of the invasion that part of the difficulties facing Iraq dated back to damage done in the Iran-Iraq conflict and in the 1991 Gulf War.[46] That was particularly important because of the scope and nature of those conflicts, in which a wide array of facilities were targeted, among other things spilling a variety of pollutants into the soil and waterways of a

nation without the water treatment facilities in operation to begin to protect against long-term pollution. Much of that pollution was left on or in
the soil. The situation was rendered more difficult by the deterioration of
the environment, the social conditions, and the economy in the period after the 1991 war. Little had been done to address the environmental degradation from industrial facilities that had been struck earlier and that continued to discharge toxic substances onto the ground and ultimately into
the water. The ships that had been sunk in the earlier conflicts that contained toxic substances from oil to battery acid had not been salvaged or remediation efforts attempted.

The actions taken by the international community in the wake of the
1991 conflict were principally aimed at security concerns. There were restrictions on importation of a variety of materials that were considered potentially useful for military purposes but that were also essential for other
legitimate civilian needs, such as chlorine required for water treatment.[47] At
the same time, the Oil-for-Food program created by the United Nations was
subverted by corruption both within the Iraqi regime and outside it.[48] That,
in turn, meant that Iraqi citizens suffered. In fact, the regime used the impact of sanctions on the health and well-being of children as an argument
to eliminate or at least to loosen restrictions.

Whatever was intended, the sanctions provided a setting in which virtually all significant social and economic indicators declined dramatically. In
terms of health issues, economic security, and food security, Iraq's citizens
were vulnerable going into the 2003 war and the country's environment
was still very much under stress. All of these issues were raised even as the
conflict raged and even though some of the arguments had been presented
by some NGOs before the attack was launched. Indeed, the October 2003
UNEP Progress Report confirmed the fears expressed in the earlier assessments.[49] The World Bank and the United Nations released at about the
same time a *Joint Iraq Needs Assessment*, which provided further confirmation of these concerns.[50]

What was also clear, both before and after the attack, was that any delays
in ensuring the availability of such basic infrastructure operations as water
and sewage treatment would have devastating impacts, including significantly increased health and environmental damage. The Future of Iraq Project had warned about these dangers well before the attack was launched.[51]
The project had also explained that security would be essential in order for
the civilian population to seek to rebuild their lives and economic activity.
However, it quickly became obvious that there were insufficient forces in
place to both address the growing insurgency and all of the other challenges
that existed.[52]

The Attack on Soft Targets: Social Warfare in Iraq

In addition to some direct engagements and the use of improvised explosive devices (IEDs) against coalition troops, the insurgents would often choose to attack so-called soft targets, including essential infrastructure, civilian Iraqis, and international aid workers. The lack of security and effective law and order in the wake of the initial military actions saw a combination of crime, sectarian violence, and increasingly intense insurgent action. Iraqi citizens faced threats ranging from growing sectarian violence to criminal activity such as kidnapping. The large numbers of civilian contractors, brought in primarily by the United States to work on various projects, quickly became targets. The inability to provide government protection for these workers prompted the dramatic growth of private security firms that charged substantial fees to companies with projects in Iraq. So important and costly were these services that a Government Accountability Office (GAO) report found that, by 2005, they were taking as much as 15 percent of contracts just for the security protection component.[53] Later reports increased those estimates substantially.

Then there were the growing attacks on civilians working for international institutions and nongovernmental aid agencies. Given the circumstances and lack of resources provided by the United States and its allies, there was a clear need for and growing expectations of international agencies, both official and nongovernmental. These agencies included:

- The UN Assistance Mission for Iraq (UNAMI)
- The Humanitarian Information Center (HIC) for Iraq
- The UN Mine Action Program—Iraq Update
- UNICEF (United Nations Children's Fund)
- UNICEF Programs in South and Central Iraq
- UN Development Programme (UNDP) in Iraq
- UNDP's Electricity Network Rehabilitation Programme (ENRP) in Northern Iraq
- World Food Programme (WFP) Country Involvement—Iraq
- World Health Organization (WHO)
- Office for the Coordination of Humanitarian Affairs (OCHA)
- UN Environment Programme (UNEP)
- UN High Commissioner for Refugees (UNHCR)
- U.S. Agency for International Development (USAID)
- USAID Office of Foreign Disaster Assistance (OFDA)
- Iraq: Humanitarian Aid and Reconstruction Assistance
- USAID Office of Food for Peace (FFP)

- USAID Office of Transition Initiatives (OTI)
- U.S. Department of State, Bureau of Population, Refugees, and Migration (PRM)
- Coalition Provisional Authority (CPA)
- U.S. Embassy in Iraq
- U.S. Department of Agriculture, International Food Aid Programs
- U.S. Department of the Treasury, Office of Foreign Assets Control (OFAC)
- U.S. Defense Security Cooperation Agency, Office of Humanitarian Assistance and Mine Action (HA/MA)
- U.S. Department of State, Office of International Information Programs (IIP)
- Doctors Without Borders (French name: Médecins Sans Frontières, or MSF)
- Human Rights Watch (HRW)
- International Committee of the Red Cross (ICRC)
- International Federation of Red Cross and Red Crescent Societies (IFRC)
- Mercy Corps International
- Oxfam International
- American Friends Service Committee (AFSC): Statement on Iraq
- CARE USA
- Catholic Relief Services
- Church World Service (CWS)
- Lutheran World Relief (LWR)
- Physicians for Human Rights (PHR)
- U.S. Committee for Refugees
- World Resources Institute (WRI)
- World Vision International[54]

In August 2003, insurgents launched a suicide bombing attack on UN headquarters in Baghdad. The blast killed the head of the UN mission, Ambassador Sergio Vieira de Mello, and more than three dozen others, prompting the UN to scale back dramatically its operational personnel in Iraq.[55] An October attack on Red Cross and Red Crescent aid workers killed thirty-three and injured nearly two hundred, raising serious questions about the organization's ability and willingness to continue its operations under such insecure conditions.[56] Médecins Sans Frontières (Doctors Without Borders) also scaled back its operations and, a year later, on November 4, 2004, announced in New York and Amman that it was withdrawing completely from Iraq. "Due to the escalating violence in the country, MSF considers it no longer acceptable to expose its staff to the serious risks that apparently come with being associated with an international humanitarian organization. . . . 'We deeply regret the fact that we will no longer be able to provide much needed medical help to the Iraqi people.'"[57] Doctors Without Borders complained that, while they sought to maintain a scrupulous political independence and therefore wanted to avoid operating with troops as security guards, they were increasingly viewed by insurgents as aligned with the coalition forces.

The "Reconstruction Gap" in Iraq and Its Causes

The lack of security had other consequences as well. The Special Inspector General for Iraq Reconstruction's (SIGIR) October 2005 report indicated that security costs were one of the primary causes of what the report termed "the reconstruction gap" in Iraq.[58] "Nearly all of the U.S. appropriated dollars—more than 93%—have already been committed to programs and projects. More than 25% of these funds have been spent on security costs related to the insurgency, which has proportionately reduced funds for other reconstruction projects."[59] Even assuming that the existing projects were completed, the SIGIR concluded that in order to ensure the capacity to sustain the operation of the infrastructure projects over time, the Iraq government would need to invest between $650 and $750 million per year, plus "[a]n additional 20–25% will be needed to cover the associated costs of security, salaries, and fuel."[60]

Media outlets reported the problems identified in the October SIGIR report, along with the announcement by U.S. officials that the Bush administration would not request any further funding for Iraq reconstruction in its FY 2007 budget proposal.[61] A *Washington Post* article quoted Brigadier General William McCory, commander of the Army Corps of Engineers in charge of management of reconstruction projects: "The U.S. never intended to completely rebuild Iraq, . . . In an interview this past week, McCoy said: 'This was just supposed to be a jump-start.'"[62]

U.S. Commitments: Redefinition or Abandonment?

As the security situation deteriorated, demands increased for reductions in U.S. troop levels. At the same time, the dramatic expenditures to support the war prompted criticism at home, particularly when the Bush administration moved to make major temporary tax cuts permanent in the face of mounting budget deficits. The federal government response to Hurricane Katrina intensified fiscal pressures.

It became increasingly clear that General Shinseki had been a far better predictor of the troop needs for post-invasion Iraq operations than the administration, but that recognition came at a time when there were already calls from conservatives as well as liberals in the United States for the administration to put forth a plan to phase down troop levels. Administration insistence that Iraqi security forces would be able to take over security in the country found little acceptance by anyone outside of the White House and Defense Department.

In the face of all of these difficulties, the administration rejected any idea that it had intended to rebuild Iraq. It became increasingly clear that the intention had only been to stabilize the country and quickly turn over responsibilities to a new Iraqi government. In other words, not only had the coalition forces not intended to support sustainable development, they had not even intended to undertake a serious reconstruction and recovery effort.

The likelihood of abandonment became a real fear for many Iraqis, sectarian violence increased, and insurgent activity became more deadly. In the interim, a new president in Iran had taken extremely dramatic positions on a host of issues. For Iraqi Sunnis, the likelihood of increasing Iranian influence among the Shia-dominated government of Iraq only heightened fears and increased anger. On December 7, 2006, the Iraq Study Group, headed by James Baker and Lee Hamilton, released its long awaited report, which began: "The situation in Iraq is grave and deteriorating. . . . Violence is increasing in scope and lethality. It is fed by a Sunni Arab insurgency, Shiite militias and death squads, al Qaeda, and widespread criminality. Sectarian conflict is the principal challenge to stability. The Iraqi people have a democratically elected government, yet it is not adequately advancing national reconciliation, providing basic security, or delivering essential services. . . . A slide toward chaos could trigger the collapse of Iraq's government and a humanitarian catastrophe."[63] At the time of this writing Iraq shows little sign of peace on the horizon or a future that is built on sustainable development principles. Indeed, the civilian death toll has grown even more dramatically than the mounting military casualties.

Whatever else it was, Iraq was not a war about terrorism when it was launched in 2003. Sadly, over time, it came to have some of those elements as outside fighters from a variety of groups, including al Qaeda, whose attack on the United States on September 11, 2001, gave it prominence among terrorist organizations and as the leading enemy of Western powers, have seen Iraq as an excellent place to exploit for their own purposes and in which to recruit others.

When Iraq reaches the point where it can look forward to post-conflict development, it will only succeed if it goes beyond the kind of simplistic idea of reconstruction that the U.S. government brought to it in May of 2003 to a sustainable development approach that recognizes that the country has suffered from a variety of types of conflict, involving a series of different types of combatants over an extended period of time.

The 9/11 Attack on New York City:
Economic and Social Warfare and Their Aftermath

Most Americans recall when and where they heard the news of the attacks on the World Trade Center in New York, the Pentagon in Arlington, Virginia, just across the river from Washington, D.C., and the plot that failed when the courageous passengers aboard United Airlines Flight 93 battled the terrorists in the skies above Pennsylvania on a plane that had been intended to attack the nation's capital. It is a story that has been recounted in many settings, but perhaps nowhere in greater detail than in the report of the so-called 9/11 Commission.[64]

And yet, in all of the major reports that have been done on nation-building and post-conflict reconstruction in the years since the attack, there is virtually no significant attention to the question of sustainable development after the 9/11 attacks in the United States, or even in New York. The same problem can be found in international reports in post-conflict settings that seem to assume there is no such challenge in other developed countries. While there are numerous studies on the impact of conflict discussed in this volume and elsewhere, they do not speak to the sustainable development challenges in the United States after 9/11, Spain, Great Britain, or other Western countries that have experienced terrorist attacks or violent civil disorder.[65] That silence speaks volumes about the lack of serious attention in the United States to post-conflict development with a perspective that goes beyond the limited objectives of foreign policy aimed at the prevention of failed states and the advancement of U.S. strategic interests abroad. It also demonstrates the failure of the international community to understand that the challenges of sustainable development after conflict apply in the developed as well as developing nations. The fact is that the United States on 9/11 in 2001, Madrid's train bombings in 2004, and Great Britain's transit attacks in 2005, to name but a few examples, were not just isolated incidents in those countries. They have had profound effects on those great nations and their people.

The failure to take a sustainable development approach in the years since 9/11 could be tied to the idea that New York City had not been destroyed and that the task of rebuilding the lost buildings, the neighborhood, and the urban infrastructure laid waste by attack would be completed in due course. But, as terrible as the loss of life and the destruction of portions of one of the nation's most important cities were, the attacks had far wider consequences for the nation and for the world. Two full-scale wars followed, an international counterterrorism effort was launched with battles fought around the globe, and the domestic governance of the United States changed in a host of critically important and troublesome ways at all levels of government.

The attacks on September 11 together comprised a terrorist plot that was aimed at real people and their nation, but it was also—and in many ways just as importantly—an attack on symbols of economic, military, and political power. It was economic and social warfare as well as a political conflict. The environment was also a casualty, even if it was not a primary target.

The Seeds of Conflict Grow: The United States as Target and the Rise of Its Attacker

Before 9/11 most Americans considered terrorism, war, and civil disorder as things that happened somewhere else. Centuries earlier there had indeed been a revolutionary war, then the burning of the nation's capitol in the War of 1812, and, later, of course, the massive loss of life and destruction of the Civil War. Yes, it was true that Americans were attacked on December 7, 1941, at their bases in Hawaii by Japan and there were battles fought in the Aleutian Islands during that war.[66] In one of the more widely publicized events of the era, two groups of German saboteurs put ashore by submarines were captured in Florida and New Jersey during WWII, convicted by military commission, and executed.[67] But, for most Americans today, those events are far off in the distant past. And despite the attacks on Pearl Harbor and the Aleutians, the United States never experienced anything like what happened in Great Britain, much of Asia, Germany, Japan, Korea, Israel, Lebanon, or Vietnam as a result of conflict.

To many Americans, even those events that were serious matters of civil disorder or domestic terrorism were generally written off as relatively localized, if deadly and horribly regrettable, criminal actions to be addressed by restoration of law and order and perhaps some consideration of social conditions. However, as the twenty-first century approached, it should have been clear to Americans that the death, destruction, and consequences of conflict were going to come to the United States.

There were, in the 1990s, many terrorist groups that targeted national governments around the world. Al Qaeda with its enigmatic leader Osama bin Laden was but one of these groups in one general subset of terrorists sometimes described in terms of their ties to a particular version of Islamic fundamentalism, though many Muslims would be quick to reject their methods and would assert the attacks were in contravention of the tenets of that faith. Although they sometimes interacted with each other, the terrorist groups developed as independent units, each with its own mission and its own set of targets.

The development of al Qaeda and Osama bin Laden is generally traced to the days when Islamic fighters went to Afghanistan to battle alongside the mujahideen against the Soviets and the Moscow-backed government. In those days, the United States was happy to cooperate with the mujahideen fighters on the long-standing Cold War premise that the enemy of my enemy is my friend. Osama bin Laden, then a young Saudi from a well-to-do family, was among those who made the journey to Afghanistan to join the jihad against the Soviet-backed regime. The Soviet forces left Afghanistan in 1988. Soon after that, the USSR collapsed.

Bin Laden and others sought to maintain the al Qaeda (or "foundation" for Islamic holy war) organization that had been built for Afghanistan for future use against what they saw as the forces of the infidels who threatened Islam. By 1989, bin Laden had become the leader of al Qaeda. Over the next few years al Qaeda and other organizations would take action in theaters of conflict as diverse as the Middle East, the former Yugoslavia, and Pakistan, among other places.

Bin Laden traveled a circuitous route that eventually took him back to Afghanistan, where he established the headquarters and training facilities for his organization. Following the fall of the Soviet regime in Afghanistan, bin Laden relocated to Sudan and used his construction company as a base to develop international funding sources and communication with other organizations. He was learning from and listening to other zealots who advocated a radical version of Islam.

Following the invasion of Kuwait by the Iraqi forces of Saddam Hussein, bin Laden attempted to convince rulers in Saudi Arabia, his home country, that he should be deputized to lead Islamic fighters in the campaign to drive Saddam Hussein out of Kuwait.[68] The Saudis, however, not only rejected his proposal but joined forces with the United States–led Operation Desert Storm coalition that drove the Iraqis back. The Saudi government also provided bases and support for U.S. forces within the Saudi kingdom. These actions were to become bin Laden's rallying points in his terrorist efforts, and he regularly denounced both the Saudis and the United States. He was able to make his way to Pakistan and from there to Afghanistan, where he operated under the protection of the Taliban, who had taken power after the Soviets departed, while the United States had turned a blind eye to events in the area.

Al Qaeda launched a variety of efforts to raise funds, build its organization, and communicate with other like-minded groups in other countries, such as the Abu Sayyaf Brigade in the Philippines and Jemaah Islamiyah based in Indonesia. In addition to its activities in Asia and the Pacific, al Qaeda also intended to use Africa as a theater of operations. By 1993 al Qaeda was operating out of Nairobi and providing support for groups in Somalia in their fight against the U.S. forces there. The departure of the United States from Somalia in 1994 encouraged al Qaeda and other terrorist groups to conclude that the United States could be defeated, as the Soviets had been in Afghanistan.

There were a variety of other important terrorist events unfolding that were led by others. In February 1993 a bomb planted in a Ryder rental van exploded in the underground garage at the World Trade Center in New York City in a blast that might very well have killed many more than the six people who died. It also left nearly 1,000 people injured.[69] Ramzi Yousef was convicted of leading the attack, setting the bomb, and leaving the van to explode in the garage. Several others were later convicted due in part to very effective law enforcement efforts but also to the strange behavior of some of the conspirators, such as the man who kept returning to the rental agency in an effort to recover his $400 deposit because, he claimed, the van had been stolen.[70] Also convicted in the 1993 bombing was Omar Abdel Rahman, a radical Egyptian cleric who came to the United States as a refugee, whose extreme rhetoric had been influential among those then building terrorist operations before he came to the United States.[71]

Still, many Americans saw the 1993 bombing as something more akin to the actions of a criminal gang than as a harbinger of a larger set of terrorist operations in the planning stages around the world. In fact, the 9/11 Commission would conclude: "An unfortunate consequence of this superb investigative and prosecutorial effort was that it created an impression that the law enforcement system was well-equipped to cope with terrorism."[72] Of course, at that time, Americans were largely unaware of Osama bin Laden and al Qaeda. Neither were they aware that Ramzi Yousef's exploits in 1993 would influence his uncle, Khalid Sheikh Mohammed, the man who would later conceive and develop the plan for the September 11, 2001, attacks.

There were, however, other terrorist activities under way that were bringing leaders in various countries around the world to an understanding that global terrorism would be more important than they had previously imagined. In 1995 there was the car bomb attack in Riyadh, Saudi Arabia. There was also a nerve gas attack in a Tokyo subway perpetrated by a cult. In April of 1995, homegrown terrorists Timothy McVeigh and Terry Nichols bombed the Alfred P. Murrah federal office building in Oklahoma City, though in the early moments after the attack many Americans immediately assumed that it had been the work of Middle Eastern terrorists.

The following year, bin Laden and al Qaeda issued the now frequently quoted fatwa against the United States that insisted that al Qaeda would seek to "cut off the head of the snake."[73] Also in 1996 there was another attack in Saudi Arabia, this time a truck bomb that devastated the Khobar Towers housing complex for U.S. Air Force personnel, leaving nineteen Americans dead and 372 injured.[74]

By 1998, al Qaeda was ready to launch its own large-scale efforts, and bin Laden's operatives launched their simultaneous attacks on the U.S. embassies in Kenya and Tanzania. It was also in that year that al Qaeda surfaced as a major factor for the United States among all of the terrorist groups targeting the West. In February of 1998 bin Laden announced a fatwa for publication and in May gave an interview in which he made it clear that: "[W]e do not differentiate between those dressed in military uniforms and civilians; they are all targets in this *fatwa*."[75] On August 7, al Qaeda demonstrated its willingness to kill civilians, Muslims included, as part of its operations against the U.S. embassies. A dozen Americans were killed but over two hundred others from the host nations lost their lives in the attacks, and more than 5,000 were wounded in Nairobi and Dar es Salaam.[76] The United States struck back with cruise missile attacks on al Qaeda training camps in Afghanistan. Battle had been joined between the United States and al Qaeda.

Even so, the United States was surprised in October 2000 when the American destroyer U.S.S. *Cole* was attacked by al Qaeda suicide bombers in a small boat as the ship lay at anchor in the port of Aden in Yemen. This bold attack on a U.S. warship killed seventeen and left forty injured.[77]

Still, these clashes appeared to many Americans to be part of a battle that was being waged abroad, and few foresaw a direct attack on the United States itself. Al Qaeda had in fact been actively developing a plan for more than two years to launch just such an attack on American soil. Khalid Sheikh Mohammed later reported that he began to focus on the plan for an attack on the World Trade Center using hijacked aircraft soon after his nephew Ramzi Yousef went back to Pakistan after he led the first attack on the World Trade Center in 1993. There was little doubt economic warfare was a central feature of the plan. The 9/11 Commission later explained the decisions as to the targets to be hit as follows: "Like Yousef, KSM [Khalid Sheikh Mohammed] reasoned he could best influence U.S. policy by targeting the country's economy. KSM and Yousef reportedly brainstormed together about what drove the U.S. economy. New York, which KSM considered the economic capital of the United States, therefore became the primary target."[78]

Khalid Sheikh Mohammed then pitched the idea of such an attack to bin Laden, who ultimately approved the plan in the spring of 1999, and the final discussions of targets followed. Their preferred target list included "the White House, the U.S. Capitol, the Pentagon, and the World Trade Center."[79] It was to be a serious attack intended to produce massive casualties and serious damage to the economy, but it was also very much designed to be a symbolic assault—one that would strike the symbols of U.S. economic, political, and military power.

At 8:46 a.m. on September 11, 2001, American Airlines Flight 11 crashed into the North Tower of the World Trade Center, and just minutes later, at 9:03, United Airlines Flight 175 slammed into the South Tower. That was followed soon afterward by another attack by a hijacked aircraft; this time it was American Airlines Flight 77 that crashed into the Pentagon. Across the nation Americans watched their television sets in horror as the South Tower of the World Trade Center collapsed at 9:59 a.m. Then, shortly after 10:00, United Airlines Flight 93 crashed into a field in Shanksville, Pennsylvania, as determined passengers fought desperately to defeat the hijackers. Less than half an hour later, the North Tower of the World Trade Center came down in a cloud of dust and debris. As the 9/11 Commission put it, "On September 11, the nation suffered the largest loss of life—2,973—on its soil as a result of hostile attack in its history."[80] In addition to those tragic deaths, the injuries to those who survived and the families of those who were killed or injured were intense and life-changing. The impacts were not only physical and psychological, but also economic, and they affected not just the residents of the greater New York metropolitan area, but the entire nation and beyond.

The 9/11 Attacks as Economic Warfare

As the story of the attacks indicates, New York had been a target for a decade in significant part because of its importance to the U.S. economy. The September 11 attacks on the World Trade Center were more than symbolic, though, for they did have major economic impacts, only some of which were fully appreciated. The attacks shut down the major markets in the United States and dramatically affected international trading, given the importance of the city's financial district not only in stock markets, but also in currency trading, banking, and a host of other financial activities. Months after the attack, the Federal Deposit Insurance Corporation (FDIC) observed:

> The attack destroyed or significantly damaged many businesses in Downtown Manhattan. Business confidence, already shaken by the nation's slowing economy, was temporarily shattered as the stock market closed for four days and uncertainty reigned. Advertising, travel, tourism, and retailing suffered immediate declines. Airline traffic came to a standstill, and New York City's hotels suffered significant declines in revenues per room, which declined 34 percent from fourth quarter 2000 to fourth quarter 2001 due to sharply lower occupancy and room rates. Many Manhattan companies returned large tracts of office space to the market in anticipation of leaner times ahead. Local income and business tax collections were disrupted. The City's fiscal situation also deteriorated significantly such that the local government currently faces the largest budget deficit in decades.[81]

The U.S. Government Accountability Office concluded that direct costs included: "Human lives; property loss: buildings, business fixtures, computer equipment, phone and power utilities, subway stations, planes, vehicles; costs to respond to the emergency, remove debris, stabilize buildings, and clean up; health effects, injuries, and emotional distress; and costs to provide temporary living assistance." Indirect costs included: "Lost employee income and business profits associated with firms closed or cut back, temporarily or permanently, because office space and infrastructure were destroyed or damaged; lost employee income and business profits associated with other firms that depended on those that closed or cut back; spending reductions from other income losses triggered by the firms that closed or cut back; fiscal impacts such as reduced tax revenues; and delays to travelers and commuters." Adding those factors up, the GAO estimated in May 2002 that the local direct and indirect expenses would be approximately $83 billion.[82]

The attackers hit critical infrastructure, such as the telecommunications systems needed to support the operation of modern markets. They killed scores of financial professionals and devastated the firms that employed them. Ultimately, they eliminated, at least for a time, thousands of jobs. And also, at least temporarily, they forced dramatic decisions about relocation of businesses. All of that naturally affected tax revenues to the city and the state at a time when those governments needed to have predictable revenue streams.

But beyond the obvious impacts, the nation's airlines were grounded at a time when several of the major carriers were already in serious financial trouble. Even after they resumed relatively normal operation, the two largest carriers were facing the threat of massive lawsuits as a result of the attacks themselves, as well as the likelihood of dramatically increased insurance costs for the future.

For their part, insurance companies faced a host of uncertainties. In the face of unknown levels of claims following 9/11 and other terrorist attacks around the world, there was a tendency to constrict coverage and contemplate major premium increases. In fact, in the early days, one of the serious problems of which the public was generally unaware was that the companies that quickly answered the call to work on the cleanup and disposal of materials from the disaster could not find any insurance firms that would cover the risks to their employees, their equipment, and others who might be affected by what might occur as the firms worked to clear the tangled mess that was now known as "Ground Zero."[83] The city itself was unable to obtain coverage for its part in the process.

The immediate local impacts were but one part of a much larger set of financial decisions and economic analyses that would be needed. The true financial impacts of the attacks extended far beyond the obvious requirements. Joshua Bolten, then deputy chief of staff in the George W. Bush White House, convened a meeting of a group pulled together under the title of the domestic consequences group. The immediate agenda for that group included:

- Organizing federal emergency assistance. . . .
- Compensating victims. . . .
- Restoring civil aviation. . . .
- Reopening the financial markets. . . .
- Deciding when and how to return border and port security to more normal operations.
- Evaluating legislative proposals to bail out the airline industry and cap its liability.[84]

The question of federal assistance was an obvious expectation, but just how much aid there would be, what form it would take, and through what means and over what period it would be provided was anything but clear. Nevertheless, there were immediate demands, led by Senator Charles E. Shumer (D-NY), for a commitment of $20 billion to the city, in addition to the fact that the White House very quickly assumed that a minimum of $20 billion would be needed beyond the specific requirements of the city.[85] The GAO later determined that this was the first time that the national government had committed to a sum as large as that without first determining just how the money would be used.[86] Two years after the attacks, the GAO found that:

Initial response efforts, which includes search and rescue operations, debris removal, emergency transportation, and utility system repairs, totaled $2.55 billion. The largest single amount—$1 billion—has been set aside for the establishment of an insurance company to cover claims resulting from debris removal operations.

Compensation for disaster-related costs and losses, which includes aid to individuals for housing costs, loans to businesses to cover economic losses, and funding to the city and state for disaster-related costs, totaled about $4.81 billion.

Infrastructure restoration and improvement, which includes restoration and enhancement of the lower Manhattan transportation system and permanent utility repair and improvement, totals $5.57 billion.

Economic revitalization, which includes the Liberty Zone tax benefits and business attraction and retention programs, is estimated to total $5.54 billion. The amount of this funding is estimated, and will likely remain so, because the tax benefit amounts are not being tracked.[87]

These figures represent $18.47 billion of the total of $20 billion (with just over $1.5 billion not obligated two years after the attack), but the actual amounts were far from clear. The GAO cautioned, "The $20 billion federal assistance to New York does not include financial assistance to victims as part of the September 11 Victim Compensation Fund of 2001. It also does not include financial benefits being provided by the Internal Revenue Service (IRS) providing administrative tax relief to individuals and businesses in the period following the terrorist attacks."[88] Further, the actual cost for the Liberty Zone tax benefits program in terms of lost revenue to the federal government was uncertain two years after the attacks because the IRS was not required to attempt to track the use of those benefits over time.[89]

The airlines were able to use their considerable lobbying power to obtain both limits on liability and financial support from the federal government. The Air Transportation Safety and System Stabilization Act was signed into law just eleven days after the attacks.[90] It not only provided protection for increased insurance premiums, but it also authorized subsidies and lines of credit for the airlines, and limited their liability. Title IV of the act was known as the "September 11 Victim Compensation Fund of 2001." The special master who was assigned to administer the fund reported that: "97% of the families of deceased victims who might otherwise have pursued lawsuits for years have received compensation through the Fund. . . . In total, the Fund distributed over $7.049 billion to survivors of 2,880 persons killed in the September 11th attacks and to 2,680 individuals who were injured in the attacks or in the rescue efforts conducted thereafter."[91]

It was anyone's guess just how much security measures to protect the United States against future attacks would cost or what expenses would be incurred in military actions taken in response to the attacks. That is particularly true since the Bush administration, copying a practice used by President George Herbert Walker Bush in Operation Desert Storm, took these operations off-budget, using supplementary appropriations bills and other devices to avoid building the overall figures into the president's formal budget request to Congress.

All of this came at an already difficult financial period for the United States. The U.S. economy was headed downward in 2000 and by 2001 was in a recession.[92] In New York, the combination of the recession and the impacts of the 9/11 attacks produced estimates by 2002 of tax revenue losses of some $3 billion for 2002 and 2003 and the state comptroller's office had estimated losses for the two-year period at $5.8 billion.[93] Later studies revised the figures downward in an attempt to untangle just how much of the tax revenue shortfall was attributable to the attack and how much resulted from the recession.[94] As a practical matter, though, at a time when there were extremely high demands for services and post-9/11 action, both the state and city governments had significantly less income from taxes than what would otherwise be needed and expected in normal operating conditions.

In sum, the economic warfare evidenced by the 9/11 attack on the World Trade Center was important symbolically, but also constituted a major assault on the economy, fiscal integrity, and market infrastructure not only of the city and the state but of the nation as a whole.

Social Warfare in New York and the Nation as a Whole: People, Their Governments, and the Impact of the Attacks on U.S. Policy

The impacts went well beyond the economy. The attacks were also social warfare, assaults on a system of beliefs, governing principles and processes, and a way of life. In the early hours after the attack, many Americans were heard to say that, while the nation would fight back to protect the social order against terrorists, the terrorists would win if, in the battle, the nation forgot its foundation principles of liberty, equality, and the rule of law. Unfortunately, the attacks prompted an array of behaviors that threatened to make just the mistakes about which so many Americans were concerned.

Immediately after the attacks, the military naturally went to a war footing, with demands from the White House for military action in response to the 9/11 attacks by al Qaeda and the Taliban regime in Afghanistan that sheltered them. Congress quickly provided the authority for that action in the Authorization for the Use of Military Force (AUMF). Congress resolved: "That the President is authorized to use all necessary and appropriate force against those nations, organizations, or persons he determines planned, authorized, committed, or aided the terrorist attacks that occurred on September 11, 2001, or harbored such organizations or persons, in order to prevent any future acts of international terrorism against the United States by such nations, organizations or persons."[95]

The invasion of Afghanistan would soon follow, but, as the Iraq case study explained, some saw Afghanistan merely as phase I in what the president declared to be the war on terror. Several administration officials plainly had in mind a phase II that would include an invasion of Iraq.

While foreign policy and military action were in motion abroad, at home many policies were rapidly formulated and adopted—in some cases they were essentially thrown together in ways that would pose a host of issues for the future. The White House indicated the administration's intention to create an entirely new policy domain referred to as homeland security policy. Instead of calling for legislation, the president issued Executive Order 13228 on October 8, 2001, creating something the administration termed the Office of Homeland Security within the Executive Office of the President. Then governor of Pennsylvania, Tom Ridge was quickly appointed to the new position of assistant to the president for homeland security and given the unenviable "mission . . . to develop and coordinate the implementation of a comprehensive national strategy to secure the United States from terrorist threats or attacks."[96]

Of course, because the administration chose not to use the legislative offer of support, the new office lacked either statutory authority or its own appropriations; and yet it was supposed to coordinate and rationalize activities by a host of other agencies at all levels of government, each of which did have those legislative supports. Within a year, the White House would realize the weakness of its creation and would work with Congress to produce the Homeland Security Act of 2002.[97]

The new Department of Homeland Security (DHS) consumed not only political attention but also resources that were not available to spend on such issues as health care and education. The fiscal 2003 budget allocated $28.2 billion to the Department of Homeland Security and in FY 2005 President Bush requested a 29 percent increase above the 2003 figure;[98] an additional 7 percent increase for FY 2006; and another 7 percent increase for the FY 2007 budget.[99] In fact agencies like the Department of Health and Human Services presented some of their spending requests in terms of homeland security in order to maintain funding or perhaps to attract new dollars.

While it is difficult to track actual costs because many defense expenditures for the conflicts in Iraq and Afghanistan have not been treated as normal parts of the budget, the spending requested for the DOD in the FY 2007 budget is $504.9 billion.[100] The administration was quick to point out that the discretionary dollars requested for FY 2007 represent "a 48-percent increase over 2001."[101] Again, that excludes the full costs of the military operations in Afghanistan or Iraq.

The dramatic increases in homeland security and defense spending came during a period in which the president was attempting to hold domestic spending to increases of less than two percent overall. In fact, in his FY 2007 proposed budget, President Bush wrote, "Again, I am proposing to hold overall discretionary spending below the rate of inflation and to cut spending in non-security discretionary programs below 2006 levels."[102] That means further stress, particularly in health care and education, as well as support for a variety of state and local programs, many of which are mandated by the federal government.

As is so often true in times of emergency, there quickly developed an ends-justifies-the-means mentality that produced dangerous policy and excused abuses of authority. The White House quickly sought—and Congress quickly provided support for—sweeping expansions of surveillance authority and other powers intended to enhance the domestic as well as the international search for terrorist threats, but that also posed dramatic threats to privacy. Some of these came in the form of what became known simply as the USA Patriot Act.[103] For example, it was some time before it was learned that the Department of Justice (DOJ) was using something called "national security letters" under the Patriot Act to avoid the requirements for obtaining warrants or even standard subpoenas for information. The letters were issued to individuals demanding information about a third party. The person receiving the warrant was legally compelled to comply and legally prohibited from complaining about the demand on pain of criminal prosecution.[104]

Even though Congress was willing to work with the White House to provide such sweeping authority, the administration concluded that the Patriot Act and the Foreign Intelligence Surveillance Act (FISA) (which had been created earlier and set up a secret process for issuing warrants outside the normal judicial processes for such things[105]) were not sufficient to the administration's needs and promptly created extremely controversial programs through the National Security Agency (NSA) to monitor telephone conversations that involved international calls and, allegedly, the collection of telephone records to be used for computer searches that might yield pattern information. Until the controversy brought on by the NSA programs, few Americans outside some legal circles were even aware that there was such a thing as a secret FISA court, a body whose judges had already complained at what they regarded as overreaching and in some cases simply unprofessional conduct by some FBI agents and other justice department operatives.[106] The NSA actions were quickly challenged in a memorandum prepared by attorneys in the Congressional Research Service who argued that the president lacked the authority to undertake such programs and that they presented a host of serious legal problems under both the Constitution and statutes like FISA.[107]

These programs were disclosed by newspaper stories, but at least one of them was later confirmed and defended by the White House and the Department of Justice on two grounds. The first claim was that Congress had provided authority to take such actions in the AUMF and, second, that in any event, the president had the inherent power to institute such programs.[108]

Actions were also taken that were not clearly debated or publicized outside the administration. On September 21, 2001, Chief Administrative Law Judge Michael Creppy sent a memorandum via e-mail to all immigration judges and immigration court administrators that read as follows: "As some of you already know, the Attorney General has implemented additional security procedures for certain cases in the Immigration Court. These procedures require us to hold the hearings individually, to close the hearings to the public, and to avoid discussing the case or otherwise disclosing any information about the case to anyone outside the immigration court."[109]

The individuals whose cases came before the immigration court and for whom special interest had been indicated found that no one except their attorney could be present with them in the hearing and no information about the hearing would be disclosed, including whether or not it had ever happened.[110] By the middle of 2003 there had been some six hundred secret hearings carried out according to the Creppy memorandum and Justice Department guidelines.[111] In fact, immigration laws were used as tools not to enforce immigration policies, but as convenient tools to round up people and place them in custody. Professor David Cole wrote: "The government has selectively subjected foreign nationals to interviews, registration, automatic detention, and deportation based on their Arab or Muslim national origin; detained thousands of them, here and abroad; tried many of them in secret, and refused to provide any trials or hearings whatsoever to others; interrogated them for months on end under highly coercive, incommunicado conditions and without access to lawyers; authorized their exclusion based on pure speech; made them deportable for wholly innocent political associations with disfavored groups; and authorized their indefinite detention on the attorney general's say-so."[112] Many of those arrested were never charged, or at least not charged with any offenses related to terrorism. A significant number were jailed under conditions that the U.S. Department of Justice inspector general later determined had abused detainees' rights.[113]

Then there was the manner in which the United States decided to deal with international figures or Americans who fit the new category that the Bush administration labeled "illegal combatants." Most of those who were considered by the administration to be suspected al Qaeda operatives or Taliban fighters, and who were not U.S. citizens, were taken to a newly created prison at Guantanamo Bay, Cuba, in order to keep them outside the United States with the hope that U.S. law would not reach them there. Some of these individuals were captured on the battlefield in Afghanistan. Others were turned over to the U.S. forces as alleged fighters or al Qaeda members, in some cases to collect a reward offered for that kind of information. Still others had been arrested in other places and taken to Guantanamo. It was later alleged that not all such prisoners were taken to Cuba and that some had been moved to other countries through a process known as "extraordinary rendition." Later, in September 2006, the president acknowledged that a group of so-called "high value" prisoners had just been transferred from other detention facilities, though the precise details have yet to be disclosed. The concern by critics has been that some people may have been taken for interrogation to countries known for their willingness to exceed the boundaries of the International Convention against Torture.[114] The administration's actions largely flowed from a military order issued by the president authorizing detention and trial by a military commission issued in November 2001.[115]

Within the administration, legal justifications were written for the kinds of detentions and interrogations that would generally be regarded elsewhere in the world as illegal detentions and interrogations that might very well fit the definition of torture. In fact, there were a variety of documents prepared by a group of lawyers in the White House, the Department of Justice, and the Department of Defense that, once revealed, created outrage among Republicans as well as Democrats. This series of materials began in January of 2002 with a memorandum prepared for the general counsel of the Department of Defense by then Deputy Assistant Attorney General John Yoo, a man who would become well known for his defenses of dramatic claims to executive power, that detainees were not protected by the Geneva Conventions.[116]

There followed a series of memoranda on the question of the boundaries of interrogation techniques that could be used with detainees. In August 2002, Assistant Attorney General Jay S. Bybee wrote a memorandum that pushed matters so far as to precipitate an outraged response from members of both political parties. The memo, later known simply as "the torture memo," considered just how far interrogators might go without violating the Convention against Torture and Other Cruel, Inhuman or Degrading Treatment or Punishment or the U.S. legislation that implemented that treaty.[117] The lengthy memorandum focused on three extreme conclusions clearly designed to give the administration carte blanche in its treatment of detainees. First, it defined torture in terms so extreme that they exclude conduct that would generally be seen as cruel, inhuman, or degrading.

> [W]e conclude that torture . . . covers only extreme acts. Severe pain is generally of the kind difficult for the victim to endure. Where the pain is physical, it must be of an intensity akin to that which accompanies serious physical injury such as death or organ failure. Severe mental pain requires suffering not just at the moment of infliction but it also requires lasting psychological harm, such as seen in lasting mental disorders such as posttraumatic stress disorder. . . .[118]

Second, the administration did not need to be concerned about the restrictions of the U.S. statute prohibiting torture with respect to the detainees because that law would be unconstitutional if it interfered with actions that the president determined were necessary as part of his commander-in-chief powers under Article II.[119] Third, even if the statute did stand, officials could protect themselves from criminal liability by claiming "necessity or self-defense."[120]

Then, in the spring of 2004, the military announced to the media that disciplinary actions were being brought against six soldiers who were members of the military police unit responsible for prisoners at the Abu Ghraib detention facility in Iraq, an institution that had developed an infamous reputation during the Saddam Hussein regime.[121] Once the pictures taken by some of those involved in the abuses were made public, there was condemnation and revulsion at the thought that American soldiers would be involved in such behavior. That was followed by investigations by the military and Congress.[122]

When the so-called torture memorandum became public in June 2004 on the heels of the revelations about prisoner abuse at Abu Ghraib, even stalwarts of the president's own political party demanded that the administration reject such behavior and repudiate what purported to be legal rationalizations to support it. However, the formal memorandum from the Justice Department that rejected and replaced the Bybee memo was not completed until December 20, 2004.[123]

The 2004 election was over and the revelations of abuse persisted well into 2005. Led by Senator John McCain (R-AZ), a bipartisan statement against the administration's policy came in an October legislative action that overwhelmingly approved a ban on torture with a vote in the Senate. However, even after that the administration pursued an effort led by Vice President Cheney to exempt the CIA from the torture ban. Finally, on December 15, 2005, the White House appeared to capitulate to the congressional demands to stop the administration's policies and to the continuous and growing chorus of national and international editorial opinion challenging the Bush policies. The president stood with Senator McCain at the White House and announced his decision to support McCain's legislation.

However, when Americans awoke from their New Year's celebrations, they found that the White House had something else in mind. On December 30, as most people headed off for the holiday, the president had issued a presidential signing statement in which, while he signed the legislation into law, he also indicated that it would be administered according to the administration's understanding of the president's obligations and authority under the commander-in-chief powers of the Constitution.[124] It also asserted that detainees would have no legal right to bring action in court to enforce the detainee protection provisions of the act.

The legislation had two parts that were important to the debates about detainees. First, there were the specific prohibitions against the use of torture that McCain had championed. Then there was a portion of the statute that dealt with whether detainees at Guantanamo could bring suit in federal court for a writ of habeas corpus—requiring the government to demonstrate that it was holding the person lawfully—which was the result of the efforts of Senators Carl Levin (D) of Michigan and Lindsey Graham (R) of South Carolina. The idea of the latter provision was to permit cases that were already in the courts to move through the appellate process in order to resolve the question of legality of the detention and the processes by which decisions were made with respect to the status of detainees at Guantanamo Bay. The signing statement effectively said that the president would do as he thought best with respect to the anti-torture provisions and pronounced that all suits brought by detainees, including those then pending in the courts, would be terminated. Senator Levin reacted sharply, accusing the White House of attempting to "end-run the legislative process. . . . As I pointed out when we passed the bill, . . . the provision is prospective in its application, and does not apply to pending cases."[125]

It happened that the news of the presidential signing statement on the torture prevention legislation surfaced at the beginning of the week when then Judge Samuel Alito was to appear before the Senate Judiciary Committee for confirmation hearings on his appointment to the United States Supreme Court. Members of the committee, both Democrats, led by Senator Patrick Leahy (D-VT), and Republicans, led by then Judiciary Committee chair, Senator Arlen Specter (R-PA), peppered Alito with questions about the use of presidential signing statements. They also used that forum to express concern with the news of the December 30 statement issued by the Bush White House. While working for the Justice Department in the Reagan administration, Alito had issued a memorandum on how to use presidential signing statements to expand executive power.[126]

But the dramatic impacts on American law, government, and society from the 9/11 attacks had not ended. While Judge Alito was answering questions before the Judiciary Committee, Congressional Research Service lawyers issued their memorandum that laid out a powerful legal case against the NSA surveillance of telephone calls without the use of FISA court support.[127] The *New York Times* had revealed the existence of the program on December 16, 2005, the same day that newspapers reported the agreement between the White House and Senator McCain on the anti-torture legislation.[128] The president acknowledged the existence of the program and the attorney general defended the president on grounds that the program was justified by virtue of the AUMF passed just after the attacks of 9/11. If the AUMF is not enough, he said, "we also believe the President has the inherent authority under the Constitution, as Commander in Chief, to engage in this kind of activity."[129] The Justice Department published what amounted to a reply brief two weeks after the Congressional Research Service memorandum was issued. And, although it discussed the AUMF in detail, the argument began with the assertion that: "The NSA activities are supported by the President's well-recognized inherent constitutional authority as Commander in Chief and sole organ for the Nation in foreign affairs. . . ."[130] Additional stories hit the news in May 2006 on another NSA program, this time allegedly designed to gather and research calling patterns.

While the courts worked through these cases, though, there emerged yet another assertion of barriers to the exercise of checks on power in the post-9/11 era as the administration moved to block lawsuits that might challenge some of the programs on grounds of the state secret privilege. There had been discussion of the use of the state secret privilege for some time as a vehicle to block court action in cases that might have revealed information that would jeopardize national security. Indeed, the Justice Department argued in a case brought against AT&T in one of the NSA telephone records lawsuits that the case should be dismissed on grounds of the state secret privilege, but Judge Vaughn R. Walker of the United States District Court for the Northern District of California rejected that argument.[131] The contemporary foundations of the privilege go back to 1953.[132] Just how this doctrine will be applied in the wake of the 9/11 attacks is unclear.

The fact is that the entire nation, its government, and the civil rights and civil liberties of its citizens and others with whom the government came into contact were radically altered in many important respects, and all criticisms were met with the incantation of the magic words "September 11." By any reasonable assessment, the attack led to a dramatic transformation of the social order in the United States.

There were other social impacts of the 9/11 attacks in addition to the deaths and injuries and the changes that came to American government and politics. There were physical injuries and health issues and, less tangible but nevertheless very real, intangible factors such as social stress, including on those who suffered discrimination in the aftermath of the attacks.

The physical injuries that followed the 9/11 attacks were many and varied. Indeed, five years after the attacks it is still unclear how many people suffered what types of injuries as a result of the attacks. In addition to those who suffered immediate physical injuries in the event itself or in escaping from it, one of the most complex questions had to do with environmental health effects for those who live and work in the vicinity of the attacks. First, and most obviously, there were large numbers of first responders and cleanup workers at the World Trade Center site itself. Second, there were the local residents.

When the Twin Towers collapsed, there was an overwhelming cloud of smoke, dust, and debris that blanketed the area, including the pollutants mixed in with the building rubble from the burning airplanes that had struck the building.[133] After the initial events settled, there was a veritable army of first responders, construction workers, and volunteers who spent long hours at a time engaged first in what they hoped would be search-and-rescue operations, but that became body-recovery operations. Along with that work, there were the efforts to clean up the site, including the damage below ground level and the impacts to surrounding buildings. Those working on "the pile" were exposed all along to the pollutants in the air from the fires that continued to burn and from the materials they encountered as they worked to remove the debris.[134] (See Table 2.1.) Estimates of those immediately affected or exposed during search operations range from 250,000 to 400,000 people, both residents and workers.[135] The total estimate of workers at the site ran to some 40,000. "Physical health effects included injuries and respiratory conditions, such as sinusitis, asthma, and a new syndrome called WTC cough, which consists of persistent coughing accompanied

Table 2.1. Contaminants Potentially Present* at the World Trade Center Site

Contaminant	Health Effects	Source
Asbestos	Carcinogenic. Causes tissue scarring in the lungs when inhaled over long periods and can lead to asbestosis, mesothelioma, and lung cancer.	Used as an insulator and fire retardant, applied to steel beams.
Benzene	Flammable and carcinogenic. Short-term effects include dizziness, headaches, and tremors. Long-term exposure can lead to leukemia.	Combustion of plastics.
Biohazards	Exposure to blood and body parts can transmit infectious diseases such as hepatitis and AIDS. After long periods, they may pose little hazard to health, although finding human remains can cause psychological trauma.	Human remains of the victims trapped in the rubble (less than 15% of the bodies have been recovered).
Chromium	Carcinogenic when inhaled at high concentrations. Dermal contact can cause skin ulcers.	Video and computer monitors.
Copper	In large amounts can cause dizziness, headaches, vomiting, and damage to the kidneys and liver.	Electrical wiring and cables.
Diesel fumes	Asthma trigger. Can aggravate symptoms in asthmatics.	Truck traffic and heavy machinery from the cleanup effort.

Dioxins	Chloracne is a short-term effect of exposure. Strong evidence for carcinogenic, teratogenic, reproductive, and immunosuppressive effects. Persist and bioaccumulate in the environment and food chain.	Combustion of polyvinyl chloride found in electrical cables and other insulating materials and some plastics.
Freon	Damages the ozone layer. When burned, can produce phosgene, a potent cause of severe and life-threatening pulmonary edema.	Refrigeration and air-conditioning equipment.
Lead	Neurotoxic. Damages the central nervous system, especially in children. Can also cause kidney and reproductive damage in adults.	Video and computer monitors, rust proofing paint used on steel beams.
Mercury	Neurotoxic. Damages the peripheral nervous system, especially in children.	Thermometers and other precision instruments.
Particulate matter	Asthma trigger. Can aggravate symptoms in asthmatics. Can also aggravate cardiovascular disease. Smaller particles (PM 2.5) may be more potent than larger particles (PM 10).	Pulverized concrete and other materials (large particles); smoke, dust, and soot from combustion (small particles).
Polychlorinated biphenyls	Carcinogenic. May also cause hormonal problems and reproductive and developmental abnormalities. Persist in the human body and the environment.	Transformers and other electrical equipment.
Sulfur dioxide	Pulmonary toxicant. Can cause severe airway obstructions when inhaled at high concentrations. Can burn the nose and throat.	Combustion of many materials.

* Not all of the pollutants listed are currently being tested for at the World Trade Center site, and final data are not yet available for pollutants that are being tested for.
Source: "Focus: Environmental Aftermath," *Environmental Health Perspectives* 109, no. 11 (November 2001): A530.

by severe respiratory symptoms. Almost all firefighters who responded to the attack experienced respiratory effects, including WTC cough, and hundreds had to end their firefighting careers due to WTC-related respiratory illnesses."[136]

Three programs were established by local governments and the state of New York with the support of federal funding. The federal government instituted a program to screen those federal employees affected by the attacks. A World Trade Center Health Registry program was also created to maintain the data over time as a base for research. That registry was closed to new parties in 2004. Those in the database would be available to provide information for ongoing research. The first of those studies carried out for the Centers for Disease Control was published in 2006.[137]

The GAO concluded that the New York Fire Department program examined some 15,000 firefighters and the local program for workers and volunteers on the site saw another 14,000. The state program for state workers served 1,700 workers. The federal government program saw only 394 federal employees of the roughly 10,000 who were at 9/11 at one point or another, but stopped screening employees in 2003.[138] The U.S. Army and the U.S. Marshal Service established their own programs for their employees when the Department of Health and Human Services ended its program after seeing such a small number of the many federal employees who had been on the site. The difficulties here have to do with the unknowns in terms of actual exposure coupled with the probability that there would be illnesses and disabilities that might affect those involved years down the road. The state and local program administrators were also worried that the federal government might be unwilling to continue to provide financial support.[139] A related concern was that health care and other necessary supports would not be available over the long term to support those who were injured or became ill with chronic conditions that threatened their ability to earn a living.

The city health department also undertook a community needs assessment soon after the immediate emergency had subsided. The survey of residents in the affected residential areas was followed at the end of October 2001 with some 414 interviews in those neighborhoods. Among its findings, the needs assessment determined that: "First, residents of lower Manhattan [have] . . . tremendous concern about the air quality and its potential effects on health. The high proportion of the population experiencing symptoms likely to be related to respiratory irritants contributes to this concern. Second, the majority of households have not been cleaned according to recommendations, possibly increasing the exposure to respiratory irritants."[140]

However, what the needs assessment had to say about mental health issues was at least as significant as the discussion of potential respiratory concerns. This was not a matter of collateral damage. The mental health and sense of well-being was precisely a core target of terrorists, and evidence shows that they succeeded in causing the kind of fear and the sense of a lack of security they intended to create. The community needs assessment report concluded:

- Almost 40% of those interviewed reported symptoms suggestive of Post Traumatic Stress Disorder (PTSD), indicating a potential for thousands of people in lower Manhattan who could benefit from supportive counseling.
- Less than a third of those interviewed have received any supportive counseling, and of those at high risk for PTSD, about 40% have received supportive counseling.
- Many residents do not have access to or are not aware of the availability of mental health services.[141]

In addition to those who self-reported, respondents were administered a screening tool for PTSD, with 40 percent scoring at or above the level indicating the presence of PTSD.[142] Post-traumatic stress disorder is an often underappreciated challenge to post-conflict development. Chapter 4 deals with PTSD in considerable detail. For the moment, it is important to know that this is a persistent and pervasive challenge to those seeking to deal with life after conflict.

The U.S. Department of Health and Human Services' Substance Abuse and Mental Health Services Administration (SAMHSA) held a conference a month after the 9/11 attacks entitled "When Terror Strikes: Strengthening the Homeland through Recovery, Resilience, and Readiness." The SAMHSA newsletter published a series of articles reporting on the conference. The first of these made the point that it was time to recognize the importance of the fact that terror produces more impact on mental health than it does physical injuries.

When terrorism strikes, it's natural to focus first on those who have been physically injured or killed. But large-scale attacks produce more psychological casualties than physical ones, some of the conference presenters observed. . . . [T]he ratio of behavioral to physical casualties following a mass biological attack, in a best-case scenario, could be as low as 4 to 1. In a worst-case scenario, it could jump to as much as 10 to 1, [a presenter] said.

The shocking events of September 11 had an especially profound effect. In a RAND Corporation survey in the days following the attack, 44 percent of American adults reported substantial symptoms of stress, and 9 out of 10 had some degree of stress reactions. More than one-third of children age 5 and older had stress symptoms, and almost half said they worried about their safety or that of their families.[143]

The impacts are not only on the victims of the attack but also fall heavily on the first responders who seek to help the survivors. "After the Murrah Building bombing, Oklahoma City's firefighters saw a 300-percent increase in their divorce rate, and five of the city's rescue workers committed suicide after the event, according to Chief Johnson."[144]

At hearings conducted by members of the Subcommittee of the Senate Committee on Health, Education, Labor, and Pensions a year after the attack, New York schools chancellor Harold Levy testified that: "In fact, we now estimate 190,000 children in grades four through twelve exhibit at least one mental health problem which may inhibit their productivity in school, which subsequently requires some form of intervention."[145] Principals and teachers testified about how they waited for parents or rescuers to take children away from the area of the disaster but had to lead the children out themselves. In the process, they saw things no child should ever have to see. "'Look' [one said], 'the birds are on fire.' The truth of what he was seeing was too awful to understand."[146]

Among the many people whose sense of safety and security had been undermined, whose ability to rebound from the 9/11 tragedy was tested, were many Arab Americans and others of Middle Eastern extraction or Muslims, whatever their ethnocultural heritage. There were, to be sure, good stories in the days and weeks after the attacks that demonstrated a desire by Americans to show the world that they would not respond with hatred, bigotry, and stereotyping. The news media wrote of local residents who were not Muslims standing guard to make sure no harm came to a local mosque. Unfortunately, there were others who lashed out at those they thought were Muslim or from the Middle East. Some were called "terrorists" by coworkers, superiors, or others in the community. Still others had to live with what was clearly a growing practice of racial/ethnic profiling.[147] So significant was the concern over this situation that the cover of the Winter 2002 edition of the *Civil Rights Journal*, the journal of the U.S. Commission on Civil Rights, featured a photo of a young Arab man with the cross-hairs of a rifle scope superimposed over the picture and carried a cover story entitled "Flying while Arab: Lessons from the Racial Profiling Controversy."[148] As the strain of these behaviors affected more people, the SAMHSA conference participants noted there was an additional difficulty due to the lack of culturally sensitive and appropriate mental health services. Again, the impacts were not just in New York but around the nation.

The Lack of Attention to the Environment as Collateral Damage

It is interesting that there was little done to address environmental consequences of the World Trade Center attacks except for air pollution. This is perhaps due to the tendency of many in the environmental policy community to ignore, or at least not to focus with much intensity on, urban environments beyond specific pollution issues. Here again, the impacts can be quite unlike the kind of narrow and local focus that one might expect. Like other non-defense and non–homeland security domestic programs, the U.S. Environmental Protection Agency did not fare well in terms of its priority for resources in the president's budget requests. For example, the president's FY 2003 budget request called for a real dollar cut of almost $300 million in the agency's discretionary funds and the FY 2005 request once again called for a cut in spending. The president repeatedly made clear his intentions to cut the budget except for military and homeland security programs and the entitlement programs over which there was no discretion.

The other issue that would have important environmental impacts was the use of resources when a nation goes to war. The United States has now been at war for five years with no end to its commitments in Iraq or Afghanistan in sight. Using UNEP data in 1991, one analyst summarized the dimensions of the problem as follows:

> Nearly 85 percent of the total energy used by the United States government is for military purposes. For example, the fuel used by an F-16 . . . jet in less than one hour is nearly equivalent to what an average US motorist uses over a period of two years. The amount of energy used to produce weapons is also high: in the US it is almost equivalent to twice that of the energy directly used by the military. Further, during wartime, when high technology and sophisticated weapons are used, total energy used by the military might increase by factors of five to twenty times over the levels used during peacetime, depending on the conditions that prevail during any specific war.[149]

War production also employs strategic materials including minerals, the mining of which has a variety of environmental impacts.[150]

Over time, combat and environmental conditions have taken their toll on equipment sent to Iraq and Afghanistan, calling for a commitment of more resources to rebuild or replace it. Among the resources needed in large quantities is fossil fuels and, at a time when prices have been rising sharply, there have been calls to make available fuel from the naval oil reserve and to open more federal lands to drilling, including the Alaskan National Wilderness. Of course, the need for vast resources to support combat operations has economic impacts as well and the Federal Reserve steadily increased interest rates in an attempt to head off the inflation that generally follows in the wake of war with impacts on everything from the cost of home mortgages to credit card debt.

At the end of the day, the United States is in many important respects a country facing a need for post-conflict sustainable development. Its economy and its society, including of course its government, have been dramatically altered as a result of the conflict. Just how much the environment has been affected is not at this point clear. Civil rights and civil liberties have been dramatically affected. A host of new laws have been passed granting sweeping authority to federal officials. The flow of tax dollars has been significantly reordered to support the military and to finance homeland security policy, a field that did not exist before the attacks of 9/11. The nation is involved in combat in Afghanistan and Iraq. For all these reasons, it is essential to consider the United States and other developed countries like Great Britain and Spain as countries in need of post-conflict sustainable development.

These two case studies highlight not only the general need to address post-conflict situations with a sustainable development approach, but also the more specific need to understand social warfare, economic warfare, and environmental warfare in order to better comprehend how the three core elements of the living triangle are affected by conflict.

ENVIRONMENTAL WARFARE

When reports surfaced in the international press that Saddam Hussein had ordered oil wells in Kuwait to be set on fire in 1991, there was public outrage at the idea that someone had declared war on the environment. Years later, when the United States prepared for the 2003 invasion of Iraq, there was an expectation that oil wells would be set on fire and contractors were engaged to address the anticipated destruction of the wells and pipelines. The Iraqi regime used oil as a weapon to affect the environment once again, this time setting fires at oil facilities and in oil-filled trenches strategically located to impair the visibility of attacking forces.

Of course, the Iraqi case was an example of a wider phenomenon and one that, unfortunately, has a long history, dating back at least to the Roman empire and even earlier. That said, the state of the world's ecosystems today and the weapons of war available to large countries and also to local insurgents have intensified the need to understand what is known in military circles as environmental warfare, how it is waged, and why that matters for sustainable development in the contemporary context.

What Is Environmental Warfare?
The Need for Awareness and Careful Definition

Environmental warfare has been defined as "warfare in which the environment is manipulated for hostile military purposes."[151] In this definition, the environment becomes a weapon, either offensive or defensive, with which to face an enemy. Well understood by military commanders, the weaponry perspective is sometimes presented in language that would be sobering to most nonmilitary readers. For example, a group of U.S. Air Force officers in the mid-1990s wrote:

> In 2025, US aerospace forces can "own the weather" by capitalizing on emerging technologies and focusing development of those technologies to war-fighting applications. Such a capability offers the war fighter tools to shape the battlespace in ways never before possible. . . . From enhancing friendly operations or disrupting those of the enemy via small-scale tailoring of natural weather patterns to complete dominance of global communications and counterspace control, weather-modification offers the war fighter a wide-range of possible options to defeat or coerce an adversary.[152]

Certainly, Saddam Hussein's use of oil wells as weapons to pollute the environment, block vision of attacking forces, and clog water intakes for desalination plants fits the standard military definition of environmental warfare.

For environmentalists, environmental warfare is more often understood as an attack on the environment, either deliberately in an effort to achieve advantage or inflict harm on an adversary and its people or recklessly, perhaps thoughtlessly, as in a negligent failure to consider the environmental consequences of what commanders would term collateral damage. In this conception, the environment is under assault and becomes a casualty of war as surely as the combatants who fall in battle. The earlier description of the effects of the Iran-Iraq War, operation Desert Storm, and Operation Iraqi Freedom fit this case.

A more useful framework with which to understand environmental warfare can bridge some of these differences. This study will use the following terms. First, there is environmental weapons warfare (EWW), situations in which the environment or elements of it are used as swords or shields for active combat (a type that best fits the traditional definition of environmental warfare). Second, there is environmental high-impact warfare (EHIW). These are operations in which tactics and strategies are employed that commanders know, or reasonably should know, will have major, perhaps even catastrophic, environmental effects. At some point, the environmental consequences of military action are sufficiently grave and well-understood in advance that it is no longer adequate to describe the results simply as collateral damage. In fact, the tendency is to use the term collateral damage primarily to refer to human lives lost and not even to include serious environmental damage in that category. The EHIW concept draws a distinction that is important to consider, which is that there will still be warfare that has environmental impacts of varying degrees of seriousness that are not as obvious or acute but that result nevertheless—just as there are operations that were not expected to produce civilian casualties, but do so. This third type is environmental collateral damage (ECD). Here the term *collateral damage* is as appropriate as it is when the same concept is applied to the loss of lives.

This set of descriptions also suggests that there is not simply a dichotomy in operation in this field, but a spectrum at one end of which is the intention to use nature as a weapon, and at the other, a condition of accidental damage that is more like a natural disaster. In this conception, more of what is now either ignored or termed collateral damage will be seen as environmental warfare. It is better to address this condition forthrightly than to evade the challenges that it poses because it is distasteful to recognize the damage for what it is.

None of this is meant to suggest that environmental warfare will not be employed. It has been used since ancient times and will continue to be in the future. To suggest otherwise is naive. That said, if environmental warfare is considered forthrightly, then efforts can be advanced to place some boundaries around it, as has been true in the case of human warfare (some actions to date of this sort are noted later in this chapter). The fact that these rules may be violated is no more of a reason to avoid their creation than a similar argument would be if it were to be directed at human warfare with respect, for instance, to behaviors that have violated the Geneva Conventions.

The same problems of the doctrine of military necessity will be presented for environmental warfare as have been demonstrated in other aspects of the law of war, but that is again not a reason for avoiding the recognition that it is unacceptable merely to regard the manner in which the environment is used or injured as mere collateral damage, unfortunate but little more than one of those inevitable consequences of war.

How Is Environmental Warfare Waged?
Defensive and Offensive Approaches

There have been a variety of different approaches to environmental warfare historically. There has been the use of natural forces in the environment, deliberate disruption of natural forces, and efforts to alter natural forces. These approaches may entail the simple use of the environment, efforts at an active modification of environment, or even the intentional destruction of environment. Some combatants treat the environment as an ally, others as an obstacle, others as a target, and still others as a prize. Recent examples of the latter include conflicts in which timber, gems, oil, and water have been central features of the conflict in some African states to the point that the World Bank has focused on conflict over resources as a key element in efforts to anticipate and prevent future battles.[153]

The types and methods of environmental warfare are often divided into those used for defensive and for offensive purposes. Classically, the defensive tactics have involved the use of natural barriers, such as the use of terrain augmented by trenches or other earthworks, or the deliberate flooding of lands by the breaching of dams or levies to block or at least slow down an attacking force. These have been used repeatedly throughout history. Among the commonly cited examples of these tactics are the breaching of dikes by the Dutch in 1672 to create the "Holland Water Line" in an effort to block French attackers[154] and the decision by the Chinese in 1938 to blow up the Huayuankow dike on the Yellow River (Huang He). Westing points out that such tactics can be effective, but may also have devastating results for local residents.

> This action resulted in the drowning of several thousand Japanese soldiers and stopped their advance into China along this front. In the process, however, the flood waters also ravaged major portions of Henan, Anhui, and Jiangsu provinces. Several million hectares of farmlands were inundated in the process, and the crops and topsoil destroyed. The river was not brought back under control until 1947. In terms of more direct human impact, the flooding inundated some eleven Chinese cities and more than 4000 villages. At least several hundred thousand Chinese drowned as a result (and possibly many more), and several million were left homeless.[155]

Another frequently mentioned example was the flooding of large areas of the Netherlands with sea water in 1944.[156]

The use of the oil weapon by Saddam Hussein in 2003 was defensive in character (unlike the previous action in Kuwait) and was designed to make air attacks more difficult by blocking visibility from the air and to complicate targeting as well as the use of infrared or laser-guided weapons. While the oil fires were expected to frustrate air attacks and cover ground movements in a contemporary battlespace, the deliberate generation of smoke for such purposes was commonly employed by ships in World War II in an effort to evade air attack.

Obviously, these tactics involve both environmental weapons warfare (EWW) and environmental high-impact warfare (EHIW). One more modern defensive technique that fits the latter category is the ongoing development of high-power undersea sonar arrays (surveillance towed array sensor system low frequency active sonar [SURTASS LFAS]), the testing and deployment of which have prompted litigation by groups that have explained the impact of these powerful systems on ocean species such as whales, porpoises, and fish that make use of natural sonar systems or that are particularly sensitive to electronic signals and vibrations.[157] In 2003, the U.S. District Court for the Northern District of California issued a permanent injunction permitting the testing of the system only under limited specified conditions.[158] The Circuit Court of Appeals for the Ninth Circuit quoted an analysis published with the Navy's regulations for the sonar system.

Any human-made noise that is strong enough to be heard has the potential to reduce (mask) the ability of marine mammals to hear natural sounds at similar frequencies, including calls from conspecifics, echo-location sounds of ondontocetes, and environmental sounds such as surf noise. . . . Very strong sounds have the potential to cause temporary or permanent reduction in hearing sensitivity. In addition, intense acoustic or explosive events may cause trauma to tissues associated with organs vital for hearing, sound production, respiration, and other functions. This trauma may include minor to severe hemorrhage.[159]

Offensive environmental warfare involves a wider and more robust array of techniques. The traditional way of thinking about these tactics, Westing notes, is based on the release of "pent-up energy in the environment." "[T]he energy stored in vegetation can be released by fire, and the energy stored in water held by dams can be released by breaching the barrier."[160]

The calculated use of flood and fire to attack a foe has been used many times by many forces. So-called scorched earth tactics in which efforts were made not only to deprive an adversary of food and shelter, but to make it difficult or impossible for the enemy to counterattack or even recover from the assault have been employed in Europe and even in the United States in the case of Sherman's march to the sea in Georgia during the Civil War.

Before and after the Civil War, U.S. forces destroyed Native American crops, killed the game from which they drew sustenance, and, once they were weakened, drove them from their lands, often to relocate them to reservations that sometimes consisted of the land none of the settlers moving west wanted. In addition to the better-known Trail of Tears that moved the Cherokee and other tribes from the Southeast to the Southwestern United States with tragic loss of life on the journey, there are numerous other examples, like the so-called "Long Walk of the Navajos" in which Navajo crops and livestock were taken or destroyed and the Navajo driven off their lands under orders from General James Carleton to the Bosque Redondo. Kit Carson, the man who had lived among Native Americans and who was seen as a friend by many of them, was one of the lead officers in the campaign against the Navajo. But, of all that Carson did to them, Dee Brown asserts, the one unforgivable crime was an act of environmental warfare. "The Navahoes could forgive the Rope Thrower for fighting them as a soldier, for making prisoners of them, even for destroying their food supplies, but the one act they never forgive him for was cutting down their beloved peach trees."[161]

Brown tells the story of the reaction of the new superintendent at the Bosque Redondo reservation and his conclusions about the conditions about which Carleton had previously boasted to his superiors. "The superintendent examined the soil on the reservation and pronounced it unfit for cultivation of grain because of the presence of alkali. 'The water is black and brackish, scarcely bearable to the taste, and said by the Indians to be un-healthy, because one-fourth of their population have been swept off by dis-ease. . . . Would any sensible man select a spot for a reservation for 8,000 Indians where the water is scarcely bearable, where the soil is poor and cold, and where the muskite [mesquite] roots 12 miles distant are the only wood for the Indians to use?'"[162]

In more recent history, incendiary bomb attacks were used against Ger-man and Japanese cities in World War II and napalm was used in the Viet-nam conflict. Since the days when heavy bombing attacks from the air be-came effective in World War II, dams have been targets because they provided sources of electricity and water and because successful attacks on them sent vast quantities of water under great pressure through inhabited areas, as in the British attack on dams in May 1943 in Ruhr River Valley, leaving factories, bridges, farms, and residents decimated.[163]

As destructive as these forms of environmental warfare have been throughout history, the modern era has seen new and far more destructive variations on old themes. It is an age in which commanders have been en-couraged to think of warfare that involves aspects of the environment that humankind had little ability to manipulate in the ways that it can today. Westing lists a variety of what he terms "damage-causing manipulations of: (a) celestial bodies or space, (b) the atmosphere, (c) the land (lithosphere), (d) the oceans (hydrosphere), or (e) the biota, either terrestrial or marine (biosphere)."[164]

Well before Saddam Hussein made environmental warfare infamous, the United States implemented policies aimed at enhancing combat effective-ness in Vietnam by altering the weather and dramatically changing the ecol-ogy through the massive use of chemical defoliants. "A pilot program known as Project Popeye conducted in 1966 attempted to extend the mon-soon season in order to increase the amount of mud on the Ho Chi Minh trail thereby reducing enemy movements. A silver iodide nuclei agent was dispersed from WC-130, F4 and A-1E aircraft into the clouds over portions of the trail. . . . Positive results during this initial program led to continued operations from 1967 to 1972."[165]

The better-known of these efforts was the use of defoliants like "Agent Or-ange" in Vietnam, Laos, and Cambodia. "Between 1962 and 1971, U.S. mil-itary forces sprayed nearly 19 million gallons of herbicides over approxi-mately 3.6 million acres in Vietnam. The preparation known as Agent Orange accounted for approximately 11.2 million gallons of the total amount sprayed."[166] Most of the Agent Orange spraying was carried out as part of Operation Ranch Hand between 1965 and 1970. The intention was that Agent Orange and a variety of other defoliants named Agents Blue, White, Pink, Green, and Purple would remove the forest canopy that pro-vided cover for the enemy forces, allowing easier detection and attack.

To this day, it is unclear what the full effects of the use of these defoliants has been. However, in 1991 Congress asked the National Academy of Sciences to carry out an analysis of existing knowledge of the health implications of the use of these types of defoliants.[167] It was driven by the repeated demands of veterans of the war for recognition of a variety of health issues they contended were the result of exposure to the chemicals in Southeast Asia.[168] At the root of many of the suspected toxic reactions was a recognition that Agent Orange contained a contaminant, 2,3,7,8-tetrachlorodibenzo-p-dioxin (2,3,7,8,-TCDD), generally referred to as dioxin.[169]

Despite continuing questions, some of the health risks from the use of the defoliants were becoming clear. The Institute of Medicine study concluded: "The committee found sufficient evidence of an association with herbicides and/or TCDD for three cancers: soft tissue sarcoma, non-Hodgkin's lymphoma, and Hodgkin's disease. . . . The committee found limited/suggestive evidence of an association for three other cancers: respiratory cancers, prostate cancer, and multiple myeloma."[170] These were in addition to the already well-known danger of chloracne.

At the first of the major UN conferences on environment held in Stockholm in 1972, Sweden's Prime Minister Olaf Palme declared: "The immense destruction brought about by indiscriminate bombing and by the large-scale use of bulldozers and herbicides is an outrage that is sometimes referred to as 'ecocide.' It is shocking that only preliminary discussions of this matter have thus far been possible in the United Nations. . . . We fear that the active use of these methods is coupled with a passive resistance to discuss them."[171] International critics also insisted that the use of the chemicals constituted a violation of the 1925 chemical weapons convention, a treaty to which the United States did not accede until 1975.

In 2002, the Swedish government convened a follow-on conference on the effects of the war in Vietnam and found that the consequences of that war were long-lasting and still not fully resolved.

> The Vietnam War involved an unprecedented assault on the environment. . . . Life forms at many levels of the evolutionary scale have been significantly affected, from primitive plants and animals to human beings. . . . On an area less than eight percent that of the United States, the amount of high explosives employed was almost double the amount expended by the USA during World War II. . . . Over 72 million liters of herbicides [were sprayed]. . . . Toxic chemicals contained in the herbicides, arsenic and dioxin in particular, are expected to continue posing a significant health threat long into the future.[172]

The studies concluded that some 13 percent of the forests were devastated by the war, with 30 percent of its critically important but very sensitive mangrove forests also hard-hit.[173] The mangroves, of course, are exceedingly important not only for their role with respect to land, plants, and waters, but also because they serve as a vital nursery for the nation's fish stocks, a primary source of protein in the region. Roughly 10 percent of Vietnam, particularly the Central Highlands, was especially targeted for spraying. It must also be noted that roughly 14 percent of the defoliant was sprayed on agricultural fields to limit the availability of other food crops that might be used by the enemy.[174] The overwhelming majority of these chemicals were used in South Vietnam, the people the United States were intending to assist.

Unfortunately, the chemical agents used are persistent in the environment and recent studies indicate not only that the toxins are still present, but that even more than a quarter century after the war ended, there remain hot spots of chemical pollution.[175] The fact that much of the defoliant was used in highland areas and on a number of steep grades meant that there was significant erosion because of the loss of forest cover in twenty-eight different watersheds, and, in part for that reason, there were major floods in many areas that further eroded the already damaged areas, affecting downstream agricultural areas.[176] With the tree cover gone and soil degradation from erosion and flooding a factor, invasive grasses and other less desirable plant species took over in some of the defoliated areas. "Areas hard-hit by spraying and bombing are still dominated by such undesirable grasses as *Pennisetum polystachyon* and *Imperata cylindrica*. Examples of such areas include the Aluoi Valley, Sa Thay, Ma Da, and the Boi Loi Woods."[177] Additionally, as part of the effort to rebuild the economy, unsustainable forest practices led to destructive logging of the country's forest resources, already badly depleted by the war.

The consequences of such dramatic environmental warfare tactics can and do reach far beyond those who are specifically targeted. Thus, few Americans were aware until the Institute of Medicine study that defoliants and the means for applying them were tested locally in New York state, Puerto Rico, the Florida Everglades, and in Thailand.[178] However, Department of Defense documents explained that experiments were also conducted with herbicides (some commercial products and other newly developed compounds) from 1963 to 1965 at sites in Fort Ritchie, Fort Meade, and Aberdeen Proving Grounds, Maryland, and in Georgia and Tennessee with commercially available products along power line rights-of-way.[179]

Until recently most Americans and Canadians were unaware that the substances had also been used in Canada near a Canadian Forces Base, until the Canadian Broadcasting Corporation (CBC) presented a feature story on the facts of the spraying at CFB Gagetown, New Brunswick, and the allegations of subsequent health damage to those on the base and near it in those years and later.[180] The tests at Gagetown were carried out by U.S. personnel from Fort Detrick and the Canadian Ministry of Defense in June 1966, using Agent Orange, Agent Purple, and a number of other compounds sprayed from a helicopter on 107 plots, each of which was two hundred feet by six hundred feet[181] with a total test area that was "4 miles long and 1,200 feet wide."[182] Nine other plots in the test area were not sprayed. Additional tests were conducted at Gagetown in 1967, using fifteen different compounds, including Agents Orange and White, on thirty-seven additional plots.[183] Agent Orange and a mixture of Paraquat and Tordon were found to be the most effective.[184] Paraquat would later be used in efforts to suppress illegal drug production in Latin America.

Environmental warfare involving the use of chemical and biological tactics is not limited to what are commonly understood to be war-fighting environments. Thus, for example, broad efforts to use defoliants and herbicides to fight narco-terrorists in Colombia and elsewhere have had their own impacts and produced environmental warfare countermoves by the groups involved. What the tactic has not done is to reduce drug production to any appreciable degree. Narco-terrorists countered with their own tactics, one of which is to create no-entry zones into areas of the rainforest, not so much to protect the resources as to provide cover for their headquarters and operations. The closed areas also provide cover to hide coca-growing operations that were moved further into the forests from the areas subjected to spraying with resulting damage to those ecosystems.[185]

American homeland security officials have also been concerned ever since 9/11 about the danger that al Qaeda may have been planning chemical attacks on vulnerable targets, such as reservoirs, using aircraft normally employed for crop dusting. There is nothing new about efforts to poison water supplies. Such tactics not only result in potential harm to animals and people, but have the additional effect of leading to the danger of the spread of illnesses that often stem from inadequate or unsafe water supplies. Terrorists have also learned to employ biological organisms as weapons. Certainly the examples of anthrax attacks in the United States provide examples of that problem.

It is also clear that research and planning for new and even more dramatic environmental warfare capabilities is under way in the United States and presumably other nations as well. The Air Force 2025 and Space-CAST 2020 studies from the Air University make it clear that weather and space weapons are already considered important to future operations, and not a distant future at that. The paper entitled "Weather as a Force Multiplier" of the 2025 study argues that: "From enhancing friendly operations or disrupting those of the enemy via small scale tailoring of natural weather patterns to complete dominance of global communications and counterspace control, weather-modification offers the war fighter a wide-range of possible options to defeat or coerce an adversary." Specifically, the report argues that weather can be used to "degrade enemy forces" by "precipitation enhancement [to] flood lines of communication, reduce PGM [precision guided munitions]/recce [reconnaissance], decrease comfort level/morale[;] storm enhancement/storm modification to deny operations[;] precipitation denial [to] deny fresh water [and] induce drought[;] space weather [to] disrupt communications/radar [and] disable/destroy space assets[;] fog and cloud removal [to] deny concealment [and] increase vulnerability to PGM/Recce[; and] detect hostile weather activities."[186]

It is interesting to note that the scenario with which the paper begins is not a battle with another nation, but a planned attack on a drug cartel in Latin America. The scenario goes on to explain how the air commander would be assisted by a "weather force support element (WFSE)" that would ensure accurate predictions with regard to likely rain storms over the target and ensure the enhancement of those storms to keep the drug lords' forces on the ground. This would be done by means of unmanned aerospace vehicles (UAVs). "Simultaneously, microwave heaters create localized scintillation to disrupt active sensing via synthetic aperture radar (SAR) systems such as the commercially available Canadian search and rescue satellite-aided tracking (SARSAT) that will be widely available in 2025."[187]

To such planners, space is also understood to be a key element of environmental warfare, both in terms of providing indirect war-fighting capabilities and such direct means as "directed energy and kinetic energy weapons."[188] As with the weather example, it is revealing to read the scenario with which the space operations report begins.

> Once again a small but capably armed country is threatening to seize its smaller but resource-rich neighbor. . . . [T]he plot twists as a sophisticated satellite surveillance and reconnaissance system tracks the belligerent nation's leader. As he steps to the podium to incite his troops to greater violence, a blinding light from above vaporizes him and his podium leaving even his bodyguards untouched. His smarter brother, the second in command, countermands the invasion orders and in 12 hours the borders are restored.[189]

As Richard Tucker and Edmund Russell have observed, the environment has long been seen by military commanders and their political superiors as an ally to be enlisted in the service of combat or an enemy to be overcome or perhaps even destroyed. In fact, Herodotus related the campaign in which Cyrus II had his workers dig a canal to divert the Euphrates river flow into a marsh in order to reduce the level of the river to permit his troops to invade Babylon from the river side and thus surprise the Babylonians.[190] The most common ancient reference to environmental warfare is the report that in the Third Punic War, the Romans salted the fields in the area of Carthage to make recovery and possible rebuilding of a military force more difficult.[191] Sun Tzu's classic ancient Chinese text *The Art of War* identifies five key factors of warfare: "The first is the Tao, the second Heaven, the third Earth, the fourth generals, and the fifth the laws." He then explains that victory is most likely to go to those "Who have gained [the advantages of] Heaven and Earth."[192] Although environmental warfare has a long history, there are many new and very damaging strategies and tactics that have been in use in the contemporary era and that are contemplated for the decades immediately ahead.

Unexpected Impacts of Conflict on the Environment

Candor requires at least a recognition of a theme in the literature on environmental warfare that speaks to a counterintuitive proposition. The writers in the field assert that, in ironic ways, there can be some benefits, even if short-term, to the environment during conflict. Labeled by one scholar as "gunpoint conservation," these arguments almost all come down to the assertion that conflict creates zones in which individuals may not enter for fear of direct engagement with a hostile force or because they have been mined or otherwise set to destroy anyone or anything that enters.[193] In such areas logging or fishing will stop, animals will find a haven from hunting pressures, and plant species will have an opportunity to recover from the various pressures that come from human populations.[194] Examples to which these writers point are as diverse as the demilitarized zone between the two Koreas and Nicaragua. However, the same author who notes that the "creation of 'no-go' zones, slows or stops developments that lead to loss of biodiversity, . . . reduces pressures on some habitats, allows vegetation to recover in some areas, . . . reduc[es] hunting, and can increase biodiversity" then explains that the negative impacts include "deforestation, erosion, wildlife poaching, habitat destruction, pollution of land and water, [reduction of] funds for conservation, [stoppage of] conservation projects, [the forcing of] people onto marginal lands, and [the creation of] refugees who destroy biodiversity."[195]

Whatever these so-called positive externalities may be in the limited circumstances in which they occur, the cost can hardly be said to be worth it. A sustainable development analysis would conclude that any such positive results are more than offset by a host of other environmental, social, and economic costs.

Underestimating the Significance of Violent Conflict for the Urban Environment

Finally, much of the public discussion of environmental warfare has to do with obvious direct and often massive trauma suffered by ecosystems from bombing, armored attacks, or large-scale troop movements through a given area.[196] The ravages of large-scale battle affect many types of ecosystems. The subject elicits images of the massive tank battles of World War II, in which German panzer divisions rolled through the forests in the Battle of the Bulge and Patton led his tanks through so much of France, Belgium, and Germany; or visions of massive naval battles fought among the coral atolls of the Pacific, sending any number of ships and their crews to a watery grave. Then, of course, there were the waves of napalm attacks and massive spraying of defoliant in the jungles of Southeast Asia during the Vietnam War.

That said, there is a tendency to ignore urban ecosystems in discussions of the subject as compared to the destruction of Western forests, riparian systems, and jungle environments. Yet, there is a growing awareness, particularly in light of the fact that the majority of the world's population now lives in urban settings, that it is essential to pay more attention to the relationship between city dwellers and their ecosystems. Recall the devastation of British and German cities after World War II, the toll of a bitter war on Korean cities, and the utter destruction of Hiroshima and Nagasaki. Efforts at what is termed *precision bombing* in contemporary conflicts has still left cities devastated. Of course, such direct assaults are not limited to conventional warfare, as is demonstrated by the destruction of numerous African and Latin American coups d'état, civil wars, and terrorism. Media depictions of Kigali, the Democratic Republic of Congo, and Sierra Leone come readily to mind. To many Americans, of course, there are the searing images of "Ground Zero" in New York.

It is not sufficient to regard conflict and the urban environment as simply a matter of reconstructing the "built environment." After all, urban ecosystems are as complex as many others and, in some respects, more so. It is revealing, for example, that apart from concern with airborne particulates near and some toxic exposure at the World Trade Center site, there has been surprisingly little effort to understand what the attacks did to the environment in New York. Essentially, the discussion has been limited, as it often is in dire circumstances, to those aspects of the environment directly connected to human health or to the economy. That is too narrow an approach to ensure a sustainable future.

SOCIAL WARFARE: THE STRATEGY OF SOFT-TARGET ATTACK ON AID WORKERS AND VULNERABLE CIVILIANS

While environmental warfare may be a new concept for many people, the idea of social warfare seems intuitively obvious. The tendency is to fall back on the age-old concept of war as a formal contest of power between nation-states waged to achieve political ends. Hence, the common response is to think in terms of Carl von Clausewitz's famous dictum that: "War is a mere continuation of policy by other means. We see, therefore, that war is not merely a political act, but also a real political instrument, a continuation of political commerce, a carrying out of the same by other means."[197] And warfare, then, is but the means of conducting a war.

However, as chapter 1 argued and as the 9/11 and the Iraq case studies earlier in this chapter demonstrate, conflict today is far more diverse, and warfare is conducted by a variety of organizations against a range of targets that do not fit the classical definitions. And even where states are part of the conflict, they are often not in situations that fit the classic scenario of sovereign versus sovereign.

It is interesting that the United States government has used the formal instruments of war, including a formal adoption of an authorization of the use of military force, and the president has invoked formal powers as commander-in-chief, to engage in a "war on terror" in which the parties are not nation-states, but a group of organizations—some independent, others loosely allied, and still others closely affiliated—that speak with no authority recognized in international law. They are guilty of criminal acts of monstrous proportions, and yet they are engaged as if they were formally constituted belligerents in a war. Their actions are certainly political, but they have no lawful authority to represent a society.

While there have clearly been formal wars involving Afghanistan and Iraq recently, there remain at the time of this writing ongoing fights of several types that have come after the regimes were replaced in those two nations. In Iraq, for example, there are sectarian forces involved that have no specific political status or even a clear affiliation. The Department of Defense report to Congress as of August 2006 made the point:

> During this reporting period, attacks and civilian casualties have risen, characterized by ethno-sectarian attacks and reprisals. . . . Weekly attack levels in July 2006 were the highest to date. Coalition forces continued to attract the majority (63%) of attacks. However, the ISF and civilians continued to suffer the majority of casualties. Overall, Iraqi casualties increased by 51% compared to the previous quarter. . . .
>
> Sectarian tensions increased over the past quarter, demonstrated by the increasing number of executions, kidnappings, attacks on civilians, and internally displaced persons. According to an estimate by the United Nations, 22,977 families—137,862 individuals— have been displaced in Iraq since the February 22, 2006, Samarra Mosque bombing. . . .
>
> Executions in particular reached new highs in the month of July. The Baghdad Coroner's Office reported 1,600 bodies arrived in June and more than 1,800 bodies in July, 90% of which were assessed to be the result of executions.[198]

Although the administration insisted that the situation in Iraq "does not meet the stringent international legal standards for civil war," the report concluded that: "Sustained ethno-sectarian violence is the greatest threat to security and stability in Iraq."[199] In the memory of some of those living today, the country has seen coups d'état, several full-blown formal wars, genocide, occupation, terrorism, insurgency, and civil war.

It is also telling that the scenario employed by the Air Force 2025 paper on weather warfare did not involve a nation-state, but narco-traffickers. Indeed, fighting in Colombia may have begun as a political conflict, but it is clear that some of the parties are now primarily narco-terrorists and traffickers rather than political revolutionaries. (See chapter 3.) Finally, consider that the recent battle in the Middle East pitted Hezbollah, supplied by Iran and Syria, operating outside the Lebanese government but within its territory (though the organization also has elected members in government), and Israel, which has sent troops into Lebanon against the group. In sum, the array and character of actors is broad and complex in contemporary conflicts. This is not World War II.

To the degree that post-conflict efforts start from the assumptions about warfare that harken back to the classical formal definition in international relations, they are outdated and inadequate to address the range of conflict in the contemporary world or the variety of mechanisms and tactics of warfare by which they are waged. More to the point of this discussion, the classical approaches are inadequate to address what must be faced by those seeking to move forward after conflict. And the means of conflict are often at least as important as the ends. The post-World War II reconstruction model or contemporary approaches that focus on nation building aimed primarily at avoiding failed states are not responsive to the challenges presented by social warfare in combination with environmental and economic warfare.

In order to better respond to the need for sustainable development in a post-conflict environment, it is important to consider the types of social warfare that have been used in the contemporary context because of their consequences for those affected in recent conflicts. These include genocide, the use of rape as a common tactic, deliberate exposure to HIV, attacks on aid workers, women, and children and other so-called "soft targets," religion and ethnicity as social fault lines, identity deprivations and the creation of stateless persons, the attack on human security, and the undermining of the rule of law. The picture that has emerged in recent decades is of a collection of modes of social warfare intended to maximize individualized suffering and deprive individuals, communities, and whole societies of human security as that concept has been defined by the United Nations.

Defining Social Warfare: More than
Simply Target or Collateral Damage

First, however, it is important to be clear about the definition of social warfare. Warfare is understood as means of conflict aimed at defeating or inflicting significant damage on an enemy. Social warfare is a set of strategies or tactics that include attacks on people (other than committed combatants), their beliefs, their community, their race or ethnicity, their culture, their religion, or their government. Like environmental warfare, it is too simplistic merely to classify social warfare either as deliberate attacks or collateral damage. Social warfare may involve deliberately and directly targeted attacks on noncombatants, as in the case of terrorist attacks intended to kill or physically or psychologically injure large numbers of noncombatants. It may be social high-impact warfare in which a tactic is employed in which the natural and foreseeable consequence of the weapons or mode of attack employed is to kill or injure large numbers of noncombatants. Thus, firing from positions in the center of a community amidst large numbers of noncombatants or using heavy weapons such as artillery or large bombs in heavily populated areas would fit this category. Or the action taken may fall at the other end of the continuum and truly be collateral damage in that casualties were accidental and neither anticipated nor intended.

The 9/11 attack was not merely an attack on the government of the United States. The terrorists made clear by their choice of targets that they were attacking American society as well as its governing structures. The attackers intended to make terror a part of American life. Osama bin Laden made it clear that the intention was to ensure that life in the United States would never be the same after September 11, 2001. As the case study demonstrated, that is what has happened, even to the point of prompting the nation to move in directions that have been damaging to its historically professed principles. To bring that about, bin Laden and al Qaeda were fully prepared to kill as many civilians as possible. In a 1998 interview, bin Laden said, "We do not have to differentiate between military or civilian. As far as we are concerned, they are all targets."[200]

Genocide, Rape, and Attacks on Soft Targets:
Warfare against People and their Societies

In many countries around the world, contemporary social warfare has produced profound anger and frustration. That is not necessarily because the countries involved have not themselves engaged in it at some point in time. Neither Europeans nor the rest of the world can forget the Holocaust. In the United States, historians are quick to remind the nation of the campaign to wipe out Native Americans, not once but through several policies over a long period of time. First there was the outright slaughter of Native Americans followed by efforts to drive the survivors into lands that were alien environments inadequate to support the people forced to live there.[201] Then there were the government boarding schools where efforts were made to strip Native American children of their language, culture, and identity.[202] Then there was the Dawes Act that used a system of land allotments in an attempt to parcel out the little land that remained to tribes and nations and break the connection between tribal people and their native lands. Later still there was the decertification of tribes and nations in an effort to deny legitimacy to them as cultural, legal, and political entities.[203] Certainly World War II saw numerous examples of social warfare, ending with the delivery of two nuclear weapons on Japan designed to demonstrate destructive power rather than to take down important military targets.

However, the modern hope was that efforts made after World War II to protect noncombatants and their communities in times of conflict through the creation of a new body of laws for warfare would change the behavior of combatants and their political superiors. Certainly with respect to genocide, the repeated vow that such atrocities would never be permitted to happen again seemed to produce a common resolve to place certain types of action beyond the boundaries of behavior to be tolerated in a civilized world. New institutions such as the United Nations were created to find means to stop social warfare before it began, to limit it when possible, or to stop it as quickly as possible if and when it happened. Those factors have made it all the more difficult to comprehend the contemporary use of such means of conflict.

Indeed, it has become increasingly common, particularly since the conflicts in Bosnia-Herzegovina and Kosovo to see not one, but a series of such repulsive social warfare tactics as genocide, the deliberate use of rape, and other assaults on so-called "soft targets," though these were by no means the only or the first examples of such behavior. One study determined in fact that: "Genocides and political mass murders are recurrent phenomena. Since WWII nearly 50 such events have happened and these episodes have cost the lives of at least 12 million and as many as 22 million noncombatants, more than all victims of internal and international wars since 1945."[204] The events of the 1990s in the former Yugoslavia popularized the horrendous term *ethnic cleansing*, and the practice as well as the term have been used in a variety of other places since then. It is generally accepted that the term was taken from a Serbo-Croatian term in the 1940s, but entered contemporary parlance with use by the media to describe events in Bosnia-Herzegovina and Kosovo in the 1990s. According to the U.S. Department of State, "ethnic cleansing is defined as the systematic and forced removal of the members of an ethnic group from a community or communities in order to change the ethnic composition of a given region."[205]

By mid-1999, the State Department estimated that the action taken beginning in February 1998 by the Serb government was nothing less than "a comprehensive, premeditated, and systematic program to ethnically cleanse the Serbian province of Kosovo of its roughly 1.7 million ethnic Albanian residents."[206] While ethnic cleansing was sometimes carried out by driving people out of the area, other means were also employed, including detention and summary execution of men and boys, the organized and systematic rape of women and girls, the burning of homes and communities, and what has been termed *identity cleansing.* Identity cleansing is defined as confiscation of personal identification, passports, and other such documents in order to make it difficult or impossible for those driven out to return or even in some cases to obtain asylum in other countries due to their inability to prove their identity, citizenship, or country of origin.[207]

Even before that, the global community heard of ethnic cleansing from events in Bosnia-Herzegovina, where religion and ethnicity were closely intertwined at the core of the violence. The Bosnia-Herzegovina Human Development Report for 2000 explained the tragic labeling from the perspective of young people:

In Bosnia and Herzegovina (BiH), religion and ethnicity are almost synonymous. In most cases, when one's last name is stated or read, we all know whether that individual is a Bosnian and therefore Muslim, a Bosnian-Croat and therefore Catholic, or a Bosnian-Serb and therefore Orthodox. We are given a name at birth which brings with it powerful ethnic and religious connotations. It is irrelevant whether or not we practice the religion or choose to identify with a particular ethnicity. We are forced to accept a religious and ethnic identity, and to live with the consequences. . . .

As we grew up, others identified us with a religion or ethnicity that we did not necessarily comprehend. . . . When we were the victims of discrimination, harassment and ethnic cleansing, we were painfully defined in the context of ethnic and religious hatred. . . . The war solidified the practice of reducing someone from a human being to simply ethnic or religious stereotypes. Unfortunately, we have mostly accepted this way of thinking.[208]

In 2001, the International Criminal Tribunal for the former Yugoslavia found General Radislav Krstic guilty of genocide and other crimes in the tragedy now known internationally as Srebrenica. The court's opinion details the events leading from orders issued by Bosnian Serb President Radovan Karadzic and General Ratko Mladic that resulted in the removal from the demilitarized zone and from the protection of Dutch troops at the UN base at Potocari. What followed was the mass murder of from 7,000 to 8,000 men and the removal of women, children, and older persons with beatings, rapes, and murder to follow.[209]

The world community was also shocked by the Rwandan genocide (see chapter 5) and, even more recently, by the nightmare in Darfur, Sudan,[210] which has recently intensified, notwithstanding the fact the U.S. Secretary of State declared a state of genocide as long ago as September 2004 and a UN report on the tragedy detailed savagery and needless attacks on villagers.

> [T]he Commission established that the Government of the Sudan and the Janjaweed are responsible for serious violations of international human rights and humanitarian law amounting to crimes under international law. In particular, the Commission found that Government forces and militias conducted indiscriminate attacks, including killing of civilians, torture, enforced disappearances, destruction of villages, rape and other forms of sexual violence, pillaging and forced displacement, throughout Darfur. . . . In addition to the large scale attacks, many people have been arrested and detained, and many have been held *incommunicado* for prolonged periods and tortured. The vast majority of the victims of all of these violations have been from the Fur, Zaghawa, Massalit, Jebel, Aranga and other so-called 'African' tribes.[211]

The government of Sudan's insistence that the attacks were necessary in its battles against rebel forces was obviously untrue. However, the UN investigating commission found: "that most attacks were deliberately and indiscriminately directed against civilians. . . . Even where rebels may have been present in villages, the impact of the attacks on civilians shows that the use of military force was manifestly disproportionate to any threat posed by the rebels."[212] The evidence has been overwhelmingly clear that the government has worked in concert with the Janjaweed, providing military support on the ground and air cover.

The situation has only gotten worse since the 2004 report, and that has been true even since the signing of an accord in the spring of 2006 that was supposed to bring an end to the fighting.[213] There are no truly accurate numbers with respect to those affected by the actions of the Sudanese government, the Janjaweed militias, and actions by rebel forces. However, Human Rights Watch has estimated that as of May 2006 more than 200,000 had been killed and other press reports have suggested that the number may be more than twice that high.[214] A July 2005 UN report concluded that by that point there were some 1.88 million internally displaced persons in Darfur (which the report noted was approximately one third of the entire population of the region) and another 300,000 refugees who fled to the neighboring country of Chad.[215] A December 2006 Human Rights Watch study found that "At least two million Sudanese civilians have been displaced from their homes since mid-2003."[216]

In addition to death and injury, the social warfare described in the cases discussed also involved the deliberate use of rape and, in some cases, a deliberate infection of women with HIV. The United Nations Development Fund for Women (UNIFEM) report entitled *Women, War and Peace* began with the following striking statement of the attacks: "The strategy of forcibly impregnating women as part of an ethnic cleansing campaign has occurred in recent conflicts in Bosnia and Herzegovina, East Timor, Kosovo, Rwanda and Sudan. Tens of thousands of women in these areas (and elsewhere) suffered the trauma of being raped repeatedly and impregnated by the rapist."[217]

The awareness of the use of rape as a weapon of ethnic cleansing first came to international attention as refugees from Bosnia-Herzegovina and Kosovo told the stories of the deliberate efforts to kill off the men, rape women, and to deliberately impregnate them. Human Rights Watch described the rapes "as a tool of 'ethnic cleansing,' meant to terrorize, torture and demean women and their families and compel them to flee the area."[218]

In the early period following the first reports, even international human rights organizations were sometimes reticent to attribute these attacks as part of an intentional tactic of warfare. However, the more that testimony and later research in the area produced evidence of the scope and nature of the attacks, the intentional and systematic nature of the practice made clear the deliberate use of rape as warfare. Indeed, the International Criminal Tribunal for the former Yugoslavia issued its first convictions and findings in these cases in 2001.[219] One human rights agency put the matter in the clearest possible terms. "[R]ape and other forms of sexual violence were used in Kosovo in 1999 as weapons of war and instruments of systematic 'ethnic cleansing.' Rapes were not rare and isolated acts committed by individual Serbian or Yugoslav forces, but rather were used deliberately as an instrument to terrorize the civilian population, extort money from families, and push people to flee their homes. Rape furthered the goal of forcing ethnic Albanians from Kosovo."[220]

In the case of Rwanda, and later in Darfur, the evidence became overwhelmingly clear as to these practices, along with the additional tactic of deliberately infecting those who were raped with HIV.

[I]n Rwanda . . . , Hutu men who knew that they were infected with HIV purposely attempted to infect Tutsi women as a strategy of war. The Interahamwe leaders directly encouraged their militias to rape Tutsi women in order to dilute Tutsi ethnicity; infecting the women with a virus that would eventually kill them seemed an even more effective means of genocide. AVEGA, a support group for Rwandan women, has documented that many rape survivors were infected with HIV. Veronica . . . told us, ". . . Men in groups of between 30 and 50 would rape a woman. They would all wait their turn. This was the beginning of the spread of HIV/AIDS. Today many of us are infected because of rape."[221]

The evidence continues to grow that these attacks went on even after they were well-documented and roundly denounced by the international community. Again, Human Rights Watch found that: "[R]ape and sexual violence have been used by government forces and government-backed Janjaweed militias as a 'deliberate strategy with the aim of terrorizing the population, ensuring control of the movement of the IDP population and perpetuating its displacement.'"[222] That organization not only corroborated the findings of other international organizations on Darfur, but also independently documented numerous incidents in all regions of Darfur of such attacks "including multiple rapes by multiple attackers from government forces and militias."[223] The report points out that the impacts of these attacks extend well beyond the physical consequences of the attacks. "The legacy of these violations has had multiple consequences for the survivors and their families. In addition to the trauma of the rape itself, sexual assaults can result in serious physical injury, forced pregnancy, disease, death, and ostracism from the communities of the victims."[224]

The Darfur documents also demonstrate that the authorities in Darfur and in Sudan as a whole refused to investigate and prosecute allegations, and sought to intimidate those reporting the attacks from pressing the matter. Indeed, they stressed that human rights groups that investigated and found evidence of the attacks were also subjected to harassment and attempts at intimidation. The Office of the UN High Commissioner for Human Rights pointed, for example, to the arrest in May of 2005 in Khartoum of the Country Director of Médecins Sans Frontières (MSF; Doctors Without Borders), who was charged with espionage and other offenses, and later the regional MSF coordinator in Southern Darfur. The two were released only after international demands in June.[225]

As the Iraq case study makes clear, it has become increasingly common for humanitarian aid workers to become targets of combatants. These attacks have been employed by nation-states as well as insurgents or terrorists. The situation in Darfur is an obvious case in point. In May 2006, Human Rights Watch issued a report indicating that intimidation and deliberate interference with the work of aid agencies had put some 650,000 people who were in desperate need of assistance out of reach.[226] In the case of Darfur, the barriers have been posed both by the government of Sudan and also by rebel attacks on relief workers. To avoid the appearance that they are aligned with any of the belligerents, aid workers often refuse military security assistance and are therefore easy targets.

As the Iraq case demonstrates, even international institutions such as the Red Cross/Red Crescent and the United Nations have been driven out of some operations because of attacks on their people. That reality has more impact than is often understood, since governments and international institutions have come to rely almost completely on nongovernmental

organizations, operating on their own or under contracts or grants, to provide humanitarian and relief services and supplies around the world. The
Iraq case study also indicates that, even in countries that are active combat
zones, these NGOs are essential.

While these are some of the most obvious and dramatic examples of social warfare in the contemporary era, they are far from the only ones. Thus,
it was noted at the outset that social warfare, like its environmental coun-
terpart, ranges along a broad continuum, and the same is true of economic
warfare.

ECONOMIC WARFARE: ATTACKS ON MODERN FISCAL, INFORMATION, AND CRITICAL SYSTEMS

The 9/11 attacks provide a clear example of economic warfare outside the
traditional context of formal wars among nation-states. The attack was intended in part as a symbolic attack on a center of commerce and finance. It
was also expected to—and did—result in major financial costs, far beyond
the immediate need to restore financial infrastructure and activity in New
York City. It resulted in massive reallocations of resources and changes in
business operations, and not just in the transportation and insurance industries. It also produced massive shifts of available resources away from
domestic programs like health care and education to homeland security
and national defense. The demands were not just on federal resources but
on state and local budgets as well. Then there were the massive expenditures
required to finance the Afghanistan and Iraq wars, spending that was not
even done as a normal part of the president's budget requests but handled
outside the process, using supplemental appropriations legislation.

Of course, the idea of economic warfare is neither new nor limited to terrorists. It has been used by nation-states, including the United States. Like
the environmental and social aspects of warfare, economic warfare can be a
weapon, can target an economy for attack, or can make economic assets a
goal of conflict. As the other two dimensions, economic warfare exists along
a continuum from deliberate weapon of attack, through high-impact economic warfare, to collateral damage. Finally, like the other two dimensions,
economic warfare may have dramatic short-term consequences, but it is
also important to look to the longer-term impacts in order to think about
a sustainable future after the conflict.

Economic Warfare Then, Now, and in Years to Come

In an era when the marketplace and globalization have become central to
the day-to-day lives of so many people, and when the assumption is that

much of this reality is tied to the importance of modern computers and the Internet that connects them together, one might be forgiven for thinking that economic warfare is a recent discovery. The fact is that it is not new. One might refer to traditional conceptions of economic warfare, modern versions that emerged during and after World War II, contemporary economic conflict, and likely future forms of economic warfare.

The discussion of environmental warfare mentioned a number of cases from ancient to modern times that were partly or even significantly exemplars of economic warfare. These were in many instances contests to control resources, from food and fuel to gold. The wars of conquest and colonialism were very obvious examples of economic warfare. Not only did these battles yield valuable raw materials, they also enabled the conquerors to take control of a workforce to develop the raw materials or turn them into value-added products for consumption by the conqueror or as trade goods around the world. Sadly, of course, those practices have operated—and in some situations in the world still do operate—on the backs of slaves. Thus, examples from the former Yugoslavia reveal cases where women, in addition to being subjected to sexual assault, were also held against their will and required to serve as maids.

From the examples of the salting of the fields by Roman troops to the use of scorched-earth tactics in Georgia during the American Civil War to the contemporary era, economic warfare has aimed not only to defeat adversaries but to make it extremely difficult for the enemies to recover their economic capability later. Even the most sophisticated economy must first feed its people before it can look to them to produce and sell goods and services. In more contemporary times, when fuel is nearly as important as food, Saddam Hussein's attack on Kuwait's oil wells during the first Gulf War not only despoiled the environment, it also required major investments to bring the nation's oil industry, the core of its economy, back into production.

That said, the term *economic warfare* is one that gained prominence during and after World War II. In fact, during that conflict there was an Economic Warfare Section in the U.S. Department of Justice. Soon after WWII the Cold War came into its own, with economic warfare an integral part of the competition between the United States and the then Soviet Union. One of the most commonly used definitions of economic warfare was presented in a 1954 CIA report entitled "Soviet Bloc Economic Warfare Capabilities and Courses of Action." "Economic warfare is defined in this estimate as the use of economic measures to alter the relative power positions and alignments of opposing nations or groups of nations. This can be done by affecting either the relative economic strength of the nations in the two groups or reducing the size and effectiveness of the opposing group by causing political defections or, what is more likely, dissensions."[227]

The Reagan administration made economic warfare a central element in its Cold War strategy, but it was used by Democrats as well against Cuba. The CIA in December 1963 reported some success in the use of such weapons against the regime of Fidel Castro and called for an intensification of the effort. "These measures have been largely responsible for Castro's current economic distress, but additional effective economic warfare measures could be taken."[228]

The Reagan White House formally launched a major economic warfare campaign against the Soviet Union in 1982. The principal strategists in that campaign were Roger W. Robinson Jr., then senior director of international economic affairs in Reagan's National Security Council, William Clark, and William Casey, director of the CIA. The initial operation in that campaign came with the issuance in September of that year of National Security Decision Directive 54 entitled "United States Policy Toward Eastern Europe." This war plan laid out a set of incentives designed to encourage Eastern European countries to distance themselves from the USSR and offered them most-favored-nation status, credits, International Monetary Fund (IMF) membership, and debt restructuring to motivate them to do so. The countries that responded favorably would then also be eligible for other activities that would support their economic development, such as cultural and educational exchanges, scientific exchanges, high-level visits, supports in international organizations, and relaxation of restrictions on Eastern European diplomats and consular personnel.[229]

The second-wave attack came in November, when the administration issued National Security Decision Directive 66, which was generally known as the "Plan for Economic Warfare Against the USSR," even though its formal title was "East-West Economic Relations and Poland-Related Sanctions"; it set out to organize trade restraints by "the Allies" against the USSR.[230] While the countries that were to be allies in this effort said that "it is not their purpose to engage in economic warfare against the Soviet Union," those involved in drafting the strategy made clear that that was the intention.[231] Under NSDD 66 the idea was that "the Allies" would move to end natural gas purchases from the USSR, seek alternative sources of supply, stop sales of energy technology to the Soviets, and attempt to increase trade costs to USSR by increasing interest rates for loans and placing restraints on trade credits.[232]

In January 1983, the Reagan administration issued a third key strategy document in this economic war, National Security Decision Directive 75.[233] The strategy was to prevent "transfer of technology and equipment that would make a substantial contribution directly or indirectly to Soviet military power; . . . avoid subsidizing the Soviet economy or unduly easing the burden of Soviet resource allocation decisions, so as not to dilute pressure for structural change in the Soviet system; . . . minimize the potential for Soviet exercise of reverse leverage on Western countries based on trade, energy supply, and financial relationships; . . . permit mutual beneficial trade—without Western subsidization or the creation of Western dependence—with the USSR in non-strategic areas, such as grains."[234]

The economic warfare of today and tomorrow is more complex, sophisticated, and potentially even more devastating than ever envisioned in the past. First, in a globalized economic environment, many countries have become dependent upon the raw materials, finished products, and many types of services they need at favorable prices from foreign providers. The lines of trade and means of exchange are therefore vulnerable to interdiction, manipulation, or hostile alliances. That reliance on foreign suppliers has also led to the loss of domestic sources and services in many sectors, such that there often is not a readily available local substitute for the offshore providers. Under such conditions, the interruption of commerce can produce significant economic impacts. The problem is not merely the availability of goods and services from elsewhere, but the fact that, without them, local employment and economic activity can be significantly affected. There can be a loss of markets even for those products that can be offered in the marketplace. In addition to all of this, globalized competition adds its own set of reasons for conflict to the international mix. In fact as one military author put it, "The preeminence of politico-military competition is slowly giving way to politico-economic competition. As Shintaro Ishihara predicts, 'The twenty-first century will be a century of economic warfare.'"[235]

Second, these commercial relationships and the infrastructure that undergirds them are vulnerable to new weapons and modes of attack. Consider just two examples. More than a decade ago, Lieutenant Colonel Robert P. Kadlec explained just some of the potential of "Biological Weapons for Waging Economic Warfare."[236] Kadlec explained that relatively inexpensive and easily produced biological agents could be used to attack major agricultural sectors of the U.S. economy. He provided the following scenario, assuming a hypothetical economic warfare attack from country X.

> [Country X] is the world's second largest corn exporter. Recognizing the vulnerable situation of the United States, [it] plans an act of agricultural terrorism. Selecting a corn seed blight . . . which grows well at cool temperatures and in wet soil, they clandestinely spray this hearty spore over the US Midwest from commercial airliners flying the polar route to Chicago and Saint Louis. . . . [T]he blight is present in the soil when spring planting occurs.

> The United States . . . suffers from a crop disaster. This unexpected . . . blight decimates the US corn crop. The fall harvest is a full 30 percent below expected levels. The United States then imports corn for the first time in its history to meet domestic needs. Food prices rise sharply and cause higher-than-expected

food prices and inflation. [Country X] gains significant corn market share and
tens of billions of dollars of additional profits from their crop.[237]

Kadlec pointed out that there already had been examples of what could
happen when nonnative organisms found their way into the country, point-
ing to the devastating impact of the Mediterranean fruit fly and the white-
fly infestations that produced costs in the hundreds of millions of dollars.
Were he writing today, he could refer to the impact of hoof-and-mouth disease on the British cattle industry or the impacts of bovine spongiform en-
cephalopathy (BSE) on Canadian and U.S. beef producers. He added that
even by 1995, the "U.S. Department of Agriculture had identified 53 animal
diseases which are nonindigenous or foreign, which, if introduced into this
nation, would adversely impact the livestock industry."[238]

The other weapon of choice for economic warfare is what is sometimes
termed cyberwarfare or Net warfare based on the use of various computer
techniques and programs used to attack systems and infrastructure. Also
known as information warfare, it is defined as: "actions taken to achieve relatively greater understanding of the strengths, weaknesses, and centers of
gravity of an adversary's military, political, social, and economic infrastructure in order to deny, exploit, influence, corrupt, or destroy those adversary
information-based activities through command and control warfare and information attack."[239]

The potential for this kind of weaponry became known in nonmilitary
circles during the 1990s discussion of what was then referred to as critical
infrastructure protection. The more that the Internet became a focal point
for government and business activity and as desktop and laptop computers
became more powerful and less expensive, the clearer it was that attacks on
computer systems through the Internet could have devastating economic
and national security impacts. And that was even before the rise of the
scourge of early twenty-first century computing, identity theft. Viewed at
first as young people acting out their rebellious urges by proving they could
beat the adults and their security systems, the term "hacker" was added to
common parlance. However, breaking into computers became far less be-
nign as the intruders created viruses that could shut down or even destroy
systems and spread like wildfire through e-mail. Government agencies were
reporting rapidly growing numbers of security breaches.

The attention to computer security breaches and the consideration of the
many interdependent systems in the public arena, as well as the impact of
attacks on important private sector operations, led to the demand for critical infrastructure protection policies.[240] However, these challenges have
been made more difficult and vulnerabilities increased as both the Clinton
and George W. Bush administrations have pressed to contract out more of
the operation of public programs. Many of those contractors, in turn, sub-

contract to firms that are offshore and transmit data to those contractors over the Internet.

The E-Government Act was intended both to encourage an increase in government work done over the Internet and also to ensure greater security. While the former has happened, there is a great deal of evidence that there are serious security gaps not only in computer systems operated by public agencies, but also by contractors and subcontractors.[241] A 2006 Government Accountability Office study found that key contractors and subcontractors for federally funded health care programs subcontracted the handling of medical records to both domestic and offshore firms that had a surprising level of reported security breaches. "In responding to our survey, over 40 percent of the federal contractors and state Medicaid agencies reported that they experienced a recent privacy breach involving personal health information. By survey group, 47 percent of Medicare Advantage contractors reported privacy breaches within the past 2 years, as did 44 percent of Medicaid agencies, 42 percent of Medicare FFS contractors, and 38 percent of TRICARE contractors."[242]

There are a host of common techniques used presently to launch cyberwarfare attacks. They are summarized in Table 2.2. The techniques and knowledge needed to launch such attacks are inexpensive and widespread. They can also be difficult to defeat.

In a recent summary of the problems facing the Department of Homeland Security, the GAO noted: "As larger amounts of money are transferred through computer systems, as more sensitive economic and commercial information is exchanged electronically, and as the nation's defense and intelligence communities increasingly rely on commercially available information technology, the likelihood increases that information attacks will threaten vital national interests."[243]

Beyond the Nation-State: Economic Warfare and Other Kinds of Conflict

Economic warfare is no longer the preserve of nation-states. In fact, the World Bank project on civil war has determined that economic warfare is a central force in civil wars around the world.[244] In addition, as chapter 3 explains, there are cases in which the status of the combatants is less than clear, as in the case of Colombia, where politics may be at the origins of the conflict but cocaine profits have become the dominant force in the contemporary battles.

There are two other dimensions to economic warfare that are becoming increasingly important. The first is the presence and involvement of businesses in countries in which they become issues, key actors, or targets in

Table 2.2. Types of Cyber Attacks

Type of Attack	Description
Denial of service	A method of attack from a single source that denies system access to legitimate users by overwhelming the target computer with messages and blocking legitimate traffic. It can prevent a system from being able to exchange data with other systems or use the Internet.
Distributed denial of service	A variant of the denial-of-service attack that uses a coordinated attack from a distributed system of computers rather than from a single source. It often makes use of worms to spread to multiple computers that can then attack the target.
Exploit tools	Publicly available and sophisticated tools that intruders of various skill levels can use to determine vulnerabilities and gain entry into targeted systems.
Logic bombs	A form of sabotage in which a programmer inserts code that causes the program to perform a destructive action when some triggering event occurs, such as terminating the programmer's employment.
Phishing	The creation and use of e-mails and Web sites—designed to look like those of well-known legitimate businesses, financial institutions, and government agencies—in order to deceive Internet users into disclosing their personal data, such as bank and financial account information and passwords. The phishers then take that information and use it for criminal purposes, such as identity theft and fraud.
Sniffer	Synonymous with packet sniffer. A program that intercepts routed data and examines each packet in search of specified information, such as passwords transmitted in clear text.
Trojan horse	A computer program that conceals harmful code. A Trojan horse usually masquerades as a useful program that a user would wish to execute.
Virus	A program that infects computer files, usually executable programs, by inserting a copy of itself into the file. These copies are usually executed when the infected file is loaded into memory, allowing the virus to infect other files. Unlike the computer worm, a virus requires human involvement (usually unwitting) to propagate.
War dialing	Simple programs that dial consecutive telephone numbers looking for modems.
War driving	A method of gaining entry into wireless computer networks using a laptop, antennas, and a wireless network adaptor that involves patrolling locations to gain unauthorized access.
Worm	An independent computer program that reproduces by copying itself from one system to another across a network. Unlike computer viruses, worms do not require human involvement to propagate.

Source: U.S. Government Accountability Office, *Critical Infrastructure Protection: Department of Homeland Security Faces Challenges in Fulfilling Cybersecurity Responsibilities* (Washington, D.C.: GAO, 2005), 8.

conflict. They may be important because they operate facilities in the country or because they are important purchasers of raw products, as in the case of the infamous diamond trade in Africa.[245] The second issue is the growth of so-called international security services, including contract interrogators and other operatives, with as much as a quarter or more of all post-conflict contracting dollars going to pay for security. These firms are employed by particular principals and are not accountable to the public. However, their armed operations within a zone of conflict make them combatants—and combatants who can, under some circumstances, increase the difficulties in the country.[246]

LONG-TERM IMPLICATIONS OF ENVIRONMENTAL, SOCIAL, AND ECONOMIC WARFARE

One of the most serious problems in the post-conflict context is the danger that the costs of economic, environmental, and social warfare will be seen only in terms of their local and near-term impacts rather than the longer-term and often broad consequences. While the death of very talented and able people, the loss of thousands of highly paid jobs, the estimated $30 billion in insurance losses, the impacts on the travel and tourism industry, and all the rollover effects in the New York City economy were all very significant impacts of the 9/11 attacks, at least in economic terms, they pale in comparison with the larger national and international impacts.[247]

In fact, among the great dangers of the post-conflict reconstruction model is the focus on the immediate damage and most often the bricks-and-mortar types of damage in a specific place and at a particular time. Similarly, where there is environmental warfare, there is a tendency to focus on so-called "hot spots" and some kind of rapid remediation of the immediate circumstances, such as the lack of potable water, but here again the medium and longer term pose serious challenges.[248] As chapter 4 explains, ecosystems suffer the environmental equivalent of the post-traumatic stress disorder that affects humans, impacts that strike deep into the ecosystem and are enduring. Thus far, much of the attention on the effects of environmental warfare is viewed in terms of its human health impacts or its consequences for what is often incorrectly termed the "recovery" of the environment. It is still not clear just what the longer-term effects will be on the environment of long term, intense conflict. Vietnam has provided some preliminary evidence that the effects are manifold, complex, interconnected, and persistent more than three decades after the war.

Indeed, in many cases, as the Iraq case study, Vietnam, and many other examples indicate, a community suffers not only from one conflict, but multiple conflicts often over an extended period of time. As in the Iraq case, the Guatemala case study in chapter 4, and the Colombia case study in chapter 3 indicate, single conflicts often change over time in a variety of complex ways, not only in terms of strategies and tactics, but even in terms of the targets and the array of combatants.

Ironically, the problem of scope and temporal vision may be most difficult for those in developed countries to recognize. Thus, after the immediate reaction to the Los Angeles riots, very little happened to ensure a sustainable way forward, even for the part of the community most directly affected by the destruction. The same was true in Chicago and Detroit after the urban riots of the 1960s. At this point, it is not clear that Great Britain will respond to the 2005 attacks on its transportation system, that Spain has taken a comprehensive sustainable development route after the devastating attack on Madrid's metro system, or that France has taken such an approach in the aftermath of its own recent civil disorder.

CONCLUSION

Given our understanding of conflict over time and in the contemporary context, it should be apparent that post-conflict situations often involve more than one type of conflict and may involve an admixture of environmental, social, and economic warfare. Each of these types of conflict can be conducted across a range of possible approaches, from the intentional use of environmental, social, or economic warfare weapons through choices of weapons, strategies, and tactics that may not directly target a group, an ecosystem, or an economy, but that clearly indicate a high probability of impact in those areas, to simple collateral damage, a purely unanticipated and unintended harm. These dimensions are interrelated and interdependent. As such, real success in the post-conflict environment cannot be adequately ensured by the reconstruction, recovery, or nation-building approaches that have dominated post-conflict development policy in the post-World War II context. In fact, these approaches may in a number of important respects be counterproductive, particularly where, as has too often been the case in modern history, the powers who lead those efforts make inadequate commitments that they do not fully support and that are subject to whims of rapid political changes in the donor regimes.

Among the difficulties that stem from the reconstruction and recovery approaches is the assumption that the community is in place and that it needs only to have its infrastructure, both physical and economic, reinvigorated in a stable context. Problem solved, and the donors can then move on to the next geopolitical issue on their agendas. The fact is that conflicts not only cause death and destruction, they also tend to put people and often animals as well into flight. The fact of displacement, both within the country of conflict and outside it, has important consequences at home and around the world. These important realities and what they mean for those in flight and those who work with them are considered in chapter 3, which examines the flight, and chapter 4, which considers the post-traumatic stress that results for both people and the environment.

NOTES

1. Phillip J. Cooper and Claudia María Vargas, *Implementing Sustainable Development: From Global Policy to Local Action* (Lanham, MD: Rowman & Littlefield, 2004).

2. See, e.g., United Nations Environment Programme, Regional Office for West Asia, *A Rapid Assessment of the Iraq-Kuwait Conflict on Terrestrial Ecosystems* (Bahrain: UNEP, 1991), at www.unep.org/Documents.multilingual/Default.asp?DocumentID=307&ArticleID=3907&l=en (accessed August 26, 2005); A. R. G. Price, N. Downing, S. W. Fowler, J. T. Hardy, M. Le Tissier, C. P. Mathews, J. M. McGlade, P. A. H. Medley, B. Oregioni, J. W. Readman, C. M. Roberts, & T. J. Wrathall, *The 1991 Gulf War: Environmental Assessments of IUCN and Collaborators*, A Marine Conservation and Development Report (Gland, Switzerland: International Union for the Conservation of Nature, 1994), at www.iucn.org/themes/marine/pdf/gulfwar.pdf (accessed August 26, 2005).

3. MedAct, *Collateral Damage: The Health and Environmental Costs of War on Iraq* (London: MedAct, 2002), at www.medact.org/content/wmd_and_conflict/Medact_Iraq_report%20(1).pdf (accessed August 26, 2005); and MedAct, *Continuing Collateral Damage: The Health and Environmental Costs of War on Iraq 2003* (London: MedAct, 2003), at www.medact.org/tbx/pages/sub.cfm?id=775 (accessed August 26, 2005).

4. See World Bank, *The Economic Development of Iraq: Report of a Mission Organized by the International Bank for Reconstruction and Development at the Request of the Government of Iraq* (Washington, D.C.: World Bank, 1952), 9.

5. World Bank, *Economic Development of Iraq*, 13.

6. Library of Congress Country Studies: Iraq, "The Iran-Iraq Conflict," at http://lcweb2.loc.gov/cgi-bin/query/r?frd/cstdy:@field(DOCID+iq0024) (accessed August 29, 2005).

7. The detailed factual information on the Iran coup is taken from the CIA's own after-action report prepared by the agency's lead planner on the project. Donald N. Wilber, "Clandestine Service History: Overthrow of Premier Mossadeq of Iran, November 1952–August 1953," March 1954, published on the *New York Times* Internet site, at www.nytimes.com/library/world/mideast/iran-cia-intro.pdf (accessed August 29, 2005). See also James A. Bill, *The Eagle and the Lion: The Tragedy of American-Iranian Relations* (New Haven: Yale University Press, 1988), chapters 2–3.

8. Federation of American Scientists, "1980s Intelligence Sharing with Iraq Revisited," *Secrecy News*, from the FAS Project on Government Secrecy, vol. 2002, no. 69, July 30, 2002, at www.fas.org/sgp/news/secrecy/2002/07/073002.html (accessed August 29, 2005).

9. *Congressional Record*, November 7, 1991, vol. 137, S16305.

10. "Finding Pursuant to Section 662 of the Foreign Assistance Act of 1961, As Amended, Concerning Operations Undertaken by the Central Intelligence Agency in Foreign Countries, Other than Those Intended Solely for the Purpose of Intelligence Collection, January 17, 1986." U.S. Congress, Joint Hearings before the House Select Committee to Investigate Covert Arms Transactions with Iran and the Senate Select Committee on Secret Military Assistance to Iran and the Nicaraguan Opposition, *Iran-Contra Investigation*, 100th Cong., 1st Sess. (1987), Testimony of John M. Poindexter, 503.

11. United Nations Environment Programme, *Desk Study on the Environment in Iraq* (Nairobi: UNEP, 2003), 52.

12. UNEP, *Desk Study on the Environment in Iraq*, 53.

13. UNEP, *Desk Study on the Environment in Iraq*, 55.

14. U.S. Senate Intelligence Committee, "Postwar Findings about Iraq's WMD Programs and Links to Terrorism and How They Compare with Prewar Assessments," at http://intelligence.senate.gov/phaseiiaccuracy.pdf (accessed September 16, 2006).

15. Independent Inquiry Committee Into the United Nations Oil for Food Programme, *The Management of the United Nations Oil-for-Food Programme, Volume I Report of the Committee* (New York: Independent Inquiry Committee, 2005), at www.iic-offp.org, as of September 17, 2006. (Hereafter *Oil-for-Food Investigation*.)

16. UNEP, *Desk Study on the Environment in Iraq*, 54.

17. UNEP, *Desk Study on the Environment in Iraq*, 55.

18. "Charges Filed Against Hussein for 1982 Massacre of Shiite Villagers," *New York Times*, July 17, 2005, at www.nytimes.com.

19. National Security Directive (NSD) 54, January 15, 1991, at www.fas.org/irp/offdocs/nsd/nsd_54.htm (accessed December 26, 2006).

20. NSD 54, 1–2.

21. Jay E. Austin and Carl E. Bruch, eds., *The Environmental Consequences of War: Legal, Economic, and Scientific Perspectives* (Cambridge, UK: Cambridge University Press, 2000), 3.

22. UN Environment Programme, *Updated Scientific Report on the Environmental Effects of the Conflict between Iraq and Kuwait*, March 8, 1993, United Nations document UNEP/GC.17/lnf.9. This document summarizes the United Nations' findings on the environmental impacts of the oil fires and oil spills during the 1991 Gulf War.

23. Samira A. S. Omar, Ernest Briskey, Raafat Misak, and Adel A. S. O. Asem, "The Gulf War Impact on the Terrestrial Environment of Kuwait: An Overview," in Jay E. Austin and Carl E. Bruch, eds., *The Environmental Consequences of War: Legal, Economic, and Scientific Perspectives* (Cambridge, UK: Cambridge University Press, 2000), 320.

24. Omar et al., "Gulf War Impact," 322.

25. Mahmood Y. Abdultaheem, "War-Related Damage to the Marine Environment in the ROPME Sea Area," in Jay E. Austin and Carl E. Bruch, eds., *The Environmental Consequences of War: Legal, Economic, and Scientific Perspectives* (Cambridge, UK: Cambridge University Press, 2000), 341.

26. See, generally, United Nations, *Oil-for-Food Investigation*; and U.S. Government Accountability Office, *United Nations Oil for Food Program Audits* (Washington, D.C.: GAO, 2005).

27. United Nations Environment Programme, "Iraqi Marshlands: On the Road to Recovery," at www.unep.org/Documents.Multilingual/Default.asp?DocumentID=449&ArticleID=4902&l=en (accessed December 26, 2006). See, generally, UNEP, *The Mesopotamian Marshlands: Demise of an Ecosystem* (Nairobi: UNEP, 2001).

28. Richard A. Clarke, *Against All Enemies* (New York: Free Press, 2004), 32. Clarke was at the time of the 9/11 attacks the National Coordinator for Security, Infrastructure Protection, and Counterterrorism.

29. U.S. Department of State, *Future of Iraq Project Briefing*, November 1, 2002 (Declassified), 6, at www.gwu.edu/~nsarchiv/NSAEBB/NSAEBB163/iraq-state-02 .pdf (accessed December 26, 2006).

30. Michael R. Gordon and General Bernard E. Trainor, *Cobra II: The Inside Story of the Invasion and Occupation of Iraq* (New York: Pantheon, 2006), 4.

31. Gordon and Trainor, *Cobra II*, 19–21.

32. Gordon and Trainor, *Cobra II*, 19–30.

33. Gordon and Trainor, *Cobra II*, 38.

34. Gordon and Trainor, *Cobra II*, 38.

35. Coalition Provisional Authority, "Coalition Provisional Authority Regulation Number 6—Governing Council of Iraq," July 13, 2003, at www.cpa-iraq.org/regulations/20030713_CPAREG_6_Governing_Council_of_Iraq_.pdf (accessed December 7, 2006).

36. U.S. Department of State, *Future of Iraq Project Briefing*.

37. U.S. Department of State, *Future of Iraq Project Briefing*.

38. U.S. Department of State, *Future of Iraq Project Briefing*, 4.

39. David L. Phillips, *Losing Iraq* (Boulder, CO: Westview, 2005), 8. For extended discussions of this battle within the administration, see Bob Woodward, *State of Denial: Bush at War, Part III* (New York: Simon & Schuster, 2006).

40. Thomas E. Ricks, *Fiasco: The American Military Adventure in Iraq* (New York: Penguin, 2006), 103.

41. Testimony of General Eric K. Shinseki before the Senate Armed Services Committee, *The Fiscal Year 2004 Defense Budget*, February 25, 2003 (Washington, D.C., Federal News Service, 2003).

42. Coalition Provisional Authority, "Coalition Provisional Authority Order Number 1: De-Ba`athification of Iraqi Society," at www.cpa-iraq.org/regulations/ #Orders (accessed September 16, 2006).

43. Coalition Provisional Authority, "Coalition Provisional Authority Order Number 2: Dissoulution [*sic*] of Entities," at www.cpa-iraq.org/regulations/#Orders (accessed September 16, 2006).

44. See Ricks, *Fiasco*, 158–165.

45. U.S. Department of State, *Future of Iraq Project Briefing*, 17.

46. UNEP, *Desk Study on the Environment in Iraq*, 56–83.

47. UNEP, *Desk Study on the Environment in Iraq*, 32.

48. See United Nations, *Oil-for-Food Investigation*.

49. United Nations Environment Programme, *Environment in Iraq: Progress Report* (Geneva: UNEP, 2003).

50. United Nations and World Bank, *Joint Iraq Needs Assessment* (New York: United Nations and World Bank, 2003).

51. U.S. Department of State, *Future of Iraq Project Briefing*, 14.

52. See, e.g., Frederick M. Burkle Jr. and Eric K. Noji, "Health and Politics in the 2003 War with Iraq: Lessons Learned," *Lancet* 364 (October 9, 2004): 1371–1375.

53. U.S. Government Accountability Office, *Rebuilding Iraq: Actions Needed to Improve Use of Private Security Providers* (Washington, D.C.: GAO, 2005), 5.

54. Congressional Research Service, CRS Report for Congress, *Iraq: United Nations and Humanitarian Aid Organizations* (Washington, D.C.: CRS, 2006), 2–8, at www.usembassy.it/pdf/other/RL31766.pdf.

55. Clare Kapp, "Humanitarian Community Stunned by Red Cross Attacks in Iraq," *Lancet*, 362 (2003): 1461.

56. Kapp, "Humanitarian Community Stunned," 1461.

57. Doctors Without Borders/Médecins Sans Frontières, "MSF Stops Activities in Iraq," press release, at www.doctorswithoutborders.org/pr/2004/11-04-2004.cfm (accessed September 3, 2005).

58. Special Inspector General for Iraq Reconstruction, *Report to Congress: October 20, 2005*, 3, at www.sigir.mil/reports/quarterlyreports/Oct05/October_2005_report .pdf (accessed December 26, 2006).

59. Special Inspector General, *Report to Congress*, 3.

60. Special Inspector General, *Report to Congress*, 4.

61. See Ellen Knickmeyer, "U.S. Has End in Sight on Iraq Rebuilding: Documents Show Much of the Funding Diverted to Security, Justice System and Hussein Inquiry," *Washington Post*, January 2, 2006, A01.

62. Knickmeyer, "U.S. Has End in Sight on Iraq Rebuilding," A01.

63. Iraq Study Group, *Iraq Study Group Report* (New York: Random House, 2006), xiii–xiv, at www.usip.org/isg/iraq_study_group_report/report/1206/iraq_study_ group_report.pdf (accessed December 7, 2006).

64. See, e.g., National Commission on Terrorist Attacks upon the United States, *The 9/11 Commission Report: Final Report of the National Commission on Terrorist Attacks upon the United States* (Washington, D.C.: U.S. Government Printing Office, 2004).

65. James Dobbins, John G. McGinn, Keith Crane, Seth G. Jones, Rollie Lal, Andrew Rathmell, Rachel Swanger, and Anga Timilsina, *America's Role in Nation-Building from Germany to Iraq* (Santa Monica, CA: RAND Corporation, 2003); see also Ray Salvatore Jennings, *The Road Ahead: Lessons in Nation Building from Japan, Germany, and Afghanistan, for Postwar Iraq* (Washington, D.C.: U.S. Institute of Peace, 2003); Commission on Post-conflict Reconstruction, *Play to Win: Final Report of the Bi-partisan Commission on Post-conflict Reconstruction* (Washington, D.C.: Center for Strategic and International Studies and the Association of the U.S. Army, 2003); Elisabeth Rehn and Ellen Johnson Sirleaf, *Women, War and Peace: The Independent Experts' Assessment on the Impact of Armed Conflict on Women and Women's Role in Peace-Building* (New York: United Nations Development Fund for Women [UNIFEM], 2002).

66. National Park Service, *World War II in Alaska* (Anchorage, AK: U.S. Department of the Interior, 2000), at www.nps.gov/akso/CR/AKRCultural/CulturalMain/ 3PDF/WWII%20Resource%20Guide.pdf (accessed July 22, 2006).

67. See *Ex Parte Quirin*, 317 U.S. 1 (1942).

68. National Commission on Terrorist Attacks, *9/11 Commission Report*, 57.

69. National Commission on Terrorist Attacks, *9/11 Commission Report*, 71.

70. National Commission on Terrorist Attacks, *9/11 Commission Report*, 72.

71. National Commission on Terrorist Attacks, *9/11 Commission Report*, 72.

72. National Commission on Terrorist Attacks, *9/11 Commission Report*, 73

73. National Commission on Terrorist Attacks, *9/11 Commission Report*, 59.

74. National Commission on Terrorist Attacks, *9/11 Commission Report*, 60.

75. National Commission on Terrorist Attacks, *9/11 Commission Report*, 69.

76. National Commission on Terrorist Attacks, *9/11 Commission Report*, 70.

77. National Commission on Terrorist Attacks, *9/11 Commission Report*, 190.

78. National Commission on Terrorist Attacks, *9/11 Commission Report*, 153.

79. National Commission on Terrorist Attacks, *9/11 Commission Report*, 155.

80. National Commission on Terrorist Attacks, *9/11 Commission Report*, 311.

81. Federal Deposit Insurance Corporation, "Bank Trends—The New York City Economy: Post 9/11," May 2002, at www.fdic.gov/bank/analytical/bank/bt0204.html (accessed July 21, 2006).

82. U.S. Government Accountability Office, *Review of Studies of the Economic Impact of the September 11, 2001, Terrorist Attacks on the World Trade Center* (Washington, D.C.: GAO, 2002), 2.

83. Steven Greenhouse, "Contractors at Ground Zero Denied Insurance for Cleanup," *New York Times*, January 18, 2002, B1.

84. National Commission on Terrorist Attacks, *9/11 Commission Report*, 326–327.

85. Steven Brill, *After: The Rebuilding and Defending of America in the September 12 Era* (New York: Simon & Schuster, 2003), 49.

86. U.S. Government Accountability Office, *September 11: Overview of Federal Disaster Assistance to the New York City Area* (Washington, D.C.: GAO, 2003), 6.

87. GAO, *September 11: Overview*.

88. GAO, *September 11: Overview*, 4, n. 5.

89. GAO, *September 11: Overview*, 76–77.

90. P.L. 107-42, 115 Stat. 230 (2001).

91. Kenneth R. Fainberg, *Final Report of the Special Master for the September 11th Victim Compensation Fund of 2001*, 1, at www.usdoj.gov/final_report.pdf (accessed July 22, 2006).

92. See Congressional Research Service, *The Current Economic Recession: How Long, How Deep, and How Different from the Past?* (Washington, D.C.: CRS, 2002); Congressional Research Service, *The "Jobless Recovery" from the 2001 Recession: A Comparison to Earlier Recoveries and Possible Explanations* (Washington, D.C.: CRS, 2003).

93. U.S. Government Accountability Office, *Recent Estimates of Fiscal Impact of 2001 Terrorist Attack on New York* (Washington, D.C.: GAO, 2005), 10–11.

94. GAO, *Recent Estimates of Fiscal Impact*, 10–11.

95. P.L. 107-40, 115 Stat. 224 (2001).

96. Executive Order 13228, 66 Fed. Reg. 51812 (2001).

97. P.L. 107-296, 116 Stat. 2135 (2002).

98. Office of Management and Budget, *Budget of the United States Government, Fiscal Year 2005* (Washington, D.C.: OMB, 2004), 162.

99. Office of Management and Budget, *Budget of the United States Government, Fiscal Year 2006* (Washington, D.C.: OMB, 2005), 151.

100. Office of Management and Budget, *Budget of the United States Government, Fiscal Year 2007* (Washington, D.C.: OMB, 2006), 76.

101. OMB, *Budget of the U.S. Government 2007*, 63.

102. OMB, *Budget of the U.S. Government 2007*, 2.

103. P.L. 107-56, 115 Stat. 272 (2001).

104. See *Doe v. Gonzales*, 386 F. Supp. 2d 66 (DCT 2005); *ACLU v. Ashcroft*, 334 F. Supp. 2d 471 (SDNY 2004), *vac'd and rem'd sub nom Doe I v. Gonzales*, 449 F.3d 415 (2nd. Cir. 2006).

105. Foreign Intelligence Surveillance Act (FISA), P.L. 95-511, 92 Stat. 1783 (1978).

106. *In re All Matters Submitted to the Foreign Intelligence Surveillance Court*, 218 F. Supp. 2d 611 (Foreign Intell. Surveillance Ct. 2002), rev'd *In re: Sealed Case No. 02-001*, 310 F.3d 717 (Foreign Intell. Surveillance Ct. Rev. 2002).

107. See Elizabeth B. Bazan and Jennifer K. Elsea, *Presidential Authority to Conduct Warrantless Electronic Surveillance to Gather Foreign Intelligence Information* (Washington, D.C.: Congressional Research Service, 2006), at www.fas.org/sgp/crs/intel/m010506.pdf (accessed July 22, 2006).

108. U.S. Department of Justice, *Legal Authorities Supporting the Activities of the National Security Agency Described by the President* (Washington, D.C.: DOJ, 2006), at www.usdoj.gov/opa/whitepaperonnsalegalauthorities.pdf (accessed July 22, 2006).

109. Michael Creppy to All Immigration Judges and Court Administrators, "Memorandum: Cases Requiring Special Procedures," September 21, 2001, at http://news.findlaw.com/hdocs/docs/aclu/creppy092101memo.pdf (accessed December 26, 2006).

110. See Heidi Kitrosser, "Secrecy in the Immigration Courts and Beyond: Considering the Right to Know in the Administrative State," *Harvard Civil Rights—Civil Liberties L. Rev.* 39 (Winter 2004): 95–168.

111. Kitrosser, "Secrecy in the Immigration Courts and Beyond," 95.

112. David Cole, *Enemy Aliens: Double Standards and Constitutional Freedoms in the War on Terrorism* (New York: New Press, 2003), 5. An abbreviated version was published as "Enemy Aliens," *Stanford L. Rev.* 54 (May 2002): 953–1004.

113. See Office of the Inspector General, U.S. Department of Justice, *The September 11 Detainees: A Review of the Treatment of Aliens Held on Immigration Charges in Connection with the Investigation of the September 11 Attacks* (Washington, D.C.: U.S. Department of Justice, 2003), 158–164, at www.usdoj.gov/oig/special/03_06/full.pdf (accessed November 1, 2003).

114. "Convention against Torture and Other Cruel, Inhuman or Degrading Treatment or Punishment," Treaty Doc. 100-20, 1988 U.S.T. LEXIS 202, April 18, 1988, at www.unhchr.ch/html/menu3/b/h_cat39.htm (accessed July 22, 2006).

115. "Detention, Treatment, and Trial of Certain Non-citizens in the War against Terrorism," 66 *Fed. Reg.* 57833 (2001).

116. John Yoo to William J. Haynes II, "Memorandum: Application of Treaties and Laws to al Qaeda and Taliban Detainees," January 9, 2002, at www.slate.com/features/whatistorture/pdfs/020109.pdf (accessed July 22, 2006).

117. 18 U.S.C. §§2340-240a.

118. Jay S. Bybee to Alberto Gonzales, "Memorandum: Standards of Conduct for Interrogations under 18 U.S.C. §§2340-240a," August 1, 2002, at www.slate.com/features/whatistorture/pdfs/020801.pdf (accessed July 23, 2006), 46.

119. Bybee to Gonzales, "Memorandum: Standards of Conduct," 46.

120. Bybee to Gonzales, "Memorandum: Standards of Conduct," 46.

121. Thom Shanker, "6 G.I.'s in Iraq Are Charged with Abuse of Prisoners," *New York Times*, March 21, 2004, 14.

122. See, e.g., *Department of Defense, Investigation of the Abu Ghraib Prison and 205th Military Intelligence Brigade*, at www.defenselink.mil/news/Aug2004/d20040825fay.pdf (accessed July 22, 2006).

123. Daniel Levin to James B. Comey, "Memorandum: Legal Standards Applicable under 18 U.S.C. §§2340-240a," at www.usdoj.gov/olc/dagmemo.pdf (accessed July 23, 2006).

124. President's Statement on Signing of H.R. 2863, the "Department of Defense, Emergency Supplemental Appropriations to Address Hurricanes in the Gulf of Mexico, and Pandemic Influenza Act, 2006," December 30, 2005, at www.whitehouse.gov/news/releases/2005/12/20051230-8.html (accessed July 23, 2006).

125. Carl Levin, "Levin Statement on Administration Announcement It Will Seek Dismissal of Guantanamo Lawsuits," press release, January 4, 2006, at http://levin.senate.gov/newsroom/release.cfm?id=250235 (accessed July 23, 2006).

126. Samuel Alito to the Litigation Strategy Working Group, "Memorandum: Using Presidential Signing Statement to Make Fuller Use of the President's Constitutionally Assigned Role in the Process of Enacting Law," at www.archives.gov/news/samuel-alito/accession-060-89-269/Acc060-89-269-box6-SG-LSWG-AlitotoL-SWG-Feb1986.pdf (accessed July 23, 2006).

127. See Bazan and Elsea, *Presidential Authority*.

128. James Risen and Eric Lichtblau, "Bush Lets U.S. Spy on Callers Without Courts," *New York Times*, December 16, 2005, 1.

129. "Press Briefing by Attorney General Alberto Gonzales and General Michael Hayden, Principal Deputy Director for National Intelligence," December 19, 2005, at www.whitehouse.gov/news/releases/2005/12/20051219-1.html (accessed July 23, 2006).

130. U.S. Department of Justice, *Legal Authorities Supporting the Activities of the National Security Agency Described by the President* (Washington, D.C.: DOJ, 2006), at www.usdoj.gov/opa/whitepaperonnsalegalauthorities.pdf (accessed July 22, 2006), 1.

131. *Hepting v. AT&T Corporation*, No C-06-672 VRW ORDER, July 20, 2006, at www.cand.uscourts.gov/cand/judges.nsf/61fffe74f99516d088256d480060b72d/1dfdcaf3e81f3c54882571b10067825d/$FILE/HEPTING.SS.FINAL.ORDER.pdf (accessed July 23, 2006).

132. *United States v Reynolds*, 345 US 1 (1953).

133. See Stephen H. Gavett, "World Trade Center Fine Particulate Matter—Chemistry and Toxic Respiratory Effects: An Overview," *Environmental Health Perspectives* 111, no. 7 (2003): 971.

134. "Focus: Environmental Aftermath," *Environmental Health Perspectives* 109, no. 11 (November 2001): A528.

135. U.S. Government Accountability Office, *September 11: Monitoring of World Trade Center Health Effects Had Progressed, but Not for Federal Responders* (Washington, D.C.: GAO, 2005), 4. See also *September 11: Health Effects in the Aftermath of the World Trade Center Attack* (Washington, D.C.: GAO, 2004).

136. GAO, *September 11: Monitoring of World Trade Center Health Effects*, 5.

137. Robert M. Brackbill et al., "Surveillance for World Trade Center Disaster Health Effects among Survivors of Collapsed and Damaged Buildings," *Morbidity and Mortality Weekly Report* 55 (April 2006): 1–18.

138. GAO, *September 11: Monitoring of World Trade Center Health Effects*, 4.

139. GAO, *September 11: Monitoring of World Trade Center Health Effects*, 13.

140. Community HealthWorks, NYC Department of Health, *A Community Needs Assessment of Lower Manhattan Following the World Trade Center Attack* (New York: New York City Department of Health, 2001), 11.

141. Community HealthWorks, *A Community Needs Assessment*, 3.

142. Community HealthWorks, *A Community Needs Assessment*, 10.

143. Jane Tully, "Responding to Terrorism: Recovery, Resilience, Readiness (Part 1)," *SAMHSA News* 10 (Winter 2002), at www.samhsa.gov/SAMHSA_News/VolumeX_1/text_only/indextxt.htm (accessed July 28, 2006). The RAND study mentioned is reported at M. A. Schuster et al., "A National Survey of Stress Reactions after the September 11, 2001, Terrorist Attacks," *New England Journal of Medicine* 345, no. 20 (2001): 1507–1512.

144. Tully, "Responding to Terrorism."

145. U.S. Senate, Committee on Health, Education, Labor, and Pensions, *Children of September 11: The Need for Mental Health Services*, 107th Cong., 2nd Sess. (2002), 25.

146. U.S. Senate, *Children of September 11*, 5.

147. Deborah Goodman, "Arab Americans and American Muslims Express Mental Health Needs," *SAMHSA News* 10 (Winter 2002), at www.samhsa.gov/SAMHSA_News/VolumeX_1/article1.htm (accessed July 28, 2006).

148. David Harris, "Flying while Arab: Lessons from the Racial Profiling Controversy," *Civil Rights Journal* 6 (Winter 2002): 8–13.

149. Asit K. Biswas, "Scientific Assessment of the Long-Term Environmental Consequences of War," in Jay E. Austin and Carl E. Bruch, eds., *The Environmental Consequences of War: Legal, Economic, and Scientific Perspectives* (Cambridge, UK: Cambridge University Press, 2000), 306.

150. Biswas, "Scientific Assessment," 306–307.

151. Arthur H. Westing, "Environmental Warfare," *Environmental Law* 15 (Summer 1985): 645.

152. Col Tamzy J. House, Lt Col James B. Near Jr., Lt Col William B. Shields, Maj Ronald J. Celentano, Maj David M. Husband, Maj Ann E. Mercer, Maj James E. Pugh, "Weather as a Force Multiplier: Owning the Weather in 2025," paper prepared for Air Force 2025, vi, at http://csat.au.af.mil/2025/volume3/vol3ch15.pdf (accessed August 1, 2006).

153. Ian Bannon and Paul Collier, eds., *Natural Resources and Violent Conflict: Options and Actions* (Washington, D.C.: World Bank, 2003).

154. Westing, "Environmental Warfare," 651.

155. Westing, "Environmental Warfare," 651–652.

156. Westing, "Environmental Warfare," 652.

157. *Natural Resources Defense Council v. National Marine Fisheries Service*, 409 F. Supp. 2d 379 (SDNY 2006); *Cetacean Community v. Bush*, 386 F.3d 1169 (9th Cir. 2004).

158. *Natural Resources Defense Council v. Evans*, 364 F. Supp. 2d 1083 (NDCA 2003).

159. *Cetacean Community v. Bush*, 386 F.3d 1169, 1172 (9th Cir. 2004).

160. Westing, "Environmental Warfare," 646.

161. Dee Brown, *Bury My Heart at Wounded Knee* (New York: Holt, Rinehart and Winston, 1970), 33.

162. Brown, *Bury My Heart at Wounded Knee*, 33.

163. Westing, "Environmental Warfare," 652.

164. Westing, "Environmental Warfare," 647.

165. House et al., "Weather as a Force Multiplier," 14, citing E. M. Frisby, "Weather-Modification in Southeast Asia, 1966–1972," *Journal of Weather-Modification* 14, no. 1 (1982): 1–3.

166. Institute of Medicine, *Veterans and Agent Orange: Health Effects of Herbicides Used in Vietnam* (National Academy of Sciences, 1994), 1.

167. P.L. 102-4; 105 Stat. 11 (1991).

168. See Peter H. Schuck, *Agent Orange on Trial* (Cambridge, MA: Harvard University Press, 1986). The U.S. General Accounting Office had called for such a study in 1979 and again in 1980. U.S. General Accounting Office, *Statement of H. L. Krieger before the Committee on Veterans Affairs of the U.S. Senate* (Washington, D.C.: GAO, 1980).

169. Institute of Medicine, *Veterans and Agent Orange*, 1.

170. Institute of Medicine, *Veterans and Agent Orange*, 8–10.

171. Quoted in Environmental Conference on Cambodia, Laos, and Vietnam, *Long-Term Consequences of the Vietnam War: Ecosystems* (Stockholm: Föreningen Levande Framtid, 2002), 4, at www.nnn.se/vietnam/ecology.pdf (accessed August 18, 2006). (Note: This file is best downloaded and then opened rather than through the browser. See www.nnn.se/vietnam/environ.htm.)

172. Environmental Conference, *Long-Term Consequences of the Vietnam War*, 5.

173. Arthur H. Westing, "Assault on the Environment," in Environmental Conference on Cambodia, Laos, and Vietnam, *Long-Term Consequences of the Vietnam War: Ecosystems* (Stockholm: Föreningen Levande Framtid, 2002), at www.nnn.se/vietnam/ecology.pdf (accessed August 18, 2006), 3.

174. Westing, "Assault on the Environment," 3.

175. L. Wayne Dwernychuk, "Dioxin Hotspots in Vietnam," *Chemosphere* 60 (March 2005): 998–999, at www.hatfieldgroup.com/files/Chemosphere_HotSpots.pdf (accessed August 18, 2006); "Agent Orange/Dioxin Hot Spots—A Legacy of U.S. Military Bases in Southern Viet Nam Hotspots Overview Paper," at www.hatfieldgroup.com/files/HATFIELDAO.pdf (accessed August 18, 2006). See also Westing, "Assault on the Environment," 3.

176. Phung Tuu Boi, "Inland Plant Ecology," in Environmental Conference on Cambodia, Laos, and Vietnam, *Long-Term Consequences of the Vietnam War: Ecosystems* (Stockholm: Föreningen Levande Framtid, 2002), at www.nnn.se/vietnam/ecology.pdf (accessed August 18, 2006), 7.

177. Boi, "Inland Plant Ecology," 7.

178. Institute of Medicine, *Veterans and Agent Orange*, 25–26.

179. Kenneth D. Demaree, "Technical Memorandum 141: Defoliation Tests at CFB Gagetown, New Brunswick, Canada," Report of the Department of the Army,

Plant Sciences Laboratory, Plant Physiology Division, Fort Detrick, Frederick, Maryland, October 1968, Released by the Defense Technical Information Center, at www.hatfieldgroup.com/files/NB00070.pdf (accessed August 19, 2006), 7.

180. CBC News Online, "In Depth: Agent Orange and Agent Purple," at www.cbc.ca/news/background/agentorange (accessed August 11, 2006).

181. Demaree, "Technical Memorandum 141," 3.

182. Demaree, "Technical Memorandum 141," 7.

183. Kenneth D. Demaree, "Technical Memorandum 145: Chemical Defoliation of Northern Tree Species," Report of the Department of the Army, Plant Sciences Laboratory, Plant Physiology Division, Fort Detrick, Frederick, Maryland, October 1968, Released by the Defense Technical Information Center, at www.hatfieldgroup.com/files/NB00030.pdf (accessed August 19, 2006), 2.

184. Demaree, "Technical Memorandum 145," 10.

185. María D. Álvarez, "Forests in the Time of Turbulence: Conservation Implications of the Colombian War," in Steven V. Price, ed., *War and Tropical Forests: Conservation in Areas of Armed Conflict* (New York: Haworth, 2003), 66.

186. House et al., "Weather as a Force Multiplier," vii, Table 1.

187. House et al., "Weather as a Force Multiplier," vii, Table 1-2.

188. Lt Col Jamie G. G. Varni, Gregory M. Powers, Maj Dan S. Crawford, Maj Craig E. Jordan, and Maj Douglas L. Kendall, "Space Operations: Through the Looking Glass (Global Area Strike System)," paper prepared for Air Force 2025, vi, at http://csat.au.af.mil/2025/volume3/vol3ch14.pdf (accessed December 26, 2006), vii.

189. Varni et al., "Space Operations," 1.

190. Herodotus, *The Persian Wars*, vol. I, 191, at www.fordham.edu/halsall/ancient/greek-babylon.html (accessed July 30, 2006).

191. Austin and Bruch, *Environmental Consequences of War*, 1.

192. Sun Tzu, *The Art of War*, trans. and with a historical introduction by Ralph D. Dawyer (Boulder, CO: Westview, 1994), 167.

193. Álvarez, "Forests in the Time of Turbulence," 59.

194. Jeffrey A. McNeely, "Biodiversity, War, and Tropical Forests," in Steven V. Price, ed., *War and Tropical Forests: Conservation in Areas of Armed Conflict* (New York: Haworth, 2003), 12–14.

195. Jeffrey A. McNeely, "Biodiversity, War, and Tropical Forests," 13.

196. See, e.g., Austin and Bruch, *Environmental Consequences of War*; Richard P. Tucker and Edmund Russell, eds., *Natural Enemy, Natural Ally: Toward an Environmental History of War* (Corvallis, OR: Oregon State University Press, 2004); Steven V. Price, ed., *War and Tropical Forests: Conservation in Areas of Armed Conflict* (New York: Haworth, 2003).

197. Carl von Clausewitz, *On War*, ed. and trans. Michael Howard and Peter Paret (New York: Knopf, 1976, 1993), 99.

198. U.S. Department of Defense, *Measuring Stability and Security in Iraq; August 2006 Report to Congress in Accordance with the Department of Defense Appropriations Act 2006 (Section 9010)* (Washington, D.C.: DOD, 2006), 25–34, at www.defenselink.mil/pubs/pdfs/Security-Stabilty-ReportAug29r1.pdf (accessed September 2, 2006).

199. U.S. Department of Defense, *Measuring Stability and Security in Iraq*, 33.

200. National Commission on Terrorist Attacks, *9/11 Commission Report*, 47.

201. Dee Brown, *Bury My Heart at Wounded Knee*.

202. See David Wallace Adams, *Education for Extinction: American Indians and the Boarding School Experience 1875–1928* (Lawrence: Kansas University Press, 1995).

203. See David E. Wilkins, *American Indian Politics and the American Political System* (Lanham, MD: Rowman & Littlefield, 2002), 110–115.

204. Barbara Harff, "No Lessons Learned from the Holocaust? Assessing Risks of Genocide and Political Mass: Murder since 1955," *American Political Science Review* 97 (February 2003): 57. Professor Harff operates the "Genocide Politicide Project," with a database and other resources at www.cidcm.umd.edu/inscr/genocide (accessed December 8, 2006).

205. U.S. Department of State, *Erasing History: Ethnic Cleansing in Kosovo, May 1999*, at www.state.gov/www/regions/eur/rpt_9905_ethnic_ksvo_2.html (accessed December 8, 2006), Overview.

206. U.S. Department of State, *Erasing History*, Overview.

207. U.S. Department of State, *Erasing History*, Documenting the Abuses.

208. UNDP, *Human Development Report Bosnia Herzegovina 2000 Youth* (Sarajevo: UNDP, 2000), 57.

209. United Nations, International Criminal Tribunal for the former Yugoslavia, *Prosecutor v. Radislav Krstic*—Case No. IT-98-33-T, at www.un.org/icty/Supplement/supp27-e/krstic.htm (accessed September 4, 2006).

210. United Nations, *Report of the International Commission of Inquiry on Darfur*, pursuant to Security Council Resolution 1564 of September 18, 2004 (Geneva: United Nations, 2005), at www.ohchr.org/english/docs/darfurreport.doc (accessed September 4, 2006).

211. United Nations, *Report of the International Commission of Inquiry on Darfur*, 3.

212. United Nations, *Report of the International Commission of Inquiry on Darfur*, 3.

213. Office of the United Nations High Commissioner for Human Rights in Co-operation with the United Nations Mission in the Sudan, *Deepening Crisis in Darfur Two Months after the Darfur Peace Agreement: An Assessment*, fourth periodic report of the United Nations High Commissioner for Human Rights on the situation of human rights in the Sudan, July 2006, at www.ohchr.org/english/countries/sd/docs/4thOHCHRjuly25final.pdf#search=%22Fourth%20periodic%20report%20of%20the%20United%20Nations%20High%20Commissioner%20for%22 (accessed September 4, 2006). (Hereafter United Nations High Commissioner and Mission in the Sudan, *Deepening Crisis*.)

214. Human Rights Watch, *Darfur: Humanitarian Aid under Siege*, May 2006, at http://hrw.org/backgrounder/africa/sudan0506/darfur0506.pdf (accessed September 8, 2006), 6.

215. United Nations High Commissioner for Human Rights, *Access to Justice for Victims of Sexual Violence*, report of the High Commissioner for Human Rights, July 29, 2005, 6, at www.ohchr.org/english/countries/docs/darfur29july05_En.pdf (accessed December 26, 2006).

216. Human Rights Watch, *Darfur Bleeds: Military Attacks on Civilians in Chad*, at www.hrw.org/campaigns/darfur/pdf/darfur_bleeds.pdf (accessed April 6, 2007), 4.

217. Elisabeth Rehn and Ellen Johnson Sirleaf, *Women, War and Peace: The Independent Experts' Assessment on the Impact of Armed Conflict on Women and Women's Role in Peace-Building* (New York: United Nations Development Fund for Women [UNIFEM], 2002), 38.

218. Human Rights Watch, "Rape in Bosnia-Herzegovina," at www.hrw.org/about/projects/womrep/General-25.htm#P461_56378 (accessed September 10, 2006).

219. See *Prosecutor v. Kunarac et al.*, IT-96-23-T& IT-96-23/1-T, February 22, 2001, at www.un.org/icty/kunarac/trialc2/judgement/kun-tj010222e.pdf (accessed September 10, 2006), affm'd by the Appeals Chamber, *Prosecutor v. Kunarac et al.*, June 12, 2002, at www.un.org/icty/kunarac/appeal/judgement/kun-aj020612e.pdf (accessed September 10, 2006).

220. Human Rights Watch, "Kosovo: Rape as a Weapon of 'Ethnic Cleansing'—Summary," at www.hrw.org/reports/2000/fry/Kosov003.htm#P38_1195 (accessed September 10, 2006).

221. Rehn and Johnson Sirleaf, *Women, War and Peace*, 52.

222. Human Rights Watch, "Sexual Violence and its Consequences among Displaced Persons in Darfur and Chad: A Human Rights Watch Briefing Paper," April 12, 2005, at http://hrw.org/backgrounder/africa/darfur0505/darfur0405.pdf (accessed September 10, 2006), 10.

223. Human Rights Watch, "Sexual Violence and its Consequences," 3.

224. Human Rights Watch, "Sexual Violence and its Consequences," 9. See also Rehn and Johnson Sirleaf, *Women, War and Peace*; United Nations High Commissioner, *Access to Justice*; and United Nations High Commissioner and Mission in the Sudan, *Deepening Crisis*, cited above, for more examples than anyone would ever want to have to read. See also Stefan Elbe, "HIV/AIDS and the Changing Landscape of Africa," *International Security* 27 (Fall 2002): 159–177.

225. United Nations High Commissioner, *Access to Justice*, 30.

226. Human Rights Watch, *Darfur*, 2.

227. Central Intelligence Agency, "Soviet Bloc Economic Warfare Capabilities and Courses of Action," NIE 10–54, March 9, 1954, 1.

228. Central Intelligence Agency, "Memorandum: Current US Policy with Respect to Cuba," December 12, 1963, 4.

229. National Security Decision Directive (NSDD) 54, September 2, 1982, 2–4, at www.fas.org/irp/offdocs/nsdd/nsdd-054.htm (accessed September 12, 2006).

230. Christopher Simpson, *National Security Directives of the Reagan and Bush Administrations* (Boulder, CO: Westview, 1995), 80–81.

231. See Center for Security Policy, "Summary of the Proceedings of the Hoover Institute and Casey Institute Symposium on the Fall of the Berlin Wall: Reassessing the Causes and Consequences of the End of the Cold War," February 22, 1999, at http://security-policy.org/papers/1999/99-R47at.html (accessed August 18, 2001). See also Peter Schweizer, *Victory* (New York: Atlantic Monthly Press, 1994).

232. National Security Decision Directive (NSDD) 66, November 29, 1982, 1–2, at www.fas.org/irp/offdocs/nsdd/nsdd-066.htm (accessed September 12, 2006).

233. National Security Decision Directive (NSDD) 75, January 17, 1983, at www.fas.org/irp/offdocs/nsdd/nsdd-075.htm (accessed September 12, 2006).

234. NSDD 75, 2.

235. Lt Col Robert P. Kadlec, "Biological Weapons for Waging Economic Warfare," in Barry R. Schneider and Lawrence E. Grinter, eds., *Battlefield of the Future: 21st Century Warfare Issues* (Maxwell AFB: Air War College Studies in National Security,

1995), at www.airpower.maxwell.af.mil/airchronicles/battle/chp10.html (accessed March 20, 2006).

236. Kadlec, "Biological Weapons."

237. Kadlec, "Biological Weapons."

238. Kadlec, "Biological Weapons."

239. George J. Stein, "Information Attack: Information Warfare in 2025," paper prepared for Air Force 2025, vi, at http://csat.au.af.mil/2025/volume3/vol3ch03.pdf (accessed September 12, 2006).

240. See, e.g., "President's Commission on Critical Infrastructure Protection," E.O. 13010, 61 Fed. Reg. 37347 (1996); see Fact Sheet on Presidential Decision Directive (PDD) 62, Combating Terrorism 62, at www.fas.org/irp/offdocs/pdd-62.htm (accessed September 12, 2006); and PDD 63/NSC-63, Critical Infrastructure Protection, at www.fas.org/irp/offdocs/pdd/pdd-63.htm (accessed September 12, 2006).

241. See, e.g., Office of Management and Budget, *Federal Information Security Management Act (FISMA) 2004 Report to Congress* (Washington, D.C.: OMB, 2005).

242. U.S. Government Accountability Office, *Domestic and Offshore Outsourcing of Personal Information in Medicare, Medicaid, and TRICARE* (Washington, D.C.: GAO, 2006).

243. U.S. Government Accountability Office, *Critical Infrastructure Protection: Department of Homeland Security Faces Challenges in Fulfilling Cybersecurity Responsibilities* (Washington, D.C.: GAO, 2005), 7.

244. See Paul Collier, V. L. Elliott, Håvard Hegre, Anke Hoeffler, Marta Reynal-Querol, and Nicholas Sambanis, *Breaking the Conflict Trap: Civil War and Development Policy* (Washington, D.C.: World Bank, 2003).

245. Juliette Bennett, *Business in Zones of Conflict: The Role of the Multinational in Promoting Regional Stability* (New York: International Peace Forum, 2001), at www.unglobalcompact.org/Issues/conflict_prevention/meetings_and_workshops/Reg_stability.html (accessed December 26, 2006).

246. See, generally, Thomas E. Ricks, *Fiasco: The American Military Adventure in Iraq* (New York: Penguin, 2006).

247. On the insurance dimensions of the 9/11 attack, see Robert J. Rhee, "Terrorism Risk in a Post-9/11 Economy: The Convergence of Capital Markets, Insurance, and Government Action," *Arizona State Law Journal* 37 (Summer 2005): 435–530.

248. See United Nations Environmental Programme and United Nations Center for Human Settlements (Habitat), *The Kosovo Conflict: Consequences for the Environment and Human Settlements* (Nairobi: UNEP, 1999), 30–59.

3

People and Other
Creatures on the Move

When one examines much of the material that uses the post-conflict reconstruction and recovery model, there appears to be a tacit assumption that the community—that is the population, its demographic characteristics, and its workforce—that was in place before the conflict will be in place, intact, and that the people will be ready to resume their lives once the necessary infrastructure and political and economic processes have been restored. Similar assumptions are made with respect to the natural resources that were present in the country before conflict. However, the evidence is clear that conflict drives people into flight. Of those who do not flee, many may perish from violence or a lack of requisite food, shelter, and medical care. And when these people go on the move, there are consequences for the people, for the environment, for the shape of their society after the conflict, and for the economic, political, and social conditions that exist when it is time for post-conflict development.

Many of these consequences fall under the general category of post-traumatic stress. Chapter 4 will address the issues associated with post-traumatic stress disorder (PTSD). This chapter, however, will examine the significance of the fact of flight and displacement as well as factors in policy that can exacerbate the difficulties of those who seek asylum and challenges to natural resources in need of protection.

This analysis demonstrates that those contemplating post-conflict development should not assume that the same community, human or natural, that existed before will be in place at the end of the conflict. More fundamentally, flight takes people out of their normal environment and places them in often dramatically different contexts than what they have known. Even when they do not find themselves in foreign lands, but are internally displaced, they are generally in very different relationships with their environment. Second, the process of displacement normally means that their economic well-being and their role in the economic circumstances of their community are seriously compromised in ways that are often very difficult to resolve. Third, their social relationships, including the fabric of their immediate families, extended families, and communities are affected in a variety of ways; all the more so where they are surviving and escaping the experience of social warfare. Thus, simple assumptions about reconstruction of countries in post-conflict contexts plainly are not adequate to address these circumstances and may indeed be based upon faulty assumptions about the makeup and condition of post-conflict communities. Finally, what is true of people is often true of the nonhuman species in their own way as well. For all of these reasons, a sustainable development model of post-conflict action is essential.

COLOMBIA CASE STUDY: LIVING IN FEAR AND IN FLIGHT

Like so many other nations rich in natural resources and cultural diversity, Colombia has seen a torturous contemporary history that has driven literally millions of its people into flight, either out of the country to asylum or as internally displaced persons trying to survive in a violent land. The complex and protracted armed conflict has lasted for nearly half a century and continues at the time of this writing. It is a tragic, but very appropriate case study to understand the challenges of those living in fear and flight.

Colombia's expansive and diverse land encompasses the northern part of the Amazon and the Andes, which split and extend northward into three mountain ranges,[1] reaching out to the Atlantic and Pacific Oceans.[2] Indeed, it is the only country in South America with access to both oceans. Colombia's natural resources include richly forested mountains, flat grasslands, coastal lowlands, and rainforests. It produces oil, gold, and emeralds. Tragically, though, its major export today consists of illicit drugs, which are both a result and a source of a web of violence by shifting factions that has plagued the country for decades.

The explanations as to what has led the country on a path of destruction, civil strife, and pervasive criminal activity that has generated the highest number of displaced persons of any country in the world are relatively clear, if extremely complex. Perhaps not surprisingly, "Colombia's violence and armed conflict stem from a complex interaction of economic, social, historical, and political factors."[3] Despite its natural wealth, Colombia has long suffered from entrenched inequalities and pervasive poverty, lack of access to the polity by the majority, and weak governments, a pattern that can be traced to Colombia's colonial past. Second, there are left-wing guerrillas, right-wing paramilitary groups, drug traffickers, and the state armed forces, who have been locked in conflict with each other for long enough now that the precise initial causes have faded in face of the internal momentum of the fighting. In recent years, well-financed by the illicit drug trade, the irregular armed groups and drug traffickers have amassed an arsenal of sophisticated weaponry and satellite equipment at the level of a state military force. The most vulnerable groups have fallen victims to the cross fire as the national military battles irregular armed groups and drug cartels. Those battles continue to kill and terrorize the people, ravage the environment, and prevent the kinds of sustainable economic development that could lift so many out of poverty.

Although it is the fourth largest country in South America, Colombia is the third most populous country with 46 million inhabitants who, until recent times, were not concentrated in megacities, as has been the case in other parts of the region such as São Paolo or Mexico City.[4] Instead, it currently has five major cities, "Bogotá (4,300,000; Greater Bogotá, 6,080,000), Medellín (3,290,000), Cali (1,870,000), Barranquilla (1,358,800), and Cartagena (925,600)."[5] These five cities have grown from forced migration driven by the war, reversing the previous pattern of dispersed population in rural areas and leading to growth in other urban centers, including some thirty cities with a population of about 100,000.[6] Until recently, most of the country's population was spread throughout its 1,138,910 square kilometers, about three times the size of Montana.[7] Its beautiful, diverse, and expansive territory is also its curse, as its "fertile valleys and extensive jungle in the Pacific and Amazonian regions"[8] with access to both oceans facilitate illicit crop processing and distribution of drugs and provide convenient hideouts for irregular armed forces and drug traffickers. At the same time, such extensive and impenetrable terrain makes government law enforcement an insurmountable challenge.[9]

The protracted armed conflict in Colombia has had repercussions beyond its borders. "Today, the Colombian conflict is the longest and most geographically extended armed confrontation in Latin America; thus, achieving peace in Colombia would be a stabilizing element for the whole Andean region and the Latin American continent in general."[10] Forced displacement has uprooted millions, who have sought refuge in neighboring countries, including Panamá, Venezuela, Ecuador, and Costa Rica.[11] In fact, Colombia has led the world in numbers of internally displaced persons in recent years, which is a dramatic statement given the number and severity of conflicts in other countries.

Colombia: A Land Challenged by Inequality, Lawlessness, and Inadequate Governance

In order to understand what it means for the people and the environment of Colombia to have so many of its citizens in flight in one way or another, it is necessary to understand something about the history and politics of the country, the origins and changing character of the conflict that has been despoiling it, and the contemporary effects of the fighting on groups that have been displaced, the environment, and the economy.

Historical Roots of Contemporary Conflict: A Foundation of Inequality

As in other lands, when the Spaniards arrived in what is today Colombia, they encountered diverse indigenous groups. Some, like the highland groups, had developed sophisticated societies, and others, the lowland inhabitants, were primarily farmers.[12] Evidence of their settlements goes back over 13,000 years. There were three major civilizations: the "Chibcha, sub-Andean, and Caribbean peoples."[13] Numerous indigenous languages are still spoken today, with an estimated seventy-eight living and twenty extinct languages that originated from three major linguistic families: the Chibcha, the Carib, and the Arawak.[14]

> The most impressive civilization was that of the Chibcha-speaking Tairona, . . . [who] constructed engineering works in stone—including temples, roads, stairways, bridges, and irrigation and drainage works. . . . Farther to the south, Chibcha-speaking highland groups were mostly docile farmers. . . . The eastern highlands were controlled by the Muiscas. . . . Along with the Tairona, the Muiscas had the most hierarchically organized and territorially extensive social systems by the time the Spaniards arrived.[15]

Colombia was a land of diverse indigenous groups, but its tapestry would be changed by the arrival from Spain of the conquistadores in the early sixteenth century. While the native roots ran too deep to eradicate its ancient indigenous past, colonization augmented Colombia's diversity and offered both challenges and opportunities.[16] Unfortunately, it also sowed the seeds of the early aspects of contemporary conflict.

Notwithstanding its recent history of violence, Colombia paradoxically holds the record as the longest running democracy in Latin America. However, with its sociopolitical structure shaped in the colonial period, it was aptly "[c]haracterized by Alexander Wilde as an oligarchical conversation among gentlemen, it is a system build upon a tradition of political compromise devoted to maintenance of elitist control."[17]

The rugged topography of Colombia actually had unintended benefits, among which was the neglect of some parts of the country by Spanish conquerors, which resulted in limits on the exploitation of its natural resources. Second, the impenetrable terrain precluded the Spanish crown from building an empire in the region comparable to those in México and Perú. New Granada, which constituted what is today Venezuela, Colombia (including the territory that is today Panamá), and Ecuador, was created in 1717.[18] Its gold was exploited with the use of African slaves since European diseases had decimated the source of free labor from indigenous groups.[19] "Production of gold in New Granada grew each century, eighteenth-century production nearly tripling that of the sixteenth."[20]

The struggle for independence was fought out in stages. The first attempt failed miserably when Simón Bolívar, in concert with other leaders, gained nominal independence in 1810.[21] At that time the region became the Grand Colombia, though internal power struggles persisted. Spain was not ready to surrender such vast, rich lands and took over the territory in 1816, inflicting "brutal repression" for the next eight years.[22] Bolívar was forced to flee to Jamaica. It was not until Francisco de Miranda and Simón Bolívar mounted a renewed effort for independence in 1824 that there was a final defeat for the Spanish crown, leading to the independence of present-day Colombia, Venezuela, and Ecuador.

After independence, Colombia, like other Latin American countries, was unable to build a truly democratic system because of the entrenched oligarchy that held the nation's wealth and controlled its natural resources. The Grand Colombia disintegrated in 1830 amidst struggles between federalists and centralists like Bolívar, creating present-day Colombia. This tension produced a conflict-laden history throughout the nineteenth century.[23] These two factions became the origins of the contemporary two-party system, Liberals and Conservatives, even though the differences between the two have remained far less clear with respect to significant social policies than the labels might suggest, since both parties appeared committed to maintaining the oligarchic system with roots in colonial times. It is a legacy that has plagued efforts to develop effective political institutions.

The end of the nineteenth century was a dramatic transition with the "War of a Thousand Days," which shifted focus away from the imminent loss of that part of Colombia that is today known as Panamá.[24] Under pressure from the United States, which had decided to build the canal, the territory of Panamá declared its independence. President Theodore Roosevelt claimed, "I took Panamá!"[25] and the United States assumed control of the Canal Zone for nearly a century.

Coffee production ultimately generated positive economic growth for Colombia and allowed Colombia to be a full participant in the world market. Unlike Guatemala, where large land holdings were the norm, the small- and medium-size coffee farms in Colombia allowed the development of a middle class, though this pattern shifted to large-scale production in the 1970s. As the coffee industry became more competitive in the world market, Colombia diversified, shifting to new exports such as petroleum, fresh flowers, and processed foods, as well as traditional products such as bananas.[26]

Skidmore and Smith note that, "[i]n the early 1950s, coffee accounted for more than 10 percent of the country's gross domestic product (GDP); by the 1990s, it was down to only 2 percent."[27]

Tragically, by the end of the twentieth century, the largest export product became illicit drugs, surpassing even coffee and petroleum and generating revenues in the billions. The lack of social policies to address pervasive inequality and poverty exacerbated the inability of the government to address the drug business and resolve the violence related to its operation. Moreover, the spread of drug production, ranging from the growing of the plants to the development of processing facilities, added to contests for control over natural resources, including the forests that would serve to hide the operations, and in "Colombia [as in] Myanmar, the desire to control the production and distribution of drugs has contributed to violent conflicts."[28]

Contemporary Politics and the Violence that Came with It

It is with inequality that the discussion of the origins of the contemporary political challenges and the violence related to them must begin, even before the impact of illicit drugs became the focus of attention. Colombia ranks third in the level of inequality in Latin America,[29] as well as in terms of population density.[30] Some 62.4 percent of its people live under the poverty line and 31 percent in extreme poverty; though in rural areas the extreme poverty rate escalates to 40 percent.[31] "This means that 28,000,000 Colombians do not have enough income to cover even basic nutritional needs. Moreover, the richest 10% of the population have 80 times more wealth than the poorest 10%."[32] The World Bank's *World Development Report 2006* reported 79 percent of the rural and 55 percent of the urban population living below the poverty level, a marked increase in poverty from the 1995 figure of 48 percent each for urban and rural communities.[33]

Colombia's formal economy grew to a gross domestic product (GDP) of $118.1 billion in 2005, but the economic and social well-being of the country was troubled before and has deteriorated since. "The largest obstacles to prosperity in Colombia today are its high level of violence, armed conflict, and the ensuing disorganization of society."[34] The government's inability to control either armed conflict or the drug trade threatens all three pillars of sustainable development. Conflict-related costs are enormous, with repercussions for present as well as for future generations. Indeed, "peace costs. But war costs even more."[35]

The conflict in Colombia may be interpreted from two perspectives. On the one hand, it is perceived as a narco-democracy,[36] a democratic regime that has emerged primarily in rural areas independent of the political climate in the center of the country, which is predominantly urban. From this perspective, the uniqueness in Colombia is that the enemy of the state is not another political force, but a criminal force, the powerful drug cartels,[37] who transport the raw materials of the drugs generated in the region to be processed in Colombia. "By the late 1990s Colombia also became a major site for raising coca leaf."[38] Some of the support for paramilitary groups arises from the peasants' need to defend themselves from the three major combatants, including the insurgents, narco-traffickers, and military forces.

On the other hand, Colombia's oligarchic characteristics have persisted, pitting the Liberal and Conservative parties against each other but with neither understood to be committed to genuine social transformations. The "Era of Violence" in the middle of the twentieth century witnessed the killing of 300,000 people as a result of the feud between the Liberals and Conservatives.[39] This dual-party system, however, has not been "a true social representation,"[40] but has instead been characterized by social exclusion and "absence of viable political alternatives."[41] For example land reform was inadequate, leaving a large portion of the rural population dependent on the traditional peonage system. The two-party system faded in the second half of the twentieth century as the voters responded to personalities as opposed to active political party affiliation.[42] The populist movements that emerged in the 1930s collapsed with the assassination of an outspoken Liberal leader who championed the populist demands for reform.[43]

Contemporary foundations can be traced to the period known as *La Violencia* (The Violence), from 1948 to 1957 (for some, from 1946 to 1965).[44] Provoked by political differences between the Liberals and the Conservatives, as well as differences within the Liberal Party—between the progressive Liberals and more traditional Liberals—at the crux of it was social, economic, and political exclusion.

Peasant and working groups had pressed for change as the country moved to the mid-twentieth century. Jorge Eliécer Gaitán, a Liberal although not from a privileged background, inspired urban populism as he denounced the privileged class. His bombastic style inspired the masses with poignant rhetoric[45] that threatened the *"convivialistas"* (those who get along) who operated on compromise politics with little real change.[46] Gaitán became a symbol of a fractured polity, challenging the elite, including those of his own party. The established norms of compromise and consensus broke down. Violence followed and the assassination of Gaitán in 1948 intensified La Violencia, resulting in an estimated 300,000 deaths in the period 1948–1953 (50,000 in 1950 alone).[47] A military coup that took power in 1953 to squelch the violence held on until a coalition government arranged between the Liberals and Conservatives assumed leadership based on a "gentlemen's agreement" to alternate political power; though it was clear that the ruling class would attempt to regain control.[48]

In the years that followed there were promises of reform, but little change. Thus, the agricultural reform law enacted in 1961 promised much, but delivered little.[49] A decade after the policy was promulgated, the government had only distributed "0.25 percent of the total arable land to a paltry 0.45 percent of the farmers."[50] The lack of meaningful agricultural reform in the 1960s was "at the root of the social violence: 3 percent of landowners own more than 70 percent of the arable land as a result of the state's failure to implement a comprehensive agrarian reform."[51]

A legacy of La Violencia was the emergence as a serious force in 1966 of what became the most powerful guerrilla group originally created in 1946, Fuerzas Armadas Revolucionarias de Colombia (FARC; Revolutionary Armed Forces of Colombia). Since then, FARC has mustered political clout, economic power, and, unfortunately, an impressive military-like arsenal. Once battle was joined between the FARC and the military, millions of Colombians were caught in the cross fire.

In the last two decades of the twentieth century, the conflict expanded as drug traffickers became a major force, in addition to the rise of armed guerrilla and right-wing paramilitary groups. The pervasive and prolonged violence has led to an academic specialization in "*violentología*" (violentology)[52] in Colombia, whose scholars have explored the impact of violence on a society from a sociopolitical and economic perspective.[53]

During this prolonged violence, the state has been characterized by poor governance, lacking the institutional and legal wherewithal to directly address the armed conflict. Equally problematic has been the absence of political will to deal with ingrained socioeconomic disparities. The lack of effective legal institutions and processes, particularly in the rural areas, has made it seemingly acceptable for individuals to take the law into their own hands.[54]

Lack of Social Policies and Disillusionment of the Poor

The resurgence of violence in the 1980s, according to Cavarozzi, "led to a virtual extinction of the state."[55] Unresolved exclusion, poor governance, and brutal violence perpetrated by guerrilla groups, the drug cartels, and paramilitary groups were all factors in the break down of the state.

Unlike Guatemala, where the conflict was between government forces and insurgents, in Colombia there were three principal irregular armed groups. First, there have been three main guerrilla groups, the FARC and the Ejército de Liberación Nacional (ELN; National Liberation Army). University students established ELN in 1962 while FARC was founded much earlier by peasants.[56] Among FARC's supporters were union workers and members of the middle class. FARC originated from a "communist self-defense group which appeared during the Era of Violence of 1948–1956."[57] In the 1980s, FARC intensified its operations and later, toward the middle of the 1990s . . . became involved in drug trafficking and initiated widespread use of kidnapping to provide financing. . . . The FARC is present in all regions of the country and exercises *de facto* control over extensive areas for prolonged periods of time. . . . The FARC has employed indiscriminate violence against the population through the use of improvised explosive devices, terrorist bombings directed at civilians in urban areas, antipersonnel mines, massacres, kidnapping, extortion and forced recruitment. These tactics, together with a perceived lack of commitment to a political and social agenda have meant that the FARC now have minimal popular support in Colombia.[58]

The contested election of 1970, in which Misael Pastrana was declared the winner over Rojas Pinilla, who had created and represented an opposition party, the Acción Nacional Popular (ANAPO), gave rise to yet another insurgent group, the M-19 (April 19th Movement, from the date of that election).[59]

The second type of guerrilla organizations consisted of three minor guerrilla groups, a dissident group of the demobilized Ejército Popular de Liberación (EPL), the Ejército Revolucionario del Pueblo (ERP), and the Ejército Revolucionario Guevarista (ERG). The third factional group emerged in response to the unbridled violence and lack of protection by government authorities, "a loose confederation of paramilitary groups called, *Autodefensas Unidas de Colombia* [Self-Defense Units], with a number of dissident paramilitary groups throughout the country."[60] This armed group was legally created and trained by the state military to assist in protecting wealthy cattle ranchers from the insurgents. They also became cover for the military to avoid international criticism for rampant human rights violations. In fact, the so-called self-defense paramilitary groups have engaged in "social cleansing," murdering "people they disapproved of, such as drug addicts, homosexuals, prostitutes, the homeless, beggars and alcoholics, as well as . . . trade union leaders."[61] There were well-supported allegations that the non-state forces used their special status to take land from indigenous and Afro-Colombian groups and to enhance their economic and political power. They have enjoyed free passage at roadblocks and access to intelligence, military equipment, and communications systems.[62]

The last element of the conflict consists of disenfranchised groups engaged in gang activity who perform the dirty work for all the factions, hence the name of *sicarios*,[63] or hired killers.[64] Some of them are marginalized, unemployed youngsters, while others are former combatants of paramilitary forces.

The armed conflict, primarily active in the rural areas, forced people out of their traditional rural way of life to seek refuge in the cities, often in squalid conditions in the so-called "poverty belts."[65] One effect of the armed conflict has been forced migration to cities,[66] but the cities have not been places of refuge for displaced persons. They have often been uprooted (termed intra-urban displacement),[67] and have been destitute, insecure, victimized by gangs and other criminals or armed groups, as they endure poor housing and health conditions. "Indigenous displaced people in cities suffer high rates of malnutrition and some have died of hunger."[68] They also struggle with the psychological impacts of loss of family members, abject humiliation, torture by irregular or government forces, and loss of familial, cultural, and community anchors.

And Then Things Got Worse: Multiple Drug Traffickers and Strange Alliances

In the midst of the already deadly conditions, and in part because of them, the drug trade escalated dramatically, creating what has been aptly termed "a new nightmare."[69] As the state attempted to squelch the production of cocaine, the drug lords became significant players in the economy, eroding political and economic stability. The profitability of drug trafficking has led to a fluid merging and splitting of guerrilla groups, drug traffickers, and paramilitary groups, and in some instances, collusion of government officials and the Colombian armed forces.[70]

Colombia's first major cartel became known internationally for its brutal violence. Unresolved and entrenched labor disputes led to popular support for Pablo Escobar, leader of the Medellín Cartel, who went from a street thug to become an internationally known billionaire. Yet, he was seen by some as a Robin Hood figure for ill-treated, laid-off workers and the poor when he was given credit for the kidnapping and vicious killing of a Conservative industrialist in 1971. No evidence was ever found to link Escobar to the crime. Thus there was a surprising link between narcotics trafficking and support from the disenfranchised.[71]

Entrenched socioeconomic disparities due to pervasive underdevelopment, limited political access, and economic dependence on limited-value exports continued to plague the country. In a context of restricted options for the disenfranchised, drug production and processing became an attractive option, particularly for young males. The fact that the money was attractive did not alter the fact that the cartels were vicious and willing to use violence, bribery, or any other tactics whenever and wherever they thought them useful.

Both the Medellín and Cali Cartels also engaged in a political and armed battle with the government. "During the 1980s the 'Medellín Cartel' attempted to take the country hostage by unleashing a massive wave of violence, assassinating scores of government officials and a presidential candidate. In the early 1990s the 'Cali Cartel' employed more subtle and sophisticated tactics, relying on bribery and co-optation rather than coercion; this erupted in political scandal in 1995, when it became apparent that the nation's president had accepted large sums of drug money to help finance his electoral campaign."[72]

Military attempts to quell the violence inflicted on the country by narco-traffickers have led to ongoing multi-party warfare up to the time of this writing. In fact, late in 2006 the three major groups, narco-trafficking, paramilitary, and guerilla, merged for their own interests, primarily economic. Thus, the traditional polarized forces, guerrilla and military, have been transformed into outright criminal activity perpetrated by an ensemble of these irregular forces.

Government efforts to integrate the FARC into a more normal political relationship failed, as the group forged alliances with drug traffickers in coca production. However, the government made some gains with three insurgent groups—M-19, EPL, and Quintín Lame.[73] Even so, negotiation and disarmament was successful only with the smaller insurgent groups, e.g., M-19, and a clear failure with the two major groups, FARC and ELN. That said, "the integration of the guerrillas into parliamentary life has been unrelated to a process of democratization in this oligarchical and clientelist society."[74] Amnesty for these groups has not been accompanied by serious measures to open political space to excluded Colombians.

The blending of military skills, arms buildups, and the involvement in the drug trade has made the FARC a far more difficult and dangerous force in the country than before.

> In Colombia, the enormous profits created from the drug trade have enabled FARC to establish a vast and sophisticated military and financial network. . . . The drug trade, combined with other sources of funds (kidnapping, road tolls, and robberies), has enabled the continued purchasing of large amounts of weapons, including sophisticated surface-to-air missiles as well as heavy weaponry and military vehicles. With more than half of FARC's funds coming from the drug trade, some $250 million to $300 million annually, drug cartels have become FARC's partners in maintaining its capacity to operate against the government. FARC commonly purchases arms and equipment with large amounts of cocaine. It is believed that FARC has an annual income of $500 million to $600 million.[75]

Various mechanisms for money laundering are used by rebel groups in Colombia, as well as by others throughout the world, including bribing officials and banking in countries, such as Panamá, that have historically served for money laundering. "For example, FARC is believed to have a series of such banks [complacent or collusive banks] operating in Ecuador to facilitate the transfer of funds outside of Colombia. From there, FARC can manage its finances electronically, using computers and accessing its accounts online from the jungle. Arms shipments have frequently been arranged using this method, minimizing risk."[76]

More violent groups have emerged even as the government has tried to stop existing organizations. "Colombian authorities found evidence of the existence of a network of 162 new Colombian drug groups, directly involving at least 4,060 persons, which in turn are connected to more than 40 international criminal organisations."[77] Some use violent means while others have employed more sophisticated tactics. The Cali Cartel emphasized bribery or even the tactical use of political contributions. The fact that drug money was injected into politics worked with potential allies but it also worked with opponents who faced accusations that they were under the control of the drug cartels because of contributions. For example, President Pastrana was disgraced by accusations of drug money in his campaign finances.[78] There has also been evidence of collusion by the military.[79]

The Struggle to Squelch the Violence

Government attempts to solve the conflict have failed, although the fact that insurgent groups have also not been able to take control is a positive sign. In 1998, the government and FARC-EP negotiated a demilitarized zone (DMZ; *zona de despeje*). However, the government was forced to terminate negotiations and eliminate the DMZ in February 2002 because of a number of violations of the agreement, along with a spike in violence, as FARC took advantage of the opportunity.[80] For example, the DMZ corridor, free from government intervention, was used for coca plantation and kidnapping.

Recent governments have tried to work toward building stronger institutions, but those efforts have been undermined by attacks on judges, legislators, and presidential candidates, as well as journalists who exposed corruption. Foreign aid by the United States has focused on supporting the Colombian military and providing military personnel to fight narco-traffickers rather than on the much wider set of problems that started and later fueled the violence.

Internally Displaced Persons: Impoverished People, Imperiled Communities, and Endangered Cultures

While there may be disagreements as to the exact numbers (the reasons for which are discussed in detail later in this chapter), there is no dispute about the fact that Colombia has lived longer with more people internally displaced by conflict than any other country in the world. (The tragedy in Darfur now rivals Colombia for the total numbers of those driven into flight, a subject also discussed later in this chapter.) However, to truly comprehend the nature and meaning of the challenges for those contemplating post-conflict action, it is necessary to consider the groups affected by the displacement and the effects of the social, environmental, and economic warfare being waged among the combatants all around those displaced persons.

The Quantitative and Qualitative Story of Displacement

The protracted violence has resulted in both flight from the country and massive internal displacement. "Colombia's protracted civil war has led to one of the largest displacements since those caused by the Second World War in Europe. By 2002, 2 million people of a population of 43.5 million were refugees or internally displaced persons (IDPs)."[81] Others estimate that 3.4 to 4 million Colombians had left the country. The figures on those who have been internally displaced vary significantly (the reasons for that variation are discussed later in the chapter, with recent United Nations High Commissioner for Refugees [UNHCR] figures citing 2.5 million). International nongovernmental organizations (NGOs) estimate the number of displaced persons at as high as 3.3 million.[82] As of 2004, the United Nations Development Programme (UNDP) estimated the number of internally displaced people at between 1,575,000 and 3,410,000.[83] The Internal Displacement Monitoring Centre (IDMC) calculated the number at 3.7 million in 2005.[84] "The Colombian non-governmental organisation CODHES, which monitors displacements and human rights violations, reported an escalation of the conflict from 2004 to 2005. Almost one million people have been forced from their homes since 2002—more than 300,000 in 2005 alone."[85]

Unfortunately only 1.8 million are registered with UNHCR and therefore officially counted as displaced persons. The other half remain "stateless persons" or "persons of concern," of whom there are at least 250,000 in Ecuador and 200,000 in Venezuela, though the stream of displaced persons continues.[86] Some displaced Colombians were too afraid to surface and let their situation be known by applying for protection, fearing danger from any or all of the factions in the conflict. Still others flee without sufficient records and identity documents and therefore fear that they will be returned to their dangerous circumstances once questioned by officials in their own country, at an international border, or by international organizations.

Because the warring factions are loyal to no one and forge alliances when it is convenient, they have tended to treat virtually all groups as potential enemies or as possible informants. For government forces, it is equally difficult to assess who the enemy is. As a consequence, "[a]n estimated 35 percent of displacement is caused by persecution from illegal paramilitary organizations, 17 percent by the armed forces and police, and 24 percent by armed opposition groups. In 24 percent of the cases, the internally displaced were not able to identify those responsible (Amnesty International 1997)."[87]

Women and Children under Threat

As in other parts of the world, certain groups are particularly vulnerable to forced displacement, such as women, children, and the elderly. According to the Colombian government, 74 percent of displaced persons are women and children and 49 percent of the total are adult women,[88] which reflects the profile of refugee and displaced persons in other parts of the world. Another estimate breaks the number out in a slightly different way. "Of Colombia's internally displaced population, 58 percent are female, and 75 percent are under 25 years old (*Conferencia Episcopal Colombiana* 1994)."[89] Ethnically, the heaviest burden of forced migration has fallen on Afro-Colombians, as well as every indigenous group.

Flight amidst such terror has burdened vulnerable groups, rural families, the poor, and women, placing them at greatest risk. "Most of the displaced persons come from rural families. At least 31 of 100 displaced households are headed by women, 76 percent of them widows or women abandoned during displacement. Each of these women is responsible for an average of four children. An estimated seven out of 10 displaced households move to urban areas, most commonly to the provincial capitals of the regions of expulsion."[90]

As refugees, internally displaced women may find themselves vulnerable to a variety of violent acts, beginning with the imminent threat to their lives and their children's and including sexual violence (discussed in chapter 2). Children become victims in war in many ways, not only in terms of scarcity of schooling, poor health care, and poverty. They also fall victims to abductions or forced recruitment as child soldiers.[91] Indeed, in Colombia there have been dangers for older male children or young men, who are often forcibly recruited as soldiers, or who, for lack of better options, join insurgent groups.

Women, especially those widowed by the war, are forced to assume new roles as heads of households in cultures that have placed gender boundaries on such roles. Whether prepared or not, they have had to step into what had been traditionally defined in the culture as male roles as breadwinners or disciplinarians of children, or to confront other family responsibilities. Of course, women in such circumstances have worked with other similarly situated women to face their challenges. The study by Meertens and Segura-Escobar found that women who are internally displaced also "seem better equipped to develop support networks to continue the routines of daily survival and find new ways of earning an income, and creating social capital not with other women originating from the same area, but with those sharing the same history of displacement."[92]

Massive Displacement of Indigenous Peoples

Contemporary Colombia presents a diverse ethnocultural, racial, and linguistic profile. While the majority of the people are mestizo, a mix of indigenous and European descendants (58 percent), or white (20 percent), the various groups have intermixed, enriching the diversity with mulattos (14 percent); blacks (4 percent); mixed black-indigenous (3 percent); and indigenous (1 percent).[93] (The demographic figures vary depending on who is counting and how people are categorized.) Among its diversity, Colombia has a small group of Roma people. Their numbers and condition are scantily documented because of their traditional migratory lifestyle, hence they are scattered throughout the country. Their primary language is Romany. Like other minorities, they have endured discrimination and limited education.[94]

The conflict particularly threatens the survival of indigenous peoples, as well as of Afro-Colombians. The declining numbers of the near ninety indigenous groups constitute roughly 1 to 2 percent of the population, or about 800,000 to 1 million indigenous people, including the descendants of the Chibchas.[95] Another minority consists of 3.6 million Afro-Colombians. "These ethnic minorities are disproportionately affected by the internal armed conflict and as a result have faced increasing difficulties in preserving their culture in recent years."[96]

Unlike most other Latin America countries, Colombia's development pattern until the armed conflict was such that the majority of its population, including most indigenous people, had been scattered in rural regions. Since conflict forced migration to cities, approximately 74 percent of Colombians now live in urban areas, in contrast to 57 percent in 1951.[97]

Not only does Colombia present the highest number of internally displaced persons in the world, its indigenous groups bear a disproportionate burden of displaced persons relative to other segments of the population. While indigenous peoples comprise under 2 percent of Colombians, they make up 12 percent of displaced persons. Afro-Colombians, similarly, make up 8 percent of the population but represent 20 percent of those internally displaced.[98] The combined figures for indigenous and Afro-Colombians are as high as 40 percent, though their combined percent of total population is less than 10 percent.[99] According to the UNHCR's count of registered displaced persons, the total figure for indigenous groups for 2005 rose to 23,000.[100] Although these figures may appear small in absolute numbers, the impact can be devastating for small indigenous groups: the Nukak, between five hundred to one thousand ("a small tribe of nomadic hunter-gatherers who have lived in the rainforests of south-east Colombia for centuries"[101]); the Awá, about 1,700; and the Nasa, about 120,000, known as a community of peace.[102]

Indigenous groups have been drawn into the conflict involuntarily in various ways. Because in Colombia it is difficult to identify the enemy, "special interest organizations formed by knowledgeable Indian leaders have been accused of aiding terrorists."[103] They have been victimized by the three major factions at war through killings, death threats, invasion of their territory, and displacement from their resource-rich territories with serious threats to their cultural survival. Many have been driven off their lands when their leaders refused to produce coca for the drug trade.[104]

In 1991, Colombia ratified the Convention 169 on Indigenous and Tribal Peoples in Independent Countries formulated in 1989 by the International Labor Organization. However, the convention lacks enforcement mechanisms. Although the United Nations (UN) declared 1993 to be the International Year for the World's Indigenous People and declared an International Decade of the World's Indigenous People to begin in 1995,[105] it was not until June 2006 that the UN Human Rights Commission adopted the Declaration on the Rights of Indigenous Peoples.[106]

In addition to its participation in international negotiations and policies, Colombia has made efforts to advance the rights of indigenous peoples in terms of its stated policies, including input from indigenous peoples themselves, but many difficulties persist. In particular, the 1991 Constitution, and legislation passed to implement its provisions, recognized the right of indigenous Colombians to self-governing territories and to the recognition and protection of their languages and culture. For example, the Special Rapporteur on the Situation of Human Rights and Fundamental Freedoms of Indigenous People praised legislation pending during his mission to Colombia in 2004 that promised: "the indigenous territorial entities 'shall enjoy cultural, political, administrative and financial autonomy in the handling of their own affairs' and 'shall be governed by indigenous councils formed in accordance with the usage and custom of those peoples and communities.'"[107] However, he concluded that: "Despite the existence of a protective legal framework, the rule of law is being undermined by a consistent pattern of violations of the human rights of indigenous peoples and communities."[108] His summary of the problem criticized all the combatants.

> The Special Rapporteur heard many accounts of the conflict currently gripping the country and its devastating effects on indigenous peoples: murder and torture, mass displacement, forced disappearance, forced recruitment of young people into combat units and rape of women, as well as occupation of their lands by guerrilla, paramilitary and other illegal armed groups. There are also reports of the militarization of some indigenous communities. The Special Rapporteur is particularly concerned at the situation of some very small communities that are now on the brink of extinction as a result of the murder of their leaders, massacres, threats and the forced dispersal of their members.

After detailing numerous examples of attacks on indigenous communities, including cases in which "the military make no attempt to prevent massacres announced in advance by the paramilitaries,"[109] Stavenhagen warned of an even more sinister pattern. "Many indigenous communities report selective killings of their leaders and spokespersons, and of their traditional authorities. Such killings appear to form part of a strategy to decapitate and confuse the indigenous communities, and they certainly hasten their social and cultural disintegration. These are truly acts of genocide and ethnocide against indigenous peoples."[110]

Even apart from the direct attacks on indigenous people, the instability and displacement that came with the ongoing violence rendered the positive policies that were adopted by the government essentially meaningless in day-to-day life. In the area of education, Colombia offers bilingual education programs for indigenous communities, but their educational attainment is significantly below the national average. At the university level, although courses on bilingual education have been established at six universities,[111] the number of bilingual teachers is extremely small. In the health arena, the prospects are bleak for indigenous peoples, as well as for Afro-Colombians, whose life expectancy is significantly below the national average by ten to fifteen years.[112]

Compared to countries with the highest indigenous populations which registered the lowest spending on social policies, Colombia stands in a better light, but not by much.[113] The quality of life for indigenous people is at present far from sustainable, despite the government's efforts to redress, even to some limited degree, the social, economic, and political inequities. The questions go to policy implementation, especially in the context of devastating effects by the violence. The unrelenting violence has exacted a high price on all Colombians, but for indigenous peoples, their sheer survival is at stake. The loss of ancestral lands as they are pushed out by all armed groups and drug traffickers threatens a way of life, a culture, a people, as well as the health of the environment on which their culture is grounded. "We see that our culture is dying, our culture is disappearing," warned Eder Burgo, an Awá leader. "The solution is not a shelter with good mattresses and good food. The solution is to live in harmony in our territories."[114] For the Awá people, whose way of life is anchored on living by the river, forced migration to environmentally foreign territories renders profound alterations in cultural practices.

Others, like the Embera-Katio people of Alto Sinú, who have resisted construction of the Urrá hydroelectric dam in their territory, have suffered "murder, forced disappearances and displacements, intimidation and destruction of their property."[115] Survivors also face endangered lives, poor health, inadequate education, and poverty, as well as imminent threat of extermination—particularly groups with total population in the hundreds, such as the Nukak and the Awá.

Indigenous leaders and teachers have been particular targets of the warring factions. In March 2006, two Wounaan teachers and two leaders were murdered, representing irreparable losses. "'The death of any one of us is terrible, but we especially feel the loss of two teachers,' Ulysses, a Wounaan leader, said at that time. 'To go and study, to become a schoolteacher, this is not an easy thing for us. We have a unique language, less than a third of our children can read, older people are illiterate. To lose two of our teachers is an awful low and we feel it deeply.'"[116] The murder of the few bilingual teachers available to their communities represents a serious threat to their cultures.

The use of rape as a weapon, kidnapping, and assassination of indigenous leaders, coupled with usurpation of traditional lands, further erodes their roots. On World Indigenous Day, on August 9, 2006, five Awá registered displaced persons, three men and two women, were murdered.[117] The displaced Awá group of some 1,700 is most of their total population. The attackers did a house-to-house search during the night and shot them. One of the male victims was a former governor and Awá leader, and one of the female victims was a teacher and a mother of four.[118] The Kankuamo group also has endured heavy losses, with the assassinations of more than two hundred leaders between 2002 and 2005.[119]

For indigenous people, reversing forced migration is very complex. Displacement cannot be reversed through resettlement, not only because of dwindling numbers among all eighty-four groups, but also because their existence is intricately linked with the specific environments they inhabit and in which their cultures have evolved. "Indigenous culture is closely linked to the land and often based on the belief that the spirits of ancestors and magical beings live in the earth and water of their reservations. Forced displacement leads to the loss of tradition, culture and language—and often to the disintegration of the group's identity."[120] At this time, the indigenous groups whose cultural survival is most imperiled are "the Awa, Kofan, Siona, Paez, Coreguaje, Carijona, Guayabero, Muinane-Bora, Pasto, Embera and Witoto," who have lived in volatile territories "in the departments of Putumayo, Caquetá and Guaviare where clashes involving logging, oil drilling and mining interests have fuelled violent repression of indigenous people."[121]

Afro-Colombians Displaced by the Fighting

Descendants of slaves, Afro-Colombians continue to suffer from discrimination and past inequities in addition to the armed conflict. Their precarious life conditions—such as poverty, problems with access and quality of health care, lack of access to clean water or sewage services, poor housing, low educational attainment, and unemployment—have worsened with forced displacement.[122] Their communities have been under siege; they have faced blockades in or out of their communities and have been the victims of killings and disappearances. The high representation of Afro-

Colombians among the internally displaced persons and their deteriorating situation remained unchanged at the end of 2006. They lead in suffering the worst health consequences of coca aerial spraying by the government.[123] They have also fallen victim to bombardments by the Colombian Air Force because, paradoxically, they inhabit the least protected territories. Because of their home area, they are further imperiled by the armed conflict and illicit drug trade.

The Social, Economic, and Environmental Effects of Conflict and Displacement

Imagine a nation with millions in flight at any moment in time enduring ongoing devastating conflict decade after decade. It has been a conflict that has involved all three types of warfare discussed in chapter 2, including social, economic, and environmental warfare. Consider some of the damage to social development, economic development, and environmental protection that has been responsible, along with the direct impacts of violence, for driving Colombians into flight. These conditions have also, and in turn, been exacerbated by the fact that so many have left their home communities as refugees or internally displaced persons.

According to the UNDP's *Human Development Report 2002*, the Human Development Index (HDI) rank for Colombia was 68 out of 173. For a country with a wealth of profitable natural resources, Colombia's development has been profoundly unequal, skewed against rural areas evidenced by a lower HDI in contrast to that of urban areas. For example, the illiteracy rate is three times higher in rural regions. School enrollment is about sixty in one hundred in rural areas, compared to seventy-eight in one hundred in urban areas. Marked differences exist among provinces, the poorest provinces located on the Pacific Coast, "excluding Valle del Cauca, the southern municipalities of the Atlantic Coast, and the New Provinces, excluding their capitals."[124]

Health, Conflict, and Flight in Colombia. The deleterious effects of the violence and flight on the health of Colombians are both short-term and long-term issues (the long-term effects will be discussed further in chapter 5). Health is compromised by malnutrition, lack of immunization, increase in infectious diseases, low infant birth weight, injuries, unsanitary conditions, maternal death, and complicated with all of these factors, psychological war trauma, as well as increased risk for multiple disabilities.[125] Quality of life dramatically diminishes for the forcibly displaced, even when compared to that of poor sectors of society. In Colombia, "70% of IDP households are deficient in two or more UBN [unmet basic needs]—notably in the area [of] housing and living conditions."[126] Internally displaced persons do poorly in all of the five identified UBN factors: "(a) housing; (b) access to services; (c) living conditions . . .; (d) school enrollment; and (e) economic dependency."[127] The abandonment of their homes and lands sends them into flight with little or nothing in hand with which to build a new life. Added to that are the cramped and often unsanitary conditions in displacement camps. Displaced persons seeking refuge in urban shanty-towns often lack access to clean water or sewage services.

The incidence of rape and lack of norms of conduct in war circumstances increases vulnerability to HIV-AIDS. "According to Colombia's National Health Institute data reported in 2003, nearly 240,000 people—mostly women and displaced people—or 0.6 percent of the population, had been infected with the virus since AIDS arrived in Colombia in October 1983; AIDS is the fifth leading cause of death in the working-age population."[128] The scarcity of food and security increases the likelihood that women and young girls, particularly those outside their home communities and on the run, will be forced to perform sexual favors in exchange for food and protection for their families by irregular and state forces, conditions that have increased the prevalence of sexually transmitted diseases, HIV-AIDS, and mental disorders associated with trauma.[129] (See chapter 4 for a discussion of post-traumatic stress disorder.)

Although Colombia's infant and child health has shown some slight improvements overall,[130] for displaced families, the child morbidity is six times that of the national average.[131] Their plight is worsened by blockades by irregular forces which restrict their movement, further limiting access to health care, food supply, or the sale of their products. As recently as November 23, 2006, Awá families have fled to Ecuador to avoid getting caught in the cross fire. "'No one can go in and out.'"[132] Their flight was prompted because their community leader was killed for refusing to grow coca and fear of reprisals on the rest of the community.

The mental health status of internally displaced persons is precarious for children, adults, families, and communities, and is complicated by a lack of services. The unresolved and protracted uprooted condition gnaws at psychological as well as physical health. "IDP children suffer from emotional trauma, as 63% of them have had at least one family member murdered . . . are also victims of child labour, prostitution, and criminal activities. . . . The feeling of powerlessness among IDPs is exacerbated by the widespread impunity prevalent in Colombia, following traumatic experiences and gross violations of human rights."[133] Forced displacement erodes overall quality of life, and a number of factors associated with conflict have debilitating impacts on children, resulting in neurological and developmental disorders.

Children are also particularly vulnerable to death and injury from land mines. "The explosion of mines kills two Colombians per day. A report by the US Department of State (March 2001) estimated that there were 130,000 mines in more than 400 municipalities, in 28 of the 31 states.

Colombia and Nicaragua are the two countries in Latin America with the most antipersonnel mines."[134] Half of civilian victims of mines are children who, unknowingly, use them as toys. Approximately 83 percent of the accidents occur in rural areas.[135] Because of lack of access to proper medical care, 30 percent of victims die soon after the accident.

The poor health conditions of those internally displaced mean a bleak prospect for infants and children whose development may be permanently harmed. In a study sponsored by the Pan American Health Organization (PAHO) and the World Health Organization (WHO), in which 721 people were interviewed, 43 percent presented signs of mental distress, 40 percent presented "an imperative need for mental health treatment [and] 40 people had attempted suicide[;] 19 [had] epilepsy and 31 [had] mental retardation."[136] This is particularly significant, because in the literature on refugees and internally displaced persons, there is scant research or discussion of the needs of persons with disabilities. Yet this study demonstrates the compounded despair experienced by displaced persons who also live with some kind of disability.

However, even though Colombians in flight, and others as well, have experienced serious conflict-related health issues, there are challenges to the health care system needed to address the problems. First, clinics, community health centers, and health care providers become targets and casualties in war and conflict; thus their services diminish and trained personnel become scarce.[137] The *Colombia Human Development Report 2003* concludes that "health care itself has fallen victim of the armed conflict," and in a number of ways—through the assassination and kidnappings of health professionals, sequestering of ambulances, and theft of medical supplies.[138] These violations have overburdened health care facilities. Second, there is also a decline in resources available for health care, as limited resources are often reallocated to military expenditures.[139]

Third, health care providers leave war-stricken areas in search of safety for their families and themselves, reducing the number of health care providers available. Fourth, the lack of health care imperils prenatal, perinatal, and postnatal care, with dire repercussions on infants. For women, it translates into high mother mortality rates at 130 per 100,000 live births in 2000.[140] Fifth, the need to respond to a high number of complex injuries, requiring costly procedures, inflicted by the armed conflict has meant that health professionals in Colombia have been unable to respond to the regular health care needs of the population, for example, prenatal care.[141] Sixth, the scarcity of food resulting in starvation or malnutrition has deleterious effects on child morbidity and mortality. Children's healthy physical, cognitive, and psychological development is linked to good nutrition, without which children's growth can be stunted, intellectual development impaired, and emotional well-being threatened.

Schooling under Violence.   In the area of education Colombia has made some inroads, though it faces many challenges that have been multiplied by the armed conflict.[142] Although "primary school is free, surveys among displaced households indicate that many did not send their children to school because they could not afford to buy uniforms and textbooks or pay for their identification papers necessary for admission."[143] The violence and forced migration has posed additional problems for educators, for parents, and most of all, for children. "Parents are reluctant to send their children to school when there are security risks. In Colombia children abandon schooling at higher rates in municipalities where paramilitaries and insurgents are active than in other areas."[144] Access to school for Afro-Colombians and Indigenous groups is restricted "by a total lack of appropriate curricula."[145] Dropout rates are as high as 60 percent for early elementary school age children.[146] Not only are insecurity, discrimination, and language barriers to education, but gender as well. In fact, "insecurity linked to violent conflict is strongly associated with gender disparity in education."[147] Other intervening factors are the killing of teachers and the destruction of schools.[148]

Robbed Innocence: Children Forced into Becoming Soldiers.   The violence and forced uprooting has left children, both boys and girls, more vulnerable to recruitment by irregular forces, especially for children and adolescents in rural areas. "The Global Report 2004 of the Coalition to Stop the Use of Child Soldiers estimates that there were 14,000 child soldiers in the irregular armed groups, of which 50% were girls" in Colombia.[149] Although there have been demobilization efforts, the results are limited. For example, in 2004, only 35 percent of child soldiers had benefited. The prospect is grim for child soldiers for several reasons, including fear of familial or community rejection, retribution against their families, or mass murder if they defect from the irregular armies.[150] Children are particularly vulnerable in a number of ways. "In Colombia, for example, girls as young as 12 are reported to have submitted sexually to armed groups in order to ensure their families' safety."[151]

Governmental efforts to reintegrate child soldiers in Colombia have sought to employ a multifaceted, integrated approach. Such an approach departs from the traditional view of child soldiers as criminals and embraces a perspective on child soldiers as victims of armed conflict, hence the need to link "family, social, cultural, and productive integration."[152] This was the result of a change in the law, Law 782, adopted in 2002, that required that such efforts integrate "therapeutic, legal, and educational"[153] dimensions. In response, the Colombian Family Welfare Institute (ICBF; Instituto Colombiano de Bienestar Familiar) was given the mandate to oversee the protection and integration of child soldiers. Among the elements of this integrated approach is family reunification. If that is not feasible, youngsters are placed in shelters. For example, between 1999 and 2003, shelters served 595 child soldiers. The lack of opportunities becomes salient in the makeup of the group: "8% were from urban areas and 92% from rural areas. Nearly 80% were between 15 and 17 years old. About 595 are males and 235 females. Of these, 72% voluntarily surrendered and the rest were captured. 84% belonged to guerrilla groups, 10% to self-defense groups and the rest could not be determined."[154] Although ICBF has also established shelters for young people, the numbers are low compared to the need.

The International Migration Office set up a program that offers hope. In the Cauca region, 535 indigenous youth have benefited from sociocultural integration in which various agencies and actors, including indigenous leaders, are involved.[155] "Through blackberry plantations, growing chickens, pigs, and cows, from the hand of a cultural project, a musical group is born that sings to life; a new stage is created when boys and girls and indigenous and Afro-Colombian youngsters bet on peace."[156] Like the Rwanda model, this integration program includes social, economic, and community integration.[157] The UNDP cites the need for sustainable interventions that consider health and sexuality education for youngsters who have been sexually abused but are also at a sexually active age.

Justice Compromised: The Rule of Law or Peace? The lack of an effective rule of law system has been one of the factors that has exacerbated the plight of those who were ultimately driven into flight, as those involved in the conflict have concluded that they have nothing to fear from the law. They also know that those they victimize have little or no recourse in a meaningful forum. Like other nations plagued by genocide, civil conflict, and war, Colombia struggles with the effort to build and maintain the rule of law in a society where legal institutions have been weak or nonexistent. In Colombia, as in Guatemala and El Salvador, "the grievance-fed violent conflict gave rise to a culture of violence and lack of respect for the rule of law that facilitated the extension of violence to other spheres, opening up spaces for violence based on greed."[158]

Sadly, in addition to its place at the top of the numbers of the displaced, Colombia also holds the record for the highest murder and kidnapping rates, crimes against both men and women.[159] The fluid alliance among the irregular armed groups, drug traffickers, paramilitary, and government forces has victimized civilians with their lives, their safety, their dignity, and their property. "During 1998–2001 there were more than 100,000 homicides in Colombia—an average of 61 victims per 100,000 people each year. By comparison, there were about 5.7 homicides per 100,000 people per year in the United States in the same period. The high homicide rate in Colombia reduced life expectancy during the 1990s by an estimated 1.5–2 years."[160]

As chapter 4 explains in some detail, the cycles of collective violence reach beyond the current era as future generations are caught in the intergenerational and collective trap of post-traumatic stress disorder. "When conflicts end, roads and bridges can be swiftly rebuilt with external support. But the breakdown of institutions, loss of trust and the trauma inflicted on vulnerable people can make renewed conflict more likely. By weakening states, violent conflict can lock entire populations, and the populations of neighbouring states, into cycles of violence. Breaking these cycles is one of the greatest human development challenges facing the international community."[161]

Among the kinds of crimes that have gone unremedied that are in significant part responsible for the plight of displaced persons in Colombia are the varied techniques of land-grabbing by various parties to the conflict. "The Colombian government, in response to a 2004 judgment of the Constitutional Court, increased its 2005 budget to buy and distribute land to IDPs. But forced displacement for purpose of land-grabbing has continued and the court decision is counter-balanced by a proposed law on privatisation of forest land which would legalise land-grabbing by paramilitary officers and threatens the rights of indigenous people to recover their land."[162] The amnesty law passed in June 2005 further intensified the problem. It provided immunity to irregular armed groups and gave them property "rights" to illegally acquired property. Law and order have been lacking for IDPs, as evidenced by the assassination of IDP leaders and unwillingness of the government to tackle these issues.

However, there have been efforts to reinvigorate the judicial process to provide effective rule of law responses to at least some of the problems. Colombia's Constitutional Court ruled against the government in a case challenging policies and services directed at internally displaced persons on grounds that they violated Colombia's own constitution and its law of 1997 on internal displacement, and also that the government's actions were not in compliance with the UN Guiding Principles on Internal Displacement. The government appropriated some $2.2 billion to finance the required remedies. "While the court's decision is a legal victory for IDPs and could provide the basis for an enhanced government response, it remains unclear if the new funds allocated will be spent for the right purpose due to alleged corruption within local Colombian administrations."[163]

Environmental Warfare: Both Cause and Effect

The conflict from 1984 to the present has been fueled in part by control of resources. The United Nations Development Programme calls this type of environmental warfare (see chapter 2) the "resource curse" because the environment has become a battling ground for the insurgents, the paramilitary, organized crime, and state forces. Unfortunately, when the indigenous people who have lived sustainably in an ecosystem for generations are driven out, the effects are not only social and economic harm to the displaced, but also damage to the environment after the displacement. The sustainable lifestyles are replaced by the destructive practices of drug production and conflict. These impacts include deliberate deforestation to expand coca production into terrain that is less accessible to government forces. Those activities and the continuing conflict among factions and government have led to "forest fragmentation."[164] The newly cultivated areas are then also subject to spraying with a variety of toxic chemicals that do further damage to the water courses as well as the forests.

Urban areas do not escape environmental degradation, with consequences on displaced persons. The unsanitary conditions in which displaced families resettle present environmental health hazards. "Environmental health is awful and people have hardly any access to public services, they are exposed to disease-carrier vectors and environmental poisonous substances and live in places where the geological risk is high. All group ages show a high prevalence to illness . . . 57% of children mortality rates between August and November 2000 could have been prevented."[165] The World Bank studies demonstrate that access to sanitation plays a significant role in preventing child mortality, more than access to clean water in preventing infectious diseases, especially in infants and children.[166]

The Economy and the Conflict: Broad Impacts on the
Nation and Reduced Opportunities for the Displaced

It is also clear that "[l]ong running conflicts in Latin America have had severe impacts on economic growth."[167] Colombia's enterprises that could stimulate the economy and provide revenues for infrastructure and social development have been lost to continuous and pervasive sabotage, kidnappings, murders, and a collective climate of chaos. Further, in countries like Guatemala and Colombia with a history of profound inequalities, the economic loss from armed conflict and pervasive criminal violence further exacerbates disparities, exacting the highest price on the most vulnerable groups. And, as is clear from this case study, the displaced are, for all the reasons discussed to this point, the most vulnerable in many important respects.

The displaced, almost by definition, lose their traditional source of income and employment. Farmers are driven to cities that already have limited opportunities for gainful employment at a living wage. As transients, displaced persons are strangers in the community and may face discrimination because of their region of residence or ethnocultural heritage. They very often do not have extended family or other relatives.

Even refugees, who may find that the host countries provide some resettlement assistance, most commonly find employment well below their level of skill, education, and experience. Those who are fortunate enough to have professional training and credentials often find that their credentials are not valid in the host country. Of course, those who leave the country are not in place to assist in its development. On the positive side, some families of refugees, such as those from Central American countries that have been the scene of prolonged conflict, have benefited from cash sent home by those who managed to get to a safe country and were able to obtain employment adequate to provide some assistance.

On the other hand, many of those internally displaced may never be able to return to their homes, and many who become refugees in another country may choose not to do so. This loss is incalculable not only socially, but also economically.

The current administration seeks to bring an end to the violence and promises to take Colombia into a better future. When the opportunity comes to move to post-conflict development, it will be necessary to consider how the dramatic forces that have driven record numbers of Colombians into flight, either within the country or outside of it, have fundamentally reshaped the nation.

PEOPLE ON THE MOVE: WHO AND HOW MANY?

The United Nations High Commissioner for Refugees (UNHCR) is the international institution charged with monitoring, protecting, and serving refugees and other persons under threat or in uniquely vulnerable positions as defined by the UN Convention Relating to the Status of Refugees originally adopted in 1951, and the 1967 Protocol to that agreement.[168] One of the duties of UNHCR is to monitor the numbers of refugees, their countries of origin, and the host countries that provide them asylum and grant them refugee status with its accompanying legal protections. In addition to publishing annual statistics, UNHCR also periodically produces a volume entitled *The State of the World's Refugees*, the most recent edition of which was published in 2006.[169] The most recent data reported by UNHCR show 9,236,000 refugees, but the number of people who fit into what UNHCR calls the total population of concern is much higher, at 19,195,350.[170] Perhaps not surprisingly in the contemporary context, many of the refugees came from places that have seen extended or intense conflict.

In addition to refugees, the number of those of concern includes asylum seekers, returned refugees, internally displaced persons, and stateless persons. "UNHCR's founding mandate defines refugees as persons who are outside their country and cannot return owing to a well-founded fear of persecution because of their race, religion, nationality, political opinion or membership of a particular social group."[171] Asylum seekers, on the other hand, are people who have fled to another country and "apply for 'asylum'—

the right to be recognized as bona fide refugees and receive legal protection and material assistance."[172] Internally displaced persons are those "who are caught in situations similar to refugees, but who have stayed in their own countries rather than cross an international frontier."[173] Stateless persons are those who are "not considered a national by any state under its law."[174]

The positive news from recent reports is that current numbers of refugees and internally displaced persons are approximately half what they were in the mid-1990s. The problem with the discussion of these data is that the numbers dramatically understate, perhaps by half or more, the actual numbers of people driven into flight for a variety of reasons that even UNHCR is beginning to recognize. There are two sets of reasons that make it difficult, if not impossible, to know just how many people are in flight and what their current status and challenges might be.

First, the way that the data are collected and tabulated captures only a portion of those persons on the move. The annexes to the *State of the World's Refugees* explain limits on how the data are gathered. Thus, refugees are those persons who have been recognized as such either by a host country or are under the protection of the UNHCR in that category. That represents a small portion of those in flight, since many of the world's nations are making it much more difficult to obtain refugee status.[175] Still others are not counted for special reasons, as in the case of "Palestinian refugees residing in areas of operation of the United Nations Relief and Works Agency for Palestine Refugees in the Near East (UNRWA)."[176] In Pakistan, the only persons counted as refugees are those in refugee camps.[177]

Asylum seekers are people who have applied for refugee status but have not yet had their cases resolved. The UNHCR relies on countries in which asylum applications have been made to report the applications and the status, but the reporting is neither consistent nor systematic. "In the absence of Government figures, UNHCR has estimated the refugee population in many industrialized countries, based on recent resettlement arrivals and recognition of asylum seekers. For Canada, USA, Australia and New Zealand, estimates are based on arrivals/recognition during the past five years, whereas for most European countries a 10-year period has been applied. These periods reflect the different naturalization rates for refugees."[178] Of course, naturalization—the granting of citizenship to someone born a foreign national—is a very different matter from a conferral of refugee status.

If those factors suggest serious limitations on the data, consider UNHCR's declaration with respect to internally displaced persons that: "statistical data on IDPs is less reliable than on refugees. UNHCR statistics are limited to IDPs to whom UNHCR extends protection or assistance. As such, UNHCR statistics do not provide a comprehensive picture of global internal displacement."[179] The calculation of "returned refugees" is similarly problematic. The UNHCR notes that: "Returnees, 'returned refugees' and 'returned IDPs', refer to refugees and IDPs who have returned home but continue to receive assistance from UNHCR. . . . [O]nly refugees and IDPs who have returned during the last 12 months are included."[180] The methodology appendix recognizes that "precise figures on refugee returns and on those who are internally displaced are difficult to obtain due to unregistered movements and lack of access to those people."[181] Not surprisingly, the UN warns that "statistics on stateless persons, in particular those who are not displaced, are difficult to obtain."[182] These and other issues pointed out by UNHCR's own methodological explanations demonstrate that there are major difficulties with the figures, most of which tend to bias the numbers dramatically downward.

The second set of factors that makes it difficult to understand accurately the numbers and conditions of persons in flight is more complex and goes to contemporary changes in national and regional laws on asylum. Consider first the nature of those changes and then their consequences for our ability accurately to assess the circumstances of the millions affected by conflict and then to respond to their needs both while they are in flight and after the conflicts have ended.

Refugee Politics, Policy, and Law: The Movement from Protection of Those in Flight to Protection from Those Seen as Security Threats

The UNHCR explains the ways in which policies adopted since the 1990s have seriously undermined the ability of refugees to obtain the protections that were intended by the 1951 refugee convention and the 1967 protocol. Asylum seekers have increasingly been seen not as persons in need of protection but as security threats. The result has been to discourage many legitimate refugees from moving to a safe haven and intensifying their trauma, the effects of which endure long after the conflict ends (see chapter 4). Those problems, in addition to the changing nature of conflict, have exacerbated post-conflict challenges.

It is important to understand that these difficulties were developing prior to the attacks on 9/11, but they have been dramatically intensified since those events. In addition to the retraumatization visited upon those caught up in the refugee determination process, these changes have also had significant impacts on those who provide assistance to refugee claimants.

Refugee Policy Trends Before 9/11: Doors Quietly Closing

At the international level, although the responsibility for refugee policy and its administration rests with the UNHCR, that agency and the services it provides have been significantly influenced by the various international nongovernmental organizations that operate alongside UNHCR in the midst of crises. In the field, UNHCR depends heavily on these nonprofit relief organizations to provide humanitarian relief and financial support for refugees and internally displaced persons. Historically, these NGOs have operated within nations in conflict or in neighboring countries and in host countries to facilitate resettlement of refugees. The meaning of refugee policy on the ground is shaped by the ability and willingness of those NGOs to turn words into action, as well as by the policies adopted by both international bodies and individual nations.

The UNHCR has long had important political functions in addition to the direct assistance to refugees it provides in concert with its civil society partners. It has played an important political role in working with countries to obtain their agreement to serve as safe havens and to permit the development of refugee camps. That has often been a complex task, since the countries that agree to host UNHCR facilities and NGO operations do not want to face reprisals from the neighboring states, nor do they wish to shoulder an unfair financial burden. Above all, they do not want the refugee camps to be permanent or to have the assumption made that the refugees will be able to remain in their country over the long term. Even before the 9/11 attacks, these countries were concerned about the danger that other countries may refuse to grant refugee status, asylum, and resettlement assistance to those who have spent time in a safe country after their departure from a country in which they had a "well-founded fear of persecution on account of race, religion, nationality, membership in a particular social group or political opinion" under the doctrine known as the first asylum principle.[183] That would leave the countries closest to the fighting to bear disproportionate obligations over the long term.

The UNHCR also must work with the relevant national governments and international NGOs to meet the humanitarian needs of the refugees and internally displaced people, a task that has become increasingly challenging in the contemporary period as social warfare has become more complex and more vicious. These survivors often have complex and multifaceted needs, such as the medical and psychological needs of those, like the Bosnian and later the Kosovo refugees, who have been under threat for extended periods and faced genocide, separation of men from their wives and children, and the use of torture and use of rape as a deliberate weapon as explained in chapter 2.

Second, the agency has had to conduct ongoing policy making and supervision for resettlement work in the camps and other areas under UNHCR authority. Efforts to process refugee applications and provide resettlement in host countries have become more difficult in part because of such practices as identity cleansing (described in chapter 2), in which refugees or other displaced persons have been deliberately deprived of identity documents. Under policies adopted by many countries during the 1990s, the lack of adequate identity documents is grounds for refusal of entry at borders and truncated refugee determination processes that can lead to rapid rejection of the petitions with little hope for review.

Despite the agreement by most nations to honor the 1951 and 1967 refugee agreements, potential host countries have increasingly operated on the basis of individual sets of policy decisions, working in accord with the international agreements when it has served their purposes and ignoring them where and when they chose.[184] Even before the 9/11 attacks, the broad tendency in national policies on refugees was increasingly for national leaders to see refugees as economic or political threats and to find mechanisms to avoid accepting responsibility for them.

One of the trends that began following the flight of refugees referred to as Vietnamese "boat people" (because they fled in a variety of boats ranging from small fishing boats to small cargo carriers) and intensified during the 1990s was the tendency to see refugee issues as a foreign problem, to be managed offshore.[185] The view was less that these were people in need of rescue from danger and more an attitude that refugee claimants were really immigrants. Therefore, the claimants' applications should be processed at the host country's embassy in the country of origin. Of course, those who truly are facing "a well-founded fear of persecution" in their home country, and therefore do qualify as convention refugees, are the least likely to be able to engage in such an orderly application process and are often in no position to track down documents and witnesses.

Another aspect of these arm's-length policies is an emphasis on resettlement decisions that are to be made while the refugee is in a refugee camp in a third country. However, the nations with refugee camps are often developing countries on the borders of the troubled countries of origin, leaving the developed countries free of responsibilities. As the situation in Africa in recent decades indicates, the receiving countries have often been overwhelmed by their own military, economic, or political crises. Hence, the figures in contemporary UNHCR reports concerning returned refugees have, in several situations, involved those who fled their own country only to have to return when the neighboring nation that had initially received them found itself in turmoil. "For instance, the return of Sierra Leonean refugees from Guinea in 2000 and Liberia in 2001, prompted by hostilities in the areas where they had sought asylum, has been likened to an emergency evacuation rather than an organized repatriation movement."[186]

National policies in the 1990s also created more formidable barriers at ports of entry, even seeking to make the asylum decision at the border and not permit the applicants to enter their intended host nation even for the period of time needed to resolve the asylum claim. Those who are not rejected in a summary process may, under the changing policies of the 1990s, be detained at the port of entry, pending what was in many cases an accelerated and abbreviated adjudicative proceeding. One of the reasons to make the decision at the border was that those who are actually in a host country when their claim is decided have a wider range of substantive and procedural legal protections than one denied entry into the country in the first instance.

If the claimant is permitted to enter a host country, there follows a process for the resolution of status. This situation can arise in one of three ways, and many countries from the 1990s on have sought through policy and administrative practices to limit the first option and stop the others.[187] First, one may come as a refugee sponsored by an organization such as a church or an individual who will provide resettlement assistance. A more common approach has been for refugees to get themselves into a potential host country by any means possible and then apply to regularize their status. Many refugees have found themselves without papers, knowledge, or means of using legitimate transportation. The person who fears for her life or that of her children will walk to what she hopes will be a safe haven, get there on board an unseaworthy craft, or, if the resources are available, pay someone to help her and her children to their intended destination, and then make her claim. Some claimants who can do so leave in a low-visibility manner by obtaining a tourist visa and, once in the host country, apply for asylum. A third approach, common until the late 1990s, involved claimants who were able to make their way to the border and make a claim to refugee status at that time, with the hope that they would be paroled into a country pending resolution of an asylum application. During the late 1990s, Europe, Canada, the United States, and other countries moved to block entry without the refugee claim resolved.

At the same time that host countries, particularly in Europe and North America, were building tougher border controls, they addressed four sets of concerns in their emerging refugee policies. First, there was the humanitarian focus. Notwithstanding the many abuses and insensitivities over time, many nations have accepted large numbers of refugees who have gone on to be valuable members of those societies. Indeed, those refugees most often come with the understanding that they will work extremely hard, often at less-than-desirable jobs that are well below their level of skills and knowledge so as to provide a foundation for a better life for their children. Ironically, there have been humanitarian policy actions even as the same countries refused to cooperate in the development of effective and enforceable international refugee agreements and institutions. Thus, while the United States played an active role in negotiations for the 1951 Convention on Refugees, it did not actually become a signatory and implement the agreement until 1968. Even while it was passing harsh immigration laws, it admitted large numbers of refugees from particular countries. Canada was a willing host to significant numbers of refugees, particularly given the size of its population. Many European countries, led by Sweden and Germany, have taken substantial numbers of refugees over the years on humanitarian grounds. Thus, even as they were adopting much more restrictive refugee and immigration statutes in the 1990s, these nations welcomed refugees from Kosovo with open arms.

The second and increasingly dominant emphasis is foreign policy. It is certainly understandable that refugee policy is shaped in part by foreign policy. At the same time, the Convention on Refugees and its protocol were intended to transcend particular foreign policy moves of the moment. Indeed, they were designed to address fundamental issues precisely at the most difficult periods in international affairs. The fact that these overarching agreements have too often been ignored because of short-term issues has been nothing short of maddening to refugees and those who work with them. In 1936, James McDonald, then High Commissioner for Refugees under the League of Nations, resigned in protest. He wrote: "[W]hen domestic politics threaten the demoralization and exile of hundreds of thousands of human beings, considerations of diplomatic correctness must yield to those of common humanity."[188] European nations and the United States would not act to take Jewish refugees from Hitler's Germany. The European countries who were members of the League of Nations also would not authorize the office of the High Commissioner to act for fear that it would antagonize Germany. Far too often, foreign policy concerns have been used to refuse refugees asylum.

On the other hand, foreign policy considerations have also been the basis for generous grants of refugee status. For many years, what was then West Germany accepted anyone who escaped from East Germany. The United States accepted virtually any refugees coming from Communist countries. In particular, the policy of the United States to grant immediate refugee status and generous supports to persons coming from Cuba, while rejecting many others from Latin American and Caribbean countries, was a foreign policy–based action that generated considerable criticism.

The United States did not adopt a fully formed refugee policy until the 1980 Refugee Reform Act, providing the first major rewrite of policy in the field since the early 1950s.[189] Of course, during that period, the Vietnam war ended, which launched one of the most ambitious refugee resettlement challenges in that era.[190] The Cold War was still raging and governed most of U.S. refugee decision making. Prior to Vietnam, "[o]f the 233,436 refugees admitted between 1956 and 1968, all but 925 were from Communist countries."[191]

No sooner had the 1980 Refugee Act gone into effect than the Reagan administration took office with a foreign policy agenda that would mean that refugee issues would grow in intensity and complexity. At the top of those foreign policies priorities was the Cold War and a renewal of the idea that issues in other countries were to be understood in terms of U.S. and Soviet influence and surrogate conflict. In the Western Hemisphere, right-wing governments that enforced what the United States regarded as stability were to be supported, as in El Salvador and Guatemala, and other groups that sought change were considered Communist-inspired revolutionaries to be fought, as in Nicaragua.[192] The U.S. actions in the region included the infamous Iran-Contra affair, in which U.S. weapons were promised in exchange for assistance in money laundering as a way to get resources to the Contras.[193] Later, the Special Counsel investigating Iran-Contra found that:

- the sale of arms to Iran contravened United States Government policy and may have violated the Arms Export Control Act;
- the provision and coordination of support to the contras violated the Boland Amendment ban on aid to military activities in Nicaragua; . . .
- the Iran operations were carried out with the knowledge of, among others, President Ronald Reagan, Vice President George Bush, Secretary of Defense Caspar W. Weinberger, Director of Central Intelligence William J. Casey, and national security advisers Robert C. McFarlane and John M. Poindexter; of these officials, only Weinberger and [Secretary of State George P.] Shultz dissented from the policy decision. . . .[194]

Unfortunately, the ends-justifies-the-means approach employed by the administration in its Iran-Contra policy and its surrogate warfare in Central America extended to its implementation of refugee policy. The conflicts and ravages of death squads sent hundreds of thousands into flight. For those who came to the United States, it was soon apparent that the Immigration and Naturalization Service (INS) used its broad discretion to favor refugee claimants from Nicaragua and, at the same time, systematically excluded applicants from El Salvador and Guatemala.[195] One Senate investigation in the late 1980s found that "an estimated 62,000 innocent civilians have been killed since the start of the current civil war in El Salvador."[196]

Notwithstanding that evidence of a clear foundation for many Salvadorans to flee the situation, "[i]n the first half of FY 1987, the Immigration and Naturalization Service granted asylum to 3 percent of those Salvadoran asylum applications adjudicated and 88 percent of those by Nicaraguans."[197] Applicants from such other countries as Poland and Iran were being treated very differently, with 49 percent of claimants from Poland and 66 percent from Iran receiving asylum in the same period of time, despite the fact that there was not the kind or amount of evidence of systematic assassination of civilians that was apparent in El Salvador or Guatemala.[198]

The discriminatory treatment was obvious but nevertheless continued until a suit was filed by a church group that resulted in a consent decree in which federal authorities in effect conceded the discrimination.[199] Even though the government agreed that "foreign policy and border enforcement considerations are not relevant to the determination of whether an applicant for asylum has a well-founded fear of persecution," and that "the fact that an individual is from a country whose government the United States supports or with which it has favorable relations is not relevant to the determination of whether an application for asylum has a well-founded fear of persecution," and "whether or not the United States Government agrees with the political or ideological beliefs of the individual is not relevant to the determination of whether an applicant for asylum has a well-founded fear of persecution," it soon became apparent that the problem of discriminatory treatment based upon foreign policy considerations did not end.[200] The federal government did not take the steps necessary to ensure that the INS had the resources needed to provide the proper reconsideration for those affected and the agency continued to demonstrate arbitrary behavior in a variety of contexts.

Part of the problem concerned the unwillingness of nation-states to accept legitimate asylum seekers from friendly regimes. These policies are justified on grounds that the country of origin is a "safe country" and a claim from a person in a safe country is considered presumptively unfounded.[201] There are several factors that can affect judgments about just what is and what is not a safe country.

In some cases there can be difficulties in making decisions about whether claimants face a well-founded fear of persecution in countries that are in transition away from authoritarian regimes or emerging from conflict. Obvious examples include persons who fled from what had formerly been Soviet Socialist republics after the collapse of the former Soviet Union. The United States and European nations suddenly changed their long-standing responses to asylum seekers from those countries because they were then forming relationships with the governments in what were being called the newly independent states of the former Soviet Union, including Russia. The conditions in a number of those countries were far from secure and there were many people who had a well-founded fear that they would be persecuted because of their race, religion, or other grounds that fit the convention. Refugee claimants who would clearly have been accepted a few months earlier found themselves rejected as coming from safe countries.[202]

Another example from another part of the world is Guatemala. After years of murder and state-sponsored terror, the United States applauded election of a civilian government, but the human rights situation in Guatemala remained far from resolved, and those who had been regarded as leftists were subjected to threats and violence. A local labor leader and his family made their way to the United States, albeit with an illegal entry, and then applied for refugee status. The Immigration and Naturalization Service rejected their claims on grounds that clearly reflected U.S. foreign policy, taking only a single paragraph to dispose of the idea that there were grounds for a fear of persecution and concluding that the man's clash with officials in Guatemala was economic rather than political. The United States Circuit Court of Appeals for the D.C. Circuit reversed that finding, concluding that the lawyer for the family was correct in asserting that under the INS approach: "Aleksandr Solzhenitsyn would not have been eligible for political asylum because his dispute with the former Soviet Union is properly characterized as a literary, rather than a political, dispute."[203]

Domestic politics have also played a part in shaping refugee policy, including factors that fly in the face of the basic international commitments, such as racism and religious prejudice. Refugees from Europe have often been treated very differently and received with greater concern for the requirements of the international convention and humanitarian principles than those from other parts of the world. One need only recall that until 1967, the Convention on Refugees only applied to European refugees. However, the reaction to Somalis in Scandinavia, to Haitians in the United States, and to what have been referred to as "non-Europeans" in a number of EU countries, even in the 1990s and after, have brought accusations of discrimination.[204]

Discriminatory trends have often accompanied periods of isolationism and times when relatively extreme ideological tendencies shape domestic politics. An obvious example that shaped U.S. immigration and refugee policies for decades to come originated in the 1920s postwar isolationism. In such periods, refugees, as well as immigrants more generally, make easy targets since they lack substantial groups who will rally to their support, and those who do speak out have been accused of disloyalty or saddled with vague charges of complicity in some sort of subversive conspiracy.

A further factor has been economic. During the 1980s and 1990s, assumptions were commonly made that many of those seeking asylum were not really refugees, but economic immigrants seeking a better standard of living. Refugee policy discussion often focused on the question of sorting out legitimate asylum applicants from those who are immigrants. Such factors may play a larger role in policy debates when the host country is facing challenging economic times. It is perhaps not surprising then that such considerations were substantial political factors in the 1980s and resurfaced following the recession of 2001 and the jobless recovery that followed as the forces of globalization influenced job availability, wages, and employee benefit programs. The suggestion was that refugees were part of the larger group known as immigrants, or even more broadly, foreigners, who threatened jobs.

Of course, one of the confounding factors in this discussion is that those who flee from conflict usually left countries that, because of the conflict, did indeed face serious economic difficulties. Within those contexts, those persons who had to take flight due to a well-founded fear of persecution were viewed as threats to the regime and lost jobs, benefits from public programs, housing, business permits, and other important economic opportunities. So it is often true that one aspect of their flight may have related to economic issues. That fact does not transform refugees into economic immigrants, but it can be used as an excuse by those who argue in favor of restricting refugee arrivals and treating asylum seekers as immigrants.

The consequences of this complex set of forces was a dramatic effort, particularly during the 1990s in Western, developed countries, to create or revise policies so as to close the doors to many asylum seekers who truly had fled to avoid a well-founded fear of persecution and to render the refugee determination process more arbitrary. Some of these decisions discouraged legitimate refugee claimants as well as many NGO representatives who sought to assist them.

In the United States, Congress passed landmark legislation in 1996 that dramatically expanded Immigration and Naturalization Service discretion and reduced available procedural and substantive legal protections for asylum seekers. The new law, entitled the Illegal Immigration Reform and Immigrant Responsibility Act of 1996,[205] granted INS agents at ports of entry the authority to conduct what were called expedited removals, with very limited review available from those decisions.[206] It was so severe that the U.S. Department of Justice insisted that more protections be provided by the government than were mandated by the new statute.[207] Not only did the harsh practices continue, but the United States intensified its own efforts to block applicants and pressured others to do so even before 9/11. These actions only seemed to make the arbitrariness of U.S. behavior more apparent, since the country could and did respond rapidly and in a very welcoming way to particular groups of asylum seekers, such as those from Kosovo, in contexts that fit with current foreign policy preferences, even as it was anything but welcoming to others with meritorious claims.

Although the United States would later charge its neighbor to the north with lax enforcement of its refugee and immigration laws, the fact is that Canada, which had for many years been a country dedicated to active implementation of the international refugee law regime on humanitarian as well as political and legal grounds, moved to a more restrictive approach patterned very much on the 1996 U.S. policy. The Canadian government also stressed keeping the decision processes out of Canada and in the countries of origin or refugee camps, rendering the refugee claimant processes more rapid with fewer procedural protections for the applicant, and limiting the availability of judicial review.

Canada is one of the world's largest nations, but one with a small population, most of whom live relatively close to the U.S. border. Immigration and a strong humanitarian commitment to assisting refugees not only supported the international commitments but also served to help build a multicultural Canada. Along with Sweden and a few other countries, Canada was regarded as a leader in refugee resettlement, and its many public/private partnerships resulted in a wide range of programs particularly centered in Montreal, Ottawa, and Vancouver. In terms of numbers of refugees as a percentage of its total population, Canada ranked at the top, along with Sweden, of fourteen countries evaluated in one study.[208] Indeed, the Nansen Medal for service to refugees was awarded to the Canadian people as a political community, the only time such a thing has happened.[209]

The climate changed in the 1980s and 1990s, both because of internal political dynamics and because of outside pressure. One of the internal dynamics came with difficult times in the Canadian economy and reductions in social service programs, like health care. Like other political communities in similar situations, Canada began to see some of the tendency to blame problems on newcomers and "the Other." In January 1993, *Maclean's* reported that "regardless of age, income or level of education," four of five respondents surveyed considered increased immigration "'bad,' 'very bad,' or simply 'a fact of life.'" The respondents added that there was a clear connection between those attitudes and the state of the economy.[210]

Like other countries, Canada moved to revise its refugee law and policy, a process that has continued since then. Legislation adopted in 1988, 1992, and 1995, respectively, changed the institutions, procedures, and standards for refugee status determinations and appeals.[211] These measures were intended not only to streamline but also to restrict refugee admissions and the percentage of approvals did fall, according to the then Immigration Review Board (IRB) General Counsel Gerald Stobo, from 76 percent in 1989 to 48 percent by late 1993.[212]

Some political critics continued to claim that the Canadian refugee system was still too lenient, but refugee service organizations catalogued any number of problems with the new policies that showed increased burdens on legitimate claimants and their families, more evidence of arbitrary decision making, less assurance of rudimentary due process requirements, and limited judicial review opportunities for oversight of the refugee determination processes.

Today's policies still have some fundamental flaws. Since 1995, all adult immigrants and refugees have been charged $975 for the privilege of permanent residence, making Canada the only country in the world to charge such a fee to refugees. . . . The Canadian refugee determination system . . . fails to meet international standards in crucial ways, notably in the absence of the right to appeal on the merits of a negative determination. Canada also has in place the kinds of measures to "deter people from seeking refuge" mentioned above. In fact, the Canadian government has boasted of being a world leader in developing strategies against "illegal immigration," strategies that are blind to whether the "illegal migrant" is a refugee fleeing persecution.[213]

The response to the criticisms of the evolving refugee policies by the minister of citizenship and immigration was to appoint a legislative review advisory group whose report called for some 172 changes in the policy.[214] Citizenship and Immigration Canada (CIC) published a White Paper entitled *Building on a Strong Foundation for the 21st Century: New Directions for Refugee Policy and Legislation* in January 1999, calling for additional legislation intended to consolidate and centralize control over refugee status determinations, expand the number of situations that would be dealt with in a single expedited decision process, and introduce further policy requirements designed to push asylum decisions offshore into third-country refugee camps or the country of origin.[215]

Further fuel was added to the fire, as the new proposals were under consideration when Canadian and U.S. officials found people in cargo containers at West Coast ports, and this event came hard on the heels of the highly publicized cases in which Canadian agencies were called to intercept unseaworthy vessels, better described as hulks than as ships, carrying immigrants bound for British Columbia. Those events began in the summer of 1999, and then Citizenship and Immigration Minister Elinor Caplan was at pains to answer demands for more enforcement and stronger efforts to exclude illegal immigrants.[216]

When such demands arise in Canada or elsewhere, those demanding action are rarely sensitive to the distinctions between legitimate refugees, who come by sometimes troublesome means, and others. Although Caplan stressed the government's intention to maintain its immigration targets, she repeatedly found it necessary to respond to fears and frustrations: "I understand the concerns of many Canadians about these recent marine arrivals. . . . Early this year, the government proposed new legislative directions on immigration and refugee policy. These directions include enhancing our ability to intercept illegal migrants abroad, stiffer penalties for those who contravene our laws, and the increased use of detention of people."[217]

These and other pressures also meant that many of the minister's statements about refugees began with a recognition of the importance of the immigrant community and the humanitarian commitment to assist refugees, but those messages were increasingly qualified by warnings of the growing focus on security and enforcement. "Canadians are compassionate and generous."[218] "Our government will continue to accept refugees, while at the same time take strong measures to stem the flow of those who try to abuse our refugee programme."[219] "I want to keep the front door to this country open, but I know that to do so, we've got to make sure that we close the back door."[220]

Enforcement and the emphasis on exclusion of claimants were dominant themes in the months that followed. Thus, for example, while the chapter of the White Paper entitled "Refugee Protection" presented two issues that were associated with added protections for refugees, the other six highlighted issues that had to do with enforcement and exclusion of unqualified applicants.[221] The other chapters revealed a similar emphasis, as did the minister's speeches throughout the fall of 1999 and into the beginning of 2000.[222] There was to be increased pressure for greater identity documentation at entry, expanded use of detention, a speeding up of the hearing decision process, and streamlining of review processes that suggested that the processes were surely likely to be faster, but there were serious questions about just how fair they would be. Caplan was giving these speeches as she offered the new citizenship act C-16 and later a new refugee act. The new provisions of the Citizenship Act not only moved to implement these streamlining suggestions, but also to grant new authority to revoke citizenship (Sec. 16), as well as to block citizenship on broad assertions of public interest (Sec. 21) or national security interest assertions (Sec. 23) by the minister. It also expanded the list of those ineligible to apply for citizenship (Sec. 28). The later Refugee Act was patterned along the same policy lines. Ironically, the ministry was attempting to do a host of new things at a time when it was facing budget cuts. Within existing resources, priorities were shifted from other activities to enforcement, and when new funds were added in conjunction with the new legislation, they too were focused on enforcement efforts.[223] Thus, the new Canadian policies and the new enforcement-oriented attitude displayed during their implementation were in place before 9/11.

In sum, the charges by many in the United States that Canada has had an unchecked open door to refugee claimants and that their government had not been trying to keep their policies current in light of the contemporary international challenges, even before 9/11, was simply wrong on the facts and was propounded by critics who had not paid attention to what was happening there. It also meant for many desperate people that warnings were given that perhaps the world's leader in humanitarian application of refugee status was changing its approach and viewing them more as threats than as people who promised to make contributions to Canada in return for granting them asylum from the conflict in their countries of origin.

The European Case: When Harmonization
of Policy Means Closing the Door

Similar forces produced similar results in Europe, but with the added complexities that grew out of the evolution of the European Union. Europe was, to be sure, in a very different position from North America. Even though there was no question that many European countries had acted on humanitarian grounds over the years, it was equally clear that they had often focused on foreign policy as a rationale to exclude others, at least as much as the United States. Of course, the meaning and nature of foreign policy changed dramatically as the Cold War came to an end and the EU moved into a complex set of policy-making processes and institutional changes as a European Community.

The fall of the Berlin wall, the breakup of the Soviet Union, and the implosion of Yugoslavia placed new pressures and demands on Europe, its individual countries, and their economies. The 1980s were years of retrenchment and conservative politics in much of Europe. Nationalist groups gained strength and ugly incidents marred Western Europe's reputation as the cosmopolitan haven for a wide range of cultures. Cuts in public service programs were common throughout the region. It was also a time when Europeans saw immigrants and refugees who were, as they put it, "non-Europeans" as competitors for jobs in a Europe with rising unemployment.

While the member states wanted to ease movement of EU citizens throughout the region through changes that meant an end to traditional border controls, it also became increasingly clear that the EU countries intended to protect themselves from what they, like others in the United States and Canada, increasingly saw as economic immigrants rather than legitimate refugees. There were also fears of international crime that provided another impetus to clamp more controls on outsiders and newcomers even as Europeans sought to remove such restrictions among themselves. Just as European integration was moving forward, domestic policies in several countries took a decidedly nationalistic turn, evidencing a concern that, in periods of economic stress, governments would be concerned about the well-being of their own populations, with outsiders seen not so much as collaborators but as competitors. It was perhaps not so surprising that as 1992 approached, steps were taken toward the development of more restrictive refugee policies, policies that used a regional border locus and an economic focus.[224]

Efforts to transform border controls in Europe can be traced back to 1960, when the Netherlands, Luxembourg, and Belgium moved to open their borders to one another. In 1984, France and Germany concluded a similar accord and in 1985 were joined by the Netherlands, Luxembourg, and Belgium in an agreement signed in Schengen, Luxembourg, and known thereafter as the Schengen agreements.[225] These agreements were later transformed into the Schengen Convention and were followed by the Schengen Implementation Agreement, which took effect in 1995. By 1997, what became known as the Schengen area included over a dozen countries.

The Schengen agreements were not simply about opening borders, but involved a host of issues about which European nations saw a need to harmonize policy and concerns about the need to protect the countries of the region from crime, uncontrolled immigration, and unjustified claims to asylum. The agreements called, among other things, for harmonization of asylum policies. Under the new design a refugee could apply for asylum in only one country in the region in order to stop what was termed "asylum shopping." Just which of the member countries would be the one to render decision in any particular case would be determined not by the applicant, but by rules agreed to by the Schengen countries. Still, the Schengen agreements were not EU documents and, in late 1989 the Council of the EU called for formal action. The Dublin Convention was signed in 1990 and went into effect in 1997.[226]

As the EU came into its own, at least three significant trends became apparent. First, other countries that were contemplating joining the EU had to bring their policies into conformity with the EU agreements.[227] That meant that a cordon had been growing around Europe, a fact that sent strong signals around the world that its countries no longer welcomed refugees and that asylum seekers would face a significant set of legal barriers, along with the likelihood of abbreviated status determination proceedings, little opportunity for appeal, and the possibility of being sent to another country even before their claims were resolved.[228]

Second, once refugees got word of efforts to clamp down on borders of a growing number of European countries, they took a circuitous route through Russia to the Baltic countries, where they were smuggled into Sweden or Finland.[229] Meanwhile, both of those countries were going through hard economic times and domestic politics began to play important roles as a focus of policy. Soon efforts were made to ensure that the mere fact that a claimant made it into the country would not prevent an expeditious resolution of the claim with a quick deportation to follow in the event that the claim was denied. Indeed, while these policies were being modified, Sweden and Finland both witnessed violent incidents against immigrants and refugees.[230]

A third trend that emerged from the Dublin/Schengen regime in operation has been the tendency to shift the focus from economic to foreign policy with the rise of the so-called safe-country doctrine discussed earlier. The concept grows out of two critically important provisions of the 1951 Convention on Refugees. Article 33 provided that: "No contracting State shall expel or return ('*refouler*') a refugee in any manner whatsoever to the frontiers of territories where his life or freedom would be threatened on account of his race, religion, nationality, membership of a particular group or a political opinion."[231] This is known as the *nonrefoulement* provision and is supposed to protect a refugee from being sent back to a dangerous situation. But Article 31 states that: "The contracting states shall not impose penalties, on account of their illegal entry or presence, on refugees who, coming directly from a territory where their life or freedom was threatened in the sense of Article 1, enter or are present in their territory without authorization, provided they present themselves without delay to the authorities and show good cause for their illegal entry or presence."[232] The argument is that if a refugee was in a safe third country prior to his or her arrival in Europe, then there was an obligation to file for asylum in that country of first asylum. Under those conditions, the argument runs, it is not a violation of the nonrefoulement provisions of the convention to return an applicant to such a country after an abbreviated proceeding.

Under the Dublin/Schengen regime and existing interpretations by some EU nations, an applicant could be returned before the asylum proceedings had been concluded. Indeed, while, for example, the Netherlands required proof that the former safe country was willing to take the refugee back and treat him or her in accordance with convention requirements, the United Kingdom required no such assurances.[233] This process was explained on grounds of the safe country doctrine. The EU country immigration officers who met in 1992 in London considered this issue and produced what has come to be known as the London Resolutions. "Within the European Union, the London Resolutions establish that the return of asylum-seekers to a safe country of asylum obviates any obligation of Member States to investigate the merits of a claim to refugee status. . . . The Dublin Convention applies only if no such safe country exists."[234]

The other dimension of the safe third country doctrine is the so-called safe country of origin discussed earlier with respect to examples like Guatemala and republics that emerged when the Soviet Union collapsed.[235] Under this doctrine in the EU, as in Canada and the United States, an asylum claim lodged by a person from what is regarded as a safe country is considered manifestly unfounded and is subject to accelerated and indeed abbreviated procedures.

The Working Party on Asylum Procedures of the International Association of Refugee Law Judges examined the procedures like those in use in Europe, Canada, and the United States and found that while they may have the benefit of speed and efficiency, they pose serious risks that the rights of asylum seekers will be sacrificed in the process.[236] For reasons discussed earlier, it is often the case that asylum seekers present themselves with few documents, no witnesses other than themselves, and perhaps in the throes of post-traumatic stress disorder. Many lack proper legal representation and, for a variety of reasons, often do not understand their rights. In such circumstances, efforts to tighten adjudicative procedures and reduce the kind of flexibility that can address some of these difficulties may mean that there is due process of law in form but not in substance.

In sum, well before the attacks of 9/11, the Madrid train bombing, or the attacks on the London Underground, European countries managed to create a system that pushed the barriers to refugee claimants to borders of the region and, with the growing use of the safe country of asylum and safe country of origin doctrines, changed the focus of decision making from humanitarian considerations to political and economic priorities. And all of these changes went into effect even before the Treaty of Amsterdam took effect in 1999 and before the EU Constitution, which have in some important respects rendered the situation even more complex.[237]

The Post-9/11 Intensification of Resistance to Asylum Seekers: National Security Priority Ahead of Humanitarian Efforts

After 9/11, the picture for those driven from their normal lives by conflict around the world became far more challenging. The combined forces of foreign policy and religious and ethnic discrimination drove many of those changes.

The measures that had been enacted during the 1990s with the assurances that they would be applied carefully and with the international humanitarian commitment to refugee protection squarely in view were pushed to the maximum extent possible as elements of what the Bush administration termed "the war on terror." The 9/11 case study in chapter 2 detailed a variety of these actions, including roundups of persons presumed to be of Middle Eastern extraction, other forms of racial and religious profiling, and the deliberate and routine use of the most technical violations of the now extraordinarily complex immigration laws as the basis for deportation, exclusion, or to detain and hold persons for extended periods without charging them with terrorist activities.[238] Those detained were held in conditions and under circumstances that even the Department of Justice inspector general found unacceptable.[239]

Then there were the secret Immigration and Naturalization Service hearings conducted pursuant to the Creppy memorandum. As has historically been the case with secret adjudications, wherever they have taken place, there has been a tendency toward abuse by the government. In the secret proceedings and in open hearings in refugee cases, there have been miscarriages of justice in recent years that have been denounced as nothing short of outrageous by federal judges of both political parties, including those with very conservative ideological positions. The issue was not just the secret proceedings alone, but the more general and very clear message, communicated in no uncertain terms by then Attorney General John Ashcroft (see chapter 2), that the immigration laws were to be used aggressively and with an obvious assumption that those with pending cases were potential security threats or otherwise unworthy.

Judge Richard Posner, long considered a leading conservative judge and a member of the United States Circuit Court of Appeals for the Seventh Circuit, presented a scathing indictment of the process in a 2005 case.

In the year ending on the date of the argument, different panels of this court reversed the Board of Immigration Appeals in whole or part in a staggering 40 percent of the 136 petitions. . . . Our criticisms of the Board and of the immigration judges have frequently been severe. E.g., "the [immigration judge's] opinion is riddled with inappropriate and extraneous comments" . . . ; "this very significant mistake suggests that the Board was not aware of the most basic facts of [the petitioner's] case" . . . ; "the procedure that the [immigration judge] employed in this case is an affront to [petitioner's] right to be heard" . . . ; "the immigration judge's factual conclusion is 'totally unsupported by the record' . . . ; the immigration judge's unexplained conclusion is 'hard to take seriously'" . . . ; "there is a gaping hole in the reasoning of the board and the immigration judge" . . . ; "the elementary principles of administrative law, the rules of logic, and common sense seem to have eluded the Board in this as in other cases"). Other circuits have been as critical. . . . "[T]he tone, the tenor, the disparagement, and the sarcasm of the [immigration judge] seem more appropriate to a court television show than a federal court proceeding" . . . ; the immigration judge's finding is "grounded solely on speculation and conjecture" . . . ; the immigration judge's "hostile" and "extraordinarily abusive" conduct toward petitioner "by itself would require a rejection of his credibility finding" . . . ; "the [immigration judge's] assessment of Petitioner's credibility was skewed by prejudgment, personal speculation, bias, and conjecture" . . . ; "it is the [immigration judge's] conclusion, not [the petitioner's] testimony, that 'strains credulity.'"

This tension between judicial and administrative adjudicators is . . . due to the fact that the adjudication of these cases at the administrative level has fallen below the minimum standards of legal justice. . . .[240]

Judge Fuentes of the U.S. Circuit Court of Appeals for the Third Circuit used even stronger language in one of the cases to which Posner made reference.

Time and time again, we have cautioned immigration judges against making intemperate or humiliating remarks during immigration proceedings. Three times this year we have had to admonish immigration judges who failed to treat the asylum applicants in their court with the appropriate respect and consideration. In a case involving asylum claims similar to those raised here, . . . Judge McKee expressed his concerns about the IJ's apparent "search for ways to undermine and belittle" the alien's testimony. . . . Also this year, we described an IJ's opinion as "crude" and "cruel," and noted its "hostile" tone and sometimes "extraordinarily abusive," "bullying" and "extremely insensitive" behavior. . . .

A disturbing pattern of IJ misconduct has emerged. . . . [T]he Ninth Circuit held that an IJ violated an alien's due process rights by abandoning her role as a neutral factfinder. . . . [T]he IJ accused the alien of "moral impropriety" and "became aggressive and offered a stream of non-judicious and snide commentary." . . . [T]he IJ was rebuked for her "sarcastic commentary and moral attacks" on the alien. . . .

In yet another case of improper conduct . . . an IJ aggressively questioned an asylum applicant based on his own assumptions about Catholicism. . . .

. . . [W]e are sorely disappointed that the IJ here chose to attack Wang's moral character rather than conduct a fair and impartial inquiry into his asylum claims. The tone, the tenor, the disparagement, and the sarcasm of the IJ seem more appropriate to a court television show than a federal court proceeding. But we hasten to emphasize that our concerns about the IJ's opinion are not limited to her choice of words. Substantively, many of the issues addressed by the IJ at length, and to which she gave substantial weight, were irrelevant to Wang's asylum, withholding, and CAT claims. . . . In summary, the IJ's opinion in this case was highly improper for both its contemptuous tone and its consideration of personal issues irrelevant to the merits of Wang's asylum claim.[241]

The examples cited in these two opinions indicate quite clearly that there has emerged a broad pattern of abusive, biased, and intemperate behavior toward those before the immigration judges, about which appellate courts had warned repeatedly. These behaviors were part of the much larger pattern of the dramatic use and abuse of immigration and asylum policies in the wake of the 9/11 attacks. The message that the door was closing was not lost on anyone in the domestic or the international arenas when most of the functions of what had been the Immigration and Naturalization Service were moved to the newly created Department of Homeland Security.

However, in the wake of 9/11, political players were ready and willing to exploit fear of immigrants and asylum seekers, and the bigotry that too often came along with it, to press a variety of new policies. Thus, the Congress tacked onto the Emergency Supplemental Appropriations Act for Defense, the Global War on Terror, and Tsunami Relief adopted in 2005 something known as the Real ID Act.[242] At the time, relatively little attention was paid to the provision of the Real ID Act, and its supporters answered critics by saying that it was just a means to protect against the use of false identification or ensure that those provided with government-issued ID cards were entitled to receive them. While Title II of the Real ID Act concerned ID policies, Title I, entitled "Amendments to Federal Laws to Protect Against Terrorist Entry," was very different. Section 101 of that title is directed to "Preventing Terrorists from Obtaining Relief from Removal." However, the substance is different from the title, for it is about "conditions for granting asylum," "exceptions to eligibility for asylum," removal from the country, "standard of review for orders of removal," and "clarification of discretion." These provisions are designed to focus and increase the burden of proof on the asylum seeker, increase the discretion of the Secretary of Homeland

Security and his designees in the process, and constrain the nature and availability of judicial review.

New policies after 9/11 provided additional programs, authority, and discretion on top of those that already presented difficulties. The use of expedited removals that allowed substantial discretion for officials is an example. The United States Commission on Religious Freedom instituted a study of the expedited removals process under congressional authority. While concluding that there were policies in place that were supposed to protect asylum seekers in expedited removal situations, the study found that: "Some procedures were applied with reasonable consistency, but compliance with others varied significantly, depending upon where the alien arrived, and which immigration judges or inspectors addressed the alien's claim. Most procedures lacked effective quality assurance measures to ensure that they were consistently followed." The study also found that "asylum seekers are consistently detained in jails or jail-like facilities, which the experts found inappropriate for non-criminal asylum seekers." The study concluded that "asylum seekers without a lawyer had a much lower chance of being granted asylum (2%) than those with an attorney (25%)." There are some public-private programs in some places to provide assistance, but "[t]hese programs, however, have also been implemented unevenly."

Finally, and perhaps most ominously, the Commission reported that:

> By the end of the process—the asylum hearing—unreliable and/or incomplete documentation from CBP and USCIS is susceptible to being misinterpreted by the ICE Trial attorney, misapplied by the Immigration Judge, and may ultimately result in the denial of the asylum-seeker's claim. . . . [I]mmigration judges, even within the same court, had significantly different rates of granting or denying asylum claims. Furthermore, in denying asylum applications on the basis of credibility, immigration judges frequently cited documents which the Study found to be unreliable and incomplete records. . . . The Study also noted that Expedited Removal has been expanded twice in recent years, without first addressing the flaws in the system which undermine the protections for asylum seekers.[243]

These last findings are, of course, completely consistent with what the judges reported in the cases discussed earlier.

In Canada the situation grew more intense as assurances that Canadian officials would not really engage in draconian practices, despite the ability to do so under the new legislation, were forgotten. Canada moved to end the practice of paroling refugee claimants into the country pending the resolution of their cases and worked with the United States to put in place a so-called safe third country agreement that would prohibit claimants from going through Canada to make an asylum claim in the United States and prevent anyone from going through the United States to make an asylum claim in Canada. This latter point was important because many persons who were Muslim or who came from predominantly Muslim countries feared what might happen if they attempted to make claims in the United States or to seek to change their status to permanent resident status, given what was taking place in the United States after 9/11. The safe third country doctrine provided a vehicle by which the two countries could block applicants while technically remaining within the requirements of the Refugee Convention and Protocol.

In the period before the safe third country agreement went into effect, many asylum seekers who were in the United States but wanted to make their claim in Canada made their way to the border. When they got there, they found that, while Canadian officials would accept their claims, they would not admit the asylum seekers to the country pending resolution of the claim. Instead, they were given a date to return for the processing of their asylum claim and had to remain in the United States. One of the difficulties was that many of them remained in the communities in the border areas. Many lacked resources to house, clothe, and feed themselves and their families, forcing church groups and other nonprofit agencies to undertake major assistance programs.[244]

Canada increased its use of detention and cooperated with the United States in the process known as extraordinary rendition. In the post-9/11 period, Canadian refugee policies stressed three priorities. They included security (with an implied assumption that asylum seekers may very well be terrorists in disguise), enforcement to take a "proactive" stance against risk, as CIC Minister Denis Coderre, Caplan's successor, put it (both at the border and within the country), and more demanding review of refugee claims (with an implied expectation of increased rejection of claims).

One of the key devices that was significantly expanded in support of these security values was the increased availability and use of detention. Indeed, Minister Coderre pointed to this tool as one of Citizenship and Immigration Canada's priorities.[245] In fact, the Minister pointed to the fact that the effort to enhance the use of detentions as an enforcement tool was already under way.[246] He expected to make greater use of the tool as the infrastructure necessary to do so was put in place. "[A] key activity for CIC in 2003–2004 will be to develop a more coherent and more effective national strategy for detention. CIC will undertake further policy work to design a cost-effective detention program based on increased collaboration with other government departments and agencies.[247] The move to increased use of detention within the country and at the border was a departure in Canadian practice and one of the most serious policy trends.

Canada has also faced criticism of its own with respect to detentions, even before the CIC plan to increase the practice and create more facilities was fully implemented. Thus, for example, Matthew Behrens, in an article in the *Vancouver Association for Survivors of Torture (VAST) Quarterly*, described recent cases in Ontario involving Muslims and others of Middle Eastern ethnicity.[248] He focused in particular on the story of Mahmoud Jaballah, who was arrested in 1999 based on a security certificate and then held for seven months without trial. After a federal court ordered his release, he was rearrested and remained in confinement on a security certificate from 2001 until 2003. Judge MacKay found the government had committed "abuse of process" because it had delayed for an unconscionable period the production of evidence and materials ordered by the court. "While notice from the Minister of his decision on that application has not yet been received by the Court, it is now determined that the delay in providing that [PRRA] notice, while Mr. Jaballah remains in detention, in solitary confinement, and is not sufficiently explained, and without a reasonable forecast of its termination, in the circumstances of this case constitutes an abuse of process."[249] In the process, MacKay concluded that Canadians might be surprised to learn that they had the equivalent of a "Guantanamo Bay in the heart of Toronto."

The process allowed a judge to rule on the security certificate without opportunity for disclosure of the evidence to the person detained or their lawyers. MacKay, in fact, upheld the "reasonableness" of the security certificate in May 2003. Jaballah's wife and children had been granted refugee status, but he remained in jail. The court concluded that he would likely face torture or death if he were to be returned to Egypt. However, his refugee claim has been rejected and he was found to be excludable, leaving him in a kind of legal limbo. A number of others have found themselves in similar circumstances, and their families have waited with no sense of their future. Since then, the security letter process has been found by the Supreme Court of Canada to be in violation of the Canadian Charter of Rights and Freedoms, but those detained have not been ordered released.[250]

Whatever the nature of the cases themselves, holding a person in solitary confinement for periods of more than a year and a half is an extreme form of punishment usually reserved for the most hardened of convicted felons who cannot be controlled in any other manner. Normally, extended periods of solitary confinement or administrative segregation are used as punishment for which special procedures are required. Solitary confinement is a psychosocial punishment that deprives those incarcerated of social stimulation. Given the way in which such confinements are administered, they also usually ensure the most limited forms of environmental stimulation. It is equally well known that such confinement can engender serious psychological consequences or exacerbate existing conditions.[251] One of the effects has been termed "Reduced Environmental Stimulation Syndrome" (RES).[252] Justice Cory of the Supreme Court of Canada put the special and severe nature of solitary confinement plainly in *Winters v. Legal Services Society*:

65. The consequences and effects of solitary confinement on prisoners demonstrate that it is not simply an alternative type of incarceration. . . .

66. Professor Jackson points out the difficulty of accurately describing or measuring the effects of solitary confinement on the human psyche. . . . He notes that prisoner complaints stress the deeply depressing psychological repercussions even more than the physical deprivations of solitary confinement. . . .

67. It is clear that solitary confinement is not simply a different yet similar form of incarceration than that experienced by the general prison population. Its effects can be serious, debilitating and possibly permanent. . . .[253]

There is an added pressure on those detained. They must attempt to participate in legal processes that will determine their fate under the most difficult of conditions. As any experienced criminal attorney would testify, the difficulty of preparing a case increases when those involved are unable to obtain bail to remove themselves from confinement. Such conditions increase frustration and anxiety and can easily exacerbate depression. There is every reason to expect those suffering the effects of PTSD will have their conditions seriously intensified in such circumstances.

The impacts of detention are not limited to the detainee alone. Detentions in the post-9/11 context are sometimes of indeterminate length. They may split children and parents and husband and wife. They may also mean extremely limited opportunity for communication and visitation. Depending upon where and under what conditions someone is held, although visitation may technically be possible, it can be extremely difficult. The wife of one detainee made her frustration clear. She said, "I'm a Canadian citizen. I should be able to know why the government wants to separate me from my husband."[254] Jaballah's seven-year-old daughter and fourteen-year-old son put the matter in equally stark terms that suggest some of the potential impacts of the detention on them. "'I thought this country was free, but it's not,' said Afnan. Her older brother said his school grades have fallen since his father's arrest in 2001 and then added, 'I feel that my life is over.'"[255]

Part of what is creating new tensions in Canada, the United States, and Europe is the clearly announced intention to streamline the refugee determination process. What this means in practice is a considerable modification of what it means to have due process of law in the claims process. Limits on hearing processes and appeals leave room for greater discretion on the part of hearing officers and less opportunity for what had been regarded as a full adjudication of claims.

Another major feature of the move to emphasize security has been a commitment to expedite and intensify removals from Canada, the United States, and Europe. In Canada, for example, changes in the process were matched with a more aggressive approach to removals. In fact, Minister

Coderre pointed out that: "In 2001, departmental employees . . . effected 9,542 detentions and 9,165 removals."[256] He made it clear that this was an area in which Canada was taking these steps in concert with the United States and other countries. "CIC will continue to work with international partners, particularly the U.S., the U.K. and Australia, to share best practices and coordinate efforts to expedite removals. The Department will also continue to encourage cooperation from targeted source countries to issue travel documents and accept the return of their nationals."[257]

These kinds of issues were evolving not only in the United States and Canada but in a variety of other developed nations. Thus, the treatment of refugee claimants in Australia, including detention and conditions of confinement, brought considerable criticism.[258] The situation in Europe has been in flux for reasons noted above, but has been moving in the same directions as those demonstrated in the United States and Canada.

These changing policies and their manner of implementation have been so dramatic and significant as to prompt UNHCR, an institution which for obvious reasons has tended to be extremely careful in how it characterizes the behavior of the member states of the UN, to issue a strong statement about the impacts on those in flight of the closing of the doors and what might even be characterized as an international effort to undermine the efficacy of the 1951 Convention and its protocol. The UNHCR has concluded that: "the emergence of new security concerns for states, particularly since the events of 11 September 2001, has led to the 'securitization' of asylum practices."[259] Chapter 2 of the 2006 report, entitled Safeguarding Asylum, noted that in addition to the need for the concern about the treatment of refugees, the behavior of many of the 146 countries of the world that have acceded to the convention and protocol (including those countries that have also joined the Organisation of African Unity [OAU] 1969 Convention Governing the Specific Aspects of Refugee Problems in Africa and the 1984 Cartagena Declaration on Refugees in Latin America) suggests a need to defend the very institution of asylum and refugee status in fact as well as in law.

While the number of such asylum seekers has diminished significantly in recent years, and while the majority originate from countries that are affected by armed conflict and political violence, governments and electorates in the developed world tend to perceive these new arrivals in very negative terms. They are seen as people who submit 'bogus' claims to refugee status, threaten the sovereignty of the state by entering it in an illegal manner and force governments to spend large amounts of money on asylum and welfare systems. Furthermore, these arrivals are widely believed to put unacceptable pressure on scarce resources such as jobs, housing, education and healthcare. Finally, it is a commonly held perception that even if their application for refugee status is rejected, most asylum seekers will remain illegally in the country. During the past decade, and more specifically since the 11 September 2001 attacks in the

United States, the problem of asylum fatigue in both developing countries and industrialized states has been exacerbated by a growing concern that foreign nationals and members of ethnic minorities represent a potential threat to national security and public safety. As a result, asylum seekers and refugees have come under a growing degree of public suspicion and are subject to increasingly rigorous state controls. In a context where governments and electorates are unable to draw a clear distinction between the victims of persecution and the perpetrators of terrorist violence, there is an evident need to safeguard the principle of asylum.[260]

The UNHCR recognized the concerns with security and the other forces that have played a role in the reactions against refugees. The report also asserted that while many potential host countries have repeated their commitments to the convention and protocol, they have taken actions that have involved "violations of the principle of non-refoulement; lack of admission and access to asylum procedures; detention practices that violate international standards; lack of registration and documentation; and shortcomings in refugee status determination procedures."[261] While there can often be an economic aspect to the plight of the claimant, although the conditions that sent the refugees into flight were violence or other threats, the fact is that "these causes often overlap with, or may themselves be provoked or aggravated by, economic marginalization and poverty, environmental degradation, population pressure and poor governance."[262] It is true that many, if not most, asylum seekers in the contemporary context lack travel documents, but the report acknowledged as well that many refugees are desperate enough, and lacking in knowledge of how to escape, that they pay traffickers to get them out of their predicament and help them to safety. However:

> By resorting to the services of a smuggler, an asylum seeker seriously compromises his or her claim in the eyes of many states. This also leads to an imputation of double criminality: not only do refugees flout national boundaries, they consort with criminal gangs to do so. Therefore, it is argued, their claims must be bogus and measures to restrict their basic rights are justified. Such sentiments have played into the hands of politicians who have ridden the anti-foreigner sentiments that were aggravated by the 11 September attacks. This has fuelled xenophobic attitudes, to the detriment of refugees and asylum seekers.[263]

Recognizing that many countries have developed what they euphemistically call streamlined processes for adjudication and invoke other devices to avoid their obligations to admit legitimate claimants, UNHCR observed: "In some states there has been a gradual movement away from a rights-based approach towards more discretionary forms of refugee protection. Such mechanisms have included the notions of 'safe country of origin', 'internal flight alternative', 'effective protection elsewhere' and 'safe third country'."[264] The efforts to tighten the requirements for documents and to push the examination of documents offshore to points of origin by such practices as fining airlines that transport anyone without documents has also made it that much more difficult for legitimate refugee claimants to get out of their condition of threat to a safe harbor where they have an opportunity for a full and fair consideration of their asylum claims.[265] In other cases, the fact is that countries have simply blocked movement or returned claimants to situations that were clearly and obviously dangerous.

> In 2002, in the Great Lakes Region of Africa, tens of thousands of refugees from the Democratic Republic of Congo were returned to their country of origin under conditions that were far from secure. In 2003, several hundred refugees fleeing renewed fighting in the Indonesian province of Aceh were removed from neighbouring Malaysia on the grounds that they were illegal migrants. In the same year, South America witnessed a number of efforts to remove Colombian refugees from countries where they enjoyed temporary protection.[266]

While it is not possible to know how much of the dramatic reductions in asylum seekers since 9/11 is due to the policy and practice changes and how much is due to a decrease in the number of those who would like to avail themselves of refugee protections, there is little doubt that the effects of those policy actions have been dramatic. First, there is the evidence of the decline itself.

> Member states of the European Union received nearly 20 per cent fewer asylum claims in 2004 than in the previous year, and 36 per cent fewer claims than in 2001. Most countries are now reporting their lowest annual total for several years. The number of applications lodged in Germany was 30 per cent lower in 2004 than in 2003, and the United Kingdom saw a drop of 33 per cent in 2004 when compared to the year before. New asylum claims fell by 26 per cent in North America and 28 per cent in Australia and New Zealand during the same period.[267]

Second, the numbers of rejections of asylum applications have been up sharply in those countries. Third, there has been a dramatic increase in the numbers of internally displaced persons, and those are the ones about which UNHCR is aware. If the decline in refugees were due principally to a reduction in the level of international conflict and threats, one would expect both numbers to decline.

THOSE INTERNALLY DISPLACED: THE OTHER REFUGEES

The plight of those who must flee but remain within their home country may, in some respects at least, be even worse than that of refugees, and the growing numbers of such people who are displaced within their own countries are likely to exacerbate that situation. There are several key factors to bear in mind when contemplating the growing phenomenon of internal displacement and its significance for what comes after the conflict, including: (1) the difficulty of developing an accurate assessment of the scope and scale of the problem in any given country at any moment in time during a conflict; (2) the particular vulnerabilities of those who are internally displaced to a wide variety of difficulties that may affect them and their country for years to come; (3) the challenges that come for those displaced during the period of demobilization and initial post-conflict development efforts; and (4) the impact of the presence and movement of large numbers of internally displaced persons on the environment.

The Scope and Scale of Internal Displacement

The total number of internally displaced persons is impossible to know with any degree of precision, but it is clear that the numbers are dramatic and increasing. "While nearly 5.6 million internally displaced persons were 'of concern' to UNHCR in 2004, the total number of internally displaced persons worldwide was estimated at 25 million—more than twice the number of recognized refugees."[268] Colombia alone, according to the UNHCR, is estimated to have more than 2 million internally displaced persons (with some estimates in excess of 3 million), many of whom are indigenous persons.[269] Those estimates, though, are clearly low. The UNHCR qualified its estimates, noting that "Government estimates [are] between 2.5 and 3 [million]; some NGOs estimate up to 3.3 [million]."[270] The International Displacement Monitoring Centre (IDMC) found that "More than 3.5 million out of the country's 40 million people have been displaced during the last two decades. . . ."[271] While the government numbers are well below that, IDMC points out that the government did not start registering internally displaced persons until 2000 and refused to accept the numbers developed by the leading NGO for the period from 1985 to 2000.[272]

The IDMC found that countries that were supposedly not producing as many refugees, or where a substantial number of refugees had reportedly returned, such as Afghanistan and Iraq, have more recently seen dramatic increases in internally displaced populations as a result of significantly increased violence, a lack of a fully functioning economy, the near absence in many areas of adequate housing in anything that could be described as safe communities, and a general lack of basic public services from water and power to health care.[273] But even in countries like these, where there are large numbers of outside aid workers and agencies operating, the numbers and locations of displaced persons are continuously changing and very difficult to track.

Among the complex dynamics of this phenomenon is the nature of contemporary conflict. The UNHCR states the problem succinctly. "In many situations of severe instability, including those in Burundi, Colombia, Sri Lanka and northern Uganda, the dominant trend is one of short-term, short-distance, repetitive dislocation rather than large-scale displacement into camps. It is often extremely difficult to distinguish between displaced and non-displaced populations. . . ."[274]

Other problems explained in chapter 2 include recent tactics of social warfare such as the deliberate displacement of people within a country. Also, the use of identity cleansing makes it extremely difficult for the victims to cross borders and perfect an asylum claim once they have been driven out of their home community.

Yet another difficulty arises from the fact that the number of internally displaced persons who find their way into a government- or NGO-operated facility is often but the tip of the iceberg, since many persons in that situation will attempt to find family or friends with whom they can seek temporary shelter—people who may themselves be in difficult circumstances. Consider the following example from Sri Lanka. "According to government statistics, at the end of September 1995 there were 141,992 displaced families consisting of 570,453 persons. Of those, 37,532 families (152,275 persons) were housed in 483 welfare centers and 104,460 families (418,178 persons) were with families and relatives."[275] Family or friends often can help only for a short time. Many others are even less fortunate. Writing of Colombia, the IDMC observed that: "Typically, they flee from rural areas to shantytowns around larger towns and struggle to make a living. However, increasing control by paramilitary groups and crime-related violence often force the IDPs to flee again within the urban areas."[276] This population, then, is quite literally a moving target, hopefully hidden from those who would prey upon them or seek to use them politically, but also hidden from those who seek to identify and help them.

Particular Vulnerabilities of the Internally Displaced

Whatever the precise numbers, they are massive and the problem is increasing for a variety of reasons, including the growing tendency toward civil wars and other internal conflicts as compared to formal wars between nation-states. It is equally clear that the plight of the internally displaced may be even more challenging than that of refugees. At least, once refugees are able to reach a host country and successfully qualify for refugee status, they are presumably safe and, in some countries at least, may receive a degree of resettlement and integration assistance. However, for those who are internally displaced, there most often is no safe haven, and the protected situations that are identified are often only temporary, as conflicts move within the country and because, in some circumstances, the belligerents may seek to use the displaced persons for their own political or military purposes.

Apart from this broad reality, there are a range of more particular dangers faced by those internally displaced. Roberta Cohen and Francis Deng point out that:

> Of the world's populations at risk, internally displaced persons tend to be among the most desperate. They may be forcibly resettled on political or ethnic grounds or find themselves trapped in the midst of conflicts and in the direct path of armed attack and physical violence. On the run and without documents, they are easy targets for roundups, arbitrary detention, forced conscription, and sexual assaults. Uprooted from their homes and deprived of the resource base, many suffer from profound physical and psychological trauma. They are more often deprived of shelter, food, and health services than other members of the population. The U.S. Centers for Disease Control reports that death rates among the internally displaced have been as much as sixty times higher than those of nondisplaced within the same country. In fact, the highest mortality rates ever recorded during humanitarian emergencies have involved internally displaced persons.[277]

Currently, the clearest example of this situation is Darfur where, as chapter 2 explained, the displaced are being killed and the women who have not been murdered outright have become the prey for a variety of fighters and criminals. Certainly Colombia is another country where countless innocent displaced persons have been killed and others forced to try to subsist in conditions that pose high risks of injury or death and the likelihood of long-term serious diseases. The United Nations Special Rapporteur on the Situation of Human Rights and Fundamental Freedoms of Indigenous People, Rodolfo Stavenhagen, concluded in his 2004 report on his mission to Colombia that:

> At least 60 per cent of displaced women lack access to health services. Displaced children present high rates of malnutrition, respiratory diseases, diarrhoea and dehydration, and many of them are forced to migrate to urban areas to avoid recruitment by the armed groups. . . . The Special Rapporteur received reports of abuses and violations of the rights of indigenous women, who are frequently subjected to physical violence, usually accompanied by sexual assault, by the armed groups in the socio-political conflict.[278]

Because displaced persons are so scattered and fearful, it can be difficult even for those governments and aid organizations that can and want to provide assistance to do so. That is all the more true where the displaced continue to be vulnerable to attack, as in the case of Darfur. And for those governments that are trying to help, there are added challenges from attempting to serve these needy populations and prosecute armed conflict at the same time. The communities or regions of the country that are asked to play host to the displaced also face additional burdens at a time when it is often difficult for them to maintain their normal operations in a nation in conflict, with the economic, social, and environmental stresses that entails.

Those who are displaced face some specific issues in addition to the general challenges of food, shelter, safety, and health. One set of these problems comes from the fact that children have particular needs. Among the difficulties is that of ensuring that they continue to receive educational services. This is important not only because of its obvious significance for the children's development, but also because it provides some kind of routine and structured activity at a time in their lives when everything else is in turmoil. The scope and scale of these problems for children are often dramatic. For example, in the recent clash between Hezbollah and Israel, one estimate of displacement in Lebanon concluded: "The rough estimate is between three-quarters of a million and one million people, of whom 50% are children. The United Nations Interim Force in Lebanon (UNIFIL) reports that only 18% of those living in southern Lebanon remain."[279]

Related to this set of concerns about social issues is the challenge of attempting to maintain the identity and cohesiveness of families, or what is left of them, amidst the conditions of conflict. That includes, as is evident in the case of indigenous displaced persons in Colombia, the challenge of maintaining cultural identity. There is also the fact that the displaced often suffer property losses and are scattered such that it is difficult to ensure that property rights can be restored once the conflict has ended. Of course, where properties were deliberately destroyed as part of social and economic warfare, the effort to find a starting point for post-conflict discussions of property requires an ability to communicate with those who were driven out. The conflicts over property that remain can be intense where others— sometimes known as "secondary occupants"—have taken over property taken from or abandoned by those who had to take flight, as was true in Kosovo and Bosnia and Herzegovina.[280] Related to that problem is the need to locate the displaced as the conflict ends and demobilization begins, not only so they can rejoin other members of their family who have survived but were scattered by the conflict and reclaim their homes and places in their communities of origin, but also so that they can establish the bona fides to participate in public participation activities that may be part of efforts to construct a new government or restore the legitimacy and authority of the governing institutions that existed before the conflict.

It was for all these reasons that the United Nations Office for the Coordination of Humanitarian Affairs prepared its *Guiding Principles on Internal Displacement*.[281] However, despite the existence of the guiding principles, the challenges remain.

THE ENVIRONMENT, REFUGEES, DISPLACED PERSONS, AND OTHER CREATURES ON THE MOVE

Of course, when large numbers of people take flight, they have profound effects on natural communities, including sending other species into movement as well. That movement may be the obvious sort in which species simply must flee from fighting as they would from wildfires, to a movement toward extinction as animals are exploited to feed those engaged in the battles and other species are simply placed in habitats in which they are unlikely to survive. In conflict, even species and habitats that are considered protected in peacetime are ravaged. These actions present the full range of environmental warfare as described in chapter 2, from the deliberate use of the environment as a weapon, to the use of tactics that will clearly have a high impact on the environment, to the other end of the continuum, in which the ecosystems become collateral damage of the fighting.

The most recent settings in which such impacts are evident are in the Great Lakes region of Africa and in the conflicts in Central and South America. In these locations, multiple conflicts, some internal and some external in character, have moved back and forth across the same areas, bringing waves of destruction. But the movement of refugees from other countries and internally displaced persons within the same country have also had significant impacts.

> When the displaced flee to rural areas, they may do irreparable damage to ecosystems, especially if they have no other options but to strip surrounding forests and grasslands to satisfy their need for housing and fuel. In Rwanda, the damage done to Akagera National Park by internally displaced persons and returning refugees will have long-term economic consequences. The temporary settlement of internally displaced persons in 1994–95 within the Nyungwi and Gishweti forests in the western part of the country has damaged those protected areas as well.[282]

Studies done in Colombia, Nicaragua, Indonesia, Rwanda, and the Democratic Republic of the Congo have documented a wide range of devastation.[283] The damage is that much worse where the exploitation of resources is one of the reasons for the conflict, where the environment is deliberately used for tactical reasons, or where populations are intentionally driven into vulnerable habitats, and when other problems such as political corruption exacerbate the situation.[284]

Setting aside the other impacts, several of which are discussed in chapters 2 and 5, even the movement of refugees and internally displaced persons who have no destructive motive and only seek to survive can have devastating effects. That is particularly true if there are other populations in the vicinity of refugees or internally displaced people who are also driven by conflict to seek food and fuel from otherwise protected animal species and national forest or park lands. When forests are denuded even by those just attempting to survive, the effects are well known, including erosion, damage to soil composition, loss of cooling, loss of protection for streams and rivers and the species they support, loss of animal cover, and, in some cases, exacerbation of desertification.

Losses to animal populations and habitat have been documented in several countries. For example:

- "In 1994, some 850,000 refugees were living around Virunga National Park, partly or completely deforesting some three hundred square kilometers of the park in a desperate search for food and firewood. Up to 40,000 people entered the park every day, taking out between 410 and 770 tons of forest products."[285]
- "Liberia's civil war has forced rural people to hunt duikers . . . , pygmy hippos . . . , forest elephants . . . , and chimpanzees . . . for food."[286]
- "In the Democratic Republic of the Congo, civil war has stopped efforts to protect the last habitat of the pygmy chimpanzee, or bonobo. . . . Fewer than 15,000 of the apes survive, and they are increasingly threatened by local people who are being forced to depend on the forest for survival. This includes hunting of bonobos for bushmeat."[287]
- Park guards in Kahuzi-Biega National Park in the Democratic Republic of the Congo were disarmed by one of the factions involved in the fighting. Before the fighting, the park contained "86% of the world's population of eastern lowland gorilla. . . . A census . . . showed that during the period in which the guards were disarmed, 40% of the gorillas and 95% of the elephants that were present in the park in 1996 had been killed for their meat and ivory."[288]

Additionally, some of the protected lands were lost when they were converted to resettlement areas. Still other ecosystems are fragmented when roads are cut through the area or other development is undertaken for military or other purposes, as in Rwanda and Sri Lanka.[289] Such construction, with the increased human access and movement it entails, can break green corridors and block the movement of animals in their traditional life patterns. Roads, bridges, and the like also make it easier for those hunting for food to get to the animals they will kill. Additionally, poachers have used the opening of the protected areas for refugees and displaced persons as an opportunity to access previously protected zones that often have little conservation staff on hand to detect or arrest these predators. When cover is lost and natural food supplies are depleted by deforestation or hunting, animals must range further than their normal patterns, with increasing likelihood that they will confront humans. That, in turn, increases the chance that they will be killed for food or from a perceived need for protection.

The impact on the environment is not limited to rural areas. Cohen and Deng capture the urban challenge effectively.

Major urban centers, too, suffer serious consequences because of displacement. Urban populations may double or triple and overload social services, water supplies, and sanitation facilities and thereby hasten the deterioration of the urban infrastructure, already weakened by conflict. Frequently, state services to the country as a whole become strained or even disrupted. Displacement thus "has ripple effects throughout entire societies," going far beyond the need for humanitarian assistance to those displaced.[290]

Cities that are themselves scenes of violence, as well as receiving communities for those in flight, are environments that endure incredible stresses of the sort described above. For example, many of those displaced by urban violence in the United States in the 1960s and after faced health and safety challenges in part because of the effects of destruction and degradation of the urban environment. The earlier volume, *Implementing Sustainable Development*, presents a case study on conditions in Detroit, where a number of problems associated with air pollution, such as high incidences of asthma, have plagued the city's children.

Another set of health problems related to overcrowding from displaced populations is associated with excessive stress on sanitation and potable water systems. Sanitation difficulties can foster rodents as well as mites and other pests that carry disease. Populations that must live in overcrowded conditions provide fertile ground for the spread of those diseases and present a difficult challenge to public health officials, even assuming that their offices are adequately supported and operating effectively during a period of conflict. Failures of electricity, so common in periods of conflict and in some developing countries, exacerbate a number of these difficulties. For all these reasons, the truism that urban environments are combinations of the natural environment and built environment carries far more implications for the three dimensions of sustainable development during and after conflict than is commonly recognized.

In sum, the movement of people across borders, within countries, and among species poses an increasingly complex set of problems during and after periods of conflict. The challenge is to provide sufficient protections of the environment to encourage receiving countries to continue to take refugees, to have enough resources available to support refugees and displaced persons, and to limit the impact on the environment so as to avoid long-term damage or injury beyond the level of ecological resilience.

It was this complex challenge that prompted a report prepared by UN-HCR's Engineering and Environmental Sciences Section based on research carried out in ten countries in 1997. The report, entitled *Refugee Operations and Environmental Management: Selected Lessons Learned*, was designed to be a sourcebook for governments in countries in conflict and others seeking to assist them.[291] In order to address these pressures on the environment, the report called for action at each stage of the conflict and its aftermath, including planning before a conflict is imminent, and discussed factors that could usefully be anticipated. The report identified a set of "cross-cutting themes" and a set of technical issue areas, all of which are important to address. The cross-cutting themes include "financial considerations, inter-agency co-ordination and co-operation, policy issues, support to local institutions/government, local participation, and gender." As to technical issues that frequently present themselves in such circumstances, the report underscores the importance of and provides recommendations for "forestry and natural resource management, community-based strategies for natural resource management, protected areas, domestic energy, organised energy supply, environmental education, refugee diet, and livestock."[292]

A DIFFERENT COMMUNITY AFTER THE FIGHTING ENDS

What is clear about all of these factors that are common to nations in conflict is that the community that is in place at the end of the conflict is not the same as what existed before. That is true of both the human community and the natural community. Many of the people who existed before, in some cases hundreds of thousands, are dead. Many others have sought asylum elsewhere, and even if some of them return after the conflict ends, they will be changed by the experiences they have endured, within their home country before their departure, during their flight as refugees, and in the host country that granted them asylum. Many more people who could not or would not leave, either because of their personal circumstances or changing international and national refugee policy, are often even more dramatically affected than the refugees. As internally displaced persons, they often endured worse conditions than the refugees and survived within the conflict throughout its duration.

Consider, for example, the case of Rwanda. The country's *Human Development Report* for 1999 provides a glimpse of the change in the human community before and after the genocide.

[B]y 1991 the population had reached nearly 7.2 million people. . . . [T]he demographic impact of the 1994 events [saw] the population dropping from 7.5 million in 1993 to 5.2 million in 1994. This drop in population of just over 30 percent was the result of both the genocide and the out-migration of a sizeable portion of the population (not including the internally displaced). Conversely, population growth from the end of 1994 to 1997 was equally dramatic, increasing by almost 1.5 million in less than three years, as a result of the large inflows of refugees and internal population growth. The percentage ratio of men to women in the population is also significant and disturbing. Estimates before 1994 showed males and females to account for 49 percent and 51 percent of the population, respectively. After 1994, the ratio changed to 46 and 54 percent respectively. In numerical terms, in 1993 there were 3.66 million males and 3.86 million females. By 1997, there were only 3.55 million males compared to 4.11 million females. Part of this decline is reflected in the precipitous rise in the numbers of female- and child-headed households. . . . The most recent population estimate for 1998 . . . places the population at 7.88 million.[293]

Because of conflict, the natural resources of the country were also dramatically altered. They were used in various ways to support the conflict and those who waged it. The flora and the fauna were themselves likely the object of deliberate destruction, and, if not deliberately targeted, experienced insults from tactics that would clearly have intensive environmental impacts. Still other resources were affected by those in flight, even though they intended no harm and sought only to provide food, fuel, and shelter for their families. On the other hand, other animals and plants were affected by those who deliberately exploited the chaos of conflict to poach animals and plunder forests and other natural resources.

Given these kinds of changes in communities in conflict, any model of post-conflict action that assumes that the human or natural communities are basically the same at the end of the conflict and incorporates such assumptions into post-conflict action is simply inappropriate. Unlike most of these models, a sustainable development approach makes no such assumptions and works from a realistic understanding of the conditions of social development, economic development, and environmental protection.

CONCLUSION

This chapter has considered that the kinds of social, environmental, and economic warfare presented in chapter 2 often have the consequence of sending people and other species into flight. The fact of that flight, particularly in the kinds of numbers that have been present in so many conflicts, poses serious social, economic, and environmental consequences. These tensions are present with respect to refugees and internally displaced persons.

Flight and displacement and their resulting effects are driven by the nature and location of the conflicts and others by policy decisions that target asylum seekers and internally displaced persons. Still other effects result from efforts to meet the needs of those who are displaced.

It is, of course, true that resilience is one of the hallmarks of the human species and of ecosystems as well. However, there are limits to resilience.

And even if those limits are not reached, the consequences of conflict and the effort to survive through it engender post-traumatic stress disorder that is present for many years and has profound effects as communities seek sustainable development after the conflict ends. Because this phenomenon is so important, chapter 4 addresses it in depth.

NOTES

1. Library of Congress, Federal Research Division, "Country Profile: Colombia," December 2004, 4, at http://lcweb2.loc.gov/frd/cs/cotoc.html (accessed December 26, 2006).

2. Thomas E. Skidmore and Peter H. Smith, *Modern Latin America*, 6th ed. (New York: Oxford University Press, 2005).

3. Andrés Solimano, "Introduction and Synthesis," in Andrés Solimano, ed., *Colombia: Essays on Conflict, Peace, and Development* (Washington, D.C.: World Bank, 2000), 1.

4. U.S. Department of State, "Background Note: Colombia," 2006 at www.state .gov/outofdate/bgn/c/626.htm (accessed December 26, 2006).

5. Library of Congress, "Country Profile: Colombia," 4.

6. U.S. Department of State, "Background Note: Colombia."

7. U.S. Department of State, "Background Note: Colombia."

8. United Nations High Commissioner for Refugees (UNHCR), *International Protection Considerations Regarding Colombian Asylum-Seekers and Refugees* (Geneva: UNHCR, 2005).

9. UNHCR, *International Protection Considerations*.

10. Solimano, "Introduction and Synthesis," 5.

11. United Nations High Commissioner for Refugees (UNHCR), *Colombia: UNHCR's Protection and Assistance Programme for IDPs and Refugees* (New York: UNHCR, 2004).

12. Karl H. Schwerin, "The Indian Populations of Latin America," in Jan Knippers Black, ed., *Latin America, Its Problems and its Promise: A Multidisciplinary Introduction* (Boulder, CO: Westview, 1991), 39.

13. Library of Congress, "Country Profile: Colombia," 1.

14. Library of Congress, "Country Profile: Colombia," 7.

15. Skidmore and Smith, *Modern Latin America*, 6th ed., 222.

16. Library of Congress, "Country Profile: Colombia."

17. John D. Martz, "Venezuela, Colombia, and Ecuador," in Jan Knippers Black, ed., *Latin America, Its Problems and its Promise: A Multidisciplinary Introduction* (Boulder, CO: Westview, 1991), 439.

18. Martz, "Venezuela, Colombia, and Ecuador," 429.

19. E. Bradford Burns, *Latin America: A Concise Interpretative History*, 6th ed. (Englewood Cliffs, NJ: Prentice Hall, 1994), 29.

20. Burns, *Latin America: A Concise Interpretative History*, 29.

21. Library of Congress, "Country Profile: Colombia."

22. Skidmore and Smith, *Modern Latin America*, 6th ed., 224.

23. Skidmore and Smith, *Modern Latin America*, 6th ed., 225; Martz, "Venezuela, Colombia, and Ecuador," 429.

24. Skidmore and Smith, *Modern Latin America*, 6th ed., 229.

25. Skidmore and Smith, *Modern Latin America*, 6th ed., 230.

26. Skidmore and Smith, *Modern Latin America*, 6th ed., 233.

27. Skidmore and Smith, *Modern Latin America*, 6th ed., 233.

28. Etienne G. Krug, Linda L. Dahlberg, James A. Mercy, Anthony B. Zwi, and Rafael Lozano, eds., *World Report on Violence and Health* (Geneva: World Health Organization, 2002), 221.

29. UNHCR, *International Protection Considerations*, 4.

30. Library of Congress, "Country Profile: Colombia," 6.

31. Library of Congress, "Country Profile: Colombia," 8.

32. UNHCR, *International Protection Considerations*, 5.

33. World Bank, *World Development Report 2006* (New York: Oxford University Press, 2005), 278.

34. Solimano, "Introduction and Synthesis," 2.

35. United Nations Development Programme, *El Conflicto, Callejón sin Salida, Informe Nacional de Desarrollo Humano para Colombia—2003* (Bogotá: UNDP 2003), 10. (This passage was translated by Claudia María Vargas. The original in Spanish reads as follows: "La paz sí cuesta. Pero la guerra cuesta mucho más.")

36. Skidmore and Smith, *Modern Latin America*, 6th ed., 224.

37. UNDP, *El Conflicto*.

38. Thomas E. Skidmore and Peter H. Smith, *Modern Latin America*, 5th ed. (New York: Oxford University Press, 2001), 392.

39. UNHCR, *International Protection Considerations*, 5.

40. UNHCR, *International Protection Considerations*, 5.

41. UNHCR, *International Protection Considerations*, 5.

42. Skidmore and Smith, *Modern Latin America*, 6th ed.

43. Alain Touraine, Latin America: From Populism toward Social Democracy, in Menno Vellinga, ed., *Social Democracy in Latin America: Prospects for Change* (Boulder, CO: Westview, 1993), 298.

44. Skidmore and Smith, *Modern Latin America*, 6th ed.; UNDP, *El Conflicto*, 25.

45. Skidmore and Smith, *Modern Latin America*, 6th ed., 241.

46. Martz, "Venezuela, Colombia, and Ecuador," 439.

47. Skidmore and Smith, *Modern Latin America*, 6th ed., 242.

48. Juan Alberto Fuentes, "Violent Conflict and Human Development in Latin America: The Cases of Colombia, El Salvador and Guatemala," *Human Development Report 2005*, Human Development Report Office, Occasional Paper, United Nations Development Programme, 2005/10, 72. See also Martz, "Venezuela, Colombia, and Ecuador," 438.

49. Burns, *Latin America: A Concise Interpretative History*, 234.

50. Burns, *Latin America: A Concise Interpretative History*, 234.

51. Internal Displacement Monitoring Centre (IDMC), *Colombia: Government "Peace Process" Cements Injustice for IDPs: A Profile of the Internal Displacement Situation* (Geneva: IDMC, 2006), 53.

52. Caroline Moser, "Violence in Colombia: Building Sustainable Peace and Social Capital," in Andrés Solimano, ed., *Colombia: Essays on Conflict, Peace, and Development* (Washington, D.C.: World Bank, 2000), 10.

53. María D. Álvarez, "Forests in the Time of Violence: Conservation Implications of the Colombian War," in Steven V. Price, ed., *War and Tropical Forests: Conservation in Areas of Armed Conflict* (Binghamton, NY: Food Products Press, 2003), 51.

54. UNDP, *El Conflicto*, 24.

55. Marcelo Cavarozzi, "The Left in South America: Politics as the Only Option," in Menno Vellinga, ed., *Social Democracy in Latin America: Prospects for Change* (Boulder, CO: Westview, 1993), 157.

56. Skidmore and Smith, *Modern Latin America*, 6th ed., 244.

57. UNHCR, *International Protection Considerations*, 6.

58. UNHCR, *International Protection Considerations*, 7.

59. Skidmore and Smith, *Modern Latin America*, 6th ed., 244–245.

60. UNHCR, *International Protection Considerations*, 6.

61. IDMC, *Colombia: Government "Peace Process" Cements Injustice*, 15.

62. IDMC, *Colombia: Government "Peace Process" Cements Injustice*, 15–18.

63. *Economist*, "Drugs, War, and Democracy," *Economist*, April 19, 2001, at www.economist.com/surveys/PrinterFriendly.cfm?story_id=5 (accessed November 14, 2006).

64. UNHCR, *International Protection Considerations*, 6.

65. UNHCR, *Colombia: UNHCR's Protection and Assistance Programme.*

66. UNHCR, *International Protection Considerations*, 4.

67. IDMC, *Colombia: Government "Peace Process" Cements Injustice.*

68. IDMC, *Colombia: Government "Peace Process" Cements Injustice*, 155.

69. Fernando Henrique Cardoso, "Challenges of Social Democracy in Latin America," in Menno Vellinga, ed., *Social Democracy in Latin America: Prospects for Change* (Boulder, CO: Westview, 1993), 281.

70. Skidmore and Smith, *Modern Latin America*, 6th ed., 250.

71. Skidmore and Smith, *Modern Latin America*, 6th ed., 248.

72. Skidmore and Smith, *Modern Latin America*, 5th ed., 392.

73. Cavarozzi, "Left in South America," 158.

74. Cavarozzi, "Left in South America," 158.

75. Jonathan M. Winer and Trifin J. Roule, "Follow the Money: The Finance of Illicit Resource Extraction," in Ian Bannon and Paul Collier, eds., *Natural Resources and Violent Conflict: Options and Actions* (Washington, D.C.: World Bank, 2003), 205.

76. Winer and Roule, "Follow the Money," 206.

77. IDMC, *Colombia: Government "Peace Process" Cements Injustice*, 50.

78. Skidmore and Smith, *Modern Latin America*, 6th ed., 433.

79. IDMC, *Colombia: Government "Peace Process" Cements Injustice.*

80. UNHCR, *International Protection Considerations*, 6.

81. United Nations Development Programme, *Human Development Report 2005* (New York: UNDP, 2005) 160.

82. United Nations High Commissioner for Refugees, *2005 Global Refugee Trends* (Geneva: UNHCR, 2006), 9.

83. UNDP, *Human Development Report 2005*, 294.

84. Internal Displacement Monitoring Center, *Internal Displacement: Global Overview of Trends and Developments in 2005* (Geneva: IDMC, 2006), 6. (Hereafter IDMC, *Internal Displacement 2005*.)

85. IDMC, *Colombia: Government "Peace Process" Cements Injustice*, 19.

86. UNHCR, *2005 Global Refugee Trends*, 10.

87. Moser, "Violence in Colombia," 17.

88. UNHCR, *Colombia: UNHCR's Protection and Assistance Programme*.

89. Moser, "Violence in Colombia," 15.

90. Moser, "Violence in Colombia," 17.

91. UNDP, *Human Development Report 2005*, 160.

92. Moser, "Violence in Colombia," 34, citing D. Meertens and N. Segura-Escobar, "Gender, Violence and Displacement in Colombia," *Singapore Journal of Tropical Geography*, 17, no. 2 (1996): 165–178.

93. U.S. Department of State, "Background Note: Colombia."

94. Alfredo Sarmiento Gómez, Lucía Mina Rosero, Carlos Alonso Malaver, and Sandra Álvarez Toro, "Background Papers, *Human Development Report 2003*, Colombia: Human Development Progress towards the Millennium Development Goals," Occasional Paper, United Nations Development Programme, June 2003, 15.

95. U.S. Department of State, "Background Note: Colombia."

96. UNHCR, *International Protection Considerations*, 4.

97. Library of Congress, "Country Profile: Colombia," 6.

98. UNHCR, *International Protection Considerations*, 33.

99. IDMC, *Colombia: Government "Peace Process" Cements Injustice*.

100. UNHCR, "Colombia: Indigenous Day," UNHCR Briefing Notes, August 8, 2006, at www.unhcr.org/news/NEWS/44d875994.html.

101. UNHCR, "UNHCR Urges Armed Groups to Leave Colombia's Indigenous Peoples Alone," UNHCR News Stories, August 9, 2006, at www.unhcr.org/cgi-bin/texis/vtx/print?tbl=NEWS&id=44d9ef9c4.

102. IDMC, *Colombia: Government "Peace Process" Cements Injustice*, 81.

103. Schwerin, "Indian Populations of Latin America," 46–47.

104. IDMC, *Colombia: Government "Peace Process" Cements Injustice*, 52.

105. Gillete Hall, Heather Marie Layton, and Joseph Shapiro, "Introduction," in Gillete Hall and Harry Anthony Patrinos, eds., *Indigenous Peoples, Poverty and Human Development in Latin America* (New York: Palgrave Macmillan, 2006), 8.

106. UN General Assembly, "Report to the General Assembly on the First Session of the Human Rights Council," June 30, 2006, at http://daccessdds.un.org/doc/UNDOC/LTD/G06/128/65/PDF/G0612865.pdf?OpenElement (accessed December 15, 2006).

107. Rudolfo Stavenhagen, "Indigenous Issues: Human Rights and Indigenous Issues—Mission to Colombia," report of the Special Rapporteur on the Situation of Human Rights and Fundamental Freedoms of Indigenous People, November 10, 2004, 7, at www.afsc.org/colombia/learn-about/documents/UN_Report_on_Indigenous.pdf (accessed December 15, 2006).

108. Stavenhagen, "Indigenous Issues," 5.

109. Stavenhagen, "Indigenous Issues," 9.

110. Stavenhagen, "Indigenous Issues," 9–10.

111. Hall et al., "Introduction," 16.

112. Hall et al., "Introduction," 17.

113. Hall et al., "Introduction," 22.

114. UNHCR, "Little for Colombia's ethnic Awá to Celebrate on World Indigenous Day," UNHCR News Stories, August 8, 2006, at http://www.unhcr.org/cgi-bin/texis/vtx/print?tbl=NEWS&id=44d8a9a54 (accessed August 14, 2006).

115. IDMC, *Colombia: Government "Peace Process" Cements Injustice*, 53–54.

116. UNHCR, "UNHCR Urges Armed Groups."

117. UNHCR, "Colombia: Indigenous Murders," UNHCR Briefing Notes, August 11, 2006, at www.unhcr.org/cgi-bin/texis/vtx/print?tbl=NEWS&id=44dc609b7 (accessed August 14, 2006).

118. UNHCR, "Colombia: Indigenous Murders."

119. IDMC, *Colombia: Government "Peace Process" Cements Injustice*, 50.

120. UNHCR, "Colombia: Indigenous Day."

121. IDMC, *Colombia: Government "Peace Process" Cements Injustice*, 71.

122. Gómez et al., "Background Papers, *Human Development Report 2003*," 15–18.

123. IDMC, *Colombia: Government "Peace Process" Cements Injustice*, 71.

124. Gómez et al., "Background Papers, *Human Development Report 2003*," 4.

125. Flavia Bustreo, Eleonora Genovese, Elio Omobono, Herik Axelsson, and Ian Bannon, *Improving Child Health in Post-conflict Countries: Can the World Bank Contribute?* (Washington, D.C.: World Bank, 2005).

126. IDMC, *Colombia: Government "Peace Process" Cements Injustice*, 148.

127. IDMC, *Colombia: Government "Peace Process" Cements Injustice*, 148.

128. Library of Congress, "Country Profile: Colombia," 8.

129. IDMC, *Colombia: Government "Peace Process" Cements Injustice*, 124.

130. UNICEF, *The State of the World's Children 2006: Excluded and Visible* (New York: UNICEF, 2005), 98.

131. IDMC, *Colombia: Government "Peace Process" Cements Injustice*, 147.

132. UNHCR, "Colombian Indigenous Seek Refuge from Violence in Ecuador," UNHCR, November 23, 2006, at: www.unhcr.org/cgi-bin/texis/vtx/print?tbl=NEWS&id=4565adac4 (accessed November 27, 2006).

133. IDMC, *Colombia: Government "Peace Process" Cements Injustice*, 159.

134. UNDP, *El Conflicto*, 124.

135. UNDP, *El Conflicto*, 122.

136. IDMC, *Colombia: Government "Peace Process" Cements Injustice*, 159.

137. Bustreo et al., *Improving Child Health*, 12.

138. UNDP, *El Conflicto*, 106.

139. Fuentes, "Violent Conflict."

140. World Bank, *World Development Report 2006: Equity and Development* (New York: Oxford University Press, 2005) 294.

141. UNDP, *El Conflicto*, 106.

142. UNDP, *Human Development Report 2005*, 161.

143. IDMC, *Internal Displacement 2005*, 29.

144. UNDP, *Human Development Report 2005*, 159.

145. IDMC, *Colombia: Government "Peace Process" Cements Injustice*, 174.

146. IDMC, *Colombia: Government "Peace Process" Cements Injustice*, 174.

147. UNDP, *Human Development Report 2005*, 159.

148. UNDP, *El Conflicto*, 105–106.

149. UNHCR, *International Protection Considerations*, 34.

150. UNHCR, *International Protection Considerations,* 34–35.

151. UNICEF, *The State of the World's Children 2005: Childhood under Threat* (New York: UNICEF, 2004) 45.

152. UNDP, *El Conflicto,* 252.

153. UNDP, *El Conflicto,* 252.

154. UNDP, *El Conflicto,* 251.

155. UNDP, *El Conflicto,* 258.

156. UNDP, *El Conflicto,* 258 (original in Spanish; translated by Claudia María Vargas).

157. UNDP, *El Conflicto,* 256.

158. Fuentes, "Violent Conflict," 11–12.

159. *Economist,* "Drugs, War, and Democracy."

160. UNDP, *Human Development Report 2005,* 161.

161. UNDP, *Human Development Report 2005,* 162.

162. IDMC, *Internal Displacement 2005,* 34.

163. IDMC, *Internal Displacement 2005,* 42.

164. Álvarez, "Forests in the Time of Violence."

165. IDMC, *Colombia: Government "Peace Process" Cements Injustice,* 163.

166. Bustreo et al., *Improving Child Health,* 13.

167. UNDP, *Human Development Report 2005,* 155.

168. United Nations High Commissioner for Refugees, "Convention and Protocol Relating to the Status of Refugees," providing documents and information on the Convention Relating to the Status of Refugees, 189 U.N.T.S. 150 (1951) and the Protocol Relating to the Status of Refugees, 606 U.N.T.S. 267 (1967), at www.unhcr .org/protect/3c0762ea4.html (accessed December 26, 2006).

169. United Nations High Commissioner for Refugees, *State of the World's Refugees 2006* (New York: UNHCR, 2006).

170. UNHCR, *State of the World's Refugees 2006,* 10.

171. UNHCR, "Refugees by the Numbers 2006," at www.unhcr.org/cgi-bin/texis/ vtx/basics/opendoc.htm?tbl=BASICS&id=3b028097c (accessed December 26, 2006).

172. UNHCR, "Refugees by the Numbers 2006."

173. UNHCR, "Refugees by the Numbers 2006."

174. UNHCR, *State of the World's Refugees 2006,* 204.

175. UNHCR, *State of the World's Refugees 2006,* chapter 2.

176. UNHCR, *State of the World's Refugees 2006,* 210.

177. UNHCR, *State of the World's Refugees 2006,* 212.

178. UNHCR, *State of the World's Refugees 2006,* 212.

179. UNHCR, *State of the World's Refugees 2006,* 203.

180. UNHCR, *State of the World's Refugees 2006,* 203.

181. UNHCR, *State of the World's Refugees 2006,* 204.

182. UNHCR, *State of the World's Refugees 2006,* 204.

183. Quoted in Bo Cooper, "Procedures for Expedited Removal and Asylum Screening under the Illegal Immigration Reform and Immigrant Responsibility Act of 1996," *Connecticut Law Review* 19 (Summer 1997): 1501.

184. A number of researchers have explored aspects of this problem. James C. Hathaway and R. Alexander Neve, "Making International Refugee Law Relevant

Again: A Proposal for Collectivized and Solution-Oriented Protection," *Harvard Human Rights Journal* 10 (Spring 1997): 115–211; Joan Fitzpatrick, "Revitalizing the 1951 Refugee Convention," *Harvard Human Rights Journal* 9 (Spring 1996): 229–253; Dennis McNamara, "The Protection of Refugees and the Responsibilities of States: Engagement or Abdication?" *Harvard Human Rights Journal* 11 (Spring 1998): 355–361.

185. For an in-depth discussion of flow of refugees from Vietnam, see Roger Winter, *Terms of Refuge: The Indochinese Exodus and the International Response* (New York: Zed Books, 1998).

186. UNHCR, *State of the World's Refugees 2006*, 19.

187. See, e.g., Illegal Immigration Reform and Immigrant Responsibility Act, P.L. 104-208, 8 U.S.C. §1101, et seq. This statute was adopted in 1996, a full five years before the 9/11 attacks and during the Clinton administration.

188. Gil Loescher, *Beyond Charity: International Cooperation and the Global Refugee Crisis* (New York: Oxford University Press, 1993), 44.

189. U.S. Senate, Committee on the Judiciary, *U.S. Immigration Law and Policy: 1952–1986*, 100th Cong., 1st Sess. (1987).

190. Winter, *Terms of Refuge*.

191. Loescher, *Beyond Charity*, 59.

192. See, e.g., Martha Honey, *Hostile Acts: U.S. Policy in Costa Rica in the 1980s* (Gainesville: University Press of Florida, 1994).

193. See Lawrence E. Walsh, *Iran-Contra: The Final Report of the Independent Counsel* (New York: Random House, 1993).

194. Walsh, *Iran-Contra*, xiii–xiv.

195. See, e.g., U.S. Senate, *Central American Migration to the United States*, hearing before the Subcommittee on Immigration and Refugee Affairs of the Committee on the Judiciary, 101st Cong., 1st Sess. (1989); U.S. House of Representatives, *Central American Asylum-Seekers*, hearing before the Subcommittee on Immigration, Refugees, and International Law of the Committee on the Judiciary, 101st Cong., 1st Sess. (1989).

196. U.S. Senate, *Providing for a GAO Study on Conditions of Displaced Salvadorans and Nicaraguans, and For Other Purposes*, report of the Committee on the Judiciary to accompany S. 332 as amended, 100th Cong., 1st Sess. (1987), 3.

197. U.S. Senate, *Providing for a GAO Study*, 4.

198. U.S. Senate, *Consultation on Refugee Admissions for Fiscal Year 1989*, hearing before the Committee on the Judiciary, 100th Cong., 2nd Sess. (1989), 18.

199. *American Baptist Churches v. Thornburgh*, 760 F.Supp. 796 (NDCA 1991).

200. *American Baptist Churches v. Thornburgh*, 799.

201. See Rosemary Byrne and Andrew Shacknove, "The Safe Country Notion in European Asylum Law," *Harvard Human Rights Journal* 9 (Spring 1996): 185–228.

202. *Gailius v. Immigration and Naturalization Service*, 147 F.3d 34 (1st Cir. 1998).

203. *Osorio v. Immigration and Naturalization Service*, 18 F.3d 1017, 1029 (2nd Cir. 1994).

204. Janice D. Villiers, "Closed Borders, Closed Ports: The Plight of Haitians Seeking Political Asylum in the United States," *Brooklyn Law Review* 60 (Fall 1994): 841–901.

205. P.L. 104-208, 110 Stat. 3009, 8 U.S.C. §1101, et seq.

206. See U.S. General Accounting Office, *Illegal Aliens: Changes in the Process of Denying Aliens Entry into the United States* (Washington, D.C.: GAO, 1998).

207. Bo Cooper, "Procedures for Expedited Removal and Asylum Screening under the Illegal Immigration Reform and Immigrant Responsibility Act of 1996," *Connecticut Law Review* 19 (Summer 1997): 1501–1524.

208. Gerald H. Stobo, "The Canadian Refugee Determination System," *Texas International Law Journal* 29 (Summer 1994): 384.

209. Named after Fridtjof Nansen, who was the first High Commissioner for Refugees under the League of Nations.

210. "A Reluctant Welcome," *Maclean's*, January 4, 1993, 26.

211. The IRB summarized those developments in its priorities for 1999–2000: "The Immigration and Refugee Board (IRB) is an independent agency which was created by the adoption of *An Act to amend the Immigration Act, 1976* and to amend other acts in consequence thereof, S.C. 1988, c. 35 (commonly referred to as C-55), which came into force on January 1, 1989. Further amendments were brought to the *Immigration Act* with the coming into force of S.C. 1992, c. 49 (commonly referred to as C-86) on February 1, 1993, and S.C. 1995, c. 15 (commonly referred to as C-44) on July 10, 1995. In its present form, the IRB is composed of three divisions, each with its own tribunal; these divisions are the Convention Refugee Determination Division (CRDD), the Immigration Appeal Division (IAD) and the Adjudication Division (AD)." Immigration and Refugees Board of Canada (1999: 1).

212. Stobo, "Canadian Refugee Determination System," 383.

213. Canadian Council for Refugees, *Refugees in Canada: Canadian Refugee and Humanitarian Immigration Policy 1997 to mid-1998* (Montreal: Canadian Council for Refugees, 1998), 2.

214. Legislative Advisory Review Group, Citizenship and Immigration Canada, *Not Just Numbers: A Canadian Framework for Future Immigration* (Ottawa: Citizenship and Immigration Canada, 1998).

215. Citizenship and Immigration Canada publicized the report and promptly called for comment on the proposals. Citizenship and Immigration Canada, *Building on a Strong Foundation for the 21st Century: New Directions for Refugee Policy and Legislation* (Ottawa: Citizenship and Immigration Canada, 1999), at http://cicnet .ci.gc.ca/english/about/policy/lr/e_lr.html. Citizenship and Immigration Canada, "Minister Lucienne Robillard Announces New Directions for Immigration and Refugee Protection Legislation and Policy," news release 99-01, January 6, 1999, at www.cic.gc.ca/english/press/99/9901-pre.html (accessed December 26, 2006); Citizenship and Immigration Canada, "Strengthening the Refugee Protection System," news release 99-05, January 6, 1999, at www.cic.gc.ca/english/press/99/9905-pre .html (accessed December 26, 2006).

216. Elinor Caplan, "Notes for an Address to the Maytree Foundation Trends in Global Migration Forum," Toronto, January 12, 2000 at http://cicnet.ci.gc.ca/english/ press/speech/maytree-e.html (accessed March 2000).

217. Elinor Caplan, "Statement by Minister Elinor Caplan on Illegal Human Smuggling to Canada," Toronto, August 11, 1999, 1 at http://cicnet.ci.gc.ca/english/ press/speech/smuggle-e.html (accessed March 2000).

218. Elinor Caplan, "Remarks to the Canadian Club," Vancouver, British Columbia, September 9, 1999, 4 at http://cicnet.ci.gc.ca/english/press/speech/canclub-e .html (accessed March 2000).

219. Elinor Caplan, "Remarks to a News Conference on Year 2000 Immigration Levels," November 1, 1999, 2 at http://cicnet.ci.gc.ca/english/press/levels2000-e .html (accessed March 2000).

220. Elinor Caplan, "Notes for an Address to the Maytree Foundation Trends in Global Migration Forum," 7 at http://cicnet.ci.gc.ca/english/press/speech/maytree-e.html (accessed March 2000).

221. Citizenship and Immigration Canada, *Building on a Strong Foundation*, 41–42.

222. See, e.g., Elinor Caplan, "Notes for an Address to the Canadian Bar Association, B.C. Immigration Section Refugee Symposium," Vancouver, British Columbia, November 26, 1999, at http://cicnet.ci.gc.ca/english/press/speech/cha-e.html (accessed March 2000). The document has since been removed from the Internet, but the speech is referenced in CBC News, "Immigration Minister Ready to Go after People Smugglers," November 26, 1999, at www.cbc.ca/news/story/1999/11/26/bc_immigration991126.html (accessed October 28, 2006).

223. See, e.g., Immigration and Refugees Board of Canada, *1999/2000 Report on Planning and Priorities: Regulatory Initiatives* (Ottawa: Immigration and Refugee Board, 1999).

224. Kenneth Regensburg, "Refugee Law Reconsidered: Reconciling Humanitarian Objectives with the Protectionist Agendas of Western Europe and the United States," *Cornell Internal Law Journal* 29 (1996): 225–261.

225. Claus Thiery, "The Schengen Agreements," Centre for International and European Law on Immigration and Asylum, University of Konstanze, paper prepared for workshop entitled "Managing Migration in the 21st Century," 1998; Netherlands Ministry of Foreign Affairs, "The Netherlands and the Schengen Agreement," 1999.

226. Juliet M. Hanna, "Implementing the Dublin Convention on Asylum," *Columbia Journal of European Law* 4 (Winter/Spring 1998): 182–191.

227. Amy L. Elson, "Baltic State Membership in the European Union: Developing a Common Asylum and Immigration Policy," *Indiana Journal of Global Legal Studies* 5 (Fall 1997): 317–339.

228. See Rosemary Byrne and Andrew Shacknove, "The Safe Country Notion"; Regensburg, "Refugee Law Reconsidered."

229. Interviews by the authors with the Director of Immigration and Head of Refugee Services, Ministry of Social Services, Helsinki, Finland, July 1994, and with Head of Refugee Section, Ministry of Culture, Stockholm, Sweden, July 1994.

230. Interviews with the Director of Immigration and Head of Refugee Services, Finland, and with Head of Refugee Section, Sweden.

231. Quoted in Byrne and Shacknove, "The Safe Country Notion," 186 n. 5.

232. Quoted in Byrne and Shacknove, "The Safe Country Notion," 189.

233. Judge E. Stendijk, "Interim Report of the Working Party on Chain Refoulement," 1998 Conference of the International Association of Refugee Law Judges (IARLJ), 2, at www.cisr.gc.ca/IARLJ/wp-cr.htm (accessed November 26, 1999).

234. Byrne and Shacknove, "The Safe Country Notion," 192.

235. Byrne and Shacknove, "The Safe Country Notion," 192.

236. Jacek Chlebny, "Interim Report of the Working Party on Asylum Procedures," 1998 Conference of the International Association of Refugee Law Judges (IARLJ), at www.irb.gc.ca/IARLJ/wp-asylum.htm (accessed November 26, 1999).

237. European Community, *Treaty of Amsterdam Amending the Treaty on European Union, the Treaties Establishing the European Community and Related Acts, Official Journal C 340, 10 November 1997,* at http://eur-lex.europa.eu/en/treaties/dat/ 11997E/htm/11997E.html#0093010004 (accessed October 29, 2006). European Community, *Treaty Establishing a Constitution for Europe, Official Journal C310, 16 December 2004,* at http://eur-lex.europa.eu/JOHtml.do?uri=OJ:C:2004:310:SOM:EN: HTML (accessed October 29, 2006).

238. See David Cole, *Enemy Aliens: Double Standards and Constitutional Freedoms in the War on Terrorism* (New York: New Press, 2003).

239. Office of the Inspector General, U.S. Department of Justice, *The September 11 Detainees: A Review of the Treatment of Aliens Held on Immigration Charges in Connection with the Investigation of the September 11 Attacks* (Washington, D.C.: U.S. Department of Justice, 2003), at www.usdoj.gov/oig/special/03_06/full.pdf (accessed November 1, 2003).

240. *Benslimane v. Gonzales,* 430 F.3d 828, 829-830 (7th Cir. 2005).

241. *Qun Wang v. Attorney General,* 423 F.3d 260, 270 (3rd Cir. 2005).

242. Division B of the Emergency Supplemental Appropriations Act for Defense, the Global War on Terror, and Tsunami Relief, 2005, P.L. 109-13, 119 Stat. 231 (2005).

243. United States Commission on International Religious Freedom, *Asylum Seekers in Expedited Removal: A Study Authorized by Section 605 of the International Religious Freedom Act of 1998,* "Executive Summary" (Washington, D.C.: United States Commission on International Religious Freedom, 2005), 4–5.

244. Michael Powell, "Pakistani Exodus to Canada Brings Waits, Crowding," *Washington Post,* February 1, 2003, A03; "Vermont Refugee Aid Group Says Policy Thins Resources," *New York Times,* March 13, 2003, A17.

245. Citizenship and Immigration in Canada, *Report on Plans and Priorities, 2003–2004* (Ottawa: Citizenship and Immigration Canada, 2003), 31.

246. *Plans and Priorities, 2003–2004,* 9.

247. *Plans and Priorities, 2003–2004,* 35.

248. Matthew Behrens, "Growing Concerns about Civil Liberties in Canada," *VAST Quarterly* 4 (September 2003): 8–9.

249. *In the Matter of Jaballah,* 2003 A.C.W.S.J. LEXIS 4031 (Federal Court Trial Division, Toronto 2003), 12.

250. *Charkaouri v. Canada (Citizenship and Immigration),* 2007 SCC 9 (2007).

251. See, generally, Michael Jackson, *Prisoners of Isolation: Solitary Confinement in Canada* (Toronto: University of Toronto Press, 1983). See also Maria A. Luise, "Solitary Confinement: Legal and Psychological Considerations," *New England Journal on Criminal and Civil Confinement* 15 (Summer 1989): 301–324; Stuart Grassian and Nancy Friedman, "Effects of Sensory Deprivation in Psychiatric Seclusion and Solitary Confinement," *International Journal of Law and Psychiatry* 8 (1986): 49–65.

252. Bryan B. Walton, "The Eighth Amendment and Psychological Implications of Solitary Confinement," *Law and Psychology Review* 21 (Spring 1997): 271–288.

253. *Winters v. Legal Services Society,* File No. 1999 Can. Sup. Ct. LEXIS 57, Cory, J., at 45-47.

254. Sophie Harkat, quoted in Sue Bailey, "Detainees' Relatives Demand Ottawa Act," *Toronto Star,* August 23, 2003, A8.

255. Tim Naumetz, "Families, Friends of Detained Muslims Lead Protest," *Ottawa Citizen*, August 26, 2003, A4.

256. *Plans and Priorities, 2003–2004*, 8.

257. *Plans and Priorities, 2003–2004*, 35.

258. See, e.g., Carmen Lawrence, "Mental Illness in Detained Asylum Seekers," *Lancet* 364 (October 2004): 1283–1284; P. N. Bhagwati, "Human Rights and Immigration Detention in Australia: Report of Justice P N Bhagwati, Regional Advisor for Asia and the Pacific of the United Nations High Commissioner for Human Rights," at www.unhchr.ch/huricane/huricane.nsf/0/bc4c8230f96684c8c1256c070032f5f1/$FILE/Report.doc (accessed November 2, 2006).

259. UNHCR, *State of the World's Refugees 2006*, 5.

260. UNHCR, *State of the World's Refugees 2006*, 32–33.

261. UNHCR, *State of the World's Refugees 2006*, 33.

262. UNHCR, *State of the World's Refugees 2006*, 24.

263. UNHCR, *State of the World's Refugees, 2006*, 2.

264. UNHCR, *State of the World's Refugees 2006*, 2.

265. UNHCR, *State of the World's Refugees 2006*, 35–37.

266. UNHCR, *State of the World's Refugees 2006*, 33.

267. UNHCR, *State of the World's Refugees 2006*, 14.

268. UNHCR, *State of the World's Refugees 2006*, 17.

269. UNHCR, "Who Is an Internally Displaced Person," at www.unhcr.org/protect/3b84c7e23.html (accessed November 10, 2006).

270. UNHCR, "Who Is an Internally Displaced Person."

271. IDMC, *Colombia: Government "Peace Process" Cements Injustice*, 10.

272. IDMC, *Colombia: Government "Peace Process" Cements Injustice*, 10.

273. UNHCR, *State of the World's Refugees 2006*, 20.

274. UNHCR, *State of the World's Refugees 2006*, 14.

275. Roberta Cohen and Francis M. Deng, eds., *The Forsaken People: Case Studies of the Internally Displaced* (Washington, D.C.: Brookings, 1998), 361.

276. IDMC, *Colombia: Government "Peace Process" Cements Injustice*, 10.

277. Roberta Cohen and Francis M. Deng, *Masses in Flight: The Global Crisis of Internal Displacement* (Washington, D.C.: Brookings, 1998), 2.

278. Rodolfo Stavenhagen, *Report of the Special Rapporteur on the Situation of Human Rights and Fundamental Freedoms of Indigenous People, Addendum: Mission to Colombia* (New York: United Nations Commission on Human Rights, 2004), 18, at www.iwgia.org/graphics/Synkron-Library/Documents/InternationalProcesses/UNCHR/Specialrapporteur/SpecialrapperteurColombia.pdf (accessed November 10, 2006).

279. Brookings Institution—University of Bern Project on Internal Displacement, "Seminar: Displacement, Protection of Civilians, and the Law of Armed Conflict in the Current Middle East Crisis," Washington, D.C., Brookings Institution, August 15, 2006, 2–3, at www.brook.edu/fp/projects/idp/20060815_ME_Report_FINAL.pdf (accessed November 10, 2006).

280. Walter Kaelin, "Internal Displacement and the Protection of Property," in Hernando DeSoto and Francis Cheneval, *Realizing Property Rights* (Zurich: University of Zurich, 2006) 177–179. Available at www.swisshumanrightsbook.com/PDFs/Kap_11.pdf (accessed August 7, 2007).

281. United Nations Office for the Coordination of Humanitarian Affairs, *Guiding Principles on Internal Displacement*, 2nd ed. (New York: United Nations, 2004), www.unhcr.org/protect/PROTECTION/43ce1cff2.pdf (accessed November 10, 2006).

282. Cohen and Deng, *Masses in Flight*, 25.

283. Steven V. Price, ed., *War and Tropical Forests: Conservation in Areas of Armed Conflict* (New York: Food Products Press, 2003).

284. Price, *War and Tropical Forests*, xv–xvii.

285. Jeffrey A. McNeely, "Biodiversity, War, and Tropical Forests," in Steven V. Price, ed., *War and Tropical Forests: Conservation in Areas of Armed Conflict* (New York: Food Products Press, 2003), 10.

286. McNeely, "Biodiversity, War, and Tropical Forests," 11.

287. McNeely, "Biodiversity, War, and Tropical Forests," 11.

288. Andrew J. Plumptre, "Lessons Learned from On-the-Ground Conservation in Rwanda and the Democratic Republic of the Congo," in Steven V. Price, ed., *War and Tropical Forests: Conservation in Areas of Armed Conflict* (New York: Food Products Press, 2003), 81.

289. See Plumptre, "Lessons Learned from On-the-Ground Conservation," 78.

290. Cohen and Deng, *Masses in Flight*, 25.

291. UNHCR, Engineering and Environmental Sciences Section, *Refugee Operations and Environmental Management*, iv, at www.unhcr.org/protect/PROTECTION/3b03b2754.pdf (accessed December 27, 2006).

292. UNHCR, *Refugee Operations and Environmental Management*, vii.

293. United Nations Development Programme, *Rwanda: Human Development Report 1999* (Kigali: UNDP, 1999), 27.

4

Traumatic Stress

Its Features and Long-Term Challenges

Chapter 3 explained why it is that the community and the environment at the end of a conflict are so different from what existed before the violence began. That chapter focused on changes that can be more or less easily seen by those who look for them, and particularly those associated with flight to escape the conflict. However, there are other effects that may not be easily seen, but that can linger with profound effects for many years—even generations—to come. Of these, one of the most important and challenging is most commonly known by its medical diagnostic label, post-traumatic stress disorder (PTSD).[1] These effects are felt not only by those who are driven into flight but also by those who remain, by the combatants and civilians, both children and adults.

Even countries like the United States, that have not suffered the massive displacement of people common to other countries afflicted by war, have come to experience traumatic stress as a result of terrorist attacks, not only of 9/11 in New York and Washington, D.C., but also from domestic terrorism, in places like Oklahoma City, and civil disorder, as in the case of the Los Angeles riots. Native Americans still contend with post-traumatic stress that stems from a variety of causes. Similarly, many in Europe who appeared to have forgotten the traumatic experiences of World War II began to relearn its devastating effects in the comparatively recent past with the eruption of the savage violence of the Balkans, and, more recently, with the London Underground and Madrid transit bombings.

With the devastation wrought by Hurricane Katrina in 2005, however, came a glimpse of elements of the plight of refugees, as hundreds of thousands of displaced persons from the South sought safety from the affected areas in Louisiana, Mississippi, and Alabama. American audiences, through continuous television viewing, were able to learn something of the trauma of massive destruction and dislocation of thousands of families. The televised coverage of the many who were stranded in temporary shelter in the Superdome in squalid conditions; children separated from their parents; the elderly left in vulnerable and dangerous conditions; and a city all but obliterated made clear the massive displacement.

As terrible as that experience was, however, that displacement was caused by an environmental disaster and, while intensely traumatic,[2] the trauma was not induced by deliberate violence, whether war or terrorism—either state-sponsored or inflicted by terrorist organizations. While natural or man-made disasters, severe accidents, and serious illnesses are traumatic, the sequences of trauma associated with war, civil conflict, or state-sponsored terror affect a person at even more profound psychological and physiological levels.

That said, once civil disorder took hold in the city of New Orleans, with roving gangs of marauders or desperate individuals taking advantage of the lack of any effective rule of law in the city, there were those who experienced conditions that have rarely been seen in Western developed countries in recent history.

At the other end of the spectrum from natural disaster is that form of social warfare known as genocide (see chapter 2). When that term is used, of course, it is common for most people to think of the Holocaust in Hitler's Germany. And while so many who saw the devastation of the Holocaust vowed that this would never be allowed to happen again, several more have followed. The Darfur crisis in Sudan continues even though it was formally declared a genocide by former U.S. Secretary of State Colin Powell.[3] Then, of course, there was the genocidal extermination of more than 800,000 Tutsis and some Hutus considered to be sympathetic to the Tutsis, discussed at length in chapter 5.

This chapter explores the effects of conflict-generated trauma. It begins with a case study that helps to explain the factors that erode the well-being and psyche of individuals and the communities within which they reside. The goal is to understand how and why individuals and communities are affected by trauma so that these complex conditions may be considered in post-conflict efforts. It addresses what traumatic stress and cultural bereavement are, how they affect different groups within the population, the intergenerational dimensions of the problem, state-sponsored versus other kinds of trauma, and efforts aimed at healing.

A CASE STUDY OF GUATEMALA: A SECRET
GENOCIDE IN THE LAND OF THE MAYA PEOPLES

Some relatively small countries seem to have had particularly turbulent histories. That can certainly be said of Guatemala. The case study to follow considers the country's history, the sad legacy of exploitation that has been part of that history, the contemporary conflicts, and the trauma visited upon its people. In particular, it focuses on the conflict that overturned the legitimately elected government in 1954 and the violence that followed and then on what is known as the thirty-six-year war, from 1960–1996. Even within all that violence, there was another conflict that took a devastating toll on a people, the Maya. As Timothy Gulden's analysis of the latter demonstrated:

> In the early parts of the conflict, the violence was typically between middle class people of the non-indigenous Ladino group struggling for control of the government. As the conflict progressed, it moved from an urban conflict focused on Guatemala City to a rural counter-insurgency campaign. The victims of state repression shifted at this point (about 1981) from middle class Ladino dissidents to indigenous Mayan peasants who were suspected of aiding rebel groups in the northwestern highlands. The scale and nature of the conflict changed as well, becoming vastly more deadly and including many acts which have been found to meet the formal definition of genocide.[4]

The Mayans became the target as it came to be assumed that they were, as a population, aligned with the insurgents the government forces claimed to be fighting.

The Commission for Historical Clarification (CEH) was created by the 1994 Oslo agreement. After carefully examining the evidence in accordance with the Convention on the Prevention and Punishment of the Crime of Genocide, the commission concluded that what happened in Guatemala with respect to the Maya was indeed a genocide.

> 122. In consequence, the CEH concludes that agents of the State of Guatemala, within the framework of counterinsurgency operations carried out between 1981 and 1983, committed acts of genocide against groups of Mayan people which lived in the four regions analysed. This conclusion is based on the evidence that, in light of Article II of the Convention on the Prevention and Punishment of the Crime of Genocide, the killing of members of Mayan groups occurred (Article II.a), serious bodily or mental harm was inflicted (Article II.b) and the group was deliberately subjected to living conditions calculated to bring about its physical destruction in whole or in part (Article II.c). The conclusion is also based on the evidence that all these acts were committed "with intent to destroy, in whole or in part" groups identified by their common ethnicity, by reason thereof, whatever the cause, motive or final objective of these acts may have been (Article II, first paragraph).

> 123. The CEH has information that similar acts occurred and were repeated in other regions inhabited by Mayan people.[5]

Quite apart from its legal findings, however, the Commission asked of the attacks on the Maya, "Why did the violence, especially that used by the

State, affect civilians and particularly the Mayan people, whose women were considered to be the spoils of war and who bore the full brunt of the institutionalised violence? Why did defenceless children suffer acts of savagery? Why, using the name of God, was there an attempt to erase from the face of the earth the sons and daughters of Xmukane', the grandmother of life and natural creation? Why did these acts of outrageous brutality, which showed no respect for the most basic rules of humanitarian law, Christian ethics and the values of Mayan spirituality, take place?"[6]

The fact that the indigenous peoples of the country have suffered so much of that trauma is a problem that Guatemala unfortunately shares with many other countries, including advanced western states like the United States and Canada, among others.

A Proud Indigenous Culture, a Bitter Conquest, and a History of Inequality

The cradle of the Maya civilization and a place of dramatic natural beauty, Guatemala boasts picturesque highlands that crown most of its territory, flanked on the west and east by the Pacific and Atlantic oceans. Its long rainy season ensures an abundance of plant life as well as producing lush forests. Guatemala is the land of the quetzal, a bird of profound symbolic importance to the indigenous people, who see it as the messenger between humankind and the gods.

> The Mayas progressed from the pictograph to the ideograph and thus invented a type of writing, the only Indians in the hemisphere to do so. Sophisticated in mathematics, they invented the zero and devised numeration by position. Astute observers of the heavens, they applied their mathematical skills to astronomy. Their careful studies of the heavens enabled them to predict eclipses, follow the path of the planet Venus, and prepare a calendar more accurate than that used in Europe. . . . The Mayas built magnificent temples. One of the most striking features of that architecture is its extremely elaborate carving and sculpture.[7]

Guatemala's bounty in natural resources and complex history stand out among the tiny Central American nations; it is "the richest in natural resources, and it attracts the most investment dollars from the United States and the large multinational corporations in Europe and Far East."[8] The largest country in size in that region, its ecological diversity and ancient culture captivate visitors. Its territory extends over 108,889 square kilometers (42,042 square miles) and has a population of 12.3 million,[9] 44 percent of whom are indigenous.[10] Many of the latter speak one of the twenty-four Maya languages, of which the most prominent are Quiché, Kaqchikel, Q'eqchí, Tz'utujils, and Mam,[11] though the official language is Spanish. While

Spanish conquerors attempted to subjugate them, the Maya fought the invaders for more than a century. "The last Maya city held out until 1697, and some of the Caribbean lowlands were never effectively controlled by Spain."[12]

During the colonial period, Guatemala was headquarters of the Captaincy General of Guatemala, which controlled the territory known today as Central America.[13] The roots of a feudal system of land tenure were established in Guatemala then, as they were in the rest of Latin America. The Maya became a slave labor population for the Ladinos, descendants of the conquerors, who imposed the *encomienda* system, granting land title as well as control over the indigenous people living in that land as serfs.[14] It became independent in 1821. From 1824 to 1838, the five Central American states constituted a unified nation, the United Provinces of Central America.[15] As Moreno explained, this tension between the desire for regional unity and frustration over intervention in each other's political affairs has been a persistent source of conflict.[16] From the middle of the nineteenth century on, the region was besieged with dictatorships and other would-be dictators. It was also plagued by an entrenched unequal distribution of wealth, resting in significant part on badly exploited indigenous labor. The country has thus enjoyed only brief periods of what approached democratic governance and little respite from conflict since its independence.

Today, five centuries since the conquest, the sad cycle characterized by the decimation of the indigenous population by colonization and marginalization still echoes in the culture, the economy, and the recent history of governance. Deeply affected with what is called post-colonization trauma, and by the genocide of the thirty-six-year war (discussed below), today the Maya peoples nevertheless contend that they are experiencing a comeback, with a rebirth of their cultural heritage.[17] In some sense, their view is in concert with their cultural conception of time as circular, and life as cyclical.[18]

By 1990, the wheel may have turned as the Academy of Mayan Languages was created by Congress[19] and the Maya culture and languages may have finally begun to enjoy the prestige accorded to a people from an ancient civilization. However, that move did not go uncontested, with opposition in Congress as well as from other quarters, including missionaries who were not in favor of preserving Maya languages and culture.

However, the latter half of the twentieth century was for the Mayas and poor Ladinos (a group of European ancestry as well as mixed ancestry, known as mestizo in other Latin American countries) a period characterized by prolonged, persistent, and intense armed conflict, triggered by deep-rooted structural socioeconomic inequities, by failed attempts for social and civil rights reform, and by the ideologically driven politics and foreign policy of the Cold War. Civil unrest in Guatemala, and the region, rampant violation of human rights, oppression, and genocide through state-sponsored terror in which 83 percent of the victims were Maya, misguided U.S. international policies, and economic policies that perpetuated what Perez-Brignioli labeled "impoverishing growth,"[20] were pervasive in Guatemala and set the nation on a path antithetical to sustainable development and toward rounds of violent conflict. These policies were often fueled by an entrenched ruling elite supported by the military and, at times, with the blessing of the higher echelons of the Catholic Church.[21]

As the Cold War evolved, the United States was inclined to find any activity that called for significant change, along with demands for social equality or equity, as destabilizing and likely to be a Soviet-inspired Communist revolutionary effort. When such reform movements were undertaken in the Western Hemisphere, the situation was further interpreted as a violation of the so-called Truman doctrine and presumed to be intervention by the Soviet Union. These movements were to be resisted politically in every case and by force if necessary. When the United States saw such a reform effort in Guatemala, all of those fears triggered an aggressive response that ultimately was aimed at overthrowing a democratically elected government in that country. The Eisenhower administration took that step even though President Eisenhower was warned that there really was no issue of Communism involved.[22]

Economic development policies in Guatemala, such as they were, during the period focused on economic growth, exacerbated inequality and poverty, and ignored the impact on most of the country's people and its environment.[23] These policies centered on agricultural production of export products, such as sugarcane, coffee, bananas, beef, cotton, and cardamom, that were often produced at the expense of virgin tropical forests taken down to enhance agricultural land.[24] Indigenous groups were exploited, especially for coffee production, by large landowners who imposed forced labor upon them.[25]

The Context, Character, and Consequences of Violent Conflict in Guatemala

While "Guatemala has a long history of strong-man rule"[26] dating back to the nineteenth century, the more recent history witnessed particularly violent, repressive, and sustained civil strife. Scholars of conflict in Latin America often mark the beginning of the contemporary military repression more precisely to the 1954 coup, which according to Skidmore and Smith, "marked a turning point in Guatemalan history. It virtually eliminated the forces of the political center."[27] A bloody war ensued in which any opposition would be ruthlessly crushed. Reports of the level of the violence as well as the common use of kidnapping, torture, and murder by the military, working with the political leadership, might be difficult to believe were it not for the fact that they have been so carefully documented, not only by scholars but also by more than 5,000 documents revealed under the Freedom of Information Act requests by the U.S. Central Intelligence Agency.[28] The National Security Archive of George Washington University has undertaken two large-scale projects on Guatemala. The first is an electronic briefing book on the *Death Squad Diaries* that reproduces the Guatemalan records on many of those rounded up, tortured, and executed in the 1980s,[29] and the second is an electronic briefing book in two volumes that details information on the activities of the Guatemalan military from U.S. files with documents from 1966 to 1995.[30]

The basis of conflict, dating back to the Conquest, has been the entrenched poverty and inequality of the majority of the population, consisting primarily of indigenous and poor Ladino groups. The ruling elite who have distanced themselves from the majority, particularly from indigenous groups, held on to political power. Those factors, plus the ideological politics of the Cold War meant death for thousands in Guatemala.

"Project PB Success": The Overthrow of Democratically Elected Government

As the Cold War got underway, the U.S. anti-Communist campaign pictured what were in truth reform efforts in such policy domains as education, health care, agrarian reform, or labor protections in Guatemala, and in other Latin American countries, as Communist-inspired efforts to subvert existing regimes. The disenfranchised Maya, the poor, and progressive middle class became victims of the government-sponsored efforts to block such reforms. They also became victims of the military, whose goal was to crush so-called Communist "subversives," poor indigenous peasants who got caught in the cross fire and who lived and sought refuge in rural areas, or who supported the ideals of the guerrilla movements but were not actually part of those groups. Others became victims and victimizers when forced into community policing. Hence, the conflict in Guatemala has been political in nature, unlike the conflict in Colombia, where insurgent groups, and, in some cases, the military drug cartels have colluded.

Ironically, the rise of the Cold War coincided with the beginnings of a brief democratic period in Guatemala, with the free and democratic election of Juan José Arévalo Bermejo in 1945.[31] Dr. Arévalo, in power from 1945 to 1950, had initiated democratic reforms: the right to vote, access to education, and abolition of compulsory labor for Indians.[32] He also established a social security system and redistributed land to landless peasants.[33] All of these actions were in stark contrast with the fifteen-year repressive rule of General Jorge Ubico (1931–1944),[34] whose regime "'modernized' vagrancy laws," placing Indians into forced labor for one hundred days a year.[35]

Arévalo's successor, President Jacobo Arbenz Guzmán, was no Communist, but was committed to continuing reforms. Part of his efforts had to do with the need for public infrastructure during a period when some of the most important infrastructure in Guatemala was under the monopolistic control of corporations, some of which were foreign-owned. Arbenz set out to build a highway to the Atlantic coast, until then only accessible through the railroad owned by the American International Railroad of Central America, and to construct a hydroelectric plant to counterbalance the only company operating then, also owned by an American corporation, Electric Bond and Share.[36]

It was the agrarian reform he attempted to institute that sparked reaction. Because there were large numbers of landless peasants, Arbenz decided to take land, with compensation, that was not being cultivated and redistribute it (including 1,700 acres owned by Arbenz himself[37]). The United Fruit Company, a U.S.-based firm that had been a power in the region since the nineteenth century, was outraged that 400,000 acres of its uncultivated land were taken, even with compensation. The Guatemalan government paid United Fruit $3 per acre, which was the amount that the company had declared as the value of the land for purposes of its Guatemalan tax obligation. The United Fruit Company undertook a major campaign in Washington, D.C., aimed at convincing U.S. officials that the Arbenz government was Communist and that it posed a threat to other countries in Latin America.[38] While it was a fact that four of the sixty-one votes in Arbenz's coalition were Communists, that did not make his government Communist. None of the four were ministers.[39] In fact, under Arbenz's government, Communists were also barred from positions in several ministries.[40] It was because of these facts that one of President Eisenhower's friends made the point at the time that there were more Communists in San Francisco than in Guatemala.[41] Of course, the fact that then U.S. Secretary of State John Foster Dulles and his brother, Allen Dulles, who was then CIA director, both had been closely involved with the United Fruit Company was a factor as well.[42]

Equally threatened by the 1952 Agrarian Reform Law, Decree 900, was the Guatemalan rural elite whose land would also be compensated based on the tax-assessed value.[43] The Catholic Church raised its voice against these reforms as well. The landowners joined United Fruit in denouncing the reforms and labeling the Arbenz government as a Communist regime that had to be removed from power. Reputable U.S. and Latin American diplomats tried to intervene to correct the misinformation, asserting that the measures taken by President Arbenz had nothing to do with Soviet intervention, but those informed voices went unheeded. The United States government moved to topple Arbenz from power. However, "Jacobo Arbenz, accused of a communist conspiracy, was not inspired by Lenin, but by Abraham Lincoln. His agrarian reform, with the goal to modernize capitalism in Guatemala, is more moderate than the North American rural laws of almost a century ago."[44]

The United States was ready to engage in such an intervention for a variety of reasons, some of which were relatively long-standing. However, the immediate precursors were more specific. In November of 1952, British MI-6 agents came to the CIA to obtain U.S. assistance to overthrow the Mosaddeq government in Iran and to put the Shah back in power. Although Mosaddeq was not a Communist he did move to nationalize British oil interests.[45] The Truman administration refused, but only two weeks after coming to power, the Eisenhower administration agreed to the plan, which was formally authorized by the president later in July as Operation Ajax.[46] The coup, launched on August 15, succeeded, encouraging other such adventures.[47]

On August 12, only three days before the Iran operation, the U.S. National Security Council approved the Guatemala coup, and a month later the CIA had its "General Plan of Action" ready for the overthrow of the Arbenz government.[48] However, the foundations for this intervention came earlier, in March of 1953 when the president issued a national security directive, NSC 144/1, that presented U.S. policy for the region and made clear the American intention to go after what it considered to be movements "toward radical and nationalistic regimes."[49] The pretext used by the administration was the assertion that Soviet bloc countries were providing arms to the Arbenz government. However, while there was one shipment of small arms to the country, the fact is that Arbenz had previously gone to the United States asking for small arms with which to equip police and domestic security forces to maintain law and order and for modest defensive capability, but those requests had been refused. Only then did Arbenz obtain the weapons from Eastern Europe. Although the coup hatched by the United States in Guatemala nearly failed, it ultimately brought down the Arbenz government.

That American-supported coup had four dramatic consequences. First, it unleashed a long period of ruthless and oppressive military rule and rampant political repression that took its heaviest toll on the middle and poor classes, but especially decimated indigenous peoples.[50] Second, it intensified tensions in the country and the region that have lasted for decades, with a well-founded suspicion of U.S. motives from within the country and, on the U.S. side, a continuing willingness to intervene in support of stability at virtually any cost in Guatemala, including discrimination against legitimate political refugees (see chapter 3). Third, the coup was used by the CIA and the United States more generally as a success story that would be the basis for the Bay of Pigs fiasco in Cuba.[51] "Afterwards, many of those involved in the two operations linked the success in Guatemala with the failure of the Bay of Pigs. 'If the Agency had not had Guatemala,' E. Howard

Hunt, a case officer who served in both PB SUCCESS and JMARC later observed, 'it probably would not have had Cuba.'"[52] Finally, it was a foundation for an ongoing relationship with the ruthless military regimes that followed, with active engagement and support from the United States from the 1960s through the Reagan era.

The Thirty-Six-Year War: Going from Bad to Worse

Arbenz's election had been the second in which Guatemalans participated in democratic processes through legitimate elections, but that budding attempt at democracy abruptly came to an end, not to resurface for some four decades. Arbenz's overthrow was the start of an increasingly bloody era. With the support of the CIA and the blessing of the Catholic Church, Colonel Carlos Castillo Armas was sworn in as president in 1954. His government was characterized by a Communist witch hunt, expropriation of land distributed under the Arbenz presidency, a reversal of social policies, a serious decline in political openness, and corruption.[53] His term ended with his assassination in 1957, only to be replaced by another supporter of state terror, General Miguel Ydígoras Fuentes (1957–1963), whose regime featured repression against organized university student, professional, teacher, and labor groups trying to return to the constitutional rights of 1945.[54]

While the decades of the 1960s and 1970s witnessed some economic gains, repression intensified. There were human rights violations, fraudulent elections and one coup after another, and the persecution of political parties, unions, and student organizations. Violence escalated, beginning in 1966 when the death squads were created. Military actions against guerrilla activity targeted innocent and indigenous peoples as well as student movements that emerged to protect against social injustice. While a civilian was elected in 1966, Julio César Méndez Montenegro, the military under Ydígoras took control of the country. The rise of institutional repression was unbounded. In October of 1967, Thomas Hughes of the State Department's Bureau of Intelligence and Research wrote a secret memorandum to the secretary entitled "Guatemala—A Counter-Insurgency Running Wild?" in which he described such tactics as "kidnappings, torture, and summary executions" approved by President Méndez Montenegro "apparently in exchange for military support for his administration."[55] Indeed, "[a]s of 1968, there were no political prisoners any longer, only [people who had] disappeared."[56] We later learned what had happened to the so-called "disappeared" when the military's records of the arrests, tortures, and executions were found in the 1990s.[57]

On the positive side, universities became a breeding ground for innovation and social engagement, creating practicum-experiences in which students were deployed throughout the country to address national needs, including in rural areas. The School of Medicine established a multidisciplinary approach to study the national status of health "not only in reference to the biological and psychological but also in relation to a socioeconomic, historical perspective."[58]

Although economically Guatemala benefited from industrial development through the Central American Common Market created in 1960, a regional war between El Salvador and Honduras in 1969 undermined it.[59] For rural inhabitants, it meant a loss of a traditional crop subsistence as large landowners began to amass small plots to their land holdings for commercial production. An urban poor population was created in the displacement, with declining health and nutrition indicators. The economic growth of the 1960s began to fall apart at the end of the decade and came to a halt in 1973 with the oil crisis.

What was labeled a counterinsurgency escalated in 1970, coinciding with the election of Colonel Carlos Arana Osorio (1970–1974), whose nickname, "the butcher of Zacapa," came from his leadership in the massacre of 10,000 civilians by the army in Zacapa in 1968.[60] He led the military to power, wealth, and status through the creation of institutions such as the Military Bank, the Military Hospital, and economic ventures exclusive to the military.[61] Guatemala's stand against Communism meant generous U.S. foreign aid, which Arana shifted to these institutions.[62] Thus, the military became a powerful force with which the ruling class would have to contend for decades to the present. Persecution and assassinations of political leaders were common. Others were persecuted whether politically involved or not, and indiscriminate violence hit innocent bystanders. The land expropriation policy was carried out in rural areas, while in urban centers and universities, students as well as professors and university administrators became targets of political persecution because of the support they lent to labor leaders and because they denounced human rights abuses.[63] The "eye for an eye" death squad was created to attack student movements. It perpetrated innumerable kidnappings, assassinations, and even massacres.[64]

Arana was followed by General Eugenio Kjell Laugerud García (1974–1978), a close ally of Arana, whose regime briefly tempered the violence[65] but oversaw increased poverty.[66] The 1976 earthquake had a catastrophic impact, but a positive one as well. The loss of over 25,000 lives and of dwellings further entrenched poverty but raised awareness and social engagement. This political engagement engendered more political persecution,[67] especially in 1977 when the highest number of strikes in the history of Guatemala took place and rural and urban movements joined forces.[68] Laugerud García allowed demonstrations and strikes and even refurbished the "Student House" where a medical, dental, and legal clinic was operated by university students. Even so, "terror against unions, parties, students, peasant organizations, and cooperatives increased."[69]

His successor, General Romeo Lucas García, through fraudulent elections, ruled from 1978 until he was unseated by younger military officers in 1982.[70] Under Lucas García, "the doors to one of the most violent decades in the history of Guatemala were opened"[71] and repression became widespread. When he raised the price of staple goods and bus fares,[72] there were strikes with a number of deaths, but the government restored lower fares.[73] However, the student movement was decimated by attacks on its leaders and supporters. "In 1979 there were 1,371 murder and kidnapping cases; in 1980, there were 2,264 cases; and in 1981, it reached 3,426 cases" of attacks on university students.[74] The attacks extended to faculty, local and national political party leaders, and labor officials, as well as massive killings of indigenous groups.[75]

With opposition forces broken, the government struck at will. However, a peasant organization organized a peaceful demonstration with the support of a student organization, Frente Estudiantil Revolucionario Robin García (FERG; Robin García Revolutionary Student Front) and took over the Spanish Embassy to attract international attention to their plight.[76] The pleas of the Spanish ambassador, who escaped, went unheeded as Lucas attacked those inside, caused a fire, and then ordered the doors locked. The embassy personnel along with the demonstrators were burned alive as the ambassador watched helplessly.[77] Spain broke diplomatic relations with Guatemala at this point. "Despite such massive human rights violations, Guatemala continued to receive new economic assistance from the United States that totaled over $60 million from 1979 through 1981."[78]

Although it is hard to imagine that life in Guatemala could be bloodier, the next regime led by Ríos-Montt (1982–1983) took the violence to new levels. State terror escalated to a genocide category throughout Guatemala (with a formal finding to that effect by the Truth Commission, discussed below). Ríos-Montt had been seeking the presidency since 1974.[79] His flamboyant style was bolstered by the Protestant fundamentalists whom he embraced and who became his advisors. His attempts to maintain power persisted into the twenty-first century.

Under Plan Victoria 82[80] (Victory Plan 82), Ríos-Montt implemented a scorched earth policy, activated the death squads, and, under the pretense of going after the "subversives," mercilessly massacred innocent people, including women and children, especially the highland indigenous groups. "More than 440 villages were burned to the ground; 100,000 to 150,000 civilians, mainly highland Indians, were killed or 'disappeared.'"[81] Gulden reported that from 1977 to 1986, there were somewhere between 80,000 to 400,000 killings and disappearances.[82] During the 1980s, it was estimated that the civil war resulted in over 100,000 deaths and 40,000 disappearances, and generated over a million displaced Guatemalans. The short period between 1982 and 1983 produced "thousands of victims of torture and disappearance, innumerable widows, orphans, and obliterated communities."[83]

The oppression, however, catalyzed social movements once more as opposition against the widespread terror and violence under Mejía Víctores (1983–1986), who ousted Ríos-Montt. While Mejía Víctores took power, promising that a new constitution would be drafted and elections held, his rise to power also prompted opposition groups to mobilize. In 1984, Coca-Cola workers initiated a strike that lasted for a year. In that same year, Nineth Montenegro de García, a law student, and María del Rosario Godoy de Cuevas, the wives of two kidnapped student leaders, created Grupo de Apoyo Mutuo por el Aparecimiento con Vida de Nuestros Familiares (GAM; Mutual Support Group for the Live Return of Our Family Members).[84] It was a period in which, according to "Dr. Mario Guerra, forensic doctor, 30 to 40 bodies arrived at the morgue on a daily basis."[85] The group had two major goals. First, it demanded an official investigation into the disappearances, and second, an investigation of the paramilitary groups. On May 15, 1985, María del Rosario Godoy de Cuevas, her three-year-old son, and her brother were murdered.[86] Indeed, the political climate was so oppressive that families could not even report the disappearance of a loved one or request an investigation for fear of retaliation by the armed forces.[87] Mejía Victores's rule was another period of extreme political repression.

Expectations were raised when free elections were held in 1985 and Vinicio Cerezo Arévalo won. He became the first civilian president to take office after more than thirty years of military rule.[88] The elections had been called by Mejía Victores in an attempt to improve the tarnished international reputation of Guatemala as a "pariah state" based on its state-sponsored terror that became a genocide.[89] At the inauguration of Cerezo, however, Mejía Victores made it clear that the military retained full authority; "[a]ny serious tampering with the military's uncontested control of rural Guatemala would clearly exceed those limits."[90]

While repression diminished under his term, Cerezo's authority was undermined by his lack of control of the military and continued operation of the death squads. The economy was failing. Strikes and demonstrations were common. According to Burns, in "1987, Guatemala suffered the most skewed land distribution system in Latin America: 54 percent of all farmers owned but 4.1 percent of the land [and] more than 420 peasant families were landless."[91] Cerezo survived two attempts to overthrow him, first by the so-called "Mountain Officers." Student movements protested, but the secret army responded by viciously "decapitating" student movements.[92] On the other hand, Cerezo fully embraced and supported the Central American peace efforts and established the Office of Human Rights Ombudsman, though more radical measures were needed to redress human rights violations. His commitment to peace took him to México to engage

Guatemalans in exile and to invite their return. In 1989 there was another failed attempt to overthrow President Cerezo. Although the violence under his term subsided for a time, the coup attempts against Cerezo were catalysts for demands for a civilian government.[93]

The decade of the 1980s is considered the lost decade in Latin America,[94] as the entire region suffered from "economic stagnation . . . and increasing social inequality."[95] Central America experienced a significant loss in social and economic development gains made in the previous twenty-five years,[96] affected directly and indirectly by civil strife in Guatemala, El Salvador, and Nicaragua, and complicated by a global recession. The regional civil wars had a profound impact on Honduras and Costa Rica. The intransigent foreign policy of the Reagan administration blocked efforts in Guatemala, El Salvador, and Nicaragua aimed at social justice and a democratic voice for the marginalized, which the United States saw as Soviet intervention.

United States foreign policy supported oppressive right-wing governments, on grounds that they supposedly offered some sense of stability regardless of the cost to the citizens. In spite of attempts by other Latin American countries to mediate and negotiate peace agreements, it was not until the 1986 Esquipulas and 1987 Esquipulas II that a peace accord was orchestrated by the then president of Costa Rica, Dr. Óscar Arias Sánchez. At the core of this effort was the need to counterbalance the misperception that the struggle for social justice was Communist activity and the failure of the international community to come to grips with the fact that the brutal military regimes had taken economic and political power.

Economic structural measures were tightened by Cerezo's successor, Jorge Serrano Elías (1990–1993), center-right. He had initiated dialogue with the guerrillas,[97] but three years into his administration, he suspended the Congress, the Supreme Court, and civil liberties and imposed a state of siege.[98] Human rights violations flared once more in response to protests over increases in bus fares, and Guatemala City became a battleground.[99]

In 1992, the Catholic Church also took a strong public position, denouncing the atrocities committed against the Mayan people, not only in the twentieth century, but since the time of the Conquest. ". . . Although there have been exemplary bishops and missionaries, there have also been errors and contradictions in the comportment of members of the church, which have impacted unjustly on the indigenous communities. We who are the present pastors of the church, ask your forgiveness."[100] This, along with statements in support of social reforms, and a commitment to support indigenous rights, was a significant departure from the historical position taken by the Catholic Church, which had long allied itself with those in power.

Ultimately, the Central American peace process had planted a seed of hope. Jorge Serrano Elías was forced to flee the country in 1993. His successor, Ramiro de León Carpio, a former human rights ombudsman, offered some hope, but disillusionment set in as the military continued its abuses. He negotiated "an agreement to respect the rights of indigenous peoples," but without constitutional backing.[101]

In 1995, Alvaro Arzú was elected. At the end of his first year in office, a peace agreement was signed with the Unidad Revolucionaria Nacional Guatemalteca (URNG; Guatemalan National Revolutionary Unity),[102] which had amalgamated three major opposition organizations that included the Guerrilla Army of the Poor (EGP) and the Rebel Armed Forces (FAR), in 1982. Nevertheless, the repression continued and even escalated in the early 1990s. Although the thirty-six-year war formally ended when a peace accord was signed in December of 1996, the violence continued, especially as attempts were made to try the murderers and their leaders. Few believed the violence had ended, particularly when, in 1998, "Bishop Juan José Gerardi was mysteriously murdered only days after the release of a massive report on human rights abuse."[103]

The peace commission, MINUGUA (United Nations Verification Mission),[104] was established by the United Nations at the signing of the initial peace agreement in 1994 (though the final accord did not come until 1996), which labored on peace efforts for the decade of 1994–2004. Monitoring implementation of the peace process ended without bringing to justice those responsible for the genocide while UN Secretary General Koffi Anan declared that "Guatemala had made enormous progress in managing the country's problems through dialogue and institutions."[105] Many journalists became casualties of the military dictators during the civil war period (such as Irma Flaquer, who was kidnapped in 1980 and whose body was never recovered[106]).

The 1999 elections won the presidency for Alfonso Portillo with overwhelming public support (68 percent). His tenure did not witness dramatic efforts at fighting organized violence, narco-trafficking, and corruption. Instead, his government struggled with increased persecution against journalists, judges, human rights activists, and witnesses, leading the government to initiate a national dialogue on how to respond to the rising level of violence in 2001, as concern over the crime and corruption also intensified.[107] In April 2003, the United States decertified Guatemala from eligibility for some assistance because of "its lack of appropriate effort in the fight against drug trafficking."[108] Rios-Montt came back to power as president of the Congress from 2000 to 2004, and gained immunity from responsibility for the genocide committed under his earlier regime from 1981 to 1983.[109]

A new president, Oscar Berger Perdomo, was sworn in, in January 2004. Although in his inaugural speech he acknowledged the mandate ". . . to serve all Guatemalans . . . to work for the needy and the poor,"[110] the future is uncertain. He took office of a country in which "three-quarters of the population [live] in poverty and political violence is still commonplace "[111]

Post-Conflict Challenges in Guatemala:
Physical Damage and Psychosocial Injuries

The long, vicious conflict has affected Guatemala and its people in a number of ways, including complex post-traumatic stress syndrome issues. Although exact figures are not known, some estimate that the thirty-six-year civil war killed more than 200,000, displaced over a million persons, of whom 250,000 in 2005 remain in such status,[112] and generated more than 1 million refugees. The war also left "75,000 widows and 250,000 orphans."[113]

Three factors have shaped the challenges for those seeking to move Guatemala forward in the wake of the decades of violence described above. They include the history of inequality, pervasive underdevelopment in the broad sense of that term, and the dramatic destructive impacts of violence over such prolonged periods of time. The visible injuries were severe, but, as this chapter explains, there was also less visible—but dramatic—damage from the trauma of the sad history of Guatemala. Those burdens have fallen most heavily on those least able to endure them, and particularly on the indigenous people of the country.

Persistent and Profound Inequality

Inequalities between rural and urban areas and between Ladinos (non-indigenous) and indigenous peoples are substantial.[114] The inequality in health, wealth, and land tenure weighs heavily against those in rural areas, and particularly indigenous peoples.[115] By the mid-twentieth century, illiteracy was 75 percent, and in rural areas ascended to 90 percent, though by the end of the century the rates had improved, except for in indigenous groups.

Historically, most of the indigenous peoples worked for large landowners who maintained what could only be described as a feudal system. Landowners also benefited from little or no taxation. The meager tax revenues in Guatemala, the lowest in Latin America,[116] constrain the nation's ability to build infrastructure and implement development strategies. According to UN officials in Guatemala, in 2005, the top fifth of the population held 60.3 percent of the country's wealth, while the bottom fifth, or 2.2 million people, only held 1.9 percent.[117] Entrenched poverty, especially in rural areas, presents profound inequities in "income distribution, resources and opportunities."[118] In 2000, 56 percent lived in poverty and 16 percent in extreme poverty.[119]

Lengthy Violence Undermines Institutions and
Policy Development to Meet Critical Needs

The prolonged strife in Guatemala has undermined the integrity of public institutions and their ability to mount the kinds of redistributive policies needed to redress serious inequities in health, education, employment, housing, clean water access, sanitation, and safety. Guatemala's governmental agencies were weak before the civil war, but were all but destroyed by it. Even such fundamental government activities as gathering data or collecting census information are major challenges, making it difficult now for decision makers to assess and determine national priorities.[120] At the same time, deteriorating social conditions, population growth, and the destructive effects of gang activity and the drug sales, sex trade, violence, and illicit weapons sales placed more demands on public agencies. Weakened institutions have in turn undermined efforts in such areas as citizen safety, protection of human rights, and improved health care and education.

With respect to education, for example, Guatemala still presents "the highest illiteracy rates and one of the lowest school enrollment rates in Latin America."[121] One of the major challenges in education is the significant gaps between rural and urban areas, dramatically skewed against indigenous peoples.[122] In 2004, among five countries in Latin America with high indigenous populations, Guatemala had the lowest levels of education, at 2.5 years of schooling compared, for example, to 6.4 in Perú.[123] In contrast to the educational attainment of Ladinos in Guatemala, levels of education for indigenous children are not increasing at significant rates, while the school dropout rate in first grade is high: 44 percent for indigenous children, compared to 31 percent for Ladinos.[124] Though there are projects to provide bilingual and intercultural education in community-led schools, coverage extends to less than one-third of indigenous Guatemalans.[125] Remaining challenges to increase educational attainments for indigenous people include community and parental involvement in the education process, improving access and quality of education, and increasing bilingual and bicultural programs.[126] Other factors also affect educational achievement, such as health and nutrition.

The combination of poverty, social exclusion, low levels of education, and rural dwelling yields a worrisome health profile, especially for women and children.[127] Maternal mortality rates are considered "extremely high, with 270 deaths per 100,000 births . . . [and the infant mortality rate] and under-five mortality rates are estimated between 43 to 58 deaths per 100,000 live births."[128] Additionally, "56 percent of chronically malnourished children in Central America live in Guatemala. . . . The incidence of chronic malnutrition among indigenous communities and rural families is 70 percent and 56 percent respectively."[129] Malnutrition affects growth, and in Guatemala the portion of children with stunted growth (height compared to weight) is nearly double for indigenous children, at 58 percent compared to 33 percent among Ladino children.[130] Malnutrition, combined with diarrhea and acute respiratory infections are the primary causes of death among children.[131] On top of all that, indigenous groups have the lowest level of health care insurance coverage and services.[132] The level of injury from the war and its aftermath, coupled with inadequate health care, imperils the health of indigenous children in particular. The consequences of war extend to psychological as well as physical issues, and many of those affected face risks of serious mental health challenges, especially those disabled by war injuries.[133]

Violence, Inequality, and the Needs of Particular Populations: Challenges for Indigenous Peoples and Women

There are several levels of challenges in the contemporary context for the indigenous peoples of Guatemala. First, there is the need to recognize and come to grips with the genocidal attacks directed at the Maya. Second, there is the problem of equality in terms of the full recognition as well as the protection of their rights and liberties as Guatemalans. Third, there is the importance of the recognition of the need for cultural preservation, including Mayan languages and cultures.

It is easy to get lost in the violence of Guatemala, both literally and figuratively. However, the Commission for Historical Clarification sought to make clear what happened to the Maya and to remove these acts as a "Memory of Silence," as the Commission entitled its report. In particular, the CEH rejected the claim that the military was merely attempting to battle the insurgents and that some innocent Maya were caught in the cross fire.

31. However, the CEH has ascertained that, in the majority of cases, the identification of Mayan communities with the insurgency was intentionally exaggerated by the State, which, based on traditional racist prejudices, used this identification to eliminate any present or future possibilities of the people providing help for, or joining, an insurgent project.

32. The consequence of this manipulation, extensively documented by the CEH, was massive and indiscriminate aggression directed against communities independent of their actual involvement in the guerrilla movement and with a clear indifference to their status as a non-combatant civilian population. The massacres, scorched earth operations, forced disappearances and executions of Mayan authorities, leaders and spiritual guides, were not only an attempt to destroy the social base of the guerrillas, but above all, to destroy the cultural values that ensured cohesion and collective action in Mayan communities.[134]

The damage committed against the Maya extended well beyond what might be obvious to many who hear of the numbers of dead. The Commission for Historical Clarification noted that:

Mayans were obliged to conceal their ethnic identity, manifested externally in their language and dress. Militarization of the communities disturbed the cycle of celebrations and ceremonies, and concealment of their rituals became progressively more widespread. Aggression was directed against elements of profound symbolic significance for the Mayan culture, as in the case of the destruction of corn and the killing of their elders. These events had a serious impact on certain elements of Mayan identity and disturbed the transmission of their culture from generation to generation. Similarly, the culture was degraded through the use of Mayan names and symbols for task forces and other military structures.[135]

The Commission recognized these injuries to culture and identity, as well as the intergenerational effects of those losses.

While Mayans were recognized as equal citizens in 1995, with the Rights and Identity of Indigenous Peoples Accord established by President Carpio, it was not constitutionally adopted, and hence carried no authority to support a real reversal of the ethnocultural discrimination and exclusion which have been central realities of Guatemalan life from the colonial period to the present. Even when full protection for civil rights is assured, there will still be the historical effects of exclusion to be confronted, as well as the post-traumatic stress of more recent violence. Long disenfranchised groups often suffer intergenerational consequences (the clinical term is *sequelae*) of the historical exclusion and exploitation imposed upon them.[136] At the time of the conquest, there was a deliberate effort to destroy their ancient culture and to subject them to servitude. In the more recent past, there was the experience of forced labor and related abuses. In the contemporary era, there have been enduring socioeconomic disadvantages in tandem with cultural alienation. These protracted violations have led to unresolved, intergenerational mourning. While the Mayans are anchored on strong cultural foundations, they suffer, as other indigenous communities in other regions of the world, the wounds of post-colonization stress[137] aggravated by war-related trauma because of persecution, violence, torture, and death.[138]

Although human development measures have historically been abysmal for indigenous peoples, the civil conflict worsened their condition. The disparities between indigenous groups in the five Latin American countries (México, Guatemala, Bolivia, Perú, and Ecuador) with the largest indigenous populations have been significant, but they are particularly accentuated in Guatemala.[139] Because there is also a marked divide between urban and rural communities, and because 80 percent of indigenous people live in rural areas, the gap is even greater for the Mayas, regardless of the human development indicator selected for analysis.

The Mayas still lag behind the Ladino population in health, education, and employment, which contributes to their poverty.[140] Because indigenous groups have the lowest rates of health protection and services, health indicators are troubling, particularly for women and children. Women are still suffering from high levels of malnutrition, which increases the incidence of infant mortality. Their newborns tend to be vulnerable to disease, eventually affecting school performance. "Malnutrition during childhood reduces life expectancy, impairs cognitive development, undermines learning ability and increases the danger of health problems later in life."[141]

That said, projects funded by the World Bank are beginning to focus on provision of culturally appropriate child and maternal health services, such as "Birth Homes,"[142] where women in rural areas can give births in a safe environment. This is particularly important because "65 percent of rural women and 75 percent of indigenous women give birth at home."[143] In addition, access to prenatal care and birthing in a hospital are low; 27 percent of indigenous women do not get prenatal care and "only 15 per cent give birth in a hospital, compared with 51 per cent of non-indigenous women."[144] Efforts to integrate culturally appropriate practices, recruitment and training of health professionals from Mayan communities, as well as training of Ladino professionals in the language of the community they serve, use of traditional healers, and programs specifically tailored to the needs of the communities are key.[145]

Despite a slight reduction in poverty, the poverty rate for Mayas compared to the rest of the population is still profound: 74 percent for indigenous and 38 percent for non-indigenous people.[146] Indigenous people also earn one-fourth the income of non-indigenous people, especially affecting young workers, a direct result of discrimination in the labor market, making it more difficult to overcome poverty barriers, despite educational level. Other factors include "lower quality education [and] low labor market returns to schooling."[147]

Indigenous children endure other challenges in addition to malnourishment, low levels of schooling, and poverty. They also work. Child labor rates are significantly higher for indigenous children, at 80 percent in 1940 and 83 percent in 1980, while non-indigenous children experienced a decline from 70 to 62 percent.[148] Indigenous children are also less likely to get paid for their work, at 72 percent, than non-indigenous children, at 67 percent.[149] This pattern may have a cultural dimension to it: "cultural norms may in many senses be positive, instilling identity and work values in children. However, for some children, working while attending school may constrain learning."[150] Notwithstanding this positive feature, for indigenous and non-indigenous children, child labor is a necessity. Working children need to help their families with basic needs and to pay for their own educational expenses. The price is that they endure discrimination, maltreatment, and exhaustion. According to a study sponsored by the International Labor Organization, in Guatemala 83 percent of those interviewed worked in agriculture;[151] other jobs include recycling in public dumps and domestic work, but primarily in the informal sector. They work because they are poor.

Indigenous Guatemalans do see rays of hope of the return of their time, their cycle. The creation of the Academy for Mayan Languages, founded in 1990, and the awarding of the Nobel Peace Prize to Rigoberta Menchú in 1992 for her activism on behalf of the Maya peoples, constitute significant recognition of their talents and accomplishments. In the area of education, there is now a recognized need for bilingual and bicultural education and programs.

Although it has been an arduous, painful, and sorrowful journey for the past five hundred years, finally in the twenty-first century there is opportunity for political participation. Legislative representation of Mayas increased to 12.4 percent in 2000 compared to 8 percent in 1985,[152] but they are still significantly underrepresented. There are now indigenous political parties—such as Majawil Q'ij, the National Coordinating Committee of Indigenous People and Campesinos (CONIC), and Nukuj Ajpop—that have negotiated some protections regarding voting rights and placed their demands on the public agenda.[153] A small victory at the local level was the election of a mayoral candidate in 1995, when Robert Qume Chay won in the municipality of Quetzaltenango. His election broke ground as the first K'iche person in such a political seat.[154]

While the legal system is making accommodations in providing services in the languages of the Maya communities, they still confront barriers regarding accessibility to legal institutions, including sparse availability of interpreters. These are particularly important issues in light of the portion of the population they represent.

Women also often experience particular hardships as a result of conflict in Guatemala, as elsewhere. First, violence against women since the end of the thirty-six-year war in 1996 has been escalating, whether due to family violence or violence perpetrated by criminal elements. "Since 2001, more than 700 women and young girls have been killed in apparently motiveless attacks. So far this year more than 250 bodies have been found. In the past six months there have been five sets of double murders, with the tortured corpses of the young girls found together."[155] A recent report by Amnesty International asserts that the "country's leaders must share the blame for an epidemic of violence that has killed more than 1,500 women in under four years. The brutality of the killings . . . reveal that extreme forms of sexual violence and discrimination remain prevalent in Guatemalan society. . . . In the first five months of 2005, the tally reached 225—considerably more than one killing every day."[156] The total number of women and girls murdered rose to 665 in 2005 (527 in 2004, 383 in 2003). In the first five months of 2006, there were 299 cases.[157]

Second, although the prolonged civil war officially ended in 1996, the effects of post-traumatic stress disorder[158] continue, with intense manifestations such as pervasive anxiety, depression, and distorted self-concept, among others that will be discussed further below. Some of the collective symptoms that affect men and women in the society are manifest in the increased violence, especially against women at home and in public settings:

> The violence generated by the armed conflict, social violence, as well as intrafamilial abuse and abuse and aggression committed against girls and adolescents, has had a strong impact on mental health, manifesting principally in low self-esteem, trauma, academic delays, anxiety, fear, depression, emotional imbalance, etc. According to the psychological gravity of the impact, adolescents can manifest problems such as aggression, alcohol abuse, and suicide.[159]

There is the double impact that women suffer from PTSD themselves and are also subjected to the behavior of others who are acting out in part at least because they are also affected by the same disorder.

Social and Political Reconciliation, the Rule of Law,
and the Effort to Mitigate the Effects of Conflict

It is obvious that serious work aimed at social and political reconciliation is needed in order to mitigate the effects of that conflict and, further, that the successful implementation of an effective rule of law system is central to all those efforts. At the same time, the work toward reconciliation can, in turn, facilitate the development of the rule of law not merely as a system of formal rules, but also as a commitment to a system of law that in fact as well as in theory binds both the rulers and the ruled such that those seeking to move Guatemala forward can have a reasonable degree of confidence in the system. To adopt a rule of law system that will be effective and will be seen as moving toward a just society, Guatemala will have to undergo a long-term, multidimensional process toward social, political, and cultural reconciliation.[160]

An effective rule of law system requires effective institutions, such as a judiciary that is viewed not as a part of a political regime but as an independent forum in which disputes will be addressed with fairness and procedural regularity.[161] That also requires courts that are strong enough to have the requisite prestige in the society so that officials can and will be held to account, such that Guatemalans will be willing to accord legitimacy to them. It necessitates fundamental changes to the military and developing civilian security forces, who should be trained to protect rather than simply to control citizens.[162] Public institutions, like a rule of law system, are not merely mechanical devices. They manifest in their operations a set of values drawn from the society that created those institutions. They are means to achieve particular ends, but the means and the ends they were designed to achieve are clearly interrelated. Michael Sandel quite accurately observed that: "Political institutions are not simply instruments that implement ideas independently conceived; they are themselves embodiments of ideas."[163]

To date, the effort to achieve this kind of rule of law system has been challenging. The Peace Accord officially signed in December of 1996 started the process of transitional justice. Prior steps included the signing of the 1994 Human Rights Accord, the first of thirteen agreements. This accord created the truth commission, the *Comisión para el Esclarecimiento Histórico* (CEH; Historical Clarification Commission). The process also required the intervention and support of the United Nations in a ten-year peace process known by its acronym as MINUGUA (United Nations Verification Mission). While the transitional process rejected amnesty as part of the peace agreement, this position was reversed in 1996 by mutual agreement between the government and URNG, the opposition group, and was included in the Law of National Reconciliation.[164]

The CEH met with difficulties as it pursued its difficult inquiries, including obstacles the government placed on its path to obstruct investigations. For example, the CEH had to do its work without any financial support from the Guatemalan government. Even so, the commission made clear that the government and the military had been guilty of genocide against the Mayas. The CEH documented that in the early 1980s, "some 200,000 were arbitrarily executed or 'disappeared,' 200,000 became refugees, and one million were internally displaced by the end of the conflict."[165] It verified that 93 percent of the acts of violence were perpetrated by the government. On completion of its work in 1999, the CEH concluded that "the violence was fundamentally directed by the state against the excluded, the poor, and above all, the Mayan people, as well as those who struggled in favor of a just and more equitable society."[166]

During the war, legal institutions were effectively eliminated. First, thirty-six years of authoritarian regimes committed extreme illegal actions. Second, the prevalence of violence against citizens conveyed the message that violence "was a more expedited resource to solving interpersonal problems."[167] Third, "to the extreme that impunity became a tolerated practice in penal law,"[168] it announced a clear message that justice was in the hands of the beholder. Although the World Bank has funded efforts to strengthen and establish legal institutions, including a traveling court, the problems with impunity of perpetrators of mass killings have posed daunting challenges for those seeking to set Guatemala on a different course.[169] The effort to put an end to immunity from prosecution and the desire to ensure compensation for the victims continue to be obstacles to peace and reconciliation.

Another of the challenges that has surfaced during this post-conflict period has been the operation of clandestine paramilitary groups that have engaged in persecution and assassinations of human rights advocates, even during the efforts at reconciliation following the conflict. These activities clearly undermine human security as that term is used by the United Nations. In response, a commission was established to investigate clandestine activities.

[C]landestine groups have emerged that threaten and punish at will and, who are connected to criminal organizations, and linked to State organisms. These clandestine bodies operate with impunity and their attacks are clearly aimed at . . . human rights organizations and activists, creating grave conditions of fear.[170]

On the other hand, Guatemala has committed itself to work toward advancing a culture of peace as well as modernizing its national civil police and legal system. In fact, the peace accord required the Guatemalan government to address transitional justice issues. There are measures to reintegrate military personnel and child soldiers to civil society, as has been the case in other countries such as Rwanda.[171] Multilingual citizenship education regarding the judicial system is now delivered through radio programs, an effective non-formal education measure.

Specific measures have been instituted to develop and strengthen legal institutions, as well as extending their services to remote areas. Through World Bank assistance, "177 Justice of the Peace courts have been created and implemented. . . . One regional and one departmental justice center have been inaugurated, and a second regional center is in progress. . . . Two mobile courts have been in operation since 2003. Twenty-five mediation centers have opened and are providing mediation services in indigenous languages."[172] Further, training on culturally responsive legal service and anticorruption seminars have been conducted. The limited institutional capacity in the legal system has been complicated by inadequate or antiquated legal record-keeping systems. Today, twenty-four automated criminal records offices and the General Archive of Protocols are operational.[173]

Women have achieved some gains in the legal system. Specifically, women have been appointed to 17 percent of judgeships (as compared to 3 percent before efforts to improve the situation) and hold fully half of the justice of the peace positions.[174] Indeed, "For the first time in Guatemala's history the President of the Supreme Court is a woman."[175] The hope is that women in the judicial system may influence an entrenched male-dominated system in a chauvinist culture to become more sensitive to gender-related victimization.

There have been some accomplishments with respect to the protection of children and adolescents, such as the Law on Childhood and Adolescence Integral Protection (Ley de Protección Integral de la Niñez y Adolescencia), 2003.[176] This law replaced the Minors Code of 1979, which was based on a particularly punitive approach toward poor children. The 2003 law recognized and protected the rights of children, including rights to special protection. Its passage was the culmination of reform efforts in support of children and adolescents who suffer poverty, homelessness, and are too often victims of violent crime.[177]

Because the impacts of violence permeate a society at many levels, Guatemala confronts a challenging future.[178] Its people suffer from individual as well as collective intergenerational post-traumatic stress disorder.[179] Violent acts affect those who are injured in ways that, as native peoples say, affect the mind, the body, and the spirit.[180] The discussion that follows in this chapter explains in more detail the phenomenon of post-traumatic stress and its manifestations.

Perhaps the Commission for Historical Clarification provided at the outset of its report on the violence in Guatemala the best summary of what happened there and of the challenge ahead.

> Guatemala has seen periods marked by beauty and dignity from the beginning of the ancient Mayan culture to the present day; . . . However, in Guatemala, pages have also been written of shame and infamy, disgrace and terror, pain and grief, all as a product of the armed confrontation among brothers and sisters. For more than 34 years, Guatemalans lived under the shadow of fear, death and disappearance as daily threats in the lives of ordinary citizens.[181]

WHAT IS TRAUMATIC STRESS AND CULTURAL BEREAVEMENT?

In order to better understand the nature, significance, and impact of traumatic stress from violent conflict on the community in places like Guatemala, it is necessary to consider something of the origins of the concept of post-traumatic stress, the contemporary understanding of post-traumatic stress disorder, the concept of cultural bereavement, the special issues of post-traumatic stress for young people, and the intergenerational effects of traumatic stress.

An Old Problem with Recent Recognition

Although the psychological effects of trauma were explored by Sigmund Freud in the nineteenth century, it has been only relatively recently that serious consideration has been given to what is today known as post-traumatic stress disorder. During World War I, soldiers who exhibited unusual behavior after exposure to the extreme stress of violent conflict were described as experiencing "shell shock," while in World War II and the Korean conflict, those symptoms were termed "combat fatigue." However, it was not until the Vietnam era that clinicians were forced to explore seriously the impact of war and the effects of witnessing its brutality on the veterans who had fought in it.[182]

Pressured by veterans of that conflict for real answers to psychosocial impacts from the war, research on the problem moved forward, including efforts to classify and name the condition so that those who were suffering from it would be eligible for treatment. The consistency and perseverance of symptoms led to a new formal diagnosis, post-traumatic stress disorder, adopted by the American Psychiatric Association in the DSMR-III (Diagnostic Statistical Manual of Mental Disorder, Third Edition) in 1980.[183] It became clear that the veterans' families were also affected. "Traumatized people feel utterly abandoned, utterly alone, cast out of the human and divine systems of care and protection that sustain life. Thereafter, a sense of alienation, of disconnection, pervades every relationship, from the most intimate familial bonds to the most abstract affiliation of community and religion."[184]

Since the identification of post-traumatic stress disorder as a recognized diagnosis, mental health professionals have sought to learn more about the impact of trauma on individuals and groups. Clinicians generally understand PTSD one patient at a time. However, those who have studied the matter in the context of families and larger populations, particularly those associated with indigenous communities, also argue that PTSD has effects on the spirit and culture of an individual, family, community, and society.[185]

While the short-term consequences of traumatic experiences are well-established, recognition of its long-term psychological and emotional effects (the term *sequelae* is employed in the clinical community) is more recent.[186] One of the populations of interest to researchers in recent years has been the group of persons who survived the Holocaust in Germany, some of whom began to manifest symptoms of PTSD quite late in life and then to receive treatment for what was clearly PTSD. Recent studies have also included examination of a wide range of traumatic events, from traffic accidents to sexual abuse.

Clinicians have explored a wide range of treatments with varying degrees of support, including psychological, medical, or pharmacological therapies. Such complementary approaches as spiritual, cultural, or community-based therapies have also been employed and are being studied.[187] While they are the subject of continuing debate in medical circles, complementary and alternative therapies are increasingly recognized as important additions to other contemporary treatments.[188]

It is now well-established that trauma triggered by war, civil conflict, terrorism, or civil disorder will have deleterious long-term effects on many of those who experience these events. That is even true for those who may not be physically victimized, but who witness such brutality, as is common among children who witness violence against parents, siblings, or neighbors. This discussion of PTSD focuses on refugees, displaced persons, veterans, survivors of torture, and their families and communities.

While PTSD is today widely recognized such that the U.S. military has limited screening processes for those returning from conflicts in Iraq and Afghanistan, members of Congress have committed to hold hearings into well-substantiated allegations that officers and noncommissioned officers have not only failed to support proper care for service members suffering from PTSD, but have in some instances actively interfered in their opportunity to attend treatment appointments and otherwise have discouraged those in need from obtaining care. These allegations surfaced in a National Public Radio story with interviews of the noncommissioned officers (NCOs) and some officers who admitted interfering with care and even taking steps to have people removed from the military without benefits to address their mental health issues.[189] There is also a concern that there are inconsistent responses by those in charge of referrals for treatment when a returning service member answers in the affirmative on a number of items on the screening questionnaire they are given during return processing.[190]

Continuing Discussions about the Nature of and Treatments for Post-Traumatic Stress Disorder and Cultural Bereavement

Post-traumatic stress disorder consists of impaired social and psychological functioning upon exposure to a traumatic event or sequences of events.[191] Trauma can be engendered where there is a risk of violence or where one witnesses injury inflicted by another human being or the brutal death of a loved one. The personal, familial, and community experience of conflict can have psychological, physical, cultural, and social impacts. Those consequences can include depression, anxiety, hypervigilance, panic, dissociation, substance abuse, psychic numbing, nightmares, and a constellation of other symptoms.[192] Some of these symptoms may manifest in culture-specific symptoms. That is, studies indicate that some cultures may experience PTSD in different ways, such as headaches, backache, heart problems, hypertension, nostalgia, and *nervios* (a Spanish-language term that is widely understood in the culture and is far more than simply an experience of feeling nervous). There is also "a cultural category that comprises dysphoria (anxiety, fear, anger)," or what is called somatization of the trauma.[193]

Survivors of brutal political regimes and violent conflict grapple with a cluster of PTSD symptoms on the one hand, but many, and particularly those who have been driven out of their homelands or whose culture was specifically attacked—as in the case of the Maya in Guatemala—also experience a related condition known as cultural bereavement. Cultural bereavement is the loss of homeland, family, and cultural anchoring. The loss of these foundations can exacerbate the psychosocial impacts of PTSD. The experience of people who are displaced, uprooted, exiled, detained, arrested, tortured, impoverished, and cut off from a cultural world have their cultural grounding shattered. Culture provides one a sense of stability, predictability, support, and emotional and intellectual anchoring. For those uprooted, the trauma needs to be understood in the context of the cultural framework and the cosmology of the person, but also in terms of healing and mourning rituals appropriate to the cultural background of the survivor.[194]

For Marlene Young, "Culture is a double-edged sword. . . . culture provides protection at a cost. Strong attachments to persons and lifestyles leads to a deeper sense of loss when the life of the culture is disrupted."[195] Therefore, researchers recommend dealing with cultural bereavement through the integration of appropriate cultural symbols and religious persons in the mourning process. For example, Cambodian orphans in the United States "wanted to learn how to chant with the monk and the older participants, and how to 'make merit' for their dead or lost parents and ancestors for a better life in the next reincarnation and to protect themselves from vengeful spirits."[196]

The purpose here is not to engage in clinical debates but to explain the fact that persons who have experienced violent conflict often are deeply affected by PTSD for years to come, as post-conflict development efforts move forward. Nevertheless, it is important to recognize that there are debates that have involved some anthropologists and mental health professionals, who caution about the application and understanding of PTSD from Western societies in other contexts.

The participants in these debates have discussed three major criticisms of the ways in which PTSD has been applied and treated.[197] First, the use of the PTSD diagnosis has been criticized as something that was normed against and understood from a Western culture-bound perspective. However, increasingly research demonstrates that although the symptoms and the types of treatments that are appropriate must be understood in terms of the cultural context of the people affected by it, PTSD is common around the globe and among culturally diverse groups.[198] That said, "trauma-focused assessment and treatment [is] always [to be] offered within a broader context that integrates ethnocultural factors, problems of language, metaphors, and symbolism, and awareness of adaptational and acculturational pressures."[199]

The second criticism is that PTSD is not an appropriate model to understand state-sponsored terror of the sort seen in Guatemala and elsewhere. The problem here is that people who find themselves in such extreme situations of threat and observe so much violence around them may engage in a great many behaviors that might be considered abnormal in other circumstances. Untangling rational responses to a bizarre reality from mental health challenges can be extremely difficult under such circumstances.[200] Third, some analysts have seen cultural bereavement as an alternative way to understand the experience of those driven into flight, as opposed to the application of a PTSD diagnosis.[201] However, the fact is that the two are related but distinct challenges, though they are what are known as co-morbid conditions (they often occur at the same time to the same people).[202] There have been discussions of other diagnoses, but those debates go well beyond the purposes of the present discussion.[203]

With the recognition of PTSD by the World Health Organization, researchers are now exploring the different ways that persons who have been exposed to flight are affected by the problem and are searching for different kinds of treatment appropriate to the culture and to the special needs of the people affected. They are beginning to respond to differences in how people experience trauma and the stress that flows from it, sometimes according to their age, their developmental stage, their gender, and their cultural context. Other issues related to PTSD include family- and community-level PTSD, intergenerational dimensions, and the impact of state violence.[204]

PTSD in Children and Adolescents

One of the most difficult facts of conflict and challenges for post-conflict development is the impact of war trauma on children and adolescents. Cross-cultural research on PTSD in children has been sparse,[205] and generally has been carried out on "selected samples after acute or 'single blow' trauma."[206] Yet, the evidence supports the diagnosis of PTSD years after the trauma.[207] Holocaust survivors have experienced PTSD even fifty years after the trauma.[208] Post-conflict development efforts depend heavily upon the young people of the society and it is therefore essential to consider the special implications of conflict-related trauma on them.

Psychological affliction from direct, witnessed, or vicarious exposure to war trauma is injurious to children, though some health providers have assumed that children's resiliency overrides its impact. (Vicarious exposure happens when those who were survivors of or witnesses to violence recount their experiences in the presence of children.) However, other research rejects this assumption that children are so resilient that they can engage in such terrible matters and simply bounce back without adverse consequences, and underscores the need to help children at least as much as, if not more than, adults.[209] Research on children from different ethnocultural groups documents consistent evidence of PTSD, anxiety disorders, major depression, and guilt in young children, adolescents, and young adults.[210]

These studies identify three major sets of symptoms, including arousal, avoidance, and intrusion.[211] The findings parallel those of adults, although the symptoms tend to manifest in different ways and in varied degrees for adults as compared to children. Adults tend to suffer more from arousal and intrusion while children tend to be afflicted more by numbing and avoidance.[212]

Children suffering from *arousal* may experience hypervigilance, sleep disturbances, irritability, outbursts of anger, aggression, anxiety, concentration and attention deficits, and excessive startle response (fear of particular noises, such as loud fans, helicopters, the sound of microwaved popcorn, squeaky sneakers, fire alarms, etc.). A familiar response of refugee children to a helicopter flying over in big cities is to drop on the floor and duck under their desks.[213] *Avoidance* is a set of symptoms that can involve a sense of foreshortened future, decreased interest in age-appropriate activities, avoidance of reminders of bad situations, avoidance of thought about—or no memory of—trauma. Related to avoidance is psychic *numbing*, which includes loss of interest in age-appropriate activities, detachment or social withdrawal, and constricted or flat affect. A related symptom is called biological disregulation, the inability to control emotions such as anger or suicidal thoughts.[214] Detachment is described as though "*warmth is lacking.*"[215] Psychic numbing or emotional insensitivity (or shutdown) may prevent children from crying their own tears because, in order to survive, they squelch their emotions.[216] Because of developmental stage, it may be difficult for children to recognize the depth of the emotional pain they have endured until it is addressed in a safe, trusting, and therapeutic environment. Children afflicted with *intrusion* experience increased emotional reactions, intrusive thoughts, nightmares, and flashbacks.[217] They may display repetitive play (doing the same thing over and over), or have aggressive and regressive behaviors such as bed-wetting and thumb-sucking. They may also suffer separation anxiety (i.e., shadowing or clinging on parents or caretakers).[218]

There are differences in the way PTSD affects young people, related to culture, gender, resettlement situation, and stage of development.

PTSD or Culture Specific Manifestations?

Despite differences in cultural manifestations of PTSD, studies conducted in various parts of the world on diverse ethnocultural groups agree that trauma from exposure to violent conflict, whether a child is a witness or a victim, is important. These studies have examined Palestinian children;[219] Southeast Asians;[220] Iranian refugee children resettled in Sweden;[221] Middle

Eastern children resettled in Denmark;[222] Croatian displaced adolescents;[223] Bosnian children;[224] Cambodians;[225] Cambodian children and their parents;[226] Central American refugees;[227] Israeli children;[228] Cambodian youth;[229] and Iraqi children,[230] among others.

Like the literature on PTSD in children, studies of pain among children are also relatively recent explorations. Even so, the evidence suggests that there may be an impact from torture or severe trauma even at the cellular level, altering genetic information and thus creating an increased sensitivity to physiological pain.[231] Unfortunately, PTSD affects developmental processes: "Since trauma takes place in a neurodevelopmental context, attention to the interaction between trauma and developmental neurobiology is clearly imperative."[232] Trauma may alter the neurobiology of a child. "Neural systems that are activated change in permanent ways, creating 'internal' representations—literally, memories. . . . The physiological hyperarousal state associated with fear and pervasive threat results in a brain that . . . has adapted to a world of unpredictability and danger. The brains of traumatized children . . . are in a persisting state of arousal and, therefore, experience persisting anxiety."[233]

Cultural norms or behaviors do not shield the child against these deleterious effects.[234] William Sack and colleagues concluded that: "PTSD as a result of massive war trauma appears to transcend the formidable barrier of culture and language in the Khmer population,"[235] even though the effects of trauma may be channeled through culture-specific symptoms.[236] While it is important to be cautious against stereotyping, some research suggests group differences and points out similarity in psychological problems, but differences in symptomatology according to varied ethnocultural groups.[237] Depression and social withdrawal tended to be common characteristics found in Southeast Asian children, while Central American children were afflicted by depression, oppositional conduct disorders such as "acting out," and school failure. Chilean children tended to experience nightmares and anxiety.

While culture may serve as a buffer through which to understand and work out the effects of trauma, it cannot prevent trauma. Indeed, findings point to commonalities regarding the human experience of emotional and physical pain and suffering.[238] In fact, some research suggests that there are far more commonalities than differences across cultural lines. Mathew Friedman and James Jaranson state that "the PTSD model predicts that traumatized individuals from both Western and non-Western backgrounds will show similar alterations in autonomic reactivity, startle reflex, sleep disturbance, adrenergic hyperarousal, hypothalamic-pituitary-adrenocortical dysregulation, and endogenous opioid system activity."[239]

Discussions of Possible Gender Differences in Young
People Exposed to Trauma from Violent Conflict

The research to date is inconclusive with regard to the degree to which gender is a factor for young people exposed to conflict-related trauma or just how much it may influence the symptoms that children and adolescents may display. Some studies found no apparent differences based on gender,[240] while other studies suggest the contrary.[241] Still others report a higher incidence of PTSD among female adolescents related to the mother's health and a longer exile period.[242] One commonly observed gender difference is that females tend to internalize the trauma while males tend to externalize it. Girls will more likely exhibit "anxiety, dysphoria, dissociation, avoidance." Boys are more likely to exhibit "impulsivity, aggression, inattention, hyperactivity."[243]

Some researchers have found that females have higher rates of PTSD than males in adult populations.[244] However, this may be attributed to the stigma attached to mental health and that, generally, it is socially acceptable for females to exhibit emotional problems while it is still a taboo for males. Likewise, females are more likely to seek psychological help.

One interesting study of girls captured some important impacts on Palestinian children.[245] Girls who had to assume more responsibility and become more independent because they lived in high-violence areas demonstrated more resilience than their counterparts living in low-violence areas who also had more parental supervision. Positive female role models tended to buffer the impact of trauma on girls, for example, when their mothers asserted a stronger role in the home and the community. The contrary was true for boys. Resilience for boys developed from structured settings with rules and parental supervision. Male role models, however, were often missing from their lives because of imprisonment or deaths of males.

On the other hand, another study among Palestinian children found that "girls tend to suffer significantly more from symptoms of anxiety, depression, and PTSD than their male cohorts."[246] Three possible reasons were offered to explain the findings: (1) males benefit from political participation, (2) Palestinian patriarchal culture attributes females a lower rank, and (3) males channel emotional distress through culturally appropriate ways, primarily somatization.

One of the subjects that remains to be studied in greater detail is just how and to what degree the growing use of rape as a weapon of social warfare (discussed in chapters 2 and 5) will exacerbate PTSD in girls and women. It is thus important to consider its impact on females, though males[247] too are raped, for example Maya boys in Guatemala.[248] It remains to be seen just what the longer term will hold for those young women who were taken into armed forces as child soldiers and faced a range of sexual and other physical as well as psychological abuse. In addition to the repercussions of traumatic stress and sexual and physical abuse, these girls face stigmatization and rejection as unwed mothers in their communities, as is the case in Liberia, Burkina Faso, and Rwanda, among others (for a discussion on rein-tegration, see chapter 5).

The Complicated Mix Facing Young People in Flight: Depression Due to PTSD, a Result of Resettlement/Life Challenges, or All of the Above

Some research has indicated that there are significant differences between the symptoms displayed by refugee children suffering from PTSD and im-migrant children who did not come from such stressful circumstances, but who are struggling with cultural shock.[249] Cultural shock tends to be for a limited time, while depression associated with PTSD can persist over an ex-tended period. Refugee children *without* PTSD often still experience depres-sion as a consequence of resettlement or recent life events. Resettlement stressors may trigger depression related to lack of language skills and recent difficult events after resettlement, such as a natural death, accidents, or breakup of a romantic relationship. However, within a period of time, as ac-culturation proceeds, the incidence of depression drops significantly for this group.[250] On the other hand, PTSD may plague refugee children for years after the conflict ends. Further, PTSD symptoms can be exacerbated by resettlement and life-event stressors.[251]

Age Differences in Manifestations of PTSD: Children and Adolescents

Life stage affects how children and adolescents respond to traumatization based on their affective and cognitive maturity.[252] Milestones they may have achieved may be reversed by the trauma, depending on the intensity and the frequency, and the age at the time of the event(s). While there are some similarities, there are also important differences for each age group. Some of the commonalities among both children and adolescents include the "high incidence of school and health problems" among those diagnosed with PTSD.[253] The National Institute of Mental Health recognizes develop-mental differences in children on how they experience and manifest trauma.[254] The following age brackets present general symptoms children may exhibit.

Children Five Years of Age and Younger

Infants and young children cannot verbalize the trauma. Their symptoms tend to be less specific and are characterized as separation anxiety, excessive crying, and whimpering. They may reveal their trauma through facial ex-pressions or physical motionlessness. Young children may also experience regression in language and behavior and such as bed-wetting, thumb-sucking, nail-biting, fear of darkness, fear of sleeping alone, and overdependence. Other regressive behaviors include excessive clinging and shadowing of caretakers. Their ability to interact with others may become restricted as well. Just how severe the children's reactions to trauma may be affected by the parents' emotional well-being and their ability to deal with traumatic events. Children at this vulnerable age may also exhibit reactive attachment disorder, which is described as "markedly disturbed and developmentally inappropriate social relatedness in most contexts that begins before age 5 years."[255] Even though preschoolers may not exhibit common symptoms of PTSD, it is sometimes possible to assess their trauma.[256]

Children Six to Eleven Years Old

Children slightly older, six to eleven, may exhibit anxiety, irritability, and disruptive and hostile behaviors. Their hostility may manifest in outbursts of anger and propensity to engage in fighting with peers. Attention difficulties may affect school performance and teachers may report that these children appear to be in a daze. They may suffer from depression and regressive behaviors and may develop sleeping disorders, such as difficulty falling asleep or waking up during sleep, to more intense symptoms like nightmares and irrational fears, including of the dark. Trauma somatization may translate into medically unexplainable physical symptoms, headaches, stomachaches, vomiting, or numbing. Refusal to go to school may be accompanied by social withdrawal and alienation from peers. Children in these age groups are three times more susceptible to PTSD than adolescents because of their cognitive, affective, and social development.[257]

Adolescents

Adolescents with PTSD often face uncertainty about the future, referred to as having a *lack of sense of futurity*. Unable to envision life beyond their trauma, they become "frozen in the past."[258] Adolescents express their trauma in poor school performance or dropping out, promiscuous sexual behavior, eating disorders, substance abuse, teenage pregnancy, and disruptive or violent behavior. In war conditions, trauma is complicated with rape, transmissions of sexually transmitted diseases, and HIV/AIDS. Symptoms of PTSD can be disabling to youngsters due to their long-term effect.[259] Disruption of familial and community connections, essential to a healthy personality development, can add to the problem because it is a stage when adolescents are forging their individuality and autonomy. In some instances, participation in meaningful community work or social movements may serve as a protective factor, and serve as a "personal resource and as a source of resilience."[260]

The National Institute of Mental Health found behaviors of adolescents similar to those exhibited by adults: flashbacks, nightmares, psychic numbing, withdrawal, isolation, avoidance or antisocial behaviors, difficulty in peer interaction, and depression. Other adultlike behaviors include substance abuse, suicidal ideation, sleep disorders, delinquency, or disorganized thinking.[261] Survival guilt is common. "The adolescent may feel extreme guilt over his or her failure to prevent injury or loss of life, and may harbor revenge fantasies that interfere with recovery from the trauma."[262]

The severity of trauma triggered by dangerous experiences may be determined by: (1) the intensity and duration of the trauma; (2) whether the child was tortured or not; (3) whether a child directly witnessed atrocities or heard from others (vicarious traumatization); (4) developmental stage; (5) personality traits; (6) availability of family support; (7) whether one, or both parents, or siblings were tortured; (8) death of the father;[263] and (9) whether the entire family suffers from PTSD.

Martin Teicher sends an important warning not only for what happened in Guatemala but to children in countries around the world who have been subjected to conflict. "Society reaps what it sows in the way it nurtures its children. Stress sculpts the brain to exhibit various antisocial, though adaptive behaviors. Whether it comes in the form of physical abuse, emotional or sexual trauma, exposure to warfare, urban violence, famine or pestilence, stress can set off a ripple of hormonal changes that permanently wire a child's brain to cope with a malevolent world."[264]

Families under Stress

War often destroys the fabric of families, separating them by political imprisonment of a father, mother, brother, or uncle, or driving some into flight while others, whose fate may be unknown for months or even years, are left behind. Survivors often live in emotional limbo and experience survival guilt. In some cases, all the males of a family, or a community, as was the fate of Bosnians, Albanians, and Kosovars, may be imprisoned while the mother and remaining children flee from political persecution. There is also the flight of unaccompanied minors, such as the lost boys of Sudan, who lost all family members, and had only each other as family.

For these reasons it should come as no surprise that PTSD tends to cluster in families.[265] The trauma, whether experienced directly or vicariously, is rarely restricted to one family member. Even when children themselves are not tortured or beaten, they often are helpless witnesses to atrocities committed against their loved ones, unable to help those they see abused and unable to process such brutalities in their own minds.

The despair, affective disregulation, depression, nightmares, anxiety, anger, withdrawn behaviors, and other symptoms may become emotionally paralyzing for a mother or father, affecting his or her ability to be emotionally available to the children.²⁶⁶ Separation of family members is particularly damaging for children. Even when parents are on hand, "it is generally difficult for adults to maintain the kind of balanced behavior that children need."²⁶⁷

Family relationships are also distressed. For example, for Vietnam, Iraq, and Afghanistan veterans, PTSD has had disrupting consequences for families as many veterans struggled with symptoms of their trauma, such as depression, anger, and emotional withdrawal.²⁶⁸ Family traumatic stress may extend beyond the nuclear family to other family members, grandparents, grandchildren, and even to later generations.

The Intergenerational Dimension of Traumatic Stress and Cultural Bereavement

At the end of many conflicts, the survivors adamantly assert that their descendants should never have to experience the horror they have seen. As World War II was coming to an end, the world community in the Preamble to the United Nations Charter stated: "We the peoples of the United Nations, determined to save succeeding generations from the scourge of war, which twice in our lifetime has brought untold sorrows," and they therefore agreed to form the United Nations.²⁶⁹ Yet there has been one violent conflict after another and increasing evidence that the effects of past conflicts have significant effects on generations to come.

While clinicians have focused their analysis of impact of trauma on individual patients, recent research on PTSD has expanded to explore the repercussions of trauma not only on survivors but also their descendants. This research has important ramifications for a sustainable development approach in which the health and well-being are considered for current generations as well as for future generations. The research has indicated that the children of those who experienced PTSD sometimes manifest evidence of the disorder even though they had no direct exposure to the events that caused the initial trauma. For example, the National Center for PTSD of the U.S. Department of Veterans Affairs reported findings on Vietnam veterans that concluded:

> Within the group of veterans who met criteria for PTSD, those whose fathers had been exposed to combat scored significantly higher in PTSD measures and guilt than those whose fathers had not been exposed to combat. . . . Intergenerational effects of trauma, therefore, seem to emerge when the second generation itself has PTSD, and they appear to be more strongly related to intergenerational processes during the homecoming period than to differences in premilitary vulnerability.²⁷⁰

Other studies on the children of Holocaust survivors found not only behavioral evidence of transgenerational transmission of PTSD but also physiological evidence as well. Research done at the Traumatic Stress Studies Division of the Department of Psychiatry at Mount Sinai School of Medicine found a range of effects.[271] Dr. Rachel Yehuda and others documented psychological as well as biological alterations. One study found, for example, that the cortisol levels of Holocaust survivors and their offspring were similar, indicative of PTSD.[272] (Cortisol is a hormone that the body uses to stop the biochemical reaction to stress and return the body to normal functioning.) Indeed, offspring presented physiological as well as psychological reactions associated with PTSD.

Although some of the research findings attest to resilience by the children of trauma or war survivors, other findings show its transgenerational repercussions not just for the children of those who have experienced PTSD but at the community levels of ethnocultural and national groups, such as Australian Aboriginal people;[273] Native Americans;[274] First Nations Peoples of Canada;[275] people in Latin American countries such as Chile[276] and Argentina;[277] South Africans;[278] Palestinians; Cambodians;[279] Armenians;[280] people in the former Yugoslavia;[281] Japanese Americans;[282] and Holocaust survivors in the United States[283] and Israel,[284] among others.

Threats to the survival of cultural foundations such as those that result from genocide, as in the case of Guatemala, can have profound effects on whether a people can endure the impact of state-sponsored terror. "The effects of trauma can also be transmitted to succeeding generations through culture. The ways in which cultures encourage or discourage people to deal with their negative emotions will, to some extent, determine the intergenerational effects of trauma."[285] Attempts at cultural annihilation can be internalized and transmitted across generations. However, the experiences that come from surviving such violence can also serve to sustain a people and strengthen their endurance. That has certainly been true in the case of Native American peoples and the evidence is that it will also be true of the Maya in Guatemala.

State-Imposed and State-Sponsored Violence

Given that there is a recognition that trauma and cultural bereavement can and do affect not just individuals, but also larger communities and that it can do so not just in the present but over time, there has been ongoing discussion about other features that may exacerbate the problem. One of the factors that has been identified is violence carried out by the state or its surrogates, like the government-supported death squads in Guatemala.[286] These are actions not simply by rogue officers or groups, but intentional governmental violence perpetrated against entire groups or communities.

There are several factors associated with this kind of violence that are important for understanding the effects of conflict on those who remain in place, those who take flight, and the community, including: (1) the importance of the state's role in the violence; (2) the fact that reasonable people must react in unacceptable ways in order to survive; (3) the fact that the actions of the state drive groups within the community further apart and seek to inflame prejudices and discriminatory behavior; (4) the tendency of this official or state-sponsored behavior to break down expectations of truth and essential levels of trust; (5) the desire by officials to protect themselves or others may prevent full accounting for violence and closure for the families and communities affected; (6) the near-term residual effects of the violence create PTSD and other trauma-related challenges as a major public health problem; and (7) the damage done and the mode and intentionality of it add to the difficulty central to sustainable development of allowing future generations to move forward free of dysfunctional limitations from previous generations.

The Importance of the State's Role in the Violence

The official designation by the state that a group of people is inferior or not worthy of the protection of law is damaging. One of the more effective statements of the problem came in the U.S. Supreme Court's ruling in *Brown v. Board of Education,* unanimously rejecting state-imposed segregation by race. One of the debates in that case concerned the question whether there was actual evidence of harm to the children who were segregated. The National Association for the Advancement of Colored People, Legal Defense and Education Fund engaged a range of social scientists, including psychologists, to explore this question. Ultimately, they convinced the Court that the fact of discrimination on the basis of race and the equally and the even more important fact that it was discrimination sanctioned by the state meant psychological damage to the children. The Court concluded that:

> . . . To separate [these children] from others of similar age and qualifications
> solely because of their race generates a feeling of inferiority as to their status in
> the community that may affect their hearts and minds in a way unlikely ever
> to be undone. . . . "Segregation of white and colored children in public schools
> has a detrimental effect upon the colored children. The impact is greater when
> it has the sanction of the law; for the policy of separating the races is usually
> interpreted as denoting the inferiority of the negro group. . . . Segregation with
> the sanction of law, therefore, has a tendency to [retard] the educational and
> mental development of Negro children and to deprive them of some of the
> benefits they would receive in a racial[ly] integrated school system.". . . Whatever may have been the extent of psychological knowledge at [an earlier time],
> this finding is amply supported by modern authority.[287]

State-sponsored violence affects individuals, families, and communities, as well as entire societies.[288] In many such situations the state action represents a deliberate effort to rend the social fabric and to damage particular parts of it.[289] It often treats individuals as objects and breaks them off from their essential social relationships. Ignacio Martín-Baró has argued that: "Such a conception denies their existence as historical beings whose life is developed and fulfilled in a complex web of social relations."[290]

The damage is all the more complex and severe where the international community stands by and takes little or no action against policies and tactics that are plain violations of international human rights accords, as in Darfur. In such settings, the global community often responds with humanitarian efforts but does not fully engage the policies that are responsible for the humanitarian disaster.[291] Similarly, the fact that the United States not only did not move to stop the violations in Guatemala, but was actually supportive of the regime when it was fully aware of its abuses remains an ongoing issue for Guatemala and for the United States.

Reasonable People Must React in Unacceptable Ways in Order to Survive

There is a certain irony that, in a situation in which the global community clearly sees illegal and inhumane behavior by governments or their surrogates and does little or nothing about it, those same governments are willing to impose on refugee claimants and others in need of assistance a standard of conduct appropriate to a peaceful context, but that would very likely lead to death in the situations from which many asylum seekers fled. As chapter 3 pointed out, many countries have increasingly used lack of adequate identity papers, a record of criminal conduct in the country of origin, or nervous or evasive behavior when responding to inquiries from officials as bases to prohibit entry to a potential host country, or even as a basis for incarceration. These kinds of behaviors often kept the asylum seekers from torture, death, or both in their countries of origin. Chapters 3 and 5 explained practices, like identity cleansing and identity documents that labeled the bearer as a member of a target group, that have been common bases for state-sanctioned violence. The fact that a refugee had a criminal record in the country of origin often means nothing more than that the person with that record was regarded as a dissident in the country of origin. While these responses—flight-fight, fear, anxiety, paranoia, hyperactivity, dissociation, emotional numbness—may be considered abnormal, from a psychological perspective, they have too often become necessary to survival in conflict and flight.

Actions of the State Drive Groups within the Community Further Apart and Seek to Inflame Prejudices and Discriminatory Behavior

Second, Martín-Baró identified polarization of societies at war as a destructive factor for the society. The state, which is supposed to be the representative of positive community values and legitimate principles of behavior, objectifies or views the "Other" as dispossessed of values and virtues. Some of the worst savagery in human history, though, has taken place when the Other who has been identified is part of one's own community who can be singled out for blame. One can certainly look to the Holocaust, to Rwanda, and to a host of other conflicts mentioned earlier, including the Maya in Guatemala.

In other cases, the state has not necessarily moved to destroy those singled out for blame or persecution, but has isolated or even incarcerated them. Most Americans are aware, for example, that Japanese Americans were first subjected to a curfew, then exclusion from their homes and businesses in West Coast communities, and then removed to concentration camps euphemistically referred to as relocation centers. Sadder still, the U.S. Supreme Court upheld the curfew and the removal,[292] though the Court determined that the incarceration exceeded the authority delegated to War Relocation Authority.[293]

Those decisions were bad enough on their face—and the dissenters in the *Korematsu v. United States* case said so in language that is among the clearest and strongest in the history of the Court—but over time it became obvious that the actions taken against over 120,000 Americans was even more despicable than was apparent. At the time of the *Korematsu* ruling on the exclusion order, Justice Murphy wrote in dissent that: "This exclusion of 'all persons of Japanese ancestry, both alien and non-alien,' from the Pacific Coast area on a plea of military necessity in the absence of martial law ought not to be approved. Such exclusion goes over 'the very brink of constitutional power' and falls into the ugly abyss of racism."[294] He added:

> I dissent, therefore, from this legalization of racism. Racial discrimination in any form . . . is utterly revolting among a free people who have embraced the principles set forth in the Constitution. . . . All residents of this nation are kin in some way by blood or culture to a foreign land. Yet they are primarily and necessarily a part of the new and distinct civilization of the United States. They must accordingly be treated at all times . . . as entitled to all the rights and freedoms guaranteed by the Constitution.[295]

Justice Robert Jackson, who would less than a year later become the chief prosecutor at the Nuremberg War Trials, wrote that the actions taken against Korematsu resulted:

> not from anything he did, said, or thought, different than they, but only in that he was born of different racial stock. . . . Now, if any fundamental assumption underlies our system, it is that guilt is personal and not inheritable. Even if all of one's antecedents had been convicted of treason, the Constitution forbids its penalties to be visited upon him. . . . But here is an attempt to make an otherwise innocent act a crime merely because this prisoner is the son of parents

as to whom he had no choice, and belongs to a race from which there is no way to resign.[296]

Forty years later it would be discovered that the government's claim of military necessity in those Japanese exclusion cases was a fraudulent misrepresentation of the fact that General DeWitt issued those orders on the basis of racism and not from any evidence of military necessity. This awful truth was discovered quite by accident late in 1982 by Ms. Aiko Herzig-Yoshinaga, who was a researcher working for the Commission on Wartime Relocation and Internment of Civilians. She came upon the only surviving copy of the original report that had been prepared by General DeWitt to justify the orders and realized that it was different from all of the other copies of the report that had actually been used in the litigation and for other official purposes later. After these documents were examined, it became clear that there never had been any evidence of military necessity and that "broad historical causes which shaped these decisions [exclusion and detention] were race prejudice, war hysteria and a failure of political leadership."[297] When superiors had seen DeWitt's original report, soon after he prepared it, orders were issued to produce a revised report and to destroy all of the copies of DeWitt's original report. "Theodore Smith of the Civil Affairs Division of the Western Defense Command [wrote a memorandum] dated June 29, 1943, certifying that he witnessed the burning of the galley proofs, galley pages, drafts and memorandums of the original report of the Japanese Evacuation."[298] They destroyed all but one of the copies. Officials were fully aware that the report that was actually used at the time of the original litigation was not what DeWitt had said and thought about Japanese Americans and that, if that information had been provided, the argument for military necessity would very likely have fallen flat. Beyond that, a federal court later found that: "Omitted from the reports presented to the courts was information possessed by the Federal Communications Commission, the Department of the Navy, and the Justice Department which directly contradicted General DeWitt's statements."[299]

Once this information became known, Fred Korematsu and Gordon Hirabayashi went to federal court and successfully argued that they should have their convictions for violating the World War II era orders overturned. In the process of granting Fred Korematsu's petition, Judge Patel of the U.S. District Court for the Northern District of California warned about the dangers of the use of conflict as a justification for the objectification of disfavored groups in the society and the removal from those persons of legal and social protections available to every other member of the community.

Korematsu remains on the pages of our legal and political history. As a legal precedent it is now recognized as having very limited application. As historical precedent it stands as a constant caution that in times of war or declared military necessity our institutions must be vigilant in protecting constitutional guarantees. It stands as a caution that in times of distress the shield of military necessity and national security must not be used to protect governmental actions from close scrutiny and accountability. It stands as a caution that in times of international hostility and antagonisms our institutions, legislative, executive and judicial, must be prepared to exercise their authority to protect all citizens from the petty fears and prejudices that are so easily aroused.[300]

Sadly, his warning was not remembered in the aftermath of the 9/11 attacks. As chapter 2 explains, the roundups of Arab Americans and others, the willingness to stretch to the breaking point valid use of material witness warrants and technical violations of immigration laws in ways they had not previously been employed, and the use of secret immigration hearings all were actions very much in the spirit and character of the *Korematsu* case. The detention without charge and creation of military commissions not justified by law, the Supreme Court found, violated not only U.S. law, but also the Geneva Conventions.[301] Chapters 1 and 3 also explain how otherwise legitimate refugee claimants have been abused.

The tendency is to catch others up in the process of officially sanctioned hostility on grounds that there can be no innocent onlookers. One is with those in power against the target group or considered an ally of that group. As chapter 5 explains, many Hutus were killed in the 1994 genocide in Rwanda because they were perceived as sympathetic to Tutsis or were unwilling to participate in the killing. "Thus, not making a commitment to certain groups is seen as a sign of commitment to certain other ones, and identifying with neither side entails the risk of being considered an enemy of both sides. . . . But both polarization and dissociation crack the foundation of coexistence and induce an exhausting climate of socio-emotional tension."[302] The effort to move forward after the conflict toward a sustainable future will face difficult challenges in ensuring both equality and equity where, as in Guatemala, the state had previously taken extreme steps to reject both of those principles.

The Tendency of This Official or State-Sponsored Behavior to Break Down Expectations of Truth and Essential Levels of Trust

An additional problem that was underscored by Martín-Baró stems from the pervasive and continuous use by the state or its surrogates of lies or distortions of truth. This practice creates a false reality for those who lie and for those expected to believe the lies. "Almost without realizing it, we have become accustomed to institutions being exactly the opposite of what they are meant to be: those responsible for guaranteeing our safety are the main source of insecurity; those in charge of justice defend abuse and injustice, those called on to enlighten and guide are the first to deceive and manipulate."[303] The cases of Rwanda, Chile, the former Yugoslavia, Guatemala, and El Salvador (upon which Martín-Baró based his analysis) illustrate the dynamics and consequences of the use of deception too well. "Denial and silence," Martín-Baró contended, are responses imposed on families due to the fact that demands for information or protests have subjected relatives to the same fate as those who had been killed.

Both during and after the conflict, efforts are made to prevent investigation of past events or even to assassinate those who are investigating or who have provided evidence to investigators. The murders of Dr. Martín-Baró, Vice-Rector and Chair of the Psychology Department, Dr. Ignacio Ellacuría, Rector of the Universidad Centroamericana José Simeón Cañas (UCA; Central American University), along with four other Jesuit colleagues, as well as the housekeeper and her daughter, on November 16, 1989,[304] on the threshold of a peace agreement in El Salvador, and the murder of Monsignor Juan José Gerardi in 1998 in Guatemala, two days after publishing a seminal human rights report in an effort to create a memory for Guatemalans, demonstrate the lengths to which the perpetrators of state violence will go.

However, as chapter 5 explains, one of the great challenges in the postconflict context is to establish the requisite degree of trust and confidence in officials and their declarations to move toward constructive patterns of social behavior and from there to higher-order social agreements necessary to make progress on sustainable development. When people have lived under regimes where official lies are expected and where dishonest behavior or at least a refusal to acknowledge truth is an essential survival skill, the effort to establish a minimum foundation of trust takes time and considerable energy. Above all, it requires repeated demonstrations that those in positions of authority will act in a manner consistent with their rhetoric and that there will be sufficient transparency and accountability that official dishonesty will be addressed.

The Desire by Officials to Protect Themselves or Others May Prevent Full Accounting for Violence and Closure for the Families and Communities Affected

As has been true in Guatemala, there are often efforts to frustrate transparency and accountability. Part of the problem rests with issues of prosecutions for abuses, but there are even broader concerns for sustainable development. There is a larger problem of providing necessary information to answer the wide range of questions about lost family members and to resolve other issues. This lack of closure by the state regarding the whereabouts and fate of the disappeared or dead perpetuates a continuous state of grief, a collective "unresolved mourning."[305] As the Rwanda case study and the discussion in chapter 5 about peace and reconciliation processes indicate, this issue of closure is not dependent upon convictions for all those involved in atrocities, but it does require sufficient information to bring some sense of understanding of the truth and consequences of the violence that has ended.

Short-Term Effects: PTSD and Other Trauma Issues as Public Health Problems

The physical injuries and psychological effects of trauma from state-sponsored violence present a major public health problem. It has been increasingly common to understand violence, such as injuries from criminal behavior, as public health issues and the same is true where a large portion of the population is experiencing PTSD, cultural bereavement, or both.[306] One study in Colombia found that "60% of the population included in the survey presented different stages of clinical depression. The study shows that, amongst the displaced population, emotional disorders and somatic complaints are high."[307] Additionally, Colombians suffered a deterioration of health, with increased morbidity and mortality and reduced life expectancy, especially for males. Indigenous groups are at serious risk of cultural extinction from forced displacement, assassination, kidnapping, and torture, as are Afro-Colombians and subsistence farmers. It is one thing to consider the therapeutic needs of individuals suffering from these conditions, but quite another to conceptualize and implement the requisite public health strategies necessary to meet challenges of this scope and intensity.[308]

The Damage Done and Its Mode and Intentionality: Problems Central to Sustainable Development of Allowing Future Generations to Move Beyond Dysfunctional Limitations from Previous Generations

The intentional nature of the pain and death by conflict, such as in Guatemala, is a critical characteristic. It makes the harm done different from that which results from natural disasters. Left unresolved, it is becoming clearer that the next generation after the violence is likely to suffer significantly from the effects of PTSD and that ethnocultural groups that have been targeted may, if their concerns are not adequately addressed, experience cultural bereavement. The high level of stress and trauma has translated into an alarming suicide rate among indigenous youth, as well as other symptoms in both young people and adults in those communities in several countries.[309] In some cases, this condition is known as post-colonization trauma, a form of post-traumatic stress disorder that may be triggered by displacement, cultural discontinuity, disintegration, or in some cases by attempted annihilation of one's people. Post-colonization trauma is also defined as historical trauma and its associated "historical trauma response" (HTR) as well as "soul wound," which manifests as community chronic trauma and unresolved grief.[310] According to the UN High Commissioner for Refugees (UNHCR), "The 'great beast' that the elders refer to is none other than encroaching western civilization, brought by outsiders who during the last 500 years have been steadily usurping the ancestral lands of the indigenous peoples of Colombia, forcing them deeper and deeper into the forests to escape death and destruction."[311]

In an effort to counteract the likely repercussions of the relentless violence, the National Indigenous Organization of Colombia (ONIC), and CAMIZBA, a local indigenous organization, in partnership with the UNHCR, are implementing a culturally responsive project in which a variety of psychosocial supports are provided to children and their families.[312] Among these are "cultural activities to strengthen indigenous identity and traditional values in nine communities belonging to the Embera, Wounaan, Katio and Chami ethnic groups." A very critical person in working with indigenous peoples is the traditional healer or *jaibana*. These indigenous spiritual leaders "assess the causes of the high rate of suicides among young people, provide psycho-social counseling in their own languages to the families and communities affected and work to strengthen traditional values."[313] The project also provides teacher training on proper interventions for children and provides culturally affirming interventions such as family and community support, including of indigenous identity and values.

SOME INROADS TOWARD HEALING

This chapter has explained how the experience of trauma affects not only contemporary behavior, but also life after the shooting stops and even well beyond that. Effective post-conflict efforts directed toward sustainable development will require attention to these realities. Reconciliation and healing in post-conflict societies require a long-term, integrated, and multidimensional approach that depends upon a number of contextual factors. The key factors include the need to face the violent past and work toward reconciliation; efforts to ensure an official historic memory; actions aimed at explaining the fate of the disappeared; development of an effective rule of law system; attention to the problems of equity and equality for traditionally persecuted groups; and a public health effort to address mental health needs of the society.[314]

Context counts, and the efforts required in Guatemala, if they are to be successful, must respond to the unique characteristics of the country and the culture. There have been some steps taken in Guatemala toward establishing a better historical record of the violence, including attention to the story of those who disappeared. "Public investigations of traumatic events legitimize private memories, help memorialize them, and contribute to the healing process."[315] Documenting the history, as in *Guatemala, Never Again*,[316] *It Was Life We Were Pursuing*[317] (authored by the Recovery of Historical Memory Project of the Office of Human Rights of the Archdiocese of Guatemala), and *Guatemala: Memory of Silence* (authored by the Historical Clarification Commission), is an important first step. A healthy future requires reconciliation, but not, as Michael Simpson observed, "amnesia." He noted on the subject of the recognition in Guatemala and in the international agencies that have been assisting its people that: "Healing of individuals and of societies requires remembrances, truth, revelation, repentance, recognition, and mourning for what has been lost."[318] Redressing the past through concerted efforts to find massive burials can allow families, communities, and societies to provide culturally appropriate burials and to honor the deceased. These rituals can aid the society on the road toward healing through grieving, especially in cases of genocide.[319] As Yael Danielli asserts, it is essential "to transform the destructive use of culture into a healing one."[320]

While this kind of role of an effective historical record should be obvious, it is not clear that many governments are addressing the impact of PTSD and cultural bereavement as public health issues to be met with the systematic and broad-based strategies required to address other kinds of public health challenges. Complementary to this concern is the need for collective mental health as well as physical health.[321]

Among the challenges for any country that wishes to undertake such a public health offensive will be the difficulty of removing the stigma—and the discrimination that often comes with it—directed at those who are facing mental health issues. These are particularly heavy burdens for women, whose incidence of depression is twice that of men, according to the World Health Organization, and who, in many affected countries, face both barriers to access and lack of privacy where they can get services.[322] Men face important difficulties in accessing mental health services as well, especially in cultures that stigmatize men who seek physical or mental health care as weaklings, or who live in cultures that regard mental health challenges in seriously negative terms. In some settings these issues for men have been addressed by working with both traditional and modern medicine or by bringing them into treatment first through the traditional cultural approaches. Thus, some "have used American Indian purification and healing practices in the treatment of PTSD."[323]

For both children and adults traditional and informal healing practices may be used with care to augment the work of mental health professionals, particularly where those resources are limited. Examples are traditional songs, socio-drama, dancing, directed games (e.g., "Games We Like to Play"), poetry, journaling, and art (e.g., Art Inside of Me)[324] in school or orphanage settings to allow for expression of the trauma. However, it is important to understand that it is dangerous to attempt to debrief those with PTSD unless the person providing this service is a trained mental health professional, since the process may produce retraumatization or may trigger crisis memories. Thus,

> Non-professional workers can help meet some of the demand for care as long as they are competent and supervised, and can draw upon professional staff when necessary to deal with complex cases. . . . Village volunteers are another largely untapped but potentially valuable resource. In Ghana in 1999, for example, the WHO Nations for Mental Health Project launched a three-year pilot project that trained volunteers selected by their communities to identify, refer and follow-up people in their villages who had mental disorders. . . . It is important to recognize that the shift to community-based care should not overlook the other end of the continuum, i.e. specialist and sub-specialist care. . . . The shortages of specialists, such as psychiatrists, in many parts of the world, means that care is often not available.[325]

Other approaches that have been employed include the "week of expression" developed by the United Nations Children's Fund (UNICEF) to deal with massive numbers of traumatized children in Rwanda, and "prayers and telling your story to God or Allah."[326] Community healing ceremonies and rituals to restore traumatized ecological environments where massacres took place may be essential in some nations before its people are willing to return to those lands, as in Rwanda.

CONCLUSION

Chapter 3 began with a discussion of the fact that any approach to postconflict action that assumes that the community, human or ecological, that was in place when the violence began will still be in place and intact when it is time to move on after the shooting stops is doomed to failure from the outset. That chapter addressed the factors that change the lives of people who are driven into flight either across national borders or within their own countries, with a particular attention to the physical conditions and insults they bear. Chapter 4, on the other hand, focused on the psychosocial effects of trauma, both in terms of post-traumatic stress disorder and cultural bereavement that affect their minds as well as their bodies, in addition to the collective psychosocial well-being and efficacy of the larger community.

This discussion of PTSD and cultural bereavement is grounded in the case study of Guatemala, which has endured so much violence for so long, a great deal of it inflicted by the government itself while the international community looked on. Included within the larger thirty-six-year war was the genocidal attack on the Maya people, who endured not only physical attacks on their people as individuals but a clear effort to decimate them as a culture, as the truth commission concluded. In such settings, PTSD and cultural bereavement are critical challenges to post-conflict development. There are different demands for service based in part on the fact that different groups are affected differently by the experiences of violence, and meeting these needs requires creative responses.

The steps forward toward sustainable development after conflict require attention to the challenges encountered by individuals and their communities, both physical and psychosocial, discussed in chapters 3 and 4. Indeed, chapter 5 turns to the dynamics of demobilization and the ways in which some of these challenges are or are not addressed.

NOTES

1. American Psychiatric Association, *Diagnostic and Statistical Manual* (DSM-IV-TR) (Arlington, VA: American Psychiatric Association), 463–468.

2. Claude Chemtob and Tisha L. Taylor, "Treatment of Traumatized Children," in Rachel Yehuda, ed., *Treating Trauma Survivors with PTSD* (Arlington, VA: American Psychiatric Publishing, 2002), 75–126.

3. Glenn Kessler and Colum Lynch, "U.S. Calls Killings in Sudan Genocide: Khartoum and Arab Militias Are Responsible, Powell Says," *Washington Post*, September 10, 2004, A01.

4. Timothy R. Gulden, "Spatial and Temporal Patterns in Civil Violence, Guatemala 1977–1986," Brookings Institution, Center on Social and Economic Dynamics Working Paper No. 26, February 2002, 1–3, at www.refugees.org/uploadedFiles/Participate/National_Center/Resource_Library/Guatemala_1977_1986_Spatial_and_Temporal_Patterns_in_Civil_Violence.pdf (accessed December 23, 2006).

5. Commission for Historical Clarification, *Guatemala: Memory of Silence*, "Conclusions," "Part I," report of the Commission for Historical Clarification, 122–123, at http://shr.aaas.org/guatemala/ceh/report/english/conc2.html (accessed December 23, 2006).

6. Commission for Historical Clarification, *Guatemala: Memory of Silence*, "Prologue," 4.

7. E. Bradford Burns, *Latin America: A Concise Interpretative History*, 6th ed. (Englewood Cliffs, NJ: Prentice Hall), 7–8.

8. Victor Perera, *Unfinished Conquest: The Guatemalan Tragedy* (Berkeley: University of California Press, 1993), 11.

9. National Geographic Society, *National Geographic: Family Reference Atlas of the World* (Washington, D.C.: National Geographic Society, 2002), 108; World Bank, "Guatemala: Country Profile," at http://devdata.worldbank.org/external/CPProfile.asp?SelectedCountry=GTM&CCODE=GTM&CNAME=Guatemala&PTYPE=CP, http://devdata.worldbank.org/external/CPProfile.asp?PTYPE=CP (accessed December 21, 2006).

10. Craig Kauffman, "Transitional Justice in Guatemala: Linking the Past and the Future," paper prepared for the ISA-South Conference, Miami, Florida, November

3–5, 2005, at www6.miami.edu/maia/ISAS05/papers/Craig_Kauffman.pdf (accessed December 23, 2006), citing "Republic of Guatemala," in *CultureGrams 2005* (Lindon, UT: Brigham Young University, 2004), 250.

11. U.S. Department of State, "Background Note: Guatemala," at www.state.gov/r/pa/ei/bgn/2045.htm (accessed December 21, 2006); Perera, *Unfinished Conquest.*

12. Richard Millet, "Central America: Background to the Crisis," in Jan Knippers Black, ed., *Latin America, Its Problems and Promise: A Multidisciplinary Introduction* (Boulder, CO: Westview, 1991), 319.

13. Millet, "Central America," 317.

14. Perera, *Unfinished Conquest,* 6.

15. Millet, "Central America," 320.

16. Dario Moreno, *The Struggle for Peace in Central America* (Gainesville: University Press of Florida, 1994).

17. Perera, *Unfinished Conquest.*

18. Perera, *Unfinished Conquest,* 313–328.

19. Perera, *Unfinished Conquest,* 99, 335.

20. Héctor Perez-Brignioli, *A Brief History of Central America,* trans. Ricardo B. Sawrey and Susana Stettri de Sawrey (Berkeley: University of California Press, 1989).

21. Perez-Brignioli, *A Brief History of Central America,* 99, 127.

22. Nick Cullather, *Secret History: The CIA's Classified Account of Its Operations in Guatemala, 1952–1954* (Stanford: Stanford University Press, 1999), 90.

23. Pérez-Brignoli, *A Brief History of Central America,* 138.

24. Pérez-Brignoli, *A Brief History of Central America,* 138.

25. Perez-Brignoli, *A Brief History of Central America.*

26. Thomas E. Skidmore and Peter H. Smith, *Modern Latin America,* 5th ed. (New York: Oxford University Press, 2001), 348.

27. Skidmore and Smith, *Modern Latin America,* 5th ed., 352.

28. U.S. Central Intelligence Agency, "Electronic Reading Room—Guatemala," at www.foia.ucia.gov/guatemala.asp (accessed December 22, 2006). See also the documents on Guatemala from 1964–1995 in CIA, "Electronic Reading Room—Civil Rights in Latin America," at www.foia.ucia.gov/human_rights.asp (accessed December 22, 2006).

29. National Security Archive, Electronic Briefing Book No. 15, "Guatemala Death Squad Diaries: Internal Military Log Reveals Fate of 183 'Disappeared,'" at www.gwu.edu/~nsarchiv/NSAEBB/NSAEBB15/press.html (accessed December 22, 2006).

30. National Security Archive, Electronic Briefing Book No. 32, "The Guatemalan Military: What the U.S. Files Reveal," at www.gwu.edu/~nsarchiv/NSAEBB/NSAEBB32/index.html (accessed December 22, 2006). These materials are part of the National Security Archive's Guatemala Documentation Project.

31. Skidmore and Smith, *Modern Latin America,* 5th ed., 348.

32. Millet, "Central America," 325.

33. BBC News, "Chronology of the Contemporary Conflict 1954–1996," at http://news.bbc.co.uk/go/pr/fr/-/1/hi/world/americas/country_profiles/1215811.stm (accessed October 27, 2005).

34. Burns, *Latin America: A Concise Interpretative History,* 265.

35. Perera, *Unfinished Conquest*, 9.

36. Oficina de Derechos Humanos del Arzobispado de Guatemala (ODHAG), *"Era tras la vida por lo que ibamos . . ."* (Guatemala City, Guatemala: Diakonía y CRS, 2004), 36, at www.uweb.ucsb.edu/~jce2/Gale.html (accessed December 27, 2006).

37. Skidmore and Smith, *Modern Latin America*, 6th ed. (New York: Oxford University Press, 2005), 390.

38. Cullather, *Secret History*, 15–17.

39. Cullather, *Secret History*, 21.

40. Cullather, *Secret History*, 90.

41. Cullather, *Secret History*, 90.

42. Skidmore and Smith, *Modern Latin America*, 5th ed., 350.

43. Millet, "Central America," 326.

44. ODHAG, *"Era tras la vida,"* 37. This passage was translated by Claudia María Vargas. The original Spanish reads as follows: "Jacobo Arbenz, acusado de conspiración comunista, no se inspira en Lenin, sino en Abraham Lincoln. Su reforma agraria, que se propone modernizar el capitalismo en Guatemala, es más moderada que las leyes rurales norteamericanas de hace casi un siglo." by Eduardo Galeano, *En el siglo del viento*, at www.uweb.ucsb.edu/~jce2/Gale.html (accessed December 27, 2006).

45. See, generally, James A. Bill, *The Eagle and the Lion: The Tragedy of American-Iranian Relations* (New Haven: Yale University Press, 1988), chapters 2–3. The nature of the situation was well explained in Mark J. Gasiorowski, "The 1953 Coup d'Etat in Iran," unpublished paper, Department of Political Science, Louisiana State University.

46. The detailed factual information on the Iran coup is taken from the CIA's own after-action report prepared by the agency's lead planner on the project. Donald N. Wilber, "Clandestine Service History: Overthrow of Premier Mossadeq of Iran, November 1952–August 1953," March 1954, published on the *New York Times* Internet site, at www.nytimes.com/library/world/mideast/iran-cia-intro.pdf (accessed December 22, 2006).

47. Wilber, "Clandestine Service History," 77.

48. Cullather, *Secret History*, 38. The plan of action is present in Director of Central Intelligence, "Memorandum: Guatemala—General Plan of Action," September 11, 1953, CIA, Electronic Document Release Center, at www.foia.ucia.gov/frame2 .htm (accessed December 22, 2006). For this document it is necessary to go to the Electronic Reading Room, then select Guatemala, then search by title through documents 1–1000.

49. Chester J. Pach Jr. and Elmo Richardson, *The Presidency of Dwight D. Eisenhower* (Lawrence: University Press of Kansas, 1991), 89–90.

50. Burns, *Latin America: A Concise Interpretative History*, 270.

51. See, generally, Cullather, *Secret History*.

52. Cullather, *Secret History*, 110.

53. ODHAG, *"Era tras la vida,"* 38.

54. ODHAG, *"Era tras la vida."*

55. Memorandum, Thomas L. Hughes to Secretary of State, October 23, 1967, at www.gwu.edu/~nsarchiv/NSAEBB/NSAEBB32/05-01.htm (accessed December 22, 2006).

56. ODHAG, *"Era tras la vida,"* 45.

57. National Security Archive, Electronic Briefing Book No. 15, "Guatemala Death Squad Diaries: Internal Military Log Reveals Fate of 183 'Disappeared,'" at www.gwu.edu/~nsarchiv/NSAEBB/NSAEBB15/dossier-color.pdf (accessed December 22, 2006).

58. ODHAG, "*Era tras la vida*," 46. This passage was translated by Claudia María Vargas. The original in Spanish reads as follows: "Con un pensum multidisciplinario, estudiarían la salud guatemalteca, no sólo con referencia a lo biológico y lo psicológico, sino en relación con los social, económico, e histórico."

59. Skidmore and Smith, *Modern Latin America*, 5th ed., 383; Millet, "Central America," 328; Pérez-Brignoli, *A Brief History of Central America*, 140.

60. John A. Booth and Thomas W. Walker, *Understanding Central America* (Boulder, CO: Westview, 1989).

61. ODHAG, "*Era tras la vida*," 47.

62. Booth and Walker, *Understanding Central America*, 40.

63. ODHAG, "*Era tras la vida*," 47–48.

64. Skidmore and Smith, Modern Latin America, 6th ed., 393; ODHAG, "*Era tras la vida*," 48.

65. Booth and Walker, *Understanding Central America*, 40.

66. Skidmore and Smith, *Modern Latin America*, 5th ed., 352.

67. Booth and Walker, *Understanding Central America*, 40.

68. ODHAG, "*Era tras la vida*," 51.

69. Booth and Walker, *Understanding Central America*, 89.

70. Booth and Walker, *Understanding Central America*, 40; ODHAG, "*Era tras la vida*," 60.

71. ODHAG, "*Era tras la vida*," 54. This passage was translated by Claudia María Vargas. The original in Spanish reads as follows: "Se abrían las puertas hacia una de las décadas más violentas de la historia guatemalteca."

72. ODHAG, "*Era tras la vida*," 54.

73. ODHAG, "*Era tras la vida*," 55.

74. ODHAG, "*Era tras la vida*," 57.

75. Booth and Walker, *Understanding Central America*, 41, 90.

76. ODHAG, "*Era tras la vida*," 58.

77. ODHAG, "*Era tras la vida*," 58.

78. Booth and Walker, *Understanding Central America*, 41.

79. Millett, "Central America," 331.

80. Moreno, *Struggle for Peace in Central America*, 44.

81. Moreno, *Struggle for Peace in Central America*, 44.

82. Timothy Gulden, "Spatial and Temporal Patterns in Civil Violence: Guatemala 1977–1986," Center on Social and Economic Dynamic, Working Paper No. 26, February 2002, 2.

83. ODHAG, "*Era tras la vida*," 61.

84. ODHAG, "*Era tras la vida*," 62.

85. ODHAG, "*Era tras la vida*," 62.

86. ODHAG, "*Era tras la vida*," 238.

87. Perera, *Unfinished Conquest*, 43–51.

88. Skidmore and Smith, *Modern Latin America*, 5th ed.; Perera, *Unfinished Conquest*, 393.

89. Moreno, *Struggle for Peace in Central America*, 42.

90. Moreno, *Struggle for Peace in Central America*, 46.

91. Burns, *Latin America: A Concise Interpretative History*, 270.

92. ODHAG, *"Era tras la vida,"* 67.

93. Skidmore and Smith, *Modern Latin America*, 5th ed., 353.

94. Eldon Kenworthy, "Central America's Lost Decade," in Jan Knippers Black, ed., *Latin America, Its Problems and Promise: A Multidisciplinary Introduction*, 346–367 (Boulder, CO: Westview, 1991).

95. Fernando Henrique Cardoso, "The Challenges of Social Democracy in Latin America," in Menno Vellinga, ed., *Social Democracy in Latin America: Prospects for Change* (Boulder, CO: Westview, 1993), 275.

96. Edelberto Torres-Rivas, "Personalities, Ideologies and Circumstances: Social Democracy in Central America," in Menno Vellinga, ed., *Social Democracy in Latin America: Prospects for Change*, 240–251 (Boulder, CO: Westview, 1993), 245; Kenworthy, "Central America's Lost Decade," 348–350.

97. Moreno, *Struggle for Peace in Central America*, 146.

98. Skidmore and Smith, *Modern Latin America*, 5th ed., 393.

99. ODHAG, *"Era tras la vida,"* 70.

100. Perera, *Unfinished Conquest*, 350.

101. Skidmore and Smith, *Modern Latin America*, 5th ed., 353.

102. Craig Kauffman, "Transitional Justice in Guatemala," 9; Skidmore and Smith, *Modern Latin America*, 6th ed., 394.

103. Skidmore and Smith, *Modern Latin America*, 6th ed., 394.

104. Sistemas de las Naciones Unidas en Guatemala, *Guatemala: Una Agenda para el desarrollo humano 2003* (Guatemala City, Guatemala: SNU, 2003); MINUGUA, "MINUGUA's 9th and Final Report on Fulfillment of the Peace Accords in Guatemala," August 30, 2004, at www.tula.ca/health%20and%20equity/UNMinugua .htm (accessed April 7, 2007).

105. U.S. Department of State, "Background Note: Guatemala."

106. June Carolyn Erlick, *Disappeared: A Journalist Silenced* (Emeryville, CA: Seal Press, 2004).

107. U.S. Department of State, "Background Note: Guatemala."

108. Skidmore and Smith, *Modern Latin America*, 6th ed., 394.

109. Craig Kauffman, "Transitional Justice in Guatemala," 17; Skidmore and Smith, *Modern Latin America*, 6th ed., 394.

110. Skidmore and Smith, *Modern Latin America*, 6th ed., 394.

111. Skidmore and Smith, *Modern Latin America*, 6th ed., 394.

112. Flavia Bustreo, Eleonora Genovese, Elio Omobono, Henrik Axelsson, and Ian Bannon, *Improving Child Health in Post-Conflict Countries: Can the World Bank Contribute?* (Washington, D.C.: World Bank, 2005).

113. Bustreo et al., *Improving Child Health*, 39.

114. World Bank, "Increasing Rural Incomes in Guatemala," at http://web .worldbank.org/WBSITE/EXTERNAL/COUNTRIES/LACEXT/GUATEMALAEXTN/ 0,,contentMDK:20902419~pagePK:1497618~piPK:217854~theSitePK:328117,00 .html (accessed December 27, 2006).

115. Claudia María Vargas, "Women in Central America," in Nelly P. Stromquist, ed., *Women in the Third World: An Encyclopedia of Contemporary Issues* (New York: Garland, 1998), 610–617.

116. World Bank, "Guatemala Country Brief," at http://web.worldbank.org/ WBSITE/EXTERNAL/COUNTRIES/LACEXT/GUATEMALAEXTN/0,,contentMDK: 20904081~menuPK:328125~pagePK:1497618~piPK:217854~theSitePK: 328117,00.html (accessed December 27, 2006).

117. Juan Pablo Corlazzoli, "Guatemala: ¡El País que queremos! Alcanzando los Objetivos Nacionales con las Metas del Milenio" (Guatemala City, Guatemala: Naciones Unidas en Guatemala, January 24, 2005).

118. World Bank, "Guatemala Country Brief."

119. World Bank, "Guatemala Country Brief."

120. Programa de las Naciones Unidas para el Desarrollo (PNUD), *Guatemala: Desarrollo Rural y Ruralidad. Compendio estadístico 2004—Guatemala* (Guatemala City, Guatemala: Editoral Serviprensa S.A., 2004), viii.

121. World Bank, "Ensuring All Children Can Go to School in Guatemala," Universalization of Basic Education Project, at http://web.worldbank.org/WBSITE/ EXTERNAL/COUNTRIES/LACEXT/GUATEMALAEXTN/0,,contentMDK: 20899218~pagePK:141137~piPK:141127~theSitePK:328117,00.html (accessed December 27, 2006).

122. PNUD, *Guatemala: Desarrollo Humano y Ruralidad*, 53.

123. Gillete Hall and Harry Anthony Patrinos, eds., *Indigenous Peoples, Poverty and Human Development in Latin America: 1994–2004* (New York: Palgrave MacMillan, 2006).

124. Hall and Patrinos, *Indigenous Peoples*, 133.

125. Hall and Patrinos, *Indigenous Peoples*; World Bank, "Ensuring All Children."

126. Joseph Shapiro, "Guatemala," in Gillete Hall and Harry Anthony Patrinos, eds., *Indigenous Peoples, Poverty and Human Development in Latin America: 1994–2004*, 145–148 (New York: Palgrave MacMillan, 2006).

127. World Bank, "Guatemala Data Profile," at http://devdata.worldbank.org/ external/CPProfile.asp?SelectedCountry=GTM&CCODE=GTM&CNAME=Guatemal a&PTYPE=CP (accessed December 27, 2006).

128. Bustreo et al., *Improving Child Health*, 39.

129. World Bank, "Improving Health and Nutrition of Mothers and Young Children in Guatemala," at http://web.worldbank.org/WBSITE/EXTERNAL/COUNTRIES/ LACEXT/GUATEMALAEXTN/0,,contentMDK:20903253~pagePK:1497618~piPK:21 7854~theSitePK:328117,00.html (accessed December 27, 2006).

130. Gillete Hall and Harry Anthony Patrinos, "Executive Summary," in Gillete Hall and Harry Anthony Patrinos, eds., *Indigenous Peoples, Poverty and Human Development in Latin America: 1994–2004* (New York: Palgrave MacMillan, 2006), 9.

131. Bustreo et al., *Improving Child Health*, 39.

132. Shapiro, "Guatemala," 146.

133. Bustreo et al., *Improving Child Health*, 6.

134. Commission for Historical Clarification, *Guatemala: Memory of Silence*, "Conclusions," "Part II," 31–32.

135. Commission for Historical Clarification, *Guatemala: Memory of Silence*, "Conclusions," "Part II," 62.

136. See for example, Yael Danieli, ed., *International Handbook of Multigenerational Legacies of Trauma* (New York and London: Plenum, 1998).

137. Eduardo Duran, Bonnie Duran, Maria Yellow Horse Brave Heart, and Susan Yellow Horse-Davis, "Healing the American Indian Soul Wounds," in Yael Danieli, ed., *International Handbook of Multigenerational Legacies of Trauma*, 341–354 (New York and London: Plenum); Beverly Raphael, Pat Swan, and Nada Martinek, "Intergenerational Concepts of Trauma for Australian Aboriginal People," in Yael Danieli, ed., *International Handbook of Multigenerational Legacies of Trauma*, 327–339 (New York and London: Plenum).

138. Anthony J. Marsella, Thomas Bornemann, Solvig Ekblad, and John Orley, eds., *Amidst Peril and Pain: The Mental Health and Well-Being of the World's Refugees* (Washington, D.C.: American Psychological Association, 1994).

139. Hall and Patrinos, *Indigenous Peoples*, 221–224.

140. Hall and Patrinos, *Indigenous Peoples*, 1.

141. Hall and Patrinos, *Indigenous Peoples*, 141.

142. World Bank, "Guatemala Data Profile."

143. Bustreo et al., *Improving Child Health*, 40.

144. Shapiro, "Guatemala," 147.

145. Shapiro, "Guatemala," 106.

146. Hall and Patrinos, *Indigenous Peoples*, 110.

147. Hall and Patrinos, "Executive Summary," 5.

148. Hall and Patrinos, *Indigenous Peoples*, 146.

149. Hall and Patrinos, *Indigenous Peoples*, 123.

150. Hall and Patrinos, "Executive Summary," 7.

151. Oficina de Derechos Humanos del Arzobispado de Guatemala (ODHAG), *Situación de la Niñez en Guatemala* (Guatemala City, Guatemala: 2004), 115.

152. Shapiro, "Guatemala," 106.

153. Hall and Patrinos, "Executive Summary," 7.

154. Gillette Hall, Heather Marie Layton, and Joseph Shapiro, "Introduction," in Gillete Hall and Harry Anthony Patrinos, eds., *Indigenous Peoples, Poverty and Human Development in Latin America: 1994–2004*, 145–148 (New York: Palgrave MacMillan, 2006), 4.

155. Claire Marshall, "Murderers Prey on Guatemalan Women," BBC News, December 6, 2003, at http://news.bbc.co.uk/go/pr/fr/-/1/hi/world/americas/3294659.stm (accessed September 28, 2005); PNUD, *Guatemala: Desarrollo Humano y Ruralidad*, 111.

156. Adam Blenford, "Guatemala's epidemic of killing," BBC News, June 9, 2005, at http://news.bbc.co.uk/go/pr/fr/-/1/hi/world/americas/4074880.stm (accessed October 27, 2005).

157. Amnesty International USA, "Murders of Women in Guatemala Increasingly Frequent in 2006, New Amnesty International Report Finds," Amnesty International USA press release, July 18, 2006, at www.amnestyusa.org/women/document.do?id=ENGUSA20060718001 (accessed October 18, 2006).

158. American Psychiatric Association, *Diagnostic and Statistical Manual of Mental Disorders*, 4th ed., text revision (DSM-IV-TR) (Arlington, VA: American Psychiatric Association, 2000), 463–468.

159. Sistemas de las Naciones Unidas en Guatemala, *2002: Guatemala: Desarrollo Humano, Mujeres y Salud*, Guatemala, Guatemala: PNUD (Programa de las Naciones

Unidas para el Desarollo) Guatemala, 2002, 201. This passage was translated by Claudia María Vargas. The original in Spanish reads as follows: "La violencia generada por el conflicto armado interno, la violencia social, así como por el maltrato intrafamiliar, abuso y agresión que se ejerce contra las niñas y adolescentes ha tenido un fuerte impacto en su salud mental, manifestándose principalmente en una baja autoestima, trauma, retraso escolar, ansiedad, miedo, depresión, desequilibrio emocional etc. Según la gravedad del impacto psicológico, las adolescentes pueden manifestar problemas como agresión, abuso de alcohol y suicidio."

160. Phillip J. Cooper and Claudia María Vargas, *Implementing Sustainable Development: From Global Policy to Local Action* (Lanham, MD: Rowman & Littlefield, 2004), chapter 4.

161. Craig Kauffman, "Transitional Justice in Guatemala"; ODHAG, *"Era tras la vida."*

162. Kauffman, "Transitional Justice in Guatemala," 14.

163. Michael J. Sandel, *Democracy's Discontent* (Cambridge, MA: Harvard University Press, 1996), ix.

164. Kauffman, "Transitional Justice in Guatemala," 14.

165. Kauffman, "Transitional Justice in Guatemala," 9.

166. Comisión para el Esclarecimiento Histórico, *Guatemala: Memoria del Silencio*, vol. 1 (Guatemala City, Guatemala: 1999), 86.

167. Sistemas de las Naciones Unidas en Guatemala, *Guatemala: Desarrollo Humano*, 147–148.

168. Sistemas de las Naciones Unidas en Guatemala, *Guatemala: Desarrollo Humano*, 147–148.

169. Adam Blenford, "Guatemala's Epidemic of Killing," BBC News, June 9, 2005, at http://news.bbc.co.uk/go/pr/fr/-/1/hi/world/americas/4074880.stm (accessed October 27, 2005).

170. Sistemas de las Naciones Unidas en Guatemala, *Guatemala: Una Agenda*, 9.

171. Etienne G. Krug, Linda L. Dahlberg, James A. Mercy, Anthony B. Zwi, and Rafael Lozano, eds., *World Report on Violence and Health* (Geneva: World Health Organization, 2002).

172. World Bank, "Improving Access to Justice in Guatemala," at http://web .worldbank.org/WBSITE/EXTERNAL/COUNTRIES/LACEXT/GUATEMALAEXTN/0,, contentMDK:20899292~pagePK:1497618~piPK:217854~theSitePK:328117,00.ht ml (accessed December 23, 2006).

173. World Bank, "Improving Access to Justice in Guatemala."

174. World Bank, "Improving Access to Justice in Guatemala."

175. World Bank, "Improving Access to Justice in Guatemala."

176. ODHAG, *Situación de la Niñez en Guatemala*, 127.

177. ODHAG, *Situación de la Niñez en Guatemala*, 130.

178. Krug et al., *World Report on Violence and Health*.

179. See for example, Danieli, *International Handbook*; Rachael Yehuda, ed., *Treating Trauma Survivors with PTSD* (Washington, D.C.: American Psychiatric Publishing, 2002).

180. Carol Locust, "The Impact of Differing Belief Systems between Native Americans and Their Rehabilitation Service Providers," *Rehabilitation Education* 9, no. 2 (1995): 205–215.

181. Commission for Historical Clarification, *Guatemala: Memory of Silence*, "Prologue," 1.

182. Judith Herman, *Trauma and Recovery* (New York: Basic, 1997).

183. American Psychiatric Association, *Diagnostic Statistical Manual-III* (DSM-III) (Washington, D.C.: American Psychiatric Association, 1980).

184. Herman, *Trauma and Recovery*, 52.

185. Duran et al., "Healing the American Indian Soul Wounds," 341–354. See Ignacio Martín-Baró, translated by Anne Wallace, in Ignacio Martín-Baró, *Writings for a Liberation Psychology* (translated by Adrianne Aron and Shawn Corne), (Cambridge, MA: Harvard University Press, 1994).

186. Yehuda, *Treating Trauma Survivors with PTSD*; Ellen Gerrity, Terence M. Keane, and Farris Tuma, eds., *The Mental Health Consequences of Torture* (New York: Kluwer Academic/Plenum, 2001); Sepp Graessner, Norbert Gurris, and Christian Pross, eds., *At the Side of Torture Survivors: Treating a Terrible Assault on Human Dignity*, trans. Jeremiah Michael Riemer (Baltimore and London: Johns Hopkins University Press, 2001); James M. Jaranson and Michael K. Popkin, eds., *Caring for Victims of Torture* (Washington, D.C.: Amerian Psychiatric Press, 1998); Danieli, *International Handbook*; Herman, *Trauma and Recovery*.

187. Yehuda, 2002; Rachel Yehuda, "Post-traumatic Stress Disorder," *New England Journal of Medicine*, vol. 346 (2002): 108–114; Arieh Y. Shalev, "Treating Survivors in the Immediate Aftermath of Traumatic Events," in Rachel Yehuda, ed., *Treating Trauma Survivors with PTSD*, 157–188; Jaranson and Popkin, *Caring for Victims of Torture*; Søren Bøjholm and Peter Vesti, "Multidisciplinary Approach in the Treatment of Torture," in Metin Basoglu, ed., *Torture and its Consequences: Current Treatment Approaches* (Cambridge: University Press, 1992), 299–309.

188. Claudia María Vargas, Deborah O'Rourke, and Mahshid Esfandiari, "Complementary Therapies for Treating Survivors of Torture," *Refuge* 22, no. 1 (2004): 129–137; Claudia María Vargas, Deborah O'Rourke, and Mahshid Esfandiari, "A Triangle of Hope for Survivors: Integrating Psychotherapy and Bodywork for Chronic Pain and Cultural Loss," *Rehabilitation Review* 24, no. 10 (2004): 18–21.

189. Daniel Zwerdling, "Soldiers Say Army Ignores, Punishes Mental Anguish," at www.npr.org/templates/story/story.php?storyId=6576505 (accessed December 24, 2006).

190. U.S. Government Accountability Office, *Post-traumatic Stress Disorder: DOD Needs to Identify the Factors Its Providers Use to Make Mental Health Evaluation Referrals for Servicemembers* (Washington, D.C.: GAO, 2006).

191. Yehuda, *Treating Trauma Survivors with PTSD*; Gerrity et al., *Mental Health Consequences of Torture*; Graessner et al., *At the Side of Torture Survivors*; Jaranson and Popkin, *Caring for Victims of Torture*; Danieli, *International Handbook*; Herman, *Trauma and Recovery*.

192. American Psychiatric Association, *Diagnostic Statistical Manual-IV-Text Revised* (DSM-IV-TR) (Washington, D.C.: American Psychiatric Association, 2000), 463–472.

193. Maurice Lipsedge, "Commentary," *Advances in Psychiatric Treatment* 7 (2001): 222–223.

194. Maurice Eisenbruch, "From Post-traumatic Stress Disorder to Cultural Bereavement: Diagnosis of Southeast Asian Refugees," *Social Science and Medicine* 33, no. 6 (1991): 673–680.

195. Marlene A. Young, *Community Crisis Response Team Training Manual*, 2nd ed. (Washington, D.C.: National Organization for Victim Assistance, 1998).

196. Eisenbruch, "From Post-traumatic Stress Disorder to Cultural Bereavement," 674.

197. See Mathew Friedman and James Jaranson, "The Applicability of the Post-traumatic Stress Disorder Concept to Refugees," in Anthony J. Marsella, Thomas Bornemann, Solvig Ekblad, and John Orley, eds., *Amidst Peril and Pain: The Mental Health and Well-Being of the World's Refugees* (Washington, D.C.: American Psychological Association, 1994).

198. Mathew A. Friedman, "Post-traumatic Stress Disorder," *Psychopharmacology— The Fourth Generation of Progress*, 2000, at www.acnp.org/G4/GN401000111/CH109 .html (accessed July 24, 2006).

199. Friedman and Jaranson, "Applicability of the Posttraumatic Stress Disorder Concept," 220.

200. John Orley, "Psychological Disorders among Refugees: Some Clinical and Epidemiological Considerations," in Anthony J. Marsella, Thomas Bornemann, Solvig Ekblad, and John Orley, eds., *Amidst Peril and Pain: The Mental Health and Well-Being of the World's Refugees*, 193–206 (Washington, D.C.: American Psychological Association, 1994).

201. Maurice Eisenbruch, "The Mental Health of Refugee Children and Their Cultural Development," *International Migration Review* 22, no. 2 (1988): 282–300; Eisenbruch, "From Post-Traumatic Stress Disorder to Cultural Bereavement"; J. Barudy, "A Programme of Mental Health for Political Refugees: Dealing with the Invisible Pain of Political Exile," *Social Science and Medicine* 28 (1989): 715–27.

202. Orley, "Psychological Disorders among Refugees."

203. In addition to PTSD, the DSM-IV-TR includes a category of acute stress disorder (ASD). A more recent diagnosis has been identified by psychiatrists such as Herman, *Trauma and Recovery*; van der Kolk, "Assessment and Treatment of Complex PTSD"; and Ahmad et al., "Reliability and Validity," which, although not yet officially recognized by the American Psychiatric Association, is called "disorders of extreme stress not otherwise specified" (DESNOS). See Clare Pain, "PTSD and Comorbidity or Disorder of Extreme Stress Not Otherwise Specified?" *CPA (Canadian Psychiatric Association) Bulletin*, August 2002, 13. While the DESNOS category awaits inclusion into the next DSM, the Field Trial of DESNOS for the DSM-IV had a high correlation with PTSD. See Bessel van der Kolk, "Assessment and Treatment of Complex PTSD," in Rachel Yehuda, ed., *Treating Trauma Survivors with PTSD*, 127–156 (Washington, D.C.: American Psychiatric Publishing, 2002). The ICD-10 (International Classification of Disease) [World Health Organization, *ICD-10 (International Classification of Disease)* (Geneva: World Health Organization, 1992)] does include a category associated with complex post-traumatic stress disorder, thus acknowledging "lasting personality changes following catastrophic stress." See World Health Organization, *ICD-10 Classification of Mental and Behavioral Disorders*, cited in: Pain, "PTSD and Comorbidity"; and Joop T. V. M de Jong, Ivan H. Komproe, Joe Spinazzola, Bessel A. van der Kolk, and Mark H. Van Ommeren, "DESNOS in Three Post-conflict Settings: Assessing Cross-Cultural Construct Equivalence," *Journal of Traumatic Stress* 18, no. 1 (2005): 13–21. See also A. Ahmad, V. Sundelin-Wahlsten, M. A. Sofi, J. A. Qahar, and A.-L. von Knorring, "Reliability and Validity of a Child-Specific

Cross-Cultural Instrument for Assessing Posttraumatic Stress Disorder," _European Child & Adolescent Psychiatry_ 9, no. 4 (2000): 285–294.

204. World Health Organization (WHO), "Ministerial Round Tables: Mental Health," Fifty-fourth World Health Assembly, Provisional Agenda Item 10, A54/DIV/4, April 10, 2001, at http://ftp.who.int/gb/pdf_files/WHA54/ea54d4.pdf (accessed April 7, 2007).

205. See A. Baker and N. Shalhoub-Kevorkian, "Effects of Political and Military Traumas on Children: The Palestinian Case," _Clinical Psychology Review_ 19, no. 8 (1999): 935–950; Chemtob and Taylor, "Treatment of Traumatized Children"; J. David Kinzie, J. Boehnlein, and William H. Sack, "The Effects of Massive Trauma on Cambodian Parents and Children," in Yael Danieli, ed., _International Handbook of Multigenerational Legacies of Trauma_, 211–221 (New York and London: Plenum, 1998); William Yule, "Emanuel Miller Lecture From Pogroms to 'Ethnic Cleansing': Meeting the Needs of War Affected Children," _Journal of Child Psychology and Psychiatry_ 46, no. 6 (2000): 695–702.

206. William H. Sack, Gregory N. Clarke, and John R. Seeley, "Multiple Forms of Stress in Cambodian Adolescent Refugees," _Child Development_ 67 (1996): 110.

207. Yehuda, _Treating Trauma Survivors with PTSD_; van der Kolk, "Assessment and Treatment of Complex PTSD"; Danieli, _International Handbook_; Kinzie et al., "Effects of Massive Trauma"; J. David Kinzie, William H. Sack, Richard H. Angell, Spero Manson, and Ben Rath, "The Psychiatric Effects of Massive Trauma on Cambodian Children: I. The Children," _Journal of the American Academy of Child Psychiatry_ 25, no. 3 (1986): 370–376; William H. Sack, Richard H. Angell, J. David Kinzie, and Ben Rath, "The Psychiatric Effects of Massive Trauma on Cambodian Children: II. The Family, Home, and the School," _Journal of the American Academy of Child Psychiatry_ 25, no. 3 (1986): 377–383; William H. Sack, John R. Seeley, Chanrithy Him, and Gregory N. Clarke, "Psychometric Properties of the Impact of Events Scale in Traumatized Cambodian Refugee Youth," _Personality and Individual Differences_ 25, no. 1 (1998): 57–67; William H. Sack, John R. Seeley ,and Gregory N. Clarke, "Does PTSD Transcend Cultural Barriers? A Study from the Khmer Adolescent Refugee Project," _Journal of the American Academy of Child and Adolescent Psychiatry_ 36, no. 1 (1997): 49–54; Sack et al., "Multiple Forms of Stress"; William H. Sack, Gregory N. Clarke, and John R. Seeley, "Posttraumatic Stress Disorder across Two Generations," _Journal of the American Academy of Child and Adolescent Psychiatry_ 34, no. 9 (1995): 1160–1166; Kjerstin Almqvist and Margareta Brandell-Forsberg, "Refugee Children in Sweden: Post-traumatic Stress Disorder in Iranian Preschool Children Exposed to Organized Violence," _Child Abuse and Neglect_ 21, no. 4 (1997): 351–366; Edith Montgomery, "Refugee Children from the Middle East," _Scandinavian Journal of Social Medicine_ (1998), Supplement 54.

208. Richard D. Goldstein, Nina S. Wampler, and Paul H. Wise, "War Experiences and Distress Symptoms of Bosnian Children," _Pediatrics_ 100, no. 5 (1997): 873–878.

209. Ilene Hyman, Morton Beiser, and Nhi Vu, "The Mental Health of Refugee Children in Canada," in _Refuge_ 15, no. 5 (1996): 4–8.

210. Yehuda, _Treating Trauma Survivors with PTSD_; van der Kolk "Assessment and Treatment of Complex PTSD"; Danieli, _International Handbook_; Kinzie et al., "Effects of Massive Trauma"; Sack et al., "Posttraumatic Stress Disorder across Two Genera-

tions"; Sack et al., "Multiple Forms of Stress"; Sack et al., "Does PTSD Transcend Cultural Barriers?"; Sack et al., "Psychometric Properties"; Almqvist and Brandell-Forsberg, "Refugee Children in Sweden"; Jon Hubbard, George M. Realmuto, Andrea K. Northwood, and Ann S. Masten, "Comorbidity of Psychiatric Diagnoses with Posttraumatic Stress Disorder in Survivors of Childhood Trauma," *Journal of the American Academy of Child and Adolescent Psychiatry* 34, no. 9 (1995): 1167–1173; Goldstein et al., "War Experiences and Distress Symptoms"; Laura Ann McCloskey and Karen Southwick, "Psychosocial Problems in Refugee Children Exposed to War," *Pediatrics* 97, no. 3 (1996), 394–397.

211. Sack et al., "Does PTSD Transcend Cultural Barriers?"

212. Bruce D. Perry, "The Vortex of Violence," *Interdisciplinary Education Series*, January, 2000, at www.bcm.tmc.edu/cta/vortex_interd.htm (accessed July 27, 2001); Bruce D. Perry, "Effects of Traumatic Events on Children." *Interdisciplinary Education Series* 2, no. 3 (1999): 1–22, at http:www.bcm.tmc.edu/cta/effects_I.htm (accessed July 27, 2001).

213. This was confirmed to the authors in discussions with parents and with caregivers who had observed this behavior in their children.

214. Van der Kolk, "Assessment and Treatment of Complex PTSD."

215. Kinzie et al., "Effects of Massive Trauma," 214.

216. Ignacio Martín-Baró, "War and the Psychosocial Trauma of Salvadoran Children," trans. Anne Wallace, in Ignacio Martín-Baró, *Writings for a Liberation Psychology*, trans. Adrianne Aron and Shawn Corne (Cambridge, MA: Harvard University Press, 1994).

217. Van der Kolk, "Assessment and Treatment of Complex PTSD"; Sack et al., "Does PTSD Transcend Cultural Barriers?"; Kinzie et al., "Effects of Massive Trauma"; Montgomery, "Refugee Children from the Middle East"; Goldstein et al., "War Experiences and Distress Symptoms."

218. Lea Marenn, *Salvador's Children: A Song for Survival* (Columbus: Ohio State University Press, 1993).

219. Abdel Aziz Mousa Thabet and Panos Vostanis, "Post-traumatic Stress Reactions in Children of War," Gaza Community Mental Health Program (GCMHP), at www.gcmhp.net/research/Post_traumatic.html (accessed September 20, 2005); Baker and Shalhoub-Kevorkian, "Effects of Political and Military Traumas"; James Garbarino and Kathleen Kostelny, "The Effects of Political Violence on Palestinian Children's Behavior Problems: A Risk Accumulation Model," *Child Development* vol. 67, no. 1 (1996): 33–45.

220. Sack et al., "Multiple Forms of Stress," 114.

221. Almqvist and Brandell-Forsberg, "Refugee Children in Sweden."

222. Montgomery, "Refugee Children from the Middle East."

223. Marina Ajdukovic, "Displaced Adolescents in Croatia: Sources of Stress and Posttraumatic Stress Reaction," *Adolescence* 33, no. 129 (1998) 209–217.

224. Goldstein et al., "War Experiences and Distress Symptoms"; V. Papgeorgiou, A. Frangou-Garunoivic, R. Iordanidou, W. Yule, P. Smith, and P. Vostanis, "War Trauma and Psychopathology in Bosnian Refugee Children," *European Child and Adolescent Psychiatry*, vol. 9 (2000): 84–90.

225. Hubbard et al., "Comorbidity of Psychiatric Diagnoses."

226. Kinzie et al., "Effects of Massive Trauma "

227. McCloskey and Southwick, "Psychosocial Problems"; Catherine J. Locke, Karen Southwick, Laura McCloskey, and María Eugenia Fernández-Esquer, "The Psychological and Medical Sequelae of War in Central American Refugee Mothers and Children," *Archives of Pediatrics and Adolescent Medicine* 150, no. 8 (1996): 826.

228. N. Laor, L. Wolmer, and D. V. Cicchetti, "The Comprehensive Assessment of Defense Style: Measuring Defense Mechanisms in Children and Adolescents," *Journal of Nervous and Mental Disease* 189, no. 6 (2001): 360–368.

229. Sack et al., "Posttraumatic Stress Disorder across Two Generations"; Sack et al., "Multiple Forms of Stress"; Sack et al., "Does PTSD Transcend Cultural Barriers?"

230. Ahmad et al., "Reliability and Validity"; C. Gorst-Unsworth and E. Goldenberg, "Psychological Sequelae of Torture and Organized Violence Suffered by Refugees from Iraq," *British Journal of Psychiatry* 172 (1998): 90–94.

231. Yehuda, *Treating Trauma Survivors with PTSD*; Steven Southwick and Mathew J. Friedman, "Neurobiological Models of Posttraumatic Stress Disorder," in Ellen Gerrity, Terence M. Keane, and Farris Tuma, eds., *The Mental Health Consequences of Torture* (New York: Kluwer Academic/Plenum, 2001); Stephen J. Suomi and Seymour Levine, "Psychobiology of Intergenerational Effects of Trauma: Evidence from Animal Studies," in Yael Danieli, ed., *International Handbook of Multigenerational Legacies of Trauma* (New York and London: Plenum, 1998).

232. John S. March and Lisa Amaya-Jackson, "Post-traumatic Stress Disorder in Children and Adolescents," *PTSD Research Quarterly* 4, no. 4 (1993): 1–3.

233. Bruce D. Perry, "The Vortex of Violence," *Interdisciplinary Education Series*, January 7, 2000 (January 2000), at www.bcm.tmc.edu/cta/vortex_interd.htm (accessed July 27, 2001).

234. Ignacio Martín-Baró, *Writings for a Liberation Psychology*, trans. Adrianne Aron and Shawn Corne (Cambridge, MA: Harvard University Press, 1994).

235. Sack et al., "Does PTSD Transcend Cultural Barriers?" 53.

236. Friedman and Jaranson, "Applicability of the Posttraumatic Stress Disorder Concept."

237. McCloskey and Southwick, "Psychosocial Problems."

238. K. J. S. Anand, "Clinical Importance of Pain and Stress in Preterm Neonates," *Biology of the Neonate* 71 (1998): 1–9; R. C. Cassidy and G. A. Walco, "Pediatric Pain: Ethical Issues and Ethical Management," *Children's Health Care* 25 (1996): 253–264; P. J. McGrath, C. Rosmus, C. Canfield, M. Campbell, and A. Hennigar, "Behaviors Caregivers Use to Determine Pain in Non-verbal Cognitively Impaired Individuals," *Developmental Medicine and Child Neurology* 40 (1998): 340–343.

239. Friedman and Jaranson, "Applicability of the Posttraumatic Stress Disorder Concept."

240. Sack et al., "Does PTSD Transcend Cultural Barriers?"; Goldstein et al., "War Experiences and Distress Symptoms."

241. Garbarino and Kostelny, "Effects of Political Violence"; Bruce D. Perry and Ishnella Azad, "Post-traumatic Stress Disorders in Children and Adolescents," *The Child Trauma Academy*, at www.childtrauma.org/CTAMaterials/PTSD_opin6.asp (accessed April 7, 2007); Caron Zlotnick, Mark Zimmerman, Barbara A. Wolfsdorf, and Jill I. Mattia, "Gender Differences in Patients with Posttraumatic Stress Disorder in a General Psychiatric Practice," *American Journal of Psychiatry* 158, no. 11 (2001):

1923–1925; Cuffe S. P., Addy C. L., Garrison C. Z., Waller J. L., Jackson K. L., McKeown R. E., and Chilappagari S. "Prevalence of PTSD in a Community Sample of Older Adolescents." *Journal of the American Academy of Child and Adolescent Psychiatry*, 37, no. 2 (1998): 147–154; Almqvist and Brandell-Forsberg, "Refugee Children in Sweden," 363.

242. Marina Ajdukovic, "Displaced Adolescents in Croatia: Sources of Stress and Posttraumatic Stress Reaction," *Adolescence* 33, no. 129 (1998): 209–217; Syed Arshad Husain, Jyotsna Nair, William Holcomb, John C. Reid, Victor Vargas, and Satish S. Nair, "Stress Reactions of Children and Adolescents in War and Siege Conditions," *American Journal of Psychiatry* 155 (1998), 1718–1719.

243. Bruce D. Perry, "Effects of Traumatic Events on Children," *Interdisciplinary Education Series* 2, no. 3 (1999): 1–22, at www.bcm.tmc.edu/cta/effects_I.htm (accessed July 27, 2001).

244. Breslau et al., cited in Bruce D. Perry, "Effects of Traumatic Events on Children," *Interdisciplinary Education Series* 2 no. 3 (1999): 1–22, at www.bcm.tmc.edu/cta/effects_I.htm (accessed July 27, 2001).

245. Garbarino and Kostelny, "Effects of Political Violence."

246. Baker and Shalhoub-Kevorkian, "Effects of Political and Military Traumas," 943.

247. Merril D. Smith, ed., *Encyclopedia of Rape* (Westport, CT: Greenwood, 2004).

248. Claudia María Vargas, "Cultural Mediation for Refugee Children: A Comparative Derived Model," *Journal of Refugee Studies* 12, no. 3 (1999): 284–306.

249. Sack et al., "Multiple Forms of Stress."

250. Sack et al., "Multiple Forms of Stress."

251. Stevan M. Weine, Dolores Vojvoda, Daniel Becker, Thomas H. McGlashan, Emir Hodzic, Dori Laub, Leslie Hyman, Marie Sawyer, and Steven Lazrove, "PTSD Symptoms in Bosnian Refugees 1 Year After Resettlement in the United States," *American Journal of Psychiatry* 155, no. 4 (1998): 562–564; Kinzie et al., "Effects of Massive Trauma," 1998.

252. Wanda P. Fremont, "Childhood Reactions to Terrorism Induced Trauma," *Psychiatric Times* 22, issue 10 (September 2005), at www.psychiatrictimes.com/article/showArticle.jhtml? (accessed July 5, 2006).

253. Locke et al., "Psychological and Medical Sequelae," 826; Weine et al., "PTSD Symptoms in Bosnian Refugees."

254. National Institute for Mental Health, *Helping Children and Adolescents Cope with Violence and Disasters*, National Institute of Medicine, September 2001, NIH Publication No. 01-3518, 3, at www.nimh.nih.gov/publicat/violence.cfm (accessed April 22, 2002).

255. American Psychiatric Association, *Diagnostic and Statistical Manual of Mental Disorders*, 4th ed., text revision (DSM-IV-TR) (Arlington, VA: American Psychiatric Association, 2000), 127.

256. Almqvist and Brandell-Forsberg, "Refugee Children in Sweden."

257. Garbarino and Kostelny, "Effects of Political Violence."

258. Mahshid Esfandiari and Frances MacQueen, "The Vitality of Interconnectedness: Vast's Service Delivery Programme, First Alone, Then Together," *Refuge* 18, no. 6 (2000): 50–55.

259. Montgomery, "Refugee Children from the Middle East"; Kinzie et al., "Effects of Massive Trauma."

260. James Garbarino and Kathleen Kostelny, "Children's Response to War: What Do We Know?" in Lewis A. Leavitt and Nathan A. Fox, eds., *The Psychological Effects of War and Violence on Children* (Hillsdale, NJ: Erlbaum, 1992), 37.

261. Martin H. Teicher, "Scars that Won't Heal: The Neurobiology of Child Abuse," *Scientific American* (March 2002): 68–75.

262. National Institute of Mental Health, 2001. See also Fremont, "Childhood Reactions to Terrorism Induced Trauma."

263. Papageorgiou et al., "War Trauma and Psychopathology in Bosnian Refugee Children," 2000; Montgomery, "Refugee Children from the Middle East"; McCloskey and Southwick, "Psychosocial Problems."

264. Teicher, "Scars that Won't Heal."

265. Kinzie et al., "Effects of Massive Trauma"; Montgomery, "Refugee Children from the Middle East"; Sack et al., "Posttraumatic Stress Disorder across Two Generations"; McCloskey and Southwick, "Psychosocial Problems."

266. Kinzie et al., "Effects of Massive Trauma."

267. Martín-Baró, "War and the Psychosocial Trauma," 127.

268. Lynette Evans, Tony McHugh, Malcolm Hopwood, and Carol Watt, "Chronic Posttraumatic Stress Disorder and Family Functioning of Vietnam Veterans and their Partners," *Australian and New Zealand Journal of Psychiatry* 37 (2003): 765–772.

269. United Nations, *Charter of the United Nations*, Preamble, at www.un.org/aboutun/charter (accessed December 25, 2006). See also Danieli, *International Handbook*, 2.

270. U.S. Department of Veterans Affairs, National Center for PTSD, *Annual Report for Fiscal Year 1999*, at www.ncptsd.va.gov/about/annual_report/ar99.html (accessed December 25, 2006); this source reports on the work of Robert Rosenheck and Alan Fontana, published as "Transgenerational Effects of Abusive Violence on the Children of Vietnam Combat Veterans," *Journal of Traumatic Stress* 11 (1998): 731–742.

271. Mount Sinai Medical School, Department of Psychiatry, Traumatic Stress Studies Division, *Research Studies and Findings*, at www.mssm.edu/psychiatry/tssp/studiesandfindings.shtml (accessed December 25, 2006).

272. Rachel Yehuda, Jim Schmeidler, Abbie Elkin, Skye Wilson, Larry Siever, Karen Binder-Brynes, Milton Wainberg, and Dan Aferiot, "Phenomenology and Psychobiology of the Intergenerational Response to Trauma," in Yael Danieli, ed., *International Handbook of Multigenerational Legacies of Trauma* (New York and London: Plenum, 1998).

273. Beverley Raphael, Pat Swan, and Nada Martinek, "Intergenerational Aspects of Trauma for Australian Aboriginal People," in Yael Danieli, ed., *International Handbook of Multigenerational Legacies of Trauma* (New York and London: Plenum, 1998).

274. Duran et al., "Healing the American Indian Soul Wounds."

275. Marie-Anik Gagné, "The Role of Dependency and Colonialism in Generating Trauma in First Nations Citizens: The James Bay Cree," in Yael Danieli, ed., *International Handbook of Multigenerational Legacies of Trauma* (New York and London: Plenum, 1998).

276. David Becker and Margarita Diaz, "The Social Process and the Transgenerational Transmission of Trauma in Chile," in Yael Danieli, ed., *International Handbook of Multigenerational Legacies of Trauma* (New York and London: Plenum, 1998).

277. Lucila Edelman, Diana Kordon, and Dario Lagos, "Transmission of Trauma: The Argentine Case," in Yael Danieli, ed., *International Handbook of Multigenerational Legacies of Trauma* (New York and London: Plenum, 1998).

278. Michael A. Simpson, "The Second Bullet: Transgenerational Impact of the Trauma of Conflict within a South African and World Context," in Yael Danieli, ed., *International Handbook of Multigenerational Legacies of Trauma* (New York and London: Plenum, 1998).

279. Kinzie et al., "Effects of Massive Trauma."

280. Diane Kupelian, Anie Sanentz Kalayjian, and Alice Kassabian, "The Turkish Genocide of the Armenians: Continuing Effects on Survivors and Their Families Eight Decades after Massive Trauma," in Yael Danieli, ed., *International Handbook of Multigenerational Legacies of Trauma* (New York and London: Plenum, 1998).

281. Eduard Klain, "Intergenerational Aspects of the Conflict in the Former Yugoslavia," in Yael Danieli, ed., *International Handbook of Multigenerational Legacies of Trauma* (New York and London: Plenum, 1998).

282. Donna K. Nagata, "Intergenerational Effects of the Japanese American Interment," in Yael Danieli, ed., *International Handbook of Multigenerational Legacies of Trauma* (New York and London: Plenum, 1998).

283. Irit Felsen, "Transgenerational Transmission of Effects of the Holocaust: The North American Research Perspective," in Yael Danieli, ed., *International Handbook of Multigenerational Legacies of Trauma* (New York and London: Plenum, 1998).

284. Zahava Solomon, "Transgenerational Effects of the Holocust: The Israeli Research Perspective," in Yael Danieli, ed., *International Handbook of Multigenerational Legacies of Trauma* (New York and London: Plenum, 1998).

285. Gagné, "Role of Dependency and Colonialism," 369.

286. Neil Kritz, Director of the U.S. Institute of Peace, Rule of Law Program, "Remarks," presented at the conference entitled, "Memory and Truth after Genocide: Guatemala," U.S. Holocaust Museum, Washington, D.C., March 21, 2000, at www.ushm.org/conscience/analysis/details/2000-03-21/guatemala/body.htm (accessed April 15, 2007.

287. *Brown v. Board of Education of Topeka, Kansas*, 347 U.S. 483 (1954). The Court added a now famous footnote acknowledging some of the authorities advanced by the NAACP, LDF attorneys: "K. B. Clark, Effect of Prejudice and Discrimination on Personality Development (Midcentury White House Conference on Children and Youth, 1950); Witmer and Kotinsky, Personality in the Making (1952), c. VI; Deutscher and Chein, The Psychological Effects of Enforced Segregation: A Survey of Social Science Opinion, 26 J. Psychol. 259 (1948); Chein, What are the Psychological Effects of Segregation Under Conditions of Equal Facilities?, 3 Int. J. Opinion and Attitude Res. 229 (1949); Brameld, Educational Costs, in Discrimination and National Welfare (MacIver, ed., 1949), 44–48; E. Franklin Frazier, *The Negro in the United States* (New York: The MacMillan Co., 1949); Gunnar Myrdal, *An American Dilemma: The Negro Problem and Modern Democracy* (New York: Harper & Rowe, 1944)."

288. Krug et al., *World Report on Violence and Health*.

289. Alex Argenti-Pillen, "The Global Flow of Knowledge on War Trauma: The Role of the 'Colombo 7 Culture' in Sri Lanka," American Society of Anthropology, April 2000, at www.asa2000.anthropology.ac.uk/argenti/argenti.html (accessed July 24, 2006).

290. Martín-Baró, *Writings for a Liberation Psychology*, 109.

291. Derek Summerfield, "The Impact of War and Atrocity on Civilian Populations: Basic Principles for NGO Interventions and a Critique of Psychosocial Trauma Projects, Relief and Rehabilitation Network," Overseas Development Institute, London, Network Paper 14 (1996): 1–41.

292. *Hirabayashi v. United States*, 320 U.S. 81 (1943); *Korematsu v. United States*, 323 U.S. 214 (1944).

293. *Ex Parte Endo*, 323 U.S. 283 (1944).

294. *Korematsu v. United States*, 233.

295. *Korematsu v. United States*, 242.

296. *Korematsu v. United States*, 243–244.

297. *Korematsu v. United States*, 584 F. Supp. 1406, 1416–1417 (NDCA 1984).

298. *Hirabayashi v. United States*, 828 F.2d 591, 598 (9th Cir. 1987).

299. *Korematsu v. United States*, 584 F. Supp., at 1419.

300. *Korematsu v. United States*, 584 F. Supp., at 1420.

301. *Hamdan v. Rumsfeld*, 165 L. Ed. 2d 723 (2006).

302. Martín-Baró, *Writings for a Liberation Psychology*, 113.

303. Martín-Baró, *Writings for a Liberation Psychology*, 113.

304. Martín-Baró, *Writings for a Liberation Psychology*, 1.

305. Felsen, "Transgenerational Transmission of Effects of the Holocaust," 51.

306. Krug et al., *World Report on Violence and Health*.

307. IDMC, Colombia: *Government "Peace Process" Cements Injustice*, 163.

308. Krug et al., *World Report on Violence and Health*; Martín-Baró, *Writings for a Liberation Psychology*; IDMC, *Colombia: Government "Peace Process" Cements Injustice*, 163.

309. Duran et al., "Healing the American Indian Soul Wounds."

310. Duran et al., "Healing the American Indian Soul Wounds." Ethan Nebelkopf and Mary Phillips, eds., *Healing and Mental Health for Native Americans: Speaking in Red* (Walnut Creek: AltaMira Press, 2004), pp. 159–165; Dolores Subia BigFoot, "American Indian Youth: Current and Historical Trauma," at http://www.nctsn.org/nctsn_assets/pdfs/AI_Youth-CurrentandHistoricalTrauma.pdf (accessed August 14, 2007).

311. UNHCR, "Indigenous Youth Lose the Will to Live amid Conflict in Colombia," UNHCR News Stories, at www.unhcr.org/cgi-bin/texis/vtx/print?tbl=NEWS& id=40e554534 (accessed November 27, 2006).

312. UNHCR, "Indigenous Youth Lose."

313. UNHCR, "Indigenous Youth Lose."

314. Martín-Baró, *Writings for a Liberation Psychology*; Fremont, "Childhood Reactions to Terrorism Induced Trauma"; Krug et al., *World Report on Violence and Health*.

315. Atle Dyregrov, Leila Gupta, Rolf Gjestad, and Magne Raundalen, "Is Culture Always Right?" *Traumatology* 8, no. 3 (2002): 2.

316. Oficina de Derechos Humanos del Arzobispado de Guatemala (ODHAG), *Guatemala Nunca Más, Proyecto de Recuperación de la Memoria Histórica (REMHI)* (Guatemala City, Guatemala: ODHAG, 1998).

317. ODHAG, *"Era tras la vida."*

318. Michael A. Simpson, "The Second Bullet: Transgenerational Impacts of the Trauma of Conflict within a South African and World Context," in Yael Danieli, ed., *International Handbook of Multigenerational Legacies of Trauma* (New York and London: Plenum, 1998), 508.

319. Craig Kauffman, "Transitional Justice in Guatemala," 11.

320. Yael Danieli, ed., "Conclusions and Future Directions," in Yael Danieli, ed., *International Handbook of Multigenerational Legacies of Trauma* (New York and London: Plenum, 1998), 681.

321. Martín-Baró, *Writings for a Liberation Psychology*, 120.

322. WHO, "Ministerial Round Tables: Mental Health."

323. Dyregrov et al., "Is Culture Always Right?" 8.

324. Vargas, "Cultural Mediation for Refugee Children"; Ester Cole, "Supporting Refugee and Immigrant Children: Building Bridges Programme of the International Children's Institute in Canada and Overseas," *Refuge* 18, no. 6: 41–45.

325. World Health Organization, *Working Together for Health: The World Health Report 2006* (Geneva: WHO, 2006), 25–26.

326. Dyregrov et al., "Is Culture Always Right?" 3, 5.

5

Demobilization

Looking Past Disaster

To many observers from outside an area plagued by violence, it is easy to see a cease-fire, a peace pact among warring parties, or an agreement by community leaders to work to stop violence in the context of civil disorder, as a time when infrastructure can be rebuilt and the economy can recover. However, as the previous chapters have explained, the promise of an end to the shooting marks the onset of another phase of the process of conflict, which is demobilization. The period of demobilization can be long and difficult, not merely for the combatants, but for the entire society. The hold on peace can be tenuous and, if handled ineffectively, the promise of a better future may, and often does, give way to renewed conflict. Even though the shooting may stop, the dying often does not. The forces of what has been called "development in reverse" are surprisingly persistent and may or may not be recognized for what they are.[1]

Sadly, there is a tendency in some settings to once again bring to the situation an idealized post-World War II picture of the signing of a peace treaty followed by a rapid demobilization and reconstruction in the form of something like the Marshall Plan. Unfortunately, for reasons explained in chapter 1, that conception of demobilization is not even an accurate portrayal of the situation after World War II, let alone most contemporary post-conflict settings.

Properly understood, the period of demobilization is as complex as any other phase of conflict and may, in many important respects, be even more difficult for those seeking to move the community forward. Too often, donor countries and aid agencies see themselves as ready to move elsewhere once what they define as the immediate humanitarian disaster (understood as ending at the formal end of hostilities) is over. Donor nations, for their part, are often more than ready to shift their focus to the next important priority on their foreign policy agendas.

These end-of-conflict realities provide further evidence of the inadequacy of the reconstruction and redevelopment model, and the need for a more effective sustainable development approach to post-conflict action. This chapter addresses the demobilization process, with particular attention to the continuation of damage to the social, economic, and environmental aspects of life after conflict. Second, it considers the challenges of demobilization of both security forces and of the nation as a whole. Third, it discusses the factors that are essential to the movement forward. However, as in earlier chapters, the present discussion begins with a case study on demobilization in Rwanda.

RWANDA: LIFE AFTER GENOCIDE

A land of captivating beauty and diverse wildlife, and habitat for the famous mountain gorillas, Rwanda has witnessed a number of deadly conflicts, culminating with the 1994 genocide and violence that continued into the twenty-first century as the Great Lakes region of Africa has endured one convulsion after another. In this small, landlocked country, the conflict has been between the majority Hutus and minority Tutsis, a product of exclusion, discrimination, displacement, and exile.[2] At the same time, those characterics also reflect political and economic conflict.[3]

Primarily rural, Rwanda is slightly larger than the state of Vermont, but as the most densely populated country in Africa, it has, not surprisingly, witnessed struggles associated with land scarcity. In 1994 its population was 7.5 million in a territory of 26,338 square kilometers (10,169 square miles), compared to Vermont's population of 613,000 in an area of 24,903 square kilometers (9,9043 square miles).[4] A country of breathtaking beauty and verdant hills, the landscape concealed the ongoing tension between the two ethnocultural groups, intensified by extremists in the power struggles on both sides. The tensions erupted into civil conflict even as the international community was negotiating the principles of the Arusha Peace Agreement for a transitional, power-sharing government that included Tutsi representation.

Although the conflict of the 1990s in Rwanda had its immediate origins in the attack in October 1990 by the Rwandan Patriotic Front (RPF), resulting in a civil war between 1990 and 1992, the clashes and the genocide of 1994 can be traced back many years before that.[5] The more immediate history went back to the years just before Rwandan independence. The RPF was founded by the Tutsi expatriates, refugees, and their descendants based in Uganda, who had been attempting to make their way back to their homeland since they had been driven out of Rwanda in 1959. In April 1994, the

Arusha Accord was in the process of implementation when a massacre was triggered by the death of President Juvenal Habyarimana.[6] His death pre-cipitated violence directed against Tutsis and Hutus who were perceived to be sympathizers of the Tutsis, in which nearly a million people were slaugh-tered, and more than 3 million people were displaced in a matter of one hundred days.[7] In a global community that so often said "never again," these atrocities were quickly recognized as one of the worst examples of a contemporary genocide. Sanctioned and armed by the state, a criminal force, "the Interahamwe (those who attack together) and the Impuza-mugambi (those who have the same goal)," ruthlessly massacred civilians during the 1990–1992 civil war, as well as during the 1994 genocide.[8]

However, this discussion of the case of Rwanda is not so much focused on the violence itself as it is on the effort to move forward after the geno-cide, a study in demobilization in several important respects. Like all other case studies, of course, it is essential to understand the context and the con-flict that led to the demobilization in the discussion to come.

Foundations of Conflict: Rwanda's Colonial Past

In this instance past is not merely prologue, it was and is an integral part of the violence and continuing tensions, since history was used by the par-ties to justify abuses over time, including to rally those who took part in the genocide. All parties, including the European colonial rulers, the Tutsis, and the Hutus, read the country's history in their own way and for their own purposes. Of course, virtually every country has parts of its history that have had contending interpretations and, so long as this remains the province of academic historians, these debates are addressed as matters of historiogra-phy. In the case of Rwanda, though, while there have certainly been debates on historiography, the issue of the country's history has been far more po-litically and socially significant than that.[9] Indeed, the clashes became so se-rious that the teaching of Rwandan history in the schools of that country was prohibited after the genocide while the Ministry of Education worked with international nongovermental organizations (NGOs) to provide a way forward that would be part of the reconciliation process and not something that would ignite renewed conflict. That effort led to a new curriculum and teacher training during 2006.[10]

What is clear is that Europeans colonized what is today Rwanda and Bu-rundi, as well as the other parts of Africa, in the late nineteenth century. Germany claimed this territory as its own colony in 1885, although it was "French, Belgian and Swiss Roman Catholics who commenced evangelizing there at the same time. Belgian forces occupied Ruanda-Urundi towards the end of World War I, and Belgium inherited the colony when it was confis-cated from Germany after the war. Ruanda-Urundi was administratively joined to the Belgian Congo in 1925."[11] It was at this point that the labels Hutu and Tutsi began to undergo a social and political construction that ultimately played a critical role in the violence to come.[12] And it was also at this time that interpretations of that history began to diverge and to be incorporated into the political and economic self-interest of the key players in the tragedy.

Under the generally accepted European construction, there were three distinct groups who made up the population of Rwanda: the Hutu, the Tutsi, and the Twas. In this view the first residents were the Twa people. In the contemporary era, the Twa make up a small minority portion of the population. They had been a forest people, primarily hunter-gatherers who later came to be treated badly by both the Tutsis and Hutus. They viewed these people of small stature as inferior. Then, according to the Europeans, came the Hutus, who were crop farmers, later labeled by the Europeans as Bantu or indigenous people. Later still, in this version, came the Tutsis from the north to take over and dominate the country. Since the Tutsis held the ruling positions when Belgium instituted its colonial rule, they were the ones to take government positions and the Hutus were considered a lesser group. This version of history served the Tutsis well in their claims to the right to rule by virtue of their presumed superiority. It later served Hutus who sought to engender hatred of the Tutsis, who could be pictured as the invaders who subjugated the Hutus.[13]

As Alison Des Forges, who synthesized the challenges raised to this long-standing view of Rwandan history, asserted: "The collaboration resulted in a sophisticated and convincing but inaccurate history that simultaneously served Tutsi interests and validated European assumptions."[14] There is no small irony to the way that it later served the political interests of Hutus who used that story to rally compatriots to participate in the genocidal attacks on the Tutsis.

As Des Forges and others explain it, the terms *Tutsi* and *Hutu* were applied to those who raised cattle and those who grew crops, respectively, and did not originally connote ethnic differences. In fact, she argued:

> Originally organized in small groups based on lineage or on loyalty to an outstanding leader, they joined in building the complex state of Rwanda. They developed a single and highly sophisticated language, Kinyarwanda, crafted a common set of religious and philosophical beliefs, and created a culture which valued song, dance, poetry, and rhetoric. They celebrated the same heroes: even during the genocide, the killers and their intended victims sang of some of the same leaders from the Rwandan past.[15]

The terms *Tutsi* and *Hutu* came to be treated as both political and ethnocultural labels. "Unclear whether these were races, tribes, or language groups, the Europeans were nonetheless certain that the Tutsi were superior to the Hutu and the Hutu superior to the Twa—just as they knew themselves to be superior to all three."[16] As the Belgian colonizers took power, they identified the two groups in that way and required all Rwandans to identify themselves accordingly for purposes of government identification records in 1933–1934. "The fact is that the Belgian power did not arbitrarily cook up the Hutu/Tutsi distinction. What it did do was to take an existing sociopolitical distinction and racialize it."[17]

The battle to establish in the clearest terms precisely what the history of the country was during the pre-colonial period continues amidst the recognition that the outcomes of those debates have real and immediate political impacts. At the same time, there was a desire to work through this issue. Organizations like Facing History, Facing Ourselves worked with Rwandan officials to reintroduce discussions of the country's history into schools in such a way that it could be a part of reconciliation efforts rather than fuel for another round of violence.

What is clear is that the Hutus came to power in the late 1950s. "The main Hutu political party was the Mouvement Démocratique Républicain (MDR), led by Grégoire Kayibanda, who, in the name of 'social revolution,' orchestrated the first of many pogroms against Tutsis, with Belgian connivance, in 1959. Thousands were killed, and many more fled as refugees."[18] It was ironic that Belgians intervened in support of the Hutus, given their prior support for Tutsis. The Tutsi expatriates fled to other Great Lakes areas such as Burundi, Tanzania, Zaire (contemporary Democratic Republic of Congo [DRC]), and Uganda. Over time, some of the Tutsis tried to fight their way back into the country several times and years later did so.

The years after independence in 1962 were difficult even among ruling Hutus. In 1973 Juvénal Habyarimana, a Hutu, overthrew Kayibanda and set up a one-party state as the Mouvement Révolutionnaire Nationale pour le Développement (MRND). This second regime ruled for twenty years until the assassination of Habyarimana in 1994. The era of Hutu rule was beset with ethnic conflict, which drove out still more Tutsi refugees.[19] For Tutsis who remained in Rwanda, the Hutu-dominated government created ethnic categories, verifiable through identity cards, to restrict access to education and government positions.

Meanwhile, the exiled Tutsis in Uganda, Burundi, and the DRC, organized a force called the Rwandan Patriotic Front (RPF), which was itself accused of assassinations of civilians and officials. Peace talks produced the Arusha Accords, signed in Arusha, Tanzania, in 1993, with international support and UN intervention that provided for a power-sharing arrangement and the return of refugees. However, the accord was seen as a surrender by Hutu extremists.

The Genocide of 1994

Peace efforts died with the assassination of Habyarimana in April 1994, with a ruthless genocide by the Rwandan government forces, paramilitaries, and right-wing Hutu political leaders. The Rwandese Government Forces (RGF), with support from the Gendarmerie and criminal forces—the Interahamwe and the Impuzamugambi—took charge. The appointed president of the interim government, Madame Agathe Uwilingiyimana, and her husband were assassinated in their home with their children present.[20] The extreme Hutu faction attacked the moderate Hutu group for supporting inclusion of the Tutsi bloc in the newly conceived government structure.

What is most significant for the country's future, however, was that the 1994 slaughter of the Tutsis was committed by Hutu-led forces, the Mouvement Révolutionnaire Nationale pour le Développement (MRND) and the Rwandan Government Forces (RGF), the military forces under the control of Hutu political leaders. Moderate Hutus, however, attempted to stop the murders. The genocide was intensified as paramilitaries and gangs joined the annihilation of Tutsis, including children in orphanages, women, the elderly, those who sought refuge in churches, and even those who had been injured from a previous attack.[21]

A Tutsi counterattack was launched by the RPF, which entered the capital in July 1994. By the time the conflict ended after RPF forces defeated the RGF and other groups, the genocide claimed more than 800,000, and half of the population was displaced.

It is difficult to understand the violence in Rwanda and the challenges of demobilization and reconciliation that followed without an awareness of the context in the Great Lakes region, which, though endowed with natural beauty and resources, has been plagued by continuous conflict, dictatorships, coups d'état, corruption, grinding poverty, environmental degradation, civil unrest, and even massacres. These conflicts, inter-party and inter-ethnic rivalries, and the conflicts in neighboring countries exacerbated an already critical set of desperate living conditions and volatile politics. The refugees, who were in a number of instances ostracized by the host countries, in some cases generated instability and conflict in bordering regions. In other instances, the native community was victimized, raped, and robbed by rebels and criminal groups operating in the border regions, including the DRC. The paramilitary activity aimed at the Rwandan government became uncontrollable in host countries, especially the DRC.

Rwanda's Post-Genocide Challenges: Emergency Response, Demilitarization, Demobilization, and Beyond

The genocide left a people and a country adrift. The massive loss of life and talent and the broken governance structures and infrastructure seriously challenged the economy and left a badly damaged environment, militarized groups, and millions of displaced persons. A genocide committed not only by those in power but by neighbors left special challenges for Rwanda. Rwanda emerged from the 1994 disaster among the low development countries on most measures. Its gross national income (GNI) in 2001 was $745 or less. The Human Development Index (HDI) (based on the literacy rate, life expectancy, and gross domestic product [GDP]) fell during the period 1992–1995 from 134 to 156 ranking, deteriorating further by 1997 to 174 out of 175 countries rated.

At and just after the genocide, Rwanda claimed what was then the highest number of displaced people in the world, with its associated consequences (see chapters 3 and 4). In addition, there were death of loved ones, loss of property, cultural displacement, loss of schooling and health care, and a lack of human security. There was also a loss of the kind of expertise needed to move toward a positive future, as so many educated and skilled people were killed or driven out. While the 1994 genocide deliberately targeted Tutsis, others were attacked as well, such as the Batwa tribes.

It would be a dramatic understatement to say that the plight of children in Rwanda was alarming: "two-thirds of the Rwandan child population (below 14 years old) is estimated to have personally witnessed atrocities—massacres—being committed."[22] According to the Rwanda 1999 *Human Development Report*, the impact on Rwandan children can be seen in the high number of significant psychologically injurious experiences.[23] The details appear in Table 5.1[24], but what is particularly striking is the fact that almost all children witnessed someone being killed, with all of the near-term and even intergenerational issues discussed in chapter 4.[25]

The impact of psychological trauma and social and cultural discontinuity combined with poverty, scarce social services, and high incidence of HIV/AIDS. As chapter 2 explained, in Rwanda rape and infection with HIV/AIDS were used as tactics of social warfare. By 2001, there were 65,000

Table 5.1. Exposure of Rwandan Children to Traumatic Events

Exposure to Traumatic Events	Percentage of Children
Witnessed violence	95.9 %
Experienced death in the family	79.6 %
Witnessed someone being killed or injured	69.5 %
Were threatened with death	61.5 %
Believed they would die	90.6 %
Witnessed killings or injuries with machete	57.7 %
Witnessed rape or sexual assault	31.4 %
Saw dead bodies or parts of bodies	87.5 %

Source: UNICEF, *Rwanda 1999 Human Development Report* (Kigali: United Nations Development Programme, 1999), 18.

children living with HIV/AIDS.[26] These factors are particularly accentuated by large numbers of street children, child-headed households, and former child soldiers.[27]

The conditions at the time of the genocide and the events that followed meant serious pressures on the environment as well. Population density generated tensions over land scarcity and exerted additional strains on land fertility. A dramatic population growth, from 4.4 million in 1975, 8.1 million in 2001, to 8.8 million in 2003, illustrates the demands on availability of arable land.[28] Water resources have posed serious problems, especially in the dry eastern part of Rwanda. The displacement and later resettlement of refugees placed additional pressure on all aspects of the environment, including previously protected areas of the country (discussed later in this chapter). Clearing for agriculture meant a reduction of forested land from 18.5 percent in 1990 to 12.4 percent in 2000.[29]

Rwandans faced the prospect of demobilizing, demilitarizing, and developing their beautiful but now scarred nation. The United Nations Development Programme (UNDP) described the humanitarian disaster that existed in Rwanda and neighboring countries.

> Between April and July 1994, in less than a hundred days, close to a million people were murdered. More than two million fled into exile for overcrowded, insalubrious camps in neighboring countries run by UN agencies and NGOs. Some 350,000 Rwandans were also internally displaced during the period. . . . Some 95,000 children lost both parents. Some 100,000 Rwandans died in exile through disease, pandemic outbreaks and armed fighting. In mid-1994 alone about 50,000 died in a virulent outbreak of cholera in camps in the Kivu provinces of Zaire/DRC. UN agencies and NGOs managing the refugee camps faced a Solomonic dilemma when shown that some 10 to 15 percent of the 1.5 million refugees and internally displaced persons they were caring for might have participated in the violence and massacres.[30]

International agencies have learned that humanitarian aid can sometimes exacerbate tensions when aid reaches fighters who sometimes use refugee camps as safe havens for their military operations, as well sources of supply. The complex array of groups and conflicts in the region make it difficult for donors to pursue "conflict-sensitive" assistance.[31]

Regional conflict further complicated the situation. According to the *Human Development Report 2005*:

> Poor households often bear the brunt of financing the very conflicts that jeopardize their security. Both rebels and state actors fund themselves by looting assets from ordinary people or exploiting natural resources, creating a war economy that feeds the conflict. Those who benefit have a vested interest in opposing peace agreements. Illegal taxation and extortion are often preferred means of raising revenue. In eastern Democratic Republic of the Congo the

Democratic Forces for the Liberation of Rwanda (FDLR) impose illegal taxes and systematically pillage local markets. The weekly "war tax" exceeds the income of most local residents. Civilians are also sometimes forced to pay the FDLR a large part of their profit from mining coltan, one of the few income-generating activities in the area. Banditry, livestock looting and the state's inability to provide protection make insecurity a daily reality in conflict-affected regions.[32]

These types of black market strategies continue to destabilize and erode peace processes and security measures.

Domestically, Tutsi and Hutu Rwandans were asked to live together in a society soon after a genocide and to work toward national reconciliation amidst an atmosphere of fear, distrust, and resentment. These challenges, exacerbated by the traumatization of the society, were further intensified by continued armed conflict between Hutu rebel militia, the Democratic Forces for the Liberation of Rwanda (FDLR), and the Rwandan army. There was also regional tension and conflict between the Rwandan government and the Democratic Republic of Congo, as well as other border nations.[33] Demobilization was complicated by an estimated 3 million returning refugees. Rwanda and the DRC signed a peace agreement on July 30, 2002,[34] but the border conflict continued.

At the core of the conciliation process, Rwandans faced the monumental task of building a new justice system and administering it in the post-genocide period. This daunting challenge has been complicated by problems of disarmament, demobilization, and repatriation, along with the difficulties of reintegrating former Hutu army leaders and Hutu guerrilla bands. First, there has been the need to try over 120,000 imprisoned individuals accused of participating in the genocide. Second, institutional capacity was decimated, including the institutional capacity to implement the law. Third, even though the traditional community-based justice system called *gacaca* (grass) was instituted to deal with the detainees, it managed to try less than 5, 000 out of 120,000 by 2002.[35] The *gacaca* courts also have had to undertake the trials of 761,000 genocide suspects.[36] Fourth, while an amnesty led to confessions of about 60,000 detainees in 2004,[37] the collective psychological scars continue to plague survivors, both because of problems with prosecutions and due to intimidation of witnesses.[38] Fifth, there has been the slow pace of the international criminal tribunal (ICTR) prosecution of members of the *akazu* (a small group of allies of former President Habyarimana), as well as former high-ranking Hutu government officials.[39] Sixth, demobilization has been plagued by continued border clashes and, until relatively recently, violence in Rwanda itself.

Violence did not stop in the region, given local tensions and the ability of various groups of fighters to move across boundaries. In 1996, Rwanda invaded the DRC to fight former members of the FDLR, the Interahamwe, and former Rwandan army forces who had been operating against Rwanda since 1994. The guerrilla war intensified in 1998, involving other countries in the region, the DRC and Uganda. These difficulties with the DRC fueled long-running Security Council efforts to clarify exactly what was happening and then to pressure the DRC into returning fugitives, among other important steps. As of 2005, UNDP reported that: "Daily insecurities persist. Despite the All-Inclusive Peace Agreement signed in 2003, hundreds of thousands of people have still not been able to resume normal lives. In fact, since November 2004 nearly 200,000 people have fled their homes in North and South Kivu provinces, seeking safety in the forests."[40]

Finally, in 2005, there were reports that the rebel forces had expressed willingness to disarm. In fact, press reports indicated that, on March 30, 2005, the FDLR offered an apology for the 1994 genocide, accompanied by an offer to disarm prior to returning to Rwanda.[41] However, the Rwanda government made it clear that any of those who returned and who had criminal liability would face prosecution. By the end of 2005 only approximately one hundred had returned.[42] While there had not been reports of Rwandan military attacks on civilians during 2005, there were reports of savage attacks by FDLR in the DRC. The U.S. State Department indicated:

> During the year the local human rights NGO Women's Network for the Defense of Right and Peace (Reseau des Femmes pour La Defense des Droits et La Paix) detailed approximately 100 cases of rape by armed groups in the territory of Walungu, South Kivu. The women raped ranged in age from 9 to 68. All but three cases were attributed to the FDLR or the splinter group, Rastas. . . .

> During the year there were credible reports that foreign rebels killed civilians. On July 9, in the village of Ntulumamba, 43 miles northwest of Bukavu, individuals believed by MONUC to be members of the FDLR herded villagers, mostly women and children, into their homes, which the perpetrators then set on fire. The perpetrators used machetes to hack to death those who tried to escape and killed a total of 40 villagers. On July 13, a UN spokesperson said MONUC had discovered mass graves in Ntulumamba and that the remains were believed to be those of the victims of the July 9 attack. The perpetrators had not been brought to justice by year's end. On October 10, members of the FDLR/RASTAS hacked to death 15 civilians, including 8 women and 6 children, in Kaniola, South Kivu, in retaliation for measures taken by the government against the FDLR/RASTAS.[43]

Finally, the violence had also decimated the human and institutional capacity in education, health, and legal systems. "Of the 800 court magistrates, only 40 could be traced in Rwanda after the war."[44]

Rwanda has been dealing with the need to make effective an educational system whose teaching force had been reduced by half.[45] The "Education for All" policy included a deliberate effort to increase participation of girls. To improve education and nutrition, children were provided hot meals in school and females received a can of oil once a month.[46] Unfortunately, despite the goal of 100 percent school enrollment by the year 2010, thousands of children still cannot attend because they are heads of households, in child labor, or are street children.[47] Child mortality and morbidity are still high due to poverty, poor nutrition, inadequate health care, and the HIV/AIDS epidemic.

New governance mechanisms were needed after the genocide and efforts were made to include reforms in the new system. There were calls for institutions to be sensitized to gender issues in order to address the needs of women survivors of the genocide, as well as to integrate them into the development processes.[48] "On August 27th, 2003, Rwanda held the first democratic presidential election in its history, and held a referendum on the new constitution that guarantees a minimum of 30 percent of parliamentary seats to women."[49] Parliamentary elections were also held.[50] In spite of limited resources for legislators to do their job properly, the Parliament of Rwanda prides itself in having "the highest proportion of women MPs in the world (48 percent in the lower house and 30 percent in the upper house)."[51] According to the *Human Development Report 2005*: "Globally, women hold only about 15% of legislative assembly seats. In only 43 countries is the ratio of female to male parliamentarians more than 1 to 5, and in only two—Rwanda and Sweden—is the ratio even close to parity."[52] (Women had attained the right to vote in 1961.) The percentage of women in parliament in 2000 was 13.0. By 2005, women made up 35.7 percent of ministerial government positions.[53]

However, serious problems persist, as economic and social advancements are lowest for women.[54] The genocide left a legacy in which men constitute a minority of the population, with significant repercussions. For example, a high percentage of women are heads of households who experience entrenched poverty and alteration of cultural patterns. "While prisoner and widow-headed households are often amongst the poorer households, the high proportion of female household heads has also presented a challenge to the traditional gender roles in Rwanda."[55] As is common among refugees and displaced women, they struggle with responsibilities traditionally ascribed to men as breadwinners and disciplinarians of their children.

As one of the poorest countries in the world, scarcity of arable land combined with the need to address damage to the environment—for example, reforestation and land terracing efforts, restocking of fishing ponds, reversing soil erosion, among others—and inadequate food production to meet the needs of Rwandans, have made the road out of poverty more difficult. Equally demanding are the needs for education on the HIV/AIDS epidemic and reeducation to integrate former combatants and disabled soldiers. The Re-education Camp or *Ingando* was intended to work toward reconciliation and social integration. The Ingando was to provide training on "topics such as national security, human rights, genocide, the history of Rwanda, education, HIV/AIDS, gender, and micro-projects. At the end of the training, each ex-soldier receives a sum of money to start a micro business or project in his community. Since its launch the centre has handled 3,400 ex-combatants."[56]

As articulated in the Arusha Agreement, the Government of National Unity established in 1994 culminated in the first elections in 2003, as well as the adoption of its first constitution. The vision for the next fifteen years is to focus on poverty alleviation to promote Rwanda's status from a least-developed country to a middle-income country.[57] Given Rwanda's many challenges, this would be an ambitious goal under any circumstances, but achieving it in a situation in which the damage has been so great and so deep is all the more difficult. "The genocide of 1994 has left the country with deep social, psychological and economic scars; human development in this context consists primarily of building a shared sense of national identity in a divided country."[58]

Reconciliation has brought modest achievements as well as significant challenges (see Table 5.2). Positive results include elimination of ethnicity from the identity card, the repatriation of refugees, and the use of the traditional gacaca process in the justice system. Some of the negative factors may have to one degree or another been present before the conflict, including corruption in administrative and judicial bodies and questionable appointments to government positions. Others are specifically symptomatic of the conflict, such as denial of the genocide, the unresolved prosecution of suspects, and ongoing land disputes.

While Rwanda faces serious obstacles in reconciliation, it also possesses cultural traditions that can help in confronting them. According to the *Poverty Reduction Strategy Paper*, these include, "*Umuganda*, the tradition of work on public projects"; "*Ubudehe*, the tradition of mutual assistance"; "*Gacaca*, the tradition of communal resolution of disputes"; and "*Umusanzu*, the tradition of support for the needy and contribution to the achievement of a common goal." Further, unlike other African countries— South Africa has eleven official languages, Ethiopia four languages, Nigeria four languages—with multiple languages, Rwandans speak primarily Kinyarwanda, although some speak French or English, facilitating integration.[59]

Demobilization: Looking Ahead after the Disaster

Since 1994, Rwanda has moved toward restoring order, a rule of law system, and security. It has also experienced economic growth and is trying to become a high-tech center in Africa. Of course, such a goal presents the dan-

Table 5.2. The Positive and Negative Factors of Reconciliation in Rwanda

Positive Factors of Reconciliation
- Equality of opportunity in education
- The omission of ethnicity from the identity card
- The inclusion of the former regime's soldiers in the national army
- The repatriation of refugees
- The creation of the various governance commissions and processes
- The gacaca process
- Transparent elections at local levels
- Competition in recruitment
- Equal opportunities for entry into the army and police
- Gender equality
- Solidarity in response to security threats
- The return of illegally confiscated property to the owners
- The reintegration of orphans into volunteer host families with the support of the Survivors of Genocide Fund and MINALOC

Negative Factors of Reconciliation
- Land disputes
- Corruption in administrative bodies
- IBUKA (a group representing genocide survivors) is perceived as sectarian
- Hutus who died in the war have not been buried with dignity
- The trial of those accused of genocide and the compensation of victims have been long delayed
- Some people deny the impact of the genocide
- Some people go into exile and attack the Government
- Rumors from external media cause confusion
- Continued insurgency
- Segregation of orphans and widows (from the rest of society)
- Salary arrears and arbitrary appointment of teachers
- Corruption in judicial bodies
- Conflicts between pastoralists and cultivators, when the animals eat the other's crops

Source: Government of Rwanda, "Poverty Reduction Strategy Paper," National Poverty Reduction Programme (Ministry of Finance and Economic Planning, June 2002), 8.

ger of a dramatic tension between rural poverty and urban prosperity. In spite of transportation difficulties common to landlocked countries, Rwanda has benefited from increased official foreign aid assistance from 11.3 percent in 1990 to 17.3 in 2001.[60] The long-term look forward has been articulated in the "Key Objectives in Rwanda's Vision 2020," which focused on: "good political and economic governance, rural economic transformation, development of services and manufacturing, human resource development, development and promotion of the private sector, regional and international economic integration, and poverty reduction."[61]

Foreign aid will be critical in the success of government-initiated measures, which, according to the World Bank, dwindles in the post-conflict period, when it is most needed and when its benefits can be maximized. "Capacity to absorb aid is most limited in the immediate post-conflict period,
as new institutions are put in place, leading to large gaps between donor
commitments and disbursements. Research suggests that the optimal period for absorbing increased aid is about six years after a peace settlement,
by which time donor interest has moved on."[62] But, even under adverse
conditions, Rwanda can point to innovations generated by conditions of
limited resources.

> [A] fuel-efficient oven, designed and manufactured by the Kigali Institute of
> Science, Technology and Management (KIST), uses charcoal, wood or biogas,
> consuming only a fraction of the fuel normally required to fire similar ovens.
> It won the Ashden Prize or "Green Oscar," a major international prize for re-
> newable energy. UNDP is key among Rwanda's bilateral and multilateral part-
> ners that have actively backed KIST since its inception in 1997 in the develop-
> ment of several appropriate technology products such as cooking stoves, water
> pumps, solar panels, roofing sheets, nails, toilet rolls, etc. made by students
> and staff and marketed locally and in the sub-region.[63]

In terms of governance, Rwanda has instituted decentralized governmental structures combined with community participation to articulate priorities and define strategies. Decentralization became important in order to redress prior inequalities in allocation of resources. Community
participation, through an empowerment process, allows participants in
communities to do their own planning anchored on traditional structures.
"The chosen Kinyarwanda name for the action planning is *ubudehe mu kur-
wanya ubukene*—which makes use of the traditional Rwandese concept of
communal action in the fields, although here the approach is for the entire
community for any project they choose to fight poverty."[64] The first elections were held in 2003, despite an atmosphere where dissent and pluralis-
tic political stances are still in nascent stages. "Analysts suggest that the way
in which the RPF government responds to demands for greater political
freedom, and more equitably shared economic opportunities, will determine how far Rwanda's current stability is maintained in the long term."[65]

THE DESTRUCTIVE DYNAMICS OF CONFLICT
DO NOT END WITH THE CEASE-FIRE

The World Bank and international aid agencies have demonstrated that the
casualties of conflict continue long after the final engagements end. While
it should be obvious that the effects of conflict are persistent, the fact is that

the scope, intensity, and duration of the challenges that arise at a moment in time when peace should be at hand are more significant than is often recognized. Although these issues are most often noted sector-by-sector by agencies with a particular policy focus, the effects are highly interrelated across the social, environmental, and economic dimensions of sustainable development. Some of the most critical issues include morbidity and mortality, food insecurity, environmental damage and impact, economic casualties, and lingering tensions after formal conflict ends.

The Casualties Continue: The Costs in Lives and Health Goes On

Mortality and morbidity rates often continue at extremely high levels after the fighting officially ends. The spread and intensification of social warfare has meant that civilians have increasingly become targets and, hence, civilian death rates have soared during the fighting. "At the beginning of the 20th century about 90 percent of the victims were soldiers, but by the 1990s nearly 90 percent of the casualties resulting from armed conflict were civilians."[66] That said, the deaths after the war are not primarily the injuries of former combat but from other conditions. For example, the evidence indicates that "civil wars kill far more civilians even after the conflict is over than they kill combatants during the conflict."[67] Azem Adam Ghobarah, Paul Huth, and Bruce Russett discussed the loss of disability-adjusted life years (DALYs)—a concept developed by the World Health Organization (WHO)—after a civil war. They concluded that: "The direct and immediate casualties from civil wars are only the tip of the iceberg of their longer-term consequences for human misery. . . . Civil wars continue to kill people indirectly, well after the shooting stops."[68] More specifically, they examined data on the loss of DALYs from all conflict in 1999 and found that nearly as many DALYs were lost in that year "as a result of the lingering effects of civil wars during the years 1991–97."[69] The reasons identified by this and other studies fall into two categories. First, there are specific dangers of accidental death or serious injuries that may result in death and diseases that are prevalent in the countries wracked by conflict. Second, there is the common breakdown in public health and health care capabilities in the wake of conflict.[70] Infectious disease is cited by most studies as the most common cause of morbidity and mortality, including malaria, tuberculosis, other respiratory illnesses, and HIV/AIDS.[71]

Studies report that the long-term victims are women and children who face the health effects years after the formal end of hostilities.[72]

[T]he impact in 1999 of living in a country that had experienced an intense civil war a few years earlier (such as Bosnia, with 6.8 civil war deaths per 100 people) rather than in a median country with no war at all is a loss of about

28.5 healthy life-years in 1999 per 100 girls under five years of age—long after the war ended in a settlement. In Rwanda's extreme case (9.7 civil war deaths per 100 people, mostly in 1994), the subsequent losses amounted to a staggering 53 DALYs per 100 children under five—and that is in addition to the impact of all the other sociopolitical and economic variables in our model.[73]

It is still not clear just how the deliberate use of rape and both deliberate and unknowing spread of HIV/AIDS will affect women and children over time. Impacts ranging from suicide to severe depression to a host of diseases that thrive in persons with immune deficiency disorders will take some time to assess. One of the confounding factors is that the problem continues to grow as soldiers are demobilized, in some instances bringing HIV/AIDS and other health issues home with them. However, even the short-term impacts are obvious and tragic.

High infant and maternal mortality rates are clearly a continuing problem. The World Bank study found that the high rates of infant mortality during war (13 percent above the baseline) are matched by rates very nearly as high (11 percent over baseline) in the five years following the conflict.[74] In addition, there are continuing losses of children who grow up in post-conflict environments. Accidental death is a common tragedy as the children encounter unexploded ordnance, land mines, and exposure to toxic materials released into the environment by bombing or other military actions (see the discussion of toxic chemicals in the Iraq case study in chapter 2). Those toxic chemicals and other pollutants too often find their way into drinking water supplies. These conditions are particularly devastating to children, who are vulnerable not only to these immediate health risks, but also to longer-term conditions from toxins to which they may be exposed at critical and vulnerable developmental stages.

The frequent difficulties in post-conflict environments of ensuring safe water and adequate sanitation are significant factors in a wide range of diseases like cholera. Such pathogens thrive in overcrowded urban areas that often face intense pressures as those displaced by conflict come to cities in search of employment after the conflict ends. These health threats are frequently compounded by the inability, because of cost or availability, to access medical care and drugs to treat even relatively common diseases.

In addition to these obvious and immediate risks, there are the persistent impacts of contemporary social warfare, such as HIV/AIDS, noted above, and post-traumatic stress, discussed at length in the previous chapter. These difficulties are compounded by the fact that those attempting to survive and to build lives after conflict may engage in a range of risky behaviors as part of attempting to cope with life after conflict. Even activities such as farming that should be no more dangerous after conflict than before can be so because of the presence of unexploded ordnance and land mines that kill or injure thousands of adults and children, who are frequently called upon in rural communities to herd animals or to assist with farming.

Government, donor, or NGO efforts to rebuild hospital and clinic facilities, though certainly important and helpful, do not prevent these realities, and they are interwoven with environmental, economic, and other social development issues.

Food Insecurity: Conflict's Continuing Co-Morbidity

While the sheer rates of casualties may be surprising, a host of factors that give rise to them should by this point be relatively obvious. A weakened population, many of whom have been displaced from their homes and their sources of income lack the food, shelter, and protections needed to cope with health threats. Food insecurity is one of those factors that is often a serious problem not only during the conflict but after it as well.[75] The 1999 Rwanda *Human Development Report* determined that: "[A] 1996 MINISANTE/UNICEF survey (which did not include the 675,000 Rwandan refugees who returned from former Zaire later in the year) found that some 9 percent of Rwandan children suffered from acute undernutrition (wasting); nearly 42 percent suffered from stunting (height-for-age) which is an indicator of the longer-term affects (*sic*) of poor nutrition. Estimates for food availability for the country as a whole showed that, beginning in the early 1990s, Rwandans were receiving only 75 percent of their recommended consumption of 2,100 Kilocalories/day, with that figure dropping to some 60 percent of total needs in 1995."[76]

The UN Food and Agriculture Organization (FAO) has found that a recent history of conflict is one of the highest predictors of food insecurity in the countries that have experienced that problem. In its 2003 State of Food Insecurity Report, FAO found that: "Overall, conflict and economic problems were cited as the main cause of more than 35 percent of food emergencies during 1992–2003. . . . Eight countries suffered emergencies during 15 or more years during 1986–2003. War or civil strife was a major factor in all eight."[77] In its 2006 report, FAO was even more specific.

Efforts to reduce hunger in the [Sub-Saharan Africa] region have been hampered by natural and human-induced disasters, including conflicts occurring during the 1990s and the spread of HIV/AIDS. Indeed, the increase in the number of undernourished people . . . was driven mainly by five war-torn countries: Burundi, the Democratic Republic of the Congo, Eritrea, Liberia and Sierra Leone. These countries combined account for 29 million of the region's total increase of 37 million. Particularly dramatic is the worsening of food insecurity in the Democratic Republic of the Congo, where the number of undernourished people tripled, from 12 million to 36 million, and the prevalence rose from 31 to 72 percent of the population. The evident conclusion is that conflict is a major reason for lack of progress towards the WFS [World Food Security] target in sub-Saharan Africa.[78]

The food security crisis in post-conflict settings is caused by direct and indirect factors. In direct terms, the conflict and the destruction of the equipment, infrastructure, and the environment that it brings interfere with the ability to produce and distribute food. Farms can become battlegrounds and places where troops or insurgents simply take what they want. Other farms or pastures lay fallow as those who normally plant or tend herds of animals are driven off to become internally displaced persons or even refugees.

Second, the process of getting food to market requires infrastructure and favorable economic conditions to function effectively. Conflict destroys essential sources of water for irrigation or to support animal herds. Fuel for farm equipment or electricity for food processing and packing may be unavailable or unreliable. Farm labor may be unavailable, as young people are gathered for voluntary or compelled service by all sides. Wider concerns, like the lack of an effective rule of law system, undermine the ability to support both those who produce and sell food. As chapter 3 explained, one of these issues is the ability of those who were driven off their land during the fighting to reclaim their property so that they can once again put their farms back into production. If property titles are in doubt and there is not an effective rule of law system in place to address such issues as contract disputes, it can be difficult to operate food production businesses or to attract investment for farms and distribution businesses.[79]

Finally, the twin impacts of conflict and natural disaster can combine to create even more serious food shortages. Countries that have endured damage to the environment and the infrastructure designed to protect against natural disasters are more vulnerable to climatic or other disasters. "In Aceh, as in Sri Lanka, food security problems were exacerbated by long-standing conflict between the government and a separatist movement. After the tsunami, persistent insecurity complicated emergency relief and rehabilitation activities."[80]

Enduring Economic Challenges after Conflict: Casualties Both Obvious and Subtle

Vulnerabilities in the community are often exacerbated by economic factors which, like health issues, continue long after the formal hostilities end. In the economy, the period of demobilization is also often one of continuing bad news, what the World Bank refers to as "highly persistent" problems described as "a war overhang effect."[81]

The health access, quality, and cost issues, as well as nutritional and other social service programs noted above, are neglected as countries seek to address the expenses of the military and service the debts associated with waging conflict. The World Bank estimates that the average percentage of GDP spent for military expenditures in countries in civil war jumps from a prewar level of 2.8 percent to 5.0 during the conflict. Over a conflict that lasts for seven years, the estimate is that the increased military spending means a "permanent loss of around 2 percent of GDP."[82] The story does not really improve when the war ends. "However, once the war has ended, military expenditure does not return to its former level. During the first postconflict decade the average country spends 4.5 percent of GDP on the military. . . . Cumulatively over the first decade of peace some 17 percent of a year's GDP is lost in increased military spending."[83]

While demands for services and for debt service climb, revenues often fall off as the employment associated with the war declines. The World Bank estimates that the revenues lost during a five-year civil war amount to some 60 percent of GDP for a year.[84] Part of the difficulty in the post-conflict period is that many people may not return, including many of those who have the knowledge, education, skills, and capital to help development of the economy. In fact, a characteristic of conflicts like civil wars is the tendency to move assets out of the country. The Bank found that during civil wars, the percent of assets held outside the country of origin jumped from a prewar average of 9 percent to 20 percent.[85] When peace returns, the capital tends not to do so. In fact, the Bank found that: "By the end of the first decade of postconflict peace capital flight has risen further to 16.1 percent."[86] In addition, there is simply a loss of assets as the homes, possessions, and businesses are destroyed or stolen. Thus, as many as two-thirds of those responding in Uganda indicated that they had lost everything and that Mozambique had less than 20 percent of the cattle after its conflict than it had before.[87]

The decision to remove or not invest capital can come from far less dramatic confrontations than those seen in places like the Great Lakes region of Africa or the Balkans. Fiji, in its nearly bloodless 2003 coup, saw a dramatic impact on its budding clothing industry and other areas of investment. Since the coup was intended to oust the duly elected government headed by the first Indo-Fijian president under the country's new constitution by a man purporting to speak for ethnic Fijians, other countries reacted strongly. Fiji, which is reliant on tourism and agriculture as its primary sources of foreign currency, was trying to diversify its economic base. The coup hurt both the traditional tourism trade and the newly emerging light industrial developments. A more fundamental problem arose when the island states that shared in the operation of the University of the South Pacific, located in Suva, refused to send students back to the campus and claims were made that the university should be located in a more stable and less discriminatory environment. The university had not only attracted students from throughout the region but provided an important base of expertise for environmental and economic matters.

Ironically, the loss of revenue and assets, both human and capital, often arises just as inflation is fueled by the effects of spending on conflict or security. Difficulties with inflation and declining revenues coupled with debts incurred during a conflict exacerbate stresses. Inflationary pressures are also intensified in many places by the very common and often dramatic increase in corruption in the aftermath of conflict. Concern that conflict will return or that corruption will not be controlled is one of the reasons for a continuing tendency to export capital and an unwillingness by foreign firms to invest. Corruption does not affect just businesses. It is a hidden and highly regressive tax that falls heaviest on those least able to afford it.[88]

Besides corruption, the World Bank studies have concluded that the policies adopted in the aftermath of conflict may exacerbate the problems of investment and economic development. "All four policy areas are worse in postconflict societies: their macroeconomies are less stable, their structural policies such as trade and infrastructure are less conducive to growth, their social policies are less inclusive, and their public sectors are less well managed."[89] The underpinnings for once lucrative enterprises have been damaged or destroyed. Thus, in Africa, studies indicate that the killing of animals, including endangered species, for bush meat, the deforestation of lush jungle habitats, and the elimination of restrictions on once protected lands and ecosystems have resulted in dramatic losses from tourism and other environmentally related income.[90]

Environmental Shock, Post-Conflict Demands, and Long-Term Challenges

While it may seem counterintuitive, the environment, like society and the economy, may also continue to suffer significantly after the fighting stops. As Steven V. Price put it:

> [A] new maxim for conservation [was coined] by Jeffrey McNeely when he observe[d] that, "while war is bad for biodiversity, peace can even be worse." In the wake of war, the regulatory authority, norms, and customs that usually govern access to and use of natural resources may be left weakened or suspended. Armed groups often take advantage of 'peacetime' by facilitating illegal extractive enterprises or by directly engaging in the outright plunder of valuable natural resources. Refugees, internally displaced people, and local communities may be left more dependent on the local resource base—including protected areas and forest reserves—for food and basic supplies.[91]

Chapter 2 explored the problems and consequences of environmental warfare and those factors will not be repeated here. However, there are issues to be noted that specifically concern post-conflict conditions. These include diagnosis and treatment of environmental damage by those who live in those ecosystems, recognition of the long-term persistence of environmental impact, and the complexity of interactive effects.

As chapters 1 and 2 explained, one of the changes that has taken place in the past decade is the careful and deliberate attempt to assess the impacts of conflict on the environment. The United Nations Environmental Programme (UNEP) led the work in this area with its reports from the Balkans Task Force on Kosovo, which was a post-conflict assessment of impact.[92] The Balkans Task Force later took on additional studies in Serbia and Montenegro, Bosnia and Herzegovina, Macedonia, and Albania. That task force was then redesignated as the UNEP Post-Conflict Assessment Unit (PCAU), headquartered in Geneva, and converted in 2005 into what is now the Post-Conflict Branch (PcoB). The Branch operates on the basis of what it terms its six pillars: "(1) Conducting environmental assessments; (2) Building institutions for environmental governance; (3) Strengthening environmental law and policy; (4) Strengthening international and regional environmental cooperation; (5) Supporting environmental information management; and (6) Integrating environmental considerations in reconstruction."[93]

By the time of the U.S.-led invasion of Afghanistan in the wake of the 9/11 attacks, it was clear that UNEP would be on hand to undertake a post-conflict assessment. These efforts were central to the development that led the post-conflict unit to its current status.[94] By the time of the U.S. invasion of Iraq, UNEP and other organizations had already been investigating impacts of the earlier wars there to establish a baseline for postwar environmental assessments.[95]

The need for an effective assessment of the condition of affected ecosystems by people who are from the area as well as interested and well-qualified outsiders cannot be overstated. There was a problem in the early rounds of such studies of insufficient representatives who were local experts as compared to international experts. The UNEP Post-Conflict Branch now has field offices in several countries. The risks of not having people who are from the area under study are many, but even beyond whatever technical issues might be of importance, such as highly developed knowledge of local flora and fauna, there are other factors of significance. A vital consideration is an awareness of the environmental history of the area, including the history of previous impacts from conflicts. Beyond the technical issues, there is a critically important set of considerations regarding the relationship of culture to environment, a central fact of life for anyone seeking to get more than a momentary snapshot of specific technical measures in a defined

area. The interactive effects of environmental forces, as well as their connection to human behavior, are complex and may be missed by those operating with a geocentric, policentric, or ethnocentric perspective. If the assessment is to be connected to future decision making, a failure to ensure
integration of local culture into the assessment itself could effectively doom
the findings of the report to irrelevancy.

Second, it is critical to understand the dynamic and long-term environmental impact from conflict. It is one thing to consider the environmental
impacts that must be examined and addressed as a conflict ends and the society moves forward. However, there is ample evidence that the environmental consequences of violent conflict are persistent over decades, not just
a few years after the conflict.

Environmental assessments that are done soon after the end of formal
conflict are important, but only part of an ongoing and changing picture.
An inventory of damage and hot spots from chemical spills can provide a
foundation for triage, but the complex interactions of insults to the environment change over time. Recognition that effects are likely to continue
for decades is essential. It is not clear that such a long time horizon is being employed by all those who need to be including such considerations
into post-conflict development decisions.

The case of Vietnam is once again in active discussion, though for many
years the U.S. government rejected the claim that Agent Orange and other
chemicals constituted a continuing risk to health, safety, and the environment. Federal courts have rejected suits by Vietnamese veterans and their
families against manufacturers of the defoliants.[96] However, in 2006 the
Ford Foundation announced $2.2 million to support study of environmen-
tal dangers and related public health and disability issues, with a particular
attention to dioxin. The current grants include:

- Vietnam Public Health Association ($175,000) To design, test, and im-
  plement public health interventions for residents of Bien Hoa
- National Steering Committee 33, Government of Vietnam ($462,800)
  To help contain the spread of dioxin around Danang airport and to assess how to protect the health of people living in the surrounding communities
- Vietnam Veterans of America Foundation ($450,000) To conduct a sur-
  vey of health needs of people living with disabilities in eleven
  provinces and design medical interventions to meet these needs.[97]

The U.S. government is cooperating in plans for cleaning up sites, even as it
continues to insist that there should be no liability for health effects claims
from exposure to dioxin.

While Vietnam is often pictured as a prime example of the problem of
persistent environmental impact, one can find cases in the United States

that stem from as far back as the WWII era. Consider the case of the Triana Tennessee River Superfund cleanup. During World War II, allied troops suffered mightily from malaria and other insect borne diseases. The promise that dichlorodiphenyltrichloroethane (DDT) would be effective against those insects was greeted with great enthusiasm and it was used in large quantities during and in the years after the war. One of the major manufacturers of DDT was a firm known as Calabama Chemical Company, located in Alabama on the Army's Redstone Arsenal grounds, producing up to 2.25 million pounds of the product per month.[98] The Olin Corporation (then Olin Methieson Chemical Company) acquired Calabama in 1954.

Well before Olin took over, the plant manager discovered that DDT was seeping into drainage ditches on the grounds.[99] It later became clear that pollution from the plant was harming the environment. Bird population studies at the Wheeler Wildlife Refuge in the 1950s indicated a decline in some species. By the mid-1960s high concentrations of DDT were detected in river sediments. One study done for the Army Corps of Engineers suggested that as much as 837 tons of DDT were polluting local rivers and tributaries as a result of the Redstone plant's operation and disposal over the years. Fish fillets from area waterways contained as much as twenty times the acceptable Food and Drug Administration limit of five parts per million in tests conducted as the cleanup discussion unfolded. "In 1963, the Public Health Service also investigated the Huntsville situation. It released a series of reports documenting that the effluent from Olin's Huntsville plant contained toxic concentrations of DDT and that fish in the Huntsville Spring Branch, which was also polluted, were dying after exposure to the chemical."[100] In fact, the company undertook remedial measures in 1966.

Olin shut down the plant in 1970 and demolished it in 1972. The company took additional measures to try to limit the damage from the DDT on the grounds and in area waterways. The waters around the plant were a focal point for environmental concerns in this period because of the role of the Tennessee Valley Authority in administering the Tennessee River and Wheeler Reservoir. These waters were used for flood control, irrigation, food production, power generation, and recreation.

Rachel Carson's *Silent Spring*, which made the dangers of DDT to wildlife so apparent, was published in the mid-1960s. However, DDT was not banned by Environmental Protection Agency (EPA) administrator William Ruckelshaus until 1972[101] and his action was upheld in court.[102] While arguments continued over the specific level of human health risk attributable to DDT, the chemical was the very symbol of the efforts by environmentalists to protect wildlife. The EPA examined the situation at Redstone Arsenal in 1972, but no further action was taken until new reports of contamination arose in 1977.

In 1977 there were new reports of DDT in fish coming from the Huntsville Creek. The FDA found fish taken from local waters that exceeded the allowable five parts per million in markets in Chicago and Detroit. The channel catfish and bass that were commonly caught and sold by commercial fishermen were now inedible and unmarketable. At the time, there was an assumption that there might have been a spill of DDT but an investigation demonstrated that something else had occurred. The wastewater ditch at the plant was eroding and was allowing the escape of significant amounts of DDT.

On another front, the mayor of Triana called the Center for Disease Control (CDC) and asked for assistance in evaluating the situation in Triana. The reason for his concern was that the many low-income residents of the Triana area supplemented their diets with large amounts of fish from the creek, Wheeler Reservoir, and from the Tennessee River. These fish were highly contaminated and the residents were consuming significant quantities of the fish. "In late 1978, the Tennessee Valley Authority released a study documenting high levels of DDT contamination in fish downstream from the old Olin plant. The next year the Center for Disease Control ("CDC") reported that residents of Triana, Alabama, a town situated downstream from the Olin facility, had high concentrations of DDT in their blood serum."[103] The CDC issued another set of findings in early 1980 that found high levels of DDT in residents of Triana, Alabama.

The Corps of Engineers ultimately contracted for an engineering study by Water and Air Research, Inc. (WAR), to determine the extent of contamination at the Redstone site and set up an advisory committee to provide information for the WAR study. Public meetings were held involving other agencies, including the EPA, the Tennessee Valley Authority (TVA), the Redstone Arsenal, the Fish and Wildlife Service, and the State of Alabama. The so-called WAR report was presented late in 1980.

The EPA brought suit under the Rivers and Harbors Act in 1980 and in 1981, after passage of the Superfund statute. The Justice Department added a claim of violation of that law to the complaint against Olin. At about the same time, local residents, the city of Triana, and the State of Alabama brought their own suits for damages. Ultimately, the company settled with the first round of private plaintiffs for some $24 million and another $15 million for a second round of suits.[104]

The company joined a consent decree in May 1983.[105] However, the decree provided for a process to follow that would articulate the more precise nature of the cleanup requirements, including performance standards to measure levels of contaminants in local fish populations. Olin began work on the remediation in April 1986, completing the construction work in the fall of 1987. However, the consent decree set a performance standard based upon the level of DDT in the most common food fish in area waterways. While some species met the standard, others did not and the deadline was extended from 1997 to the end of 2002 for channel catfish and to the end of 2007 for smallmouth buffalo.[106]

The story of the cleanup of the Triana/Tennessee River Superfund site demonstrates why it is that the end of the fighting is but the beginning of a decades-long process of eliminating toxins and other insults to the ecosystem. In this case, the response was six decades long. Any approach to the movement toward development after conflict that fails to address this fact will be inadequate to the challenge.

Lingering Tensions after Conflict

Another major ongoing challenge as communities seek to move from conflict to peaceful development is the set of lingering tensions from the conflict that undermines the community's ability to achieve a level of trust and confidence necessary to reach and work with agreements made at the end of the conflict, as well as to make important future decisions. The nature and duration of the kinds of social warfare common in recent times have exacerbated this problem.

The United Nations Development Programme has issued a series of Kosovo Early Warning Reports, with public opinion poll findings on issues since the 1999 end of hostilities.

> In contrast to the improvement of the situation in some spheres of social and economic life in Kosovo, the relations between Albanians and Serbs in Kosovo, and to lesser extent, those between the Albanians and the Romas (Ashkalis and Egyptians) did not show marked improvement that would be encouraging for the development of better mutual relations in the near future. Ten years of tense inter-ethnic relations before the conflict, the period of conflict itself and the relations immediately after the conflict created a great division and high level of mistrust between Kosovo Albanians and Serbs and there is a perception among Kosovans that these two communities are in conflict with one another. Our opinion poll confirms this perception of the population and shows that nearly all the communities are of the opinion that the Albanians and the Serbs are "in conflict". . . . [A]nalysis of the data . . . shows that the perceptions of the conflict are rooted in the periods before and during the conflict and that the Albanians and the Serbs see the same things in totally different ways—what is acceptable to one side is almost totally unacceptable to the other. In circumstances of such high inter-ethnic tension, a major effort is needed to prevent conflict and foster a peaceful life between the communities.[107]

Indeed, in March of 2004, there was a three-day period of violence in which nineteen were killed and nine hundred injured.[108] In its 2004 Kosovo *Human Development Report*, UNDP warned: "Without a further broadening and deepening of channels for more meaningful dialogue and responsive governance, public frustration will continue to fester, derailing the development process in Kosovo."[109]

Certainly, one of the most complex situations involving lingering tensions comes from Rwanda for reasons discussed at the beginning of this chapter. In 1999, UNDP Rwanda indicated the core challenge. "By any measure, the single most important determinant affecting Rwanda's future is the tragic legacy of the social divisions which have plagued the country since ethnic distinctions were first exacerbated during the colonial era. Unlike virtually all other ethnic differences in Africa, Rwandan Tutsis and Hutus (and Twa) speak the same language, share the same religions, have lived side by side for centuries, and often inter-married; but thirty years of ethnocentric political rule and often extremist ideology precipitated what culminated in the incomprehensible events of 1994."[110]

Such challenges as those in Kosovo and Rwanda have prompted the use of two types of devices designed to take formal steps toward development of some level of trust. These include peace and reconciliation commissions and international tribunals for the trial of human rights violations or war crimes. As reports from Rwanda indicate, however, the models based on the Nuremberg model for war trials or the South Africa model for peace and reconciliation commissions may not be a good fit for every circumstance.[111] And where there are large numbers of potential defendants, as in Rwanda, the resources required to implement these programs can be substantial. Further, as time passes, it becomes more challenging both to ensure effective prosecutions and simultaneously to ensure due process of law to defendants. While these programs are intended to bring closure and healing, they may, if not conducted with great care, have perverse effects and produce either retraumatization for those who survived the violence or vicarious traumatization of those who knew of the violence indirectly. What is clear is that reconciliation is for many societies an ongoing effort over generations rather than an activity conducted within near-term deadlines.

THE CHALLENGES OF DEMOBILIZATION

Clearly, one of the greatest challenges after peace is declared comes with those activities that are formally understood as demobilization of troops and transition of the society from war to peacetime operations. Once again, there is a danger that some policy makers take a view that is not unlike the idealized version of the end of WWII, but the image is both mythical and dangerous. An effective demobilization requires an awareness of what comes next, attention to the processes and implications of demobilization of forces, contemplation of the complexity of the transition of the economy, and consideration of the importance of the environment.

Remember the Challenging Reality
of the Post-World War II Demobilization

Idealized pictures of demobilization at the end of WWII are inaccurate and do not provide a good guide for others. It is useful to recall the real situation at that time to avoid simplistic assumptions about what happens when the shooting stops. Too often today the end of World War II is depicted in repeated displays of the celebrations in the streets with overjoyed military men and women embracing civilians before the cameras. Chapter 1 spoke briefly about the terrible conditions in Europe at the time, but consider the situation in the United States.

When President Harry Truman took office in April 1945, following the death of President Franklin Delano Roosevelt, the nation was fully mobilized for the world war in which it was engaged. While cheering crowds greeted Truman after his announcement of the Japanese surrender on August 14, the situation was about to change dramatically and in a direction that made Truman recall with envy the wartime period as a time when millions were prepared to sacrifice in common pursuit of victory.[112] Only a few short weeks after the surrender, he would write: "Everybody wants something at the expense of everybody else and nobody thinks much of the other fellow."[113] With the war over, most Americans in their business and professional lives were anxious to be out from under the constraints that they had accepted as part of the price of victory. Most people expected that there would be good times and great opportunities ahead, but the reality was far more sobering than the expectation.

Certainly, there were positive aspects to the picture as demobilization began. The economy had been fueled by the war production effort and unemployment had been all but eliminated during the war years. There were constraints like rationing, price controls, and wage controls, but many Americans were doing well, particularly as compared to the years of the Great Depression that had preceded WWII. Apart from Pearl Harbor and the Aleutians, the United States had not faced the devastation of combat on home soil. In fact, the war had strengthened the infrastructure and many of the nation's governmental, social, and economic institutions. The environment had paid a heavy price in terms of impacts from wartime production needs, but not the kinds of devastation wrought by the direct and indirect effects of combat.

However, demobilization would pose ongoing challenges that came fast and lasted for years to come. First there was the challenge and consequences of shutting down war production. After World War I there had been significant economic impacts from the manner in which government called a halt to the purchases of war-related products. With that in mind, the Roosevelt administration started planning for demobilization as early as 1943 and a year later Congress adopted legislation to settle outstanding contract issues that would follow. The administration had processes in place by 1945 to move very rapidly on war contracts.

> The regulations' effectiveness was proven on V-J Day when, within five minutes of the announcement of Japan's surrender, previously prepared telegrams were dispatched directing the procurement districts to terminate war contracts. Within two days, 60,000 contracts, totaling $7.3 billion, had been cancelled. Similar actions, although not as large, had occurred three months earlier on V-E Day. In all, the government terminated $20 billion in contracts and minimized litigation. The orderly termination process helped avoid a general postwar depression.[114]

The cancellation of some $15 billion in contracts in just one month led to layoffs by Boeing and Ford alone of more than 70,000 employees.[115] Thousands of jobs were being lost just when some 12 million men and women returning from military service were in need of civilian employment. For those who had experienced the Great Depression, the rapidly cooling economy in the face of new pressures for growth and employment were frightening.

Returning service members started or expanded their young families so much that the period was labeled the "baby boom" generation. These families required housing and public services, a set of challenges magnified by the fact that there was an existing housing shortage just as the demand skyrocketed.[116]

It was also a time when business leaders who had endured constraints on the profitability of their firms wanted to increase prices to correct what they saw as distorted markets and keep pace with the competition for raw materials. They did not want what they saw as essential gains to be stymied by labor demands for increased wages. On the other hand, labor unions that had accepted limits on wages and job actions during the war were demanding improved wages. For one thing, there was fear that the present and likely growing inflation rates would rapidly erode existing wages. Labor, also, saw the market situation as distorted and wanted workers to enjoy the fruits of their efforts as management sought to enhance profits.

These competing demands would lead to major strikes, and they did, starting in the fall of 1945. Truman was not prepared to tolerate strike threats from labor leaders who, he complained, had promised to help him work through the difficult issues of demobilization to achieve a stable and prosperous postwar economy. When the railroad and coal strikes threatened to paralyze the nation and damage economic recovery efforts, Truman threatened to draft striking workers and the parties settled.[117] When United Mine Workers President John L. Lewis launched a coal strike even after he had previously agreed to favorable terms in what was known as the Krug-Lewis operating agreement, Truman moved forcefully.[118] The White House obtained contempt judgments against the union and Lewis that brought stiff fines of $10,000 against Lewis and $3.5 million against the union.[119]

Truman also went to the legislature with an ambitious set of policy proposals that included action to address the housing shortage, calls for increases in the minimum wage and unemployment benefits, and an extension of the War Powers and Stabilization Act.[120] And if the Congress was not willing to cooperate, he would use what emergency powers he had available to him. The Supreme Court supported actions based on emergency powers after war's end following WWI[121] and it did so again when Truman took action during WWII demobilization. He issued executive orders on establishment of the Wage Stabilization Board,[122] liquidation of wartime agencies,[123] and reestablishment of the Office of Economic Stabilization.[124] In 1947 in a price control case and again in 1948 in a housing policy case, the Court made it clear that: "The cessation of hostilities does not necessarily end the war power. . . . The war power includes the power 'to remedy the evils which have arisen from its rise and progress' and continues during that emergency."[125] The end of a war carried what the court considered a "winding up process." "There can be no question but that the President as a step in the winding-up process had power to transfer any or all of the price administration functions to the Attorney General."[126]

There were also sharp political reactions against the president's demobilization policy, among which was the dramatic Republican victory in the 1946 congressional elections. It was only through a force of will and personal effort that Truman managed a dramatic reelection victory in 1948. One of the issues in that election was Truman's decision to pursue civil rights policies after World War II.

It was clear that African Americans, Latinos, Asian Americans, and Native Americans had served with distinction in the war, albeit in a segregated military. When they returned home, however, they were met with discrimination and even outright violence. When Truman saw what happened to the returning soldiers, he knew things had to change. "But my very stomach turned over when I learned that Negro soldiers, just back from overseas, were being dumped out of army trucks in Mississippi and beaten. Whatever my inclinations as a native of Missouri might have been, as President I know this is bad. I shall fight to end evils like this."[127] Truman delivered his civil rights address to Congress in February 1948 and immediately received a firestorm of protest. Truman surprised the pundits and pollsters with a stunning victory in 1948.

Among his answers to the situation was to desegregate the military by executive order, an action resisted by military leaders as well as civilian politicians. Truman stuck with the effort, vowing to drag the military kicking and screaming, if necessary, into the twentieth century. It was an ongoing fight that continued not only through the post-WWII period, but through the Korean War.

Of course, the fact that war ends does not necessarily mean that all of the military forces or the entire defense sector of the economy will be demobilized. The Truman administration had to deal with a changed international relations picture and significant changes in the organization, deployment, and command structure of the military to accompany a redesign of the national security apparatus. These changes would, in their turn, evolve as well with the growing complexity of the nuclear age and the rise of the Cold War.

Thus, even the relatively clear situation confronting the United States when demobilization took place at the end of World War II was far more complex and long-lasting than the often simplistic picture of the times would indicate. Today, and in many countries that are facing post-conflict demobilization, the situation can be far less clear with far fewer resources to face the future.

It Matters What Comes Next

Clearly, the combination of demobilization of large portions of the force and redeployment of the remaining forces under the Truman administration was shaped by the circumstances on the ground at the time fighting ended. The situation in which the United States found itself, with the unconditional surrender of its adversaries and no specific threats on the immediate horizon is dramatically different from virtually all of today's post-conflict contexts.

Thus, the Korean conflict ended with an armistice rather than a treaty, a condition that created ongoing and long-lasting military obligations at the same time that it put in place important conditions that would have to be considered by those who pursued post-conflict development of that devastated country. Some conflicts come to points of cease-fire without a firm resolution, and suffer renewed fighting over time, as in the case of Sri Lanka and in several situations in the Middle East. Other conflicts have resulted in regime changes, as in the case of Vietnam and Iraq. Still other conflicts end in ways that are difficult to characterize, as in Lebanon and Palestine. In such complex circumstances there may be both conflicts between nations and rebel movements inside one or more of the countries at the same time. The Great Lakes states of Africa and Colombia discussed earlier have witnessed an array of conflict such that it becomes extremely difficult to paint a clear picture that can guide the demobilization when that opportunity arises.

Demobilization of Troops

There are some issues that are common to demobilization of forces and others that are contemporary and special problems. Common problems include the obvious difficulties that come with integrating soldiers into the economy and the community. In those countries in which the economy and the infrastructure that supports it have been destroyed in the fighting, the challenge of finding jobs is all the more difficult in the absence of significant external support. It was in part for that reason that the United States developed during 1947 what would come to be known as the Marshall Plan, named after General George C. Marshall. George F. Kennan's report entitled "Certain Aspects of the European Recovery Problem from the United States Standpoint" and Under Secretary of State William L. Clayton's report on his findings on a trip to Europe made it clear that Europe was nearing an economic meltdown that would be devastating not only for the conditions in Europe but for the United States economy as well.

Of course, returning veterans represent an important labor force and they can and do often bring energy and talent to post-conflict economic and social development. They may also bring special needs or challenges with them. Nations vary considerably on the degree to which they take responsibility for providing some degree of transitional support for demobilizing military personnel. Such programs can be very expensive, though they can also yield far more over time than they cost. The problem is finding the resources in the first instance at a time when the nation's fiscal situation is weak. There is also a varied response to veterans who sustained injuries that left them with various types of disabilities or with the need for ongoing medical care after demobilization. A contemporary issue that may come home from battle is the problem of HIV/AIDS, a challenge that is facing a variety of countries, particularly in some of the scenes of conflict in Africa. These are issues not limited to veterans but that affect spouses and children.

The major category of contemporary challenges that has been increasingly widespread is the tendency of many combatants to recruit or force into service what are simply known as child soldiers. It is virtually impossible to know the true number of children who fit under the definition of child soldiers, though international organizations such as the UN Children's Fund (UNICEF) and Human Rights Watch estimate that there are some 300,000. These children are in situations that run the gamut from combat soldiers, to children used to carry messages and do support chores for combat troops, to girls kept as workers and sexual servants to combat forces. Hence the UNICEF definition holds that:

> For the purposes of disarmament, demobilization and reintegration programmes, UNICEF defines a 'child soldier' as any child—boy or girl—under 18 years of age, who is part of any kind of regular or irregular armed force or armed group in any capacity, including, but not limited to: cooks, porters, messengers, and anyone accompanying such groups other than family members. It includes girls and boys recruited for forced sexual purposes and/or forced

marriage. The definition, therefore, does not only refer to a child who is carry-ing, or has carried, weapons. (Based on the 'Cape Town Principles', 1997)[128]

More recently, UNICEF has been careful to note that many reports and pro-grammes assume that child soldiers are boys, excluding the girls who "were part of government, militia, paramilitary and/or armed opposition forces in 55 countries between 1990 and 2003 and were actively involved in armed conflict in 38 of those countries."[129]

Since the children represent both the future of a society and also a vul-nerable and impressionable part of that society, the way they are treated during the post-conflict period is crucial. Consideration of child soldiers in the demobilization process is equally critical. International institutions and NGOs have identified the key problems and essential areas of action. These needs include family and community reintegration, education, legal pro-tections, economic resources for self-support and personal development, counseling and educational mechanisms to replace violence as a learned method of problem solving, the need to address the psychological injury of combat—particularly post-traumatic stress disorder—and their role in post-conflict war trials or peace and reconciliation tribunals.

For obvious reasons, the effort to assist demobilized child soldiers to reintegrate with their families, or surrogate families, and communities is a top priority. However, that task has often been extremely difficult. First, too often, the rest of the family of a child soldier could not be located at the end of a conflict or may have been killed. In some cases, the adults were killed and demobilized child soldiers found themselves returning not to the pro-tection and nurturing environment of the family but to take responsibility for their brothers and sisters. Thus, in Rwanda, there were large numbers of child-headed households after the genocide. Even if the family is located, there may be several barriers to reintegration that must be overcome. The social warfare tactics employed by some of those who took children into their forces sometimes required a child to commit an act of violence against family or community members so that it would be unlikely that the child would be welcomed home later. Reintegration programs in Liberia and other countries demonstrated the importance of counseling and assistance from facilitator organizations to work with the family and the community as well as the returning child soldier in order to address the resistance to his or her return home.

As in virtually any emergency situation, one of the other top items on the agenda is to get the children back into some kind of school program, how-ever informal, in order to provide something akin to a normal routine, as well as to take steps to assist the child to continue his or her cognitive and social development. For returning child soldiers, taken from the normal processes of growth and development into the extreme conditions of warfare so antithetical to healthy development, the return to school is that much more important. However, it is too often the case that those returning find that the schools in their communities have been destroyed. For example, in one month alone, 460 schools in Aceh, Indonesia, were deliberately destroyed by fire.[130] That situation can be even worse where, as has often happened, there is a combination of conflict and natural disaster. Certainly Aceh and Sri Lanka provide recent examples, as areas already torn by conflict were then hit by a deadly tsunami. One of the developments that has been used to respond to such circumstances is the creation of what UNICEF calls a "school in a box," consisting of basic materials that can be easily transported to remote areas or cities that may be employed either by trained teachers or, where necessary, volunteers, to provide a basic school experience and work.

Returning child soldiers must often support themselves or assist in supporting their families. If they cannot obtain the resources to do so, they will often not be able to return to school, but will have to take whatever work they can find where they can find it. Unfortunately, that might be work using the skills and knowledge they acquired while serving as child soldiers as part of a paramilitary organization or criminal gang, as has been seen in Colombia and the Democratic Republic of Congo. Assistance that will allow a returning child soldier to fit school into his or her package of responsibilities is a need that has been recognized by some aid organizations and governments such as Colombia, either in direct supports or through devices like microenterprise loans to allow both earning potential and flexibility.

The issue of programs to support the learning of alternative coping and problem-solving techniques as compared to the recourse to violent behavior goes hand in hand with counseling, support services, and if at all possible, substantive therapy to address the psychological impacts of combat, with PTSD as a central issue. The continuing nightmare of one sixteen-year-old African girl who was a demobilized soldier captures the challenge that is faced quite literally by tens of thousands of other children. Mary said, "I still dream about the boy from my village who I killed. I see him in my dreams, and he is talking to me, saying I killed him for nothing, and I am crying."[131] As chapter 4 explained, PTSD has varied symptoms and sequelae in children at different ages over the course of their childhood and young adulthood, and may manifest differently for boys and girls. For those who suffer from PTSD and have not learned nonviolent techniques that they find successful in problem solving, there may be serious psychosocial difficulties in the years to come. That is one reason why the process of what has come to be known as teaching peace (discussed below) has become such an important aspect of the demobilization of child soldiers.

There is one remaining element that is also related to these issues of traumatic stress and displacement, the phenomenon known as retraumatization.

As witnesses to war crimes and other violent breaches of the law, child soldiers are sometimes called as witnesses in peace and reconciliation commission proceedings. Indeed, even before such proceedings, it is not uncommon for children to be repeatedly asked to recall particular heinous events when members of their family or their community suffered torture or murder. On other occasions, these child soldiers may be treated as possible suspects, and made to defend themselves against charges. Alternatively, they may be asylum applicants who must repeatedly recount the story as part of the adjudication of their claim. Each time they place themselves back into the memory of the traumatic events, they are at risk for re-traumatization—in effect reliving the trauma. This can occur even in the context of well-meaning but uninformed requests in the hope that getting the child to talk about it will help the healing process. Unless this recounting happens in a setting with competent professional caregivers on hand, the results can be devastating.

Transitioning the Economy

While the combatants are being demobilized, the economy must be demobilized as well. And if the best-case scenario of the United States after World War II was problematic, most post-conflict situations in the world today are far more challenging. Unfortunately, the simplistic approach taken by the United States to Iraq under which the serious considerations of the Future of Iraq Project were cast aside in favor of the view that one could simply repair the infrastructure and then count on Iraq oil revenues to do the rest (see chapter 2) is all too common. Among the most common difficulties are the inflationary impact of the war with its harshest effects in the years after the conflict, the costs of demobilization of forces and the policies required to address their needs, the increase in unemployment related to demobilization, the debt that so frequently accumulates during conflicts to be paid for in the future, the costs of corruption common in post-conflict environments, and the dangers of policies in the years following conflict that may undermine economic development.

Reinvigorating Environmental Commitment

One of the characteristics of wartime economies is that they are heavily natural resource intensive. They often rely on extractive industries, industrial processes that have dramatic environmental impacts, ranging from high energy use to significant pollution challenges. Even renewable resources such as timber may not be carefully managed. In those countries that buy rather than produce military supplies, equipment, and armaments, the escalated exploitation of natural resources is often used to pay for the war related expenses and to meet debt service requirements. In the face of demands for economic growth and the array of other problems facing the nation's citizens and leaders, it can be difficult to ensure that environmental protection and conservation will be regarded as important issues on the public policy agenda.

As chapter 3 indicated, there are also complex issues of resettlement of refugees and questions of uncertain property rights. These immediate and intense demands can make it difficult to find the political will to address damage done to the environment during the conflict and protect natural resource agencies and public lands. That can be true even in countries where environmental damage and issues of pollution were well known at the end of the conflict, as in the case of Vietnam. As chapter 2 noted, economic pressures after the end of the conflict led to a tendency to use resources in unsustainable ways and issues of environmental cleanup and conservation were delayed, even though international and domestic organizations were certainly motivated to raise important questions.

FOUNDATION CONDITIONS FOR FUTURE DEVELOPMENT

There are three cross-cutting themes that arise in studies and reports on post-conflict mobilization that go to foundation conditions important for development in such a context in addition to the common challenges noted above. They include the threat to action from the problem of disappearing external assistance, the importance in many contexts of programs aimed at refocusing attention to peace rather than conflict, and a concern with human security.

The Devastating Effects of Disappearing Assistance

The reality is that most countries that must face demobilization and move toward sustainable development require outside assistance. Even countries that had strong economies, social structures, and governmental institutions before have found that they need help at the time of demobilization and after. That assistance most often comes from donor countries or NGOs, with some services and technical assistance from international institutions. Unfortunately, there are common characteristics of each that often mean the assistance falls far short of the help that is needed, even for a society that is making every effort that it is capable of mounting from within its own resources. Although one could sustain the argument that the most common problem is simply an insufficient quantity of assistance in dollar terms, that is not the focus of the criticism.

The difficulties with assistance from donor nations tend to fall into three categories. The first is that the focus is based upon the priorities of the donor rather than the needs of the country facing post-conflict demobilization and development. On the one hand, it would appear to be simply a matter of practical politics that donor nations will focus on their own interests in fashioning aid in post-conflict environments. However, if the focus on self-interest is narrowly defined, it may provide short-term domestic political support, but increase the odds that the country demobilizing from conflict will falter even with the best of effort and intentions by its leaders and citizens. Second, and related to the first point, is the dangerous tendency to provide a modest amount of aid for a brief time and then move on to the next foreign policy priority. Third, there are often restrictions on where and how funds can be spent.

Afghanistan offers an example of the first two problems. It should be remembered that while there was Western support for Afghan resistance fighters against the Soviet-backed government and the Soviet troops sent in to assist, the United States virtually abandoned Afghanistan as soon as the Soviet troops withdrew. Then, some years later, the United States attacked the Taliban regime because it was providing a safe haven for al Qaeda. After the invasion toppled the Taliban regime, the assistance from the United States and other Western countries was limited in amount, in scope, and in focus, certainly by comparison with the reasonable needs of a new government that was meeting the expectations of the donors in many important respects. Essentially and initially, the Western powers led by the United States took no responsibility for security outside the Kabul-Kandahar corridor and focused much of their direct effort on attempts near the Pakistan border to capture al Qaeda leadership.

While the Bonn conference in December 2001 laid out a plan of support for Afghanistan, it is interesting to examine the way that the United States understood its role. That understanding was set forth in the Afghanistan Freedom Support Act in 2002. The act begins with the broad and salutary statement that: "The United States and the international community should support efforts that advance the development of democratic civil authorities and institutions in Afghanistan and the establishment of a new broad-based, multi-ethnic, gender-sensitive, and fully representative government in Afghanistan." However, the Congress then goes on to make clear why the United States is providing assistance and what that assistance is intended to accomplish.

> By promoting peace and security in Afghanistan and preventing a return to conflict, the United States and the international community can help ensure that Afghanistan does not again become a source for international terrorism. . . . To foster stability and democratization and to effectively eliminate the

causes of terrorism, the United States and the international community should also support efforts that advance the development of democratic civil authorities and institutions in the broader Central Asia region.

Section 102 of the act goes on to explain the "purposes of assistance" and begins with the effort "to help assure the security of the United States and the world by reducing or eliminating the likelihood of violence against United States or allied forces in Afghanistan and to reduce the chance that Afghanistan will again be a source of international terrorism." The act makes clear the intention "to fight the production and flow of illicit narcotics, to control the flow of precursor chemicals used in the production of heroin, and to enhance and bolster the capacities of Afghan governmental authorities to control poppy cultivation and related activities." The legislation contains a host of other statements about humanitarian assistance, but the message is that the focus is on protecting U.S. security by preventing terrorism based in Afghanistan.

This type of approach fits well within the traditional conception of assistance to support the donor nation's strategic interests. It carries the international relations emphasis on supporting development to avoid what are termed unstable—even failed—states that present security challenges. However, assistance that is really needed is the sort that engages the expressed needs of the recipient state. That is not to suggest a naive approach, but one that recognizes that the failure to fully engage the needs of the nation in need will most likely lead to the kind of failure that donors say they wish to prevent.

The pattern has been for donor nations to provide inadequate levels of assistance for too short a period of time. The model here is Iraq, where, as chapter 2 explains, the United States quickly changed from a promise of support needed to ensure ongoing assistance to meet the nation's development needs after Saddam Hussein to one that spent much of the money on security and indicated that it never intended to do more than help Iraqis jump-start their new nation.

The third problem is that there has been a tendency to provide in-kind assistance or funds that must be spent for assistance from contractors in the donor country. Not only does this mode cost a great deal more than other alternatives, but it often contributes to the parachute phenomenon in which Western consultants come in for short visits as compared to hiring local experts with full credentials who will be on hand throughout the implementation process. In the case of Iraq, it also led to conflict with its European allies, who rejected U.S. claims that only U.S. contractors could do the job.

While NGOs help in many difficult situations, aid from these organizations comes with its own limitations that can surface during demobilization as the nongovernmental organizations move through what Thomas van der Heijden and others have referred to as the "relief to development continuum." The argument is that many NGOs tend to focus on relief and aid in the most intense portions of the conflict, but he points out that "NGOs are not well suited to make long term commitments. Hence, once the community transitions into the development process, NGOs tend to be less involved except on a project by project basis."[132] He also argues that once local NGOs become active in a given arena, the outside NGOs tend to move on to other matters.

Learning Peace: Less a Matter of Idealism than a Political and Social Necessity

One of the areas in which NGOs, international institutions, and some donor governments have agreed, is the need to emphasize what is known as the process of learning peace. That concept refers to the process of teaching the young and the not-so-young about how to move from the use of violent conflict to resolve problems to peaceful alternatives. While that sounds like a relatively simple observation, the reality is far more difficult to achieve, particularly in contexts in which there has been religious or ethnic violence over a long period or where a country has been more or less continuously in a state of conflict such that many of its citizens and most of its young people are no longer accustomed to peaceful resolution of serious differences and may have learned to take the law into their own hands.[133]

This challenge also arises in contexts where there may have been an imposed peace, but where there was an authoritarian regime or where there has not been an effective rule of law regime. In such settings, once the constraints or controls have been lifted, there can be a vacuum in methods of conflict resolution. In some settings, long-standing cultural norms may resurface and provide effective mechanisms, but in other instances countries with a recent history of conflict may not necessarily have any readily available and accepted alternative responses. Obviously, the most effective modes of peace education are likely to be those with the best fit to the local culture, but there may or may not be a sufficient foundation of trust for those techniques to be effectively implemented in the short term.

Human Security: Far More than Simply Security

Related to this last problem is the essential requirement for development of a fundamental requisite of human security. As described earlier, human security is more than just military security or a criminal justice sense of security. The UNDP Afghanistan *Human Development Report* for 2004 explains the concept well and is worthy of quoting at some length.

[F]or countries emerging from conflict, such as Afghanistan, sustainable peace requires a guarantee that gains made today will not be taken away tomorrow. This idea is embodied in the concept of "human security." On the one hand, it entails the notion of "safety," which goes beyond security in the traditional sense, and on the other hand, it includes the guarantees and assurances that underpin the concept of "social security." Human security, therefore, becomes both the prerequisite for human development as well as a guarantee of its sustainability. While human development is a process of widening the range of people's choices, human security means that people can exercise these safely and freely while being relatively confident that the opportunities they have today are not lost tomorrow.

In the same way that traditional economic development paradigms had failed to address the broader concerns of people, traditional "security" discourses are no longer adaptable enough to address the new threats to the safety and well-being of people within states. With a combination of new global trends, the rise of non-state actors, and new types of non-military threats to the internal stability of states and people within them, the traditional concept of "security" as a realist pact between nations became obsolete at the beginning of the 21st Century. If, in the past, existential threats were assumed to emanate from external sources, and security mainly focused on protecting the state and its sovereign territory from external attacks, new non-military threats such as poverty, infectious diseases, environmental disasters, massive population movements and drugs—all of which travel without a passport—have now become part of the "security" agenda.[134]

Simplistic conceptions of nation-state power do not provide human security, and it is human security that is essential in order to move beyond demobilization to development. When it is working at optimum levels, "[h]uman security is referred to as freedom from fear and freedom from want. Seven threats are identified: economic security, food security, health security, environmental security, personal security, community security and political security. As elaborated by the Commission on Human Security, 'the objective of human security is to safeguard the vital core of all human lives from critical (severe) and pervasive (widespread) threats, in a way that is consistent with long-term human fulfillment.'"[135]

Unfortunately, the UNDP report on Afghanistan found that, for too long, the only concerns with Afghanistan were focused on the old nation-state conception of security and stability and failed utterly to address human security. The report concluded that difficulties could lie ahead if the concept of human security is not addressed in its fullness. "The report argues that while many gains have been made in the past two years, the country could still fall into a cycle of conflict and instability unless the genuine grievances of people—the lack of jobs, health, education, income, dignity, opportunities for participation, etc.—are dealt with adequately."[136]

But the problem of inadequate concern with human security is not limited to war-torn developing countries. One of the problems with some of the most dramatic examples of civil disorder in the United States is the failure to take them with sufficient seriousness as something more than a just a breakdown of law enforcement. The Los Angeles riots in 1992 came in the wake of the acquittal of police officers charged in the beating of Rodney King. Before the rioting was over, there were forty-two deaths and over a billion dollars in property damage. Although many political figures came to Los Angeles afterward to declare their commitment to understand the situation and take steps to deal with it, the reality is that little was done that really focused on Los Angeles or other cities. Instead, there was only one major study done of the events in the immediate aftermath, and that one was carried out by the police department which, not surprisingly, sought to understand what happened in terms of the police response to lawlessness.[137] Of course, there was far more happening there than that approach would indicate.

Indeed, part of the difficulty was a failure to address the problem as one of human security and not merely security narrowly defined in law enforcement terms. While the police department and a later city report indicated that there were other factors involved that precipitated the violence, including "unemployment, crime, a high rate of school dropouts, ethnic or cultural tension, and other conditions, and that the barriers to using city services included a lack of awareness of services, fear, mistrust, language differences, and access," the response was limited and focused on so-called self-sufficiency programs.[138] The city requested an exemption to use a portion of its Community Development Block Grant Funds from the federal government for projects in the area, but over time they used those funds for a variety of purposes that did not involve the areas of the city affected by the riots and the issues of human security that fueled those events. The problems are still very much in evidence and have in some respects become worse over time.

Thus, sustainable development after conflict or civil disorder calls for a human security approach of the sort advanced by the United Nations agencies and not the outdated, narrower, and more commonly used idea of mere military- or law enforcement–based security.

CONCLUSION

The period of demobilization is not a simple ending to bad times. It is a complex period in which many of the problems of the conflict for years carry over in what has been termed an "overhang effect." Unfortunately, like the other aspects of post-conflict action, this period is too often approached with an out-of-date and inappropriate reconstruction and redevelopment model. That model is often based on an oversimplified memory of post-WWII events that were far from simple and not altogether positive.

A more effective approach requires attention to the destructive dynamics of conflict that do not end with a cease-fire. These factors include social, economic, and environmental impacts that are the ongoing legacy of conflict. The fact that all three of these elements are in play is another reason why the reconstruction model as it has been employed is completely inadequate to the challenge.

The movement from conflict to a brighter future is not a simple or instant matter, but a complex process of demobilization that has been difficult even in the best of circumstances; and many modern conflicts do not leave anything like the best of circumstances. The nature of contemporary social, economic, and environmental warfare has complicated and intensified the challenges presented in this period after the formal fighting has ended.

NOTES

1. World Bank, *Breaking the Conflict Trap: Civil War and Development Policy* (Washington, D.C.: World Bank and Oxford University Press, 2003), 13.

2. Roméo Dallaire, with Brent Beardsley, *Shake Hands with the Devil: The Failure of Humanity in Rwanda* (Toronto: Random House Canada, 2003).

3. See Barbara Harff, "No Lessons Learned from the Holocaust? Assessing Risks of Genocide and Political Mass Murder since 1955,"*American Political Science Review* 97, no. 1 (2003): 57–73; René Degni-Ségui, Special Rapporteur of the Commission on Human Rights, *Report on the Situation of Human Rights in Rwanda, Submitted under Paragraph 20 of Resolution S-3/1 of 25 May 1994*, E/CN.4/1997/61, January 20, 1997 (New York: United Nations, 1997), 18.

4. *National Geographic, National Geographic Family Reference Atlas of the World* (Washington, D.C.: National Geographic, 2002), 89, 179.

5. Valerie Percival and Thomas Homer-Dixon, "Environmental Scarcity and Violent Conflict: The Case of Rwanda," Occasional Paper, Project on Environment, Population and Security, Washington, D.C.: American Association for the Advancement of Science and the University of Toronto, June 1995.

6. Percival and Homer-Dixon, "Environmental Scarcity and Violent Conflict," part I.

7. Dallaire, *Shake Hands with the Devil*.

8. Percival and Homer-Dixon, "Environmental Scarcity and Violent Conflict," part I.

9. See Jan Vansina, "Historical Tales (Ibiteekerezo) and the History of Rwanda," *History in Africa* 27 (2000): 375–414.

10. Facing History and Ourselves, "NPR Features Rwandan Education Project," at www.facing.org/campus/reslib.usf/all/E6462A2DC4309DCB852571D20061973E? Opendocument (accessed December 17, 2006).

11. Institute for Security Studies, "Rwanda," at www.iss.co.za/AF/profiles/ Rwanda/Politics.html (accessed July 9, 2005).

12. See Cyprian F. Fisiy, "Of Journeys and Border Crossings: Return of Refugees, Identity, and Reconstruction in Rwanda," *African Studies Review* 41, no. 1 (1998): 17–28; Adrien Katherine Wing and Mark Richard Johnson, "The Promise of a Post-genocide Constitution: Healing Rwandan Spirit Injuries," *Michigan Journal of Race & Law* 7 (Spring 200): 247– 315.

13. See Nigel Eltringham, "'Invaders Who Have Stolen the Country': The Hamitic Hypothesis, Race and the Rwandan Genocide," *Social Identities* 12, no. 4 (2006): 425–446.

14. Alison Des Forges, *Leave None to Tell the Story: Genocide in Rwanda* (New York: Human Rights Watch, 1999), at www.hrw.org/reports/1999/rwanda (accessed December 27, 2006).

15. Des Forges, *Leave None to Tell the Story*, "History."

16. Des Forges, *Leave None to Tell the Story*, "History."

17. Mahmood Mamdani, *When Victims Become Killers: Colonialism, Nativism, and the Genocide in Rwanda* (Princeton: Princeton University Press, 2001), 99.

18. Institute for Security Studies, "Rwanda."

19. Percival and Homer-Dixon, "Environmental Scarcity and Violent Conflict," 9.

20. Dallaire, *Shake Hands with the Devil*, 245.

21. Dallaire, *Shake Hands with the Devil*, 71.

22. United Nations Development Programme (UNDP), *Ten Years On: Helping Rebuild a Nation, The United Nations in Rwanda* (Kigali: UNDP, 2004), 11.

23. For a sense of the degree of trauma, see Dallaire, *Shake Hands with the Devil*.

24. "[B]ased on interviews of 3,030 children." UNICEF, *National Trauma Survey, 1995*, quoted in United Nations Development Programme, *Rwanda 1999 Human Development Report* (Kigali: UNDP, 1999), 18.

25. See also Yael Danieli, ed., *International Handbook of Multigenerational Legacies of Trauma* (New York: Plenum, 1998).

26. United Nations Development Programme (UNDP), *Human Development Report 2003* (New York: UNDP, 2003), 261.

27. UNDP, *Ten Years On*, 41.

28. United Nations Development Programme (UNDP), *Human Development Report 2005* (New York: UNDP, 2005), 234.

29. UNDP, *Human Development Report 2003*, 220.

30. UNDP, *Ten Years On*, 6.

31. UNDP, *Human Development Report 2005*, 169.

32. UNDP, *Human Development Report 2005*, 161.

33. UN Security Council, Global Policy Forum, "Rwanda," at www.globalpolicy .org/security/issues/rwanindx.htm (accessed July 9, 2005).

34. World Bank, "Memorandum of the President of the International Development Association to the Executive Directors on a Country Assistance Strategy for the Republic of Rwanda," Report No. 24501-RW, Country Department 9, African Region, November 21, 2002.

35. Institute for Security Studies, "Rwanda," Pretoria, South Africa, at www.iss .co.za/AF/profiles/Rwanda/Politics.html (accessed July 9, 2005).

36. Jeevan Vasagar, "Hutu Rebels Apologize for Rwanda Genocide," *Guardian*, April 1, 2005, at www.globalpolicy.org/security/issues/rwanda/2005/0401fdlrquiindx.htm (accessed August 27, 2005).

37. Institute for Security Studies, "Rwanda."

38. Institute for Security Studies, "Rwanda."

39. Institute for Security Studies, "Rwanda."

40. UNDP, *Human Development Report 2005*, 156.

41. Vasagar, "Hutu Rebels Apologize for Rwanda Genocide."

42. U.S. Department of State, Bureau of Democracy, Human Rights, and Labor, "Congo, Democratic Republic of the Country Reports on Human Rights Practices—2005," March 8, 2006, at www.state.gov/g/drl/rls/hrrpt/2005/61563.htm (accessed December 20, 2006).

43. U.S. Department of State, "Congo."

44. UNDP, *Ten Years On*, 11.

45. UNDP, *Ten Years On*, 11.

46. UNDP, *Ten Years On*, 45.

47. UNDP, *Ten Years On*, 41.

48. UNDP, *Ten Years On*, 32.

49. UNDP, *Ten Years On*, 37.

50. United Nations Development Programme (UNDP), UNDP Country Cooperation, 2004–2008, *Project Profiles: The Government of Rwanda* (Kigali: UNDP, 2004).

51. UNDP, *Project Profiles: The Government of Rwanda*, 5.

52. UNDP, *Human Development Report 2005*, 44.

53. UNDP, *Human Development Report 2005*, 318.

54. UNDP, *Ten Years On*, 37.

55. Government of Rwanda, Ministry of Finance and Economic Planning, National Poverty Reduction Programme, "Poverty Reduction Strategy Paper" (Kigali, June 2002), 8.

56. UNDP, *Ten Years On*, 33.

57. UNDP, *Project Profiles: The Government of Rwanda*.

58. United Nations Development Programme (UNDP), *Rwanda 1999 Human Development Report* (Kigali: UNDP, 1999), iv.

59. Government of Rwanda, "Poverty Reduction Strategy Paper," 8.

60. United Nations Development Program, *Human Development Report 2003* (New York: UNDP, 2003), 229.

61. Government of Rwanda, "Poverty Reduction Strategy Paper," 9.

62. UNDP, *Human Development Report 2005*, 170.

63. UNDP, *Ten Years On*, 47.

64. Government of Rwanda, "Poverty Reduction Strategy Paper," 15.

65. Rob Walker, "Rwandans Still Divided 10 Years On," BBC News, July 4, 2004, at http://news.bbc.co.uk/go/pr/fr/-/1/hi/world/africa/3557565.stm (accessed September 28, 2005).

66. Paul Collier, V.L. Elliott, Håvard Hegre, Anke Hoeffler, Marta Reynal-Querol, and Nicholas Sambanis, *Breaking the Conflict Trap: Civil War and Development Policy* (Washington, D.C.: World Bank, 2003), 13.

67. Collier et al., *Breaking the Conflict Trap*, 25.

68. Azem Adam Ghobarah, Paul Huth, and Bruce Russett, "Civil Wars Kill and Maim People—Long After the Shooting Stops," *American Political Science Review* 97 (May 2003): 189.

69. Ghobarah et al., "Civil Wars Kill and Maim People," 189.

70. Collier et al., *Breaking the Conflict Trap*, 26.

71. Ghobarah et al., "Civil Wars Kill and Maim People," 197–200.

72. Ghobarah et al., "Civil Wars Kill and Maim People," 199.

73. Ghobarah et al., "Civil Wars Kill and Maim People," 197.

74. Collier et al., *Breaking the Conflict Trap*, 23–24.

75. During conflict the food shortages can flow from a variety of factors, from destruction of farms, to displacement of farmers, to destruction of distribution systems, to diversion from civilians of foodstuffs to the military or militias, to the deliberate use of food shortages and displacement as part of social warfare, as in the case of Darfur. "Conflict contributed to food insecurity in the Darfur region of Sudan, Somalia, the Democratic Republic of the Congo and Liberia. In Darfur alone, as many as 2.1 million conflict-affected people were dependent on food aid in June 2005 (USAID 2005), while in Somalia one million people—affected by several years of drought, floods, and recurrent civil unrest—continued to require humanitarian assistance." UNEP, *Global Environment Outlook Update 2006* (Nairobi: UNEP, 2006), 12.

76. UNDP, *Rwanda 1999 Human Development Report*, 26.

77. United Nations Food and Agriculture Organization (UNFAO), *The State of Food Insecurity in the World 2003* (Rome: FAO, 2003), 14.

78. United Nations Food and Agriculture Organization (UNFAO), *State of Food Insecurity in the World 2006* (Rome: FAO, 2006), 23.

79. United Nations Food and Agriculture Organization (UNFAO), *The State of Food Insecurity in the World 2005* (Rome: FAO, 2005), 11.

80. UNFAO, *State of Food Insecurity in the World 2005*, 13.

81. Collier et al., *Breaking the Conflict Trap*, 20–21.

82. Collier et al., *Breaking the Conflict Trap*, 14.

83. Collier et al., *Breaking the Conflict Trap*, 20–21.

84. Collier et al., *Breaking the Conflict Trap*, 21.

85. Collier et al., *Breaking the Conflict Trap*, 15.

86. Collier et al., *Breaking the Conflict Trap*, 21.

87. Collier et al., *Breaking the Conflict Trap*, 15.

88. World Bank, *World Development Report 1997: The State in a Changing World* (Washington, D.C.: World Bank, 1997), 102–103.

89. Collier et al., *Breaking the Conflict Trap*, 22.

90. See, e.g., Andrew J. Plumptre, "Lessons Learned from On-the-Ground Conservation in Rwanda and the Democratic Republic of the Congo," in Steven V. Price, ed., *War and Tropical Forests: Conservation in Areas of Armed Conflict* (New York: Food Products Press, 2003), 79.

91. Price, *War and Tropical Forests*, xv.

92. United Nations Environmental Programme and United Nations Center for Human Settlements (Habitat), *The Kosovo Conflict: Consequences for the Environment & Human Settlements* (Nairobi: UNEP and Habitat, 1999).

93. UNEP Post-conflict Branch, "About," at http://postconflict.unep.ch/about .php (accessed November 25, 2006).

94. The report that was issued after UNEP visits on the ground in 2002 was United Nations Environmental Programme, *Afghanistan: Post-conflict Environmental Assessment* (Nairobi: UNEP, 2003).

95. United Nations Environment Programme, *Desk Study on the Environment in Iraq* (Nairobi, UNEP, 2003); MedAct, *Collateral Damage: The Health and Environmental Costs of War on Iraq* (London: MedAct, 2002).

96. *In re Agent Orange Product Liability Litigation*, 2005 U.S. Dist. LEXIS 3644 (SDNY 2005).

97. Ford Foundation, "Ford Foundation Announces Important Series of Grants on Environmental Research and Public Health in Vietnam," at www.fordfound.org/newsroom/view_news_detail.cfm?news_index=180 (accessed November 26, 2006).

98. Water and Air Research, Inc., *Final Contract Report, Engineering and Environmental Study of DDT Contamination of Huntsville Spring Branch, Indian Creek, and Adjacent Lands and Waters, Wheeler Reservoir, Alabama, November 1980* (Water and Air Research Inc., 1980), 6. (Hereafter the WAR Report.)

99. *Olin Corporation v. Insurance Company of North Carolina*, 966 F.2d 718, 720 (2nd Cir. 1992).

100. *Olin Corporation v. Insurance Company of North Carolina*, 966 F.2d 718, 720 (2nd Cir. 1992).

101. 37 *Fed. Reg.* 13369 (1972).

102. *Environmental Defense Fund v. EPA*, 489 F.2d 1247 (D.C.Cir. 1973).

103. *Olin Corporation v. Insurance Company of North Carolina*, 966 F.2d 718, 720 (2nd Cir. 1992).

104. *Olin Corporation v. Insurance Company of North Carolina*, 966 F.2d 718, 721 (2nd Cir. 1992).

105. *United States v. Olin Corporation*, Civil Action No. CV80-PT-5300-NE, Consent Decree, May 31, 1983. The consent decree was upheld against a later challenge, *United States v. Olin Corporation*, 606 F. Supp. 1301 (NDAL 1985).

106. U.S. Environmental Protection Agency, "Alabama NPL/NPL Caliber Cleanup Site Summaries—Triana/Tennessee River," at www.epa.gov/Region4/waste/npl/nplal/trianaal.htm (accessed November 26, 2006).

107. UNDP, *Kosovo Early Warning Report #1, May–August 2002* (Pristina: UNDP, 2002), 16

108. UNDP, *Human Development Report—Kosovo 2004* (Pristina: UNDP, 2004), 43.

109. UNDP, *Human Development Report—Kosovo 2004*, 43.

110. UNDP, *Rwanda 1999 Human Development Report*, 17.

111. See Truth and Reconciliation Commission, *Truth and Reconciliation Commission of South Africa Report*, vol. 6 (Cape Town: Government of South Africa, 2003), at www.info.gov.za/otherdocs/2003/trc/rep.pdf (accessed November 26, 2006).

112. David McCullough, *Truman* (New York: Simon & Schuster, 1992), 467–474.

113. McCulloch, *Truman*, 467.

114. John F. Nagle, *A History of Government Contracting*, 2nd ed. (Washington, D.C.: George Washington University School of Law, Government Contracts Program, 1999), 442.

115. McCullough, *Truman*, 469.

116. *Woods v. Cloyd W. Miller Co*, 333 U.S. 138 (1948).

117. McCullough, *Truman*, 502–504.

118. McCullough, *Truman*, 528.

119. *United States v. United Mineworkers*, 330 U.S. 258, 304 (1947).

120. McCullough, *Truman*, 468.

121. *United States Grain Corporation v. Phillips*, 261 U.S. 106 (1923).

122. See E.O. 9672 December 31, 1945.

123. E.O. 9674 January 4, 1946.

124. E.O. 9699 February 21, 1946.

125. *Fleming v. Mohawk Wrecking & Lumber*, 441 U.S. 111, 116 (1947). See also *Woods v. Cloyd W. Miller*, 333 U.S. 138 (1948).

126. *United States v. Allied Oil Corp.*, 341 U.S. 1, 5 (1951).

127. McCullough, *Truman*, 588.

128. UNICEF, "Child Soldiers Fact Sheet," 4, at www.unicef.org/protection/childsoldiers.pdf (accessed December 20, 2006).

129. UNICEF, *Childhood under Threat: State of the World's Children 2005* (New York: UNICEF, 2004), 42.

130. UNICEF, *Childhood under Threat: State of the World's Children 2005*, 41.

131. U.S. Department of State, Office to Monitor and Combat Trafficking in Persons, "The Facts about Child Soldiers," August 8, 2005, at www.state.gov/g/tip/rls/fs/2005/50941.htm (accessed December 3, 2006).

132. "Health Care between War and Peace: An Exploration of Issues and Strategies," HealthNet International, Discussion Paper 1, June 15, 1997.

133. Vachel W. Miller and Friedrich W. Affolter, *Helping Children Outgrow War* (Washington, D.C.: USAID, 2002).

134. UNDP, *Afghanistan National Human Development Report 2004: Security with a Human Face* (Kabul: UNDP Afghanistan, 2004), 4–5.

135. UNDP, *Afghanistan National Human Development Report 2004*, 6.

136. UNDP, *Afghanistan National Human Development Report 2004*, vi.

137. Special Advisor to the Board of Police Commissioners, *The City in Crisis: A Report by the Special Advisor to the Board of Police Commissioners on the Civil Disorder in Los Angeles*, October 21, 1992 (Los Angeles: LADP, 1992).

138. U.S. Government Accountability Office, *Community Investment: Los Angeles's Use of a Community Development Block Grant Exemption* (Washington, D.C.: GAO, 2002), 11.

6

A Final Word

In a world with so many people in conflict or post-conflict environments, it is essential to think seriously about sustainable development in the wake of war, terrorism, and civil disorder. And given the nature of social, environmental, and economic warfare, whether conducted among nations, within nations, or by terrorists, it is inappropriate and ultimately futile to continue, as so many policy makers have, to employ a reconstruction, redevelopment, or nation-building approach to the contemporary environment. Yet those are the ideas in use.

In order to move forward after conflict in a meaningful way, it is necessary to have more than just the incantation of the term *sustainable development*. It requires, first, an understanding of the nature of contemporary social, economic, and environmental warfare, in which it is far too simplistic to assume that there are strategic or tactical targets and then the regrettable but inevitable problems of collateral damage. As chapter 2 explained, each of these dimensions of contemporary conflict is better represented by a continuum rather than a dichotomy. Second, an understanding of the interconnected nature of the impact and consequences of conflict is essential to a realistic sense of the post-conflict situation and therefore to the range of effective choices moving forward. As the 9/11 case study in chapter 2 demonstrated, the scope of economic, environmental, and social impacts and effects from the attacks on the World Trade Center, the Pentagon, and the failed effort to hit the Capitol have been far greater than has been recognized by policy makers.

Contrary to the criticisms that have sometimes been leveled at advocates of sustainable development, it is not necessary to ignore political, economic, social, or even military realities, or to engage in airy, impractical exercise. It is essential to study war to understand what it means for action when the shooting stops. It is necessary to understand the carefully developed principles of sustainable development if the effects of that fighting are truly to be addressed and preventive measures for the future are to be effective. The idea that one can fix a nation by attending to its infrastructure and the assurance that some kind of political stability will prevent what are sadly termed "failed states" is an exercise in futility and, all too often, arrogance.

Sustainable development principles can be used to consider projects, programs, and larger plans by the application of the relatively simple set of questions provided in chapter 1 and explained in much greater detail in the *Implementing Sustainable Development* book. The point is not that any proposed course of action will satisfy all principles or that it will always be possible to answer all of the questions, but the mere fact of posing that systematic set of questions ensures at least that the principles worked out over the course of more than a decade and agreed to by so many nations have been considered. Since it can be the case that there will be tensions among some of the principles as applied in certain contexts, trade-offs must be considered. It is, however, far better that they be considered forthrightly than that no clear comprehensive approach be employed at all, or that the ones that are used represent little more than the wares of consulting organizations that seek to sell their own formula rather than to apply the sustainable development framework so laboriously and effectively developed by the international community.

Of course, plans, projects, and programs are meaningless unless they are implemented, which was the central subject of the *Implementing Sustainable Development* volume, and that discussion has not been repeated here.

Chapters 3 and 4 of this volume have addressed subject matter that is central to sustainable development after conflict but that is generally not found in either the post-conflict or the sustainable development literature. It is not the case that the community—social, economic, or environmental—that existed before the conflict will be in place and intact afterwards. Conflict sends people into flight, either as refugees to other lands or, as increasingly is the case, as internally displaced persons within their country. The impacts of flight exist for the country and its environment as well as for its people. Those effects are manifest both during the conflict and afterward. While many of those factors are apparent during the fight, others, like post-traumatic stress disorder, are far less obvious in many cases and may persist long after the battles have ended.

Finally, even when the guns do fall silent, the dynamics of conflict linger for years. Any post-conflict approach that assumes a quick fix and rapid departure by aid agencies and international donors is very likely to ensure serious difficulties in the years to come. Demobilization is at once a happy time, and yet it is a process that carries with it special sets of challenges that must be understood if peace and development are to be sustainable. Casualties continue, though they are often not seen as such. The economy continues to suffer the consequences of the violence. The environment can continue to show the repercussions for decades, even in countries not directly ravaged by the fighting, as the discussion of the Alabama DDT pollution demonstrated, let alone in a place like Vietnam or the Great Lakes region of Africa.

It should be clear as well from the preceding chapters that each of these aspects of conflict and what follows afterward engages all three pillars of the living triangle. Therefore, any sustainable future must also engage the social, the economic, and the environmental dimensions if it is to succeed not only in the short term but over time. The effects of conflict, after all, like other aspects of sustainable development, are intergenerational.

There are no cookbook answers or shortcuts to sustainable development after conflict, but there most assuredly are more effective and less effective ways of understanding the challenges and evaluating the strategies and tactics. To this point, and in many circumstances, we have not done well in taking the kind of integrative and comprehensive approach offered by sustainable development, and the consequences are readily apparent to anyone who takes the time to study the results.

Selected Bibliography

Abdultaheem, Mahmood Y. "War-Related Damage to the Marine Environment in the ROPME Sea Area." In Austin and Bruch, eds., *The Environmental Consequences of War: Legal, Economic, and Scientific Perspectives.*

Adams, David Wallace. *Education for Extinction: American Indians and the Boarding School Experience 1875–1928.* Lawrence: Kansas University Press, 1995.

Ahmad, A., V. Sundelin-Wahlsten, M. A. Sofi, J.A. Qahar, and A.-L. von Knorring. "Reliability and Validity of a Child-Specific Cross-Cultural Instrument for Assessing Posttraumatic Stress Disorder." *European Child & Adolescent Psychiatry* 9, no. 4 (2000): 285–294.

Ajdukovic, Marina. "Displaced Adolescents in Croatia: Sources of Stress and Post-traumatic Stress Reaction." *Adolescence* 33, no. 129 (1998): 209–217.

Almqvist, Kjerstin, and Margareta Brandell-Forsberg. "Refugee Children in Sweden: Post-traumatic Stress Disorder in Iranian Preschool Children Exposed to Organized Violence." *Child Abuse and Neglect* 21, no. 4 (1997): 351–366.

Álvarez, María D. "Forests in the Time of Turbulence: Conservation Implications of the Colombian War." In Price, ed., *War and Tropical Forests: Conservation in Areas of Armed Conflict.*

American Psychiatric Association. *Diagnostic and Statistical Manual of Mental Disorders, Fourth Edition, Text Revision (DSM-IV-TR).* Arlington, VA: American Psychiatric Association, 2000.

Anand, K. J. S. "Clinical Importance of Pain and Stress in Preterm Neonates." *Biology of the Neonate* 71 (1998): 1–9.

Argenti-Pillen, Alex. "The Global Flow of Knowledge on War Trauma: The Role of the 'Colombo 7 Culture' in Sri Lanka." American Society of Anthropology, April 2000, at www.asa2000.anthropology.ac.uk/argenti/argenti.html (accessed July 24, 2006).

Austin, Jay E., and Carl E. Bruch, eds. *The Environmental Consequences of War: Legal, Economic, and Scientific Perspectives.* Cambridge: Cambridge University Press, 2000.

Baker, A., and N. Shalhoub-Kevorkian. "Effects of Political and Military Traumas on Children: The Palestinian Case." *Clinical Psychology Review* 19, no. 8 (1999): 935–950.

Bannon, Ian, and Paul Collier, eds. *Natural Resources and Violent Conflict: Options and Actions.* Washington, D.C.: World Bank, 2003.

Becker, David, and Margarita Diaz. "The Social Process and the Transgenerational Transmission of Trauma in Chile." In Danieli, ed., *International Handbook of Multigenerational Legacies of Trauma.*

Bhatia, Michael V. *War and Intervention: Issues for Contemporary Peace Operations.* Bloomfield, CT: Kumarian, 2003.

Biswas, Asit K. "Scientific Assessment of the Long-Term Environmental Consequences of War." In Austin and Bruch, eds., *The Environmental Consequences of War: Legal, Economic, and Scientific Perspectives.*

Booth, John A., and Thomas W. Walker. *Understanding Central America.* Boulder, CO: Westview, 1989.

Brackbill, Robert M., et al. "Surveillance for World Trade Center Disaster Health Effects among Survivors of Collapsed and Damaged Buildings." *Morbidity and Mortality Weekly Report* 55 (April 2006): 1–18.

Brill, Steven. *After: The Rebuilding and Defending of America in the September 12 Era.* New York: Simon & Schuster, 2003.

Brown, Dee. *Bury My Heart at Wounded Knee.* New York: Henry Holt, 1971.

Burkle, Frederick M., Jr., and Eric K Noji. "Health and Politics in the 2003 War with Iraq: Lessons Learned." *Lancet* 364 (October 9, 2004): 1371–1375.

Burns, E. Bradford. *Latin America: A Concise Interpretative History,* 6th ed. Englewood Cliffs, NJ: Prentice Hall, 1994.

Bustreo, Flavia, Eleonora Genovese, Elio Omobono, Herik Axelsson, and Ian Banon. *Improving Child Health in Post-conflict Countries: Can the World Bank Contribute?* Washington, D.C.: World Bank, 2005.

Byrne, Rosemary, and Andrew Shacknove. "The Safe Country Notion in European Asylum Law." *Harvard Human Rights Journal* 9 (Spring 1996): 185–228.

Cassidy, R. C., and G. A. Walco. "Pediatric Pain: Ethical Issues and Ethical Management." *Children's Health Care* 25 (1996): 253–264.

Chemtob, Claude, and Tisha L. Taylor. "Treatment of Traumatized Children." In Yehuda, ed., *Treating Trauma Survivors with PTSD.*

Citizenship and Immigration Canada. *Building on a Strong Foundation for the 21st Century: New Directions for Refugee Policy and Legislation.* Ottawa: CIC, 1999.

Clarke, Richard A. *Against All Enemies.* New York: Free Press, 2004.

Cohen, Roberta, and Francis M. Deng, eds. *The Forsaken People: Case Studies of the Internally Displaced.* Washington, D.C.: Brookings, 1998.

———. *Masses in Flight: The Global Crisis of Internal Displacement.* Washington, D.C.: Brookings Institution Press, 1998.

Cole, David. *Enemy Aliens: Double Standards and Constitutional Freedoms in the War on Terrorism.* New York: New Press, 2003.

Cole, Ester. "Supporting Refugee and Immigrant Children: Building Bridges Programme of the International Children's Institute in Canada and Overseas." *Refuge* 18, no. 6 (2000): 41–45.

Collier, Paul, V.L. Elliott, Håvard Hegre, Anke Hoeffler, Marta Reynal-Querol, and Nicholas Sambanis. *Breaking the Conflict Trap: Civil War and Development Policy.* Washington, D.C.: World Bank, 2003.

Comisión para el Esclarecimiento Histórico. *Guatemala: Memoria del Silencio.* Guatemala City, Guatemala: 1999.

Commission for Historical Clarification. Report of the Commission for Historical Clarification, *Guatemala: Memory of Silence.* Guatemala City, Guatemala: 1999. At shr.aaas.org/guatemala/ceh/report/english/conc2.html (accessed December 23, 2006).

Commission on Post-conflict Reconstruction. *Play to Win: Final Report of the Bi-partisan Commission on Post-conflict Reconstruction.* Washington, D.C.: Center for Strategic and International Studies and the Association of the U.S. Army, 2003.

Congressional Research Service. *Iraq: United Nations and Humanitarian Aid Organizations.* Washington, D.C.: CRS, 2006.

Cooper, Bo. "Procedures for Expedited Removal and Asylum Screening under the Illegal Immigration Reform and Immigrant Responsibility Act of 1996." *Connecticut Law Review* 19 (Summer 1997): 1501–1524.

Cooper, Phillip J., and Claudia María Vargas. *Implementing Sustainable Development: From Global Policy to Local Action.* Lanham, MD: Rowman & Littlefield, 2004.

Cullather, Nick. *Secret History: The CIA's Classified Account of its Operations in Guatemala, 1952–1954.* Stanford, CA: Stanford University Press, 1999.

Dallaire, Roméo, with Brent Beardsley. *Shake Hands with the Devil: The Failure of Humanity in Rwanda.* Toronto: Random House Canada, 2003.

Danieli, Yael, ed. *International Handbook of Multigenerational Legacies of Trauma.* New York: Plenum, 1998.

Degni-Ségui, René, Special Rapporteur of the Commission on Human Rights. *Report on the Situation of Human Rights in Rwanda, Submitted under Paragraph 20 of Resolution S-3/1 of 25 May 1994, E/CN.4/1997/61, January 20, 1997.* New York: United Nations, 1997.

Des Forges, Alison. *Leave None to Tell the Story: Genocide in Rwanda.* New York: Human Rights Watch, 1999. At www.hrw.org/reports/1999/rwanda (accessed December 27, 2006).

Dobbins, James, John G. McGinn, Keith Crane, Seth G. Jones, Rollie Lal, Andrew Rathmell, Rachel Swanger, and Anga Timilsina. *America's Role in Nation-Building from Germany to Iraq.* Santa Monica, CA: RAND Corporation, 2003.

Domini, Antonio, Norah Niland, and Karin Wemester, eds. *Nation-Building Unraveled? Aid, Peace and Justice in Afghanistan.* Bloomfield, CT: Kumarian, 2004.

Duran, Eduardo, Bonnie Duran, Maria Yellow Horse Brave Heart, and Susan Yellow Horse-Davis. "Healing the American Indian Soul Wounds." In Danieli, ed. *International Handbook of Multigenerational Legacies of Trauma.*

Dwernychuk, L. Wayne. "Dioxin Hotspots in Vietnam," *Chemosphere* 60 (March 2005): 998–999.

Edelman, Lucila, Diana Kordon, and Dario Lagos. "Transmission of Trauma: The Argentine Case." In Danieli, ed., *International Handbook of Multigenerational Legacies of Trauma.*

Eisenbruch, Maurice. "From Post-traumatic Stress Disorder to Cultural Bereavement: Diagnosis of Southeast Asian Refugees." *Social Science Medicine* 33, no. 6 (1991): 673–680.

Eltringham, Nigel. "'Invaders Who Have Stolen the Country': The Hamitic Hypothesis, Race and the Rwandan Genocide," *Social Identities* 12, no. 4 (2006): 425–446.

Evans, Lynette, Tony McHugh, Malcolm Hopwood, and Carol Watt. "Chronic Post-traumatic Stress Disorder and Family Functioning of Vietnam Veterans and their Partners." *Australian and New Zealand Journal of Psychiatry* 37 (2003): 765–772.

Felsen, Irit. "Transgenerational Transmission of Effects of the Holocaust: The North American Research Perspective," in Danieli, ed., *International Handbook of Multigenerational Legacies of Trauma.*

Fisiy, Cyprian F. "Of Journeys and Border Crossings: Return of Refugees, Identity, and Reconstruction in Rwanda." *African Studies Review* 41, no. 1 (1998): 17–28.

Fitzpatrick, Joan. "Revitalizing the 1951 Refugee Convention." *Harvard Human Rights Journal* 9 (Spring 1996): 229–253.

Fremont, Wanda P. "Childhood Reactions to Terrorism Induced Trauma." *Psychiatric Times* 22, no. 10 (2005). At www.psychiatrictimes.com/article/showArticle.jhtml? (accessed July 5, 2006).

Fuentes, Juan Alberto. "Violent Conflict and Human Development in Latin America: The Cases of Colombia, El Salvador and Guatemala." Human Development Report 2005, Human Development Report Office, Occasional Paper, United Nations Development Programme, October 2005.

Gagné, Marie-Anik. "The Role of Dependency and Colonialism in Generating Trauma in First Nations Citizens: The James Bay Cree." In Danieli, ed., *International Handbook of Multigenerational Legacies of Trauma.*

Garbarino, James, and Kathleen Kostelny. "The Effects of Political Violence on Palestinian Children's Behavior Problems: A Risk Accumulation Model." *Child Development* 76 (1996): 33–45.

Gavett, Stephen H. "World Trade Center Fine Particulate Matter—Chemistry and Toxic Respiratory Effects: An Overview." *Environment Health Perspectives* 111, no. 7 (2003): 971.

Gerrity, Ellen, Terence M. Keane, and Farris Tuma, eds. *The Mental Health Consequences of Torture.* New York: Kluwer Academic/Plenum, 2001.

Ghobarah, Azem Adam, Paul Huth, and Bruce Russett. "Civil Wars Kill and Maim People—Long After the Shooting Stops." *American Political Science Review* 97 (May 2003): 189–202.

Gleditsch, Kristian Skrede. "A Revised List of Wars Between and within Independent States, 1816–2002." *International Interactions* 30, no. 3 (2004): 231–262.

Goldstein, Richard D., Nina S. Wampler, and Paul H. Wise. "War Experiences and Distress Symptoms of Bosnian Children." *Pediatrics* 100, no. 5 (1997): 873–878.

Goodman, Deborah. "Arab Americans and American Muslims Express Mental Health Needs." *SAMHSA News* 10 (Winter 2002). At www.samhsa.gov/SAMHSA_News/VolumeX_1/article1.htm (accessed July 28, 2006).

Gordon, Michael R., and General Bernard E. Trainor. *Cobra II: The Inside Story of the Invasion and Occupation of Iraq.* New York: Pantheon, 2006.

Gorst-Unsworth, C., and E. Goldenberg. "Psychological Sequelae of Torture and Organized Violence Suffered by Refugees from Iraq." *British Journal of Psychiatry* 172 (1998): 90–94.

Graessner, Sepp, Norbert Gurris, and Christian Pross, eds. *At the Side of Torture Survivors: Treating a Terrible Assault on Human Dignity.* Trans. Jeremiah Michael Riemer. Baltimore and London: Johns Hopkins University Press, 2001.

Hall, Gillete, and Harry Anthony Patrinos, eds. *Indigenous Peoples, Poverty and Human Development in Latin America.* New York: Palgrave Macmillan, 2006.

Hanna, Juliet M. "Implementing the Dublin Convention on Asylum." *Columbia Journal of European Law* 4 (Winter/Spring 1998): 182–191.

Harff, Barbara. "No Lessons Learned from the Holocaust? Assessing Risks of Genocide and Political Mass Murder since 1955." *American Political Science Review* 97 (February 2003): 57–73.

Harris, David. "Flying While Arab: Lessons from the Racial Profiling Controversy." *Civil Rights Journal* 6 (Winter 2002): 8–13.

Hathaway, James C., and R. Alexander Neve. "Making International Refugee Law Relevant Again: A Proposal for Collectivized and Solution-Oriented Protection." *Harvard Human Rights Journal* 10 (Spring 1997): 115–211.

Herman, Judith. *Trauma and Recovery.* New York: Basic, 1997.

House, Col Tamzy J., Lt Col James B. Near Jr., Lt Col. William B. Shields, Maj Ronald J. Celentano, Maj David M. Husband, Maj Ann E. Mercer, Maj James E. Pugh. "Weather as a Force Multiplier: Owning the Weather in 2025." Paper prepared for Air Force 2025. At csat.au.af.mil/2025/volume3/vol3ch15.pdf (accessed August 1, 2006).

Hubbard, Jon, George M. Realmuto, Andrea K. Northwood, and Ann S. Masten. "Comorbidity of Psychiatric Diagnoses with Posttraumatic Stress Disorder in Survivors of Childhood Trauma." *Journal of the American Academy of Child and Adolescent Psychiatry* 34, no. 9 (1995): 1167–1173.

Human Rights Watch. *Darfur Bleeds: Military Attacks on Civilians in Chad.* At www.hrw.org/campaigns/darfur/pdf/darfur_bleeds.pdf (accessed April 6, 2007).

———. *Darfur: Humanitarian Aid under Siege,* May 2006. At hrw.org/backgrounder/africa/sudan0506/darfur0506.pdf (accessed September 8, 2006).

Husain, Syed Arshad, Jyotsna Nair, William Holcomb, John C. Reid, Victor Vargas, and Satish S. Nair. "Stress Reactions of Children and Adolescents in War and Siege Conditions," *American Journal of Psychiatry* 155 (1998): 1718–1719.

Hyman, Ilene, Morton Beiser, and Nhi Vu. "The Mental Health of Refugee Children in Canada." *Refuge* 15, no. 5 (1996): 4–8.

Institute of Medicine. *Veterans and Agent Orange: Health Effects of Herbicides Used in Vietnam.* National Academy of Sciences, 1994.

Internal Displacement Monitoring Centre (IDMC). *Colombia: Government "Peace Process" Cements Injustice for IDPs: A Profile of the Internal Displacement Situation.* Geneva: IDMC, 2006.

———. *Internal Displacement: Global Overview of Trends and Developments 2005.* Geneva: IDMC, 2006.

Iraq Study Group. *Iraq Study Group Report.* New York: Random House, 2006.

Jennings, Ray Salvatore. *The Road Ahead: Lessons in Nation Building from Japan, Germany, and Afghanistan, for Postwar Iraq.* Washington, D.C.: U.S. Institute of Peace, 2003.

Jones, Daniel M., Stuart A. Bremer, and J. David Singer. "Militarized Interstate Disputes, 1816–1992: Rationale, Coding Rules, and Empirical Patterns." *Conflict Management and Peace Science* 15, no. 2 (1996): 163–215.

Kadlec, Lt Col Robert P. "Biological Weapons for Waging Economic Warfare." In Barry R. Schneider and Lawrence E. Grinter, eds., *Battlefield of the Future: 21st Century Warfare Issues*. Maxwell AFB: Air War College Studies in National Security, 1995.

Kapp, Clare. "Humanitarian Community Stunned by Red Cross Attacks in Iraq." *Lancet* 362 (2003): 1461.

Kauffman, Craig. "Transitional Justice in Guatemala: Linking the Past and the Future." Paper prepared for the ISA-South Conference, Miami, Florida, November 3–5, 2005. At www6.miami.edu/maia/ISAS05/papers/Craig_Kauffman.pdf (accessed December 23, 2006).

Kinzie, J. David, J. Boehnlein, and William H. Sack. "The Effects of Massive Trauma on Cambodian Parents." In Danieli, ed., *International Handbook of Multigenerational Legacies of Trauma*.

Kinzie, J. David, William H. Sack, Richard H. Angell, Spero Manson, and Ben Rath. "The Psychiatric Effects of Massive Trauma on Cambodian Children: I. The Children." *Journal of the American Academy of Child Psychiatry* 25, no. 3 (1986): 370–376.

Kitrosser, Heidi. "Secrecy in the Immigration Courts and Beyond: Considering the Right To Know in the Administrative State." *Harvard Civil Rights—Civil Liberties L. Rev.* 39 (Winter 2004): 95–168.

Klain, Eduard. "Intergenerational Aspects of the Conflict in the Former Yugoslavia." In Danieli, ed., *International Handbook of Multigenerational Legacies of Trauma*.

Knippers Black, Jan, ed. *Latin America, Its Problems and its Promise: A Multidisciplinary Introduction*. Boulder, CO: Westview, 1991.

Kritz, Neil. Remarks Presented at the Conference, "Memory and Truth after Genocide: Guatemala." U.S. Holocaust Museum, Washington, D.C., March 21, 2000. At www.ushm.org/conscience/analysis/details/2000-03-21/guatemala/body.htm (accessed April 15, 2007).

Krug, Etienne G., Linda L. Dahlberg, James A. Mercy, Anthony B. Zwi, and Rafael Lozano, eds. *World Report on Violence and Health*. Geneva: World Health Organization, 2002.

Kupelian, Diane, Anie Sanentz Kalayjian, and Alice Kassabian. "The Turkish Genocide of the Armenians: Continuing Effects on Survivors and Their Families Eight Decades after Massive Trauma." In Danieli, ed., *International Handbook of Multigenerational Legacies of Trauma*.

Laor, N., L. Wolmer, and D. V. Cicchetti. "The Comprehensive Assessment of Defense Style: Measuring Defense Mechanisms in Children and Adolescents." *Journal of Nervous and Mental Disease* 189, no. 6 (2001): 360–368.

Lawrence, Carmen. "Mental Illness in Detained Asylum Seekers." *Lancet* 364 (October 2004): 1283–1284.

Leavitt, Lewis A., and Nathan A. Fox, eds. *The Psychological Effects of War and Violence on Children*. Hillsdale, NJ: Erlbaum, 1992.

Legislative Advisory Review Group, Citizenship and Immigration Canada. *Not Just Numbers: A Canadian Framework for Future Immigration*. Ottawa: Citizenship and Immigration Canada, 1998.

Lemke, Douglas. *Regions of War and Peace*. Cambridge: Cambridge University Press, 2002.

Locke, Catherine J., Karen Southwick, Laura McCloskey, and María Eugenia Fernández-Esquer. "The Psychological and Medical Sequelae of War in Central American Refugee Mothers and Children." *Archives of Pediatrics and Adolescent Medicine* 150, no. 8 (1996): 822–828.

Locust, Carol. "The Impact of Differing Belief Systems between Native Americans and Their Rehabilitation Service Providers." *Rehabilitation Education* 9, no. 2 (1995): 205–215.

Loescher, Gil. *Beyond Charity: International Cooperation and the Global Refugee Crisis.* (New York: Oxford University Press, 1993).

March, John S., and Lisa Amaya-Jackson. "Post-traumatic Stress Disorder in Children and Adolescents." *PTSD Research Quarterly* 4, no. 4 (1993): 1–3.

Marenn, Lea. *Salvador's Children: A Song for Survival.* Columbus: Ohio State University Press, 1993.

Marsella, Anthony J., Thomas Bornemann, Solvig Ekblad, and John Orley. *Amidst Peril and Pain: The Mental Health and Well-Being of the World's Refugees.* Washington, D.C.: American Psychological Association, 1994.

Martín-Baró, Ignacio. *Writings for a Liberation Psychology.* Ed. Adrianne Aron and Shawn Corne. Cambridge, MA: Harvard University Press, 1994.

Martz, John D. "Venezuela, Colombia, and Ecuador." In Knippers Black, ed., *Latin America, Its Problems and Promise: A Multidisciplinary Introduction.*

McCloskey, Laura Ann, and Karen Southwick. "Psychosocial Problems in Refugee Children Exposed to War." *Pediatrics* 97, no. 3 (1996): 394–397.

McCullough, David. *Truman.* New York: Simon & Schuster, 1992.

McGrath, P.J., C. Rosmus, C. Canfield, M. Campbell, and A. Hennigar. "Behaviors Caregivers Use to Determine Pain in Non-verbal Cognitively Impaired Individuals." *Developmental Medicine and Child Neurology* 40 (1998): 340–343.

McNamara, Dennis. "The Protection of Refugees and the Responsibilities of States: Engagement or Abdication?" *Harvard Human Rights Journal* 11 (Spring 1998): 355–361.

McNeely, Jeffrey A. "Biodiversity, War, and Tropical Forests." In Price, ed., *War and Tropical Forests: Conservation in Areas of Armed Conflict.*

MedAct. *Collateral Damage: The Health and Environmental Costs of War on Iraq.* London: MedAct, 2002.

Mertus, Julie A. *War's Offensive on Women: The Humanitarian Challenge in Bosnia, Kosovo, and Afghanistan.* Bloomfield, CT: Kumarian, 2000.

Miller, Vachel W., and Friedrich W. Affolter. *Helping Children Outgrow War.* Washington, D.C.: USAID, 2002.

Moreno, Dario. *The Struggle for Peace in Central America.* Gainesville: University Press of Florida, 1994.

Moser, Caroline. "Violence in Colombia: Building Sustainable Peace and Social Capital." In Solimano, ed. *Colombia: Essays on Conflict, Peace, and Development.*

National Commission on Terrorist Attacks upon the United States. *The 9/11 Commission Report: Final Report of the National Commission on Terrorist Attacks upon the United States.* Washington, D.C.: U.S. Government Printing Office, 2004.

National Institute for Mental Health. *Helping Children and Adolescents Cope with Violence and Disasters.* National Institute of Medicine. At www.nimh.nih.gov/publicat/violence.cfm (accessed April 22, 2002).

National Security Archive. Electronic Briefing Book No. 15, "Guatemala Death Squad Diaries: Internal Military Log Reveals Fate of 183 'Disappeared.'" At www.gwu.edu/~nsarchiv/NSAEBB/NSAEBB15/press.html (accessed December 22, 2006).

Office of the Inspector General, U.S. Department of Justice. *The September 11 Detainees: A Review of the Treatment of Aliens Held on Immigration Charges in Connection with the Investigation of the September 11 Attacks.* Washington, D.C.: U.S. Department of Justice, 2003. At www.usdoj.gov/oig/special/03_06/full.pdf (accessed November 1, 2003).

Oficina de Derechos Humanos del Arzobispado de Guatemala (ODHAG). *Guatemala Nunca Más, Proyecto de Recuperación de la Memoria Histórica (REMHI).* Guatemala City, Guatemala: 1998.

——. *Situación de la Niñez en Guatemala.* Guatemala City, Guatemala: 2004.

Omar, Samira A. S., Ernest Briskey, Raafat Misak, and Adel A. S. O. Asem. "The Gulf War Impact on the Terrestrial Environment of Kuwait: An Overview." In Austin and Bruch, eds., *The Environmental Consequences of War: Legal, Economic, and Scientific Perspectives.*

O'Neill, Bard E. *Insurgency and Terrorism: Inside Modern Revolutionary Warfare.* Dulles, VA: Brassey's, 1990.

Perera, Victor. *Unfinished Conquest: The Guatemalan Tragedy.* Berkeley: University of California Press, 1993.

Pérez-Brignioli, Héctor. *A Brief History of Central America.* Trans. Ricardo B. Sawrey and Susana Stettri de Sawrey. Berkeley: University of California Press, 1989.

Plumptre, Andrew J. "Lessons Learned from On-the-Ground Conservation in Rwanda and the Democratic Republic of the Congo." In Price, ed., *War and Tropical Forests: Conservation in Areas of Armed Conflict.*

Price, A.R.G., N. Downing, S. W. Fowler, J. T. Hardy, M. Le Tissier, C. P. Mathews, J. M. McGlade, P. A. H. Medley, B. Oregioni, J. W. Readman, C. M. Roberts, and T. J. Wrathall. *The 1991 Gulf War: Environmental Assessments of IUCN and Collaborators.* Gland, Switzerland: International Union for the Conservation of Nature, 1994.

Price, Steven V., ed. *War and Tropical Forests: Conservation in Areas of Armed Conflict.* New York: Haworth, 2003.

Programa de las Naciones Unidas para el Desarrollo (PNUD). *Guatemala: Desarrollo Humano y ruralidad: Compendio estadístico.* Guatemala City, Guatemala: Editoral Serviprensa, 2004.

Raphael, Beverley, Pat Swan, and Nada Martinek. "Intergenerational Aspects of Trauma for Australian Aboriginal People." In Danieli, ed. *International Handbook of Multigenerational Legacies of Trauma.*

Regensburg, Kenneth. "Refugee Law Reconsidered: Reconciling Humanitarian Objectives with the Protectionist Agendas of Western Europe and the United States." *Cornell International Law Journal* 29 (1996): 225–261.

Rehn, Elisabeth, and Ellen Johnson Sirleaf. *Women, War and Peace: The Independent Experts' Assessment on the Impact of Armed Conflict on Women and Women's Role in Peace-Building.* New York: United Nations Development Fund for Women [UNIFEM], 2002.

Report of the Environmental Conference on Cambodia, Laos and Vietnam. *Long-Term Consequences of the Vietnam War: Ecosystems.* Stockholm: Föreningen Levande Framtid, 2002. At www.nnn.se/vietnam/ecology.pdf (accessed August 18, 2006).

Rhee, Robert J. "Terrorism Risk in a Post-9/11 Economy: The Convergence of Capital Markets, Insurance, and Government Action." *Arizona State Law Journal* 37 (Summer 2005): 435–530.

Ricks, Thomas E. *Fiasco: The American Military Adventure in Iraq.* New York: Penguin, 2006.

Rosenheck, Robert, and Alan Fontana. "Transgenerational Effects of Abusive Violence on the Children of Vietnam Combat Veterans." *Journal of Traumatic Stress* 11 (1998): 731–742.

Sack, William H., Richard H. Angell, J. David Kinzie, and Ben Rath. "The Psychiatric Effects of Massive Trauma on Cambodian Children: II. The Family, Home, and the School." *Journal of the American Academy of Child Psychiatry* 25, no. 3 (1986): 377–383.

Sack, William H., Gregory N. Clarke, and John R. Seeley. "Posttraumatic Stress Disorder across Two Generations." *Journal of the American Academy of Child and Adolescent Psychiatry* 34, no. 9 (1995): 1160–1166.

———. "Multiple Forms of Stress in Cambodian Adolescent Refugees." *Child Development* 67 (1996): 107–116.

Sack, William H., John R. Seeley, and Gregory N. Clarke. "Does PTSD Transcend Cultural Barriers? A Study from the Khmer Adolescent Refugee Project." *Journal of the American Academy of Child and Adolescent Psychiatry* 36, no. 1 (1997): 49–54.

Sack, William H., John R. Seeley, Chanrithy Him, and Gregory N. Clarke. "Psychometric Properties of the Impact of Events Scale in Traumatized Cambodian Refugee Youth." *Personality and Individual Differences* 25, no. 1 (1998): 57–67.

Sandel, Michael J. *Democracy's Discontent.* Cambridge, MA: Harvard University Press, 1996.

Schuck, Peter H. *Agent Orange on Trial.* Cambridge: Harvard University Press, 1986.

Schuster, M.A., et al. "A National Survey of Stress Reactions after the September 11, 2001, Terrorist Attacks." *New England Journal of Medicine* 345, no. 20 (2001): 1507–1512.

Schwerin, Karl H. "The Indian Populations of Latin America." In Knippers Black, ed., *Latin America, Its Problems and its Promise: A Multidisciplinary Introduction.*

Simpson, Michael A. "The Second Bullet: Transgenerational Impact of the Trauma of Conflict within a South African and World Context." In Danieli, ed., *International Handbook of Multigenerational Legacies of Trauma.*

Sistemas de Naciones Unidas en Guatemala. *Guatemala: Desarrollo Humano, mujeres y salud.* Guatemala City, Guatemala: SNU, 2002.

———. *Guatemala: Una agenda para el desarrollo humano 2003.* Guatemala City, Guatemala: SNU, 2003.

Skidmore, Thomas E., and Peter H. Smith. *Modern Latin America,* 6th ed. New York: Oxford University Press, 2005.

Solimano, Andrés, ed. *Colombia: Essays on Conflict, Peace, and Development.* Washington, D.C.: World Bank, 2000.

Solomon, Zahava. "Transgenerational Effects of the Holocaust: The Israeli Research Perspective." In Danieli, ed. *International Handbook of Multigenerational Legacies of Trauma*.

Special Inspector General for Iraq Reconstruction. *Report to Congress: October 20, 2005*. At www.sigir.mil/reports/quarterlyreports/Oct05/October_2005_report.pdf (accessed December 26, 2006).

Stavenhagen, Rodolfo. *Report of the Special Rapporteur on the Situation of Human Rights and Fundamental Freedoms of Indigenous People, Addendum: Mission to Colombia*. New York: United Nations Commission on Human Rights, 2004.

Teicher, Martin H. "Scars that Won't Heal: The Neurobiology of Child Abuse." *Scientific American* (March 2002): 68–75.

Touraine, Alain. "Latin America: From Populism toward Social Democracy." In Vellinga, ed., *Social Democracy in Latin America: Prospects for Change*.

Tucker, Richard P., and Edmund Russell, eds. *Natural Enemy, Natural Ally: Toward an Environmental History of War*. Corvallis: Oregon State University Press, 2004.

Tzu, Sun. *The Art of War*. Trans. and with a historical introduction by Ralph D. Dawyer. Boulder, CO: Westview, 1994.

United Nations. *Agenda 21*. New York: United Nations, 1992.

——. *Copenhagen Declaration and Programme of Action*. New York: United Nations, 1995.

——. *Report of the International Commission of Inquiry on Darfur Pursuant to Security Council Resolution 1564 of 18 September 2004*. Geneva: United Nations, 2005.

——. *Report of the World Summit on Sustainable Development, Johannesburg, South Africa, 26 August–4 September 2002*. New York: United Nations, 2002.

United Nations Development Programme (UNDP). *Human Development Report Bosnia Herzegovina 2000 Youth*. Sarajevo: UNDP, 2000.

——. *Desarrollo Humano y Ruralidad: Compendio estadístico 2004—Guatemala*. Guatemala, Editorial Serviprensa S.A., December 2004.

——. *El Conflicto, Callejón sin Salida, Informe Nacional de Desarrollo Humano para Colombia – 2003*. Bogotá: UNDP 2003.

——. *Kosovo Early Warning Report #1, May–August 2002*. Pristina: UNDP, 2002.

——. *Rwanda: Human Development Report 1999*. Kigali: UNDP, 1999.

——. *Ten Years On: Helping Rebuild a Nation, The United Nations in Rwanda*. Kigali: UNDP, 2004.

United Nations Development Programme (UNDP), Afghanistan. *Afghanistan Human Development Report: Security with a Human Face 2004*. New York: UNDP, 2004.

United Nations Environment Programme (UNEP). *Afghanistan: Post-conflict Environmental Assessment* Nairobi: UNEP, 2003.

——. *Desk Study on the Environment in Iraq*. Nairobi: UNEP, 2003.

——. *Environment in Iraq*. Geneva: UNEP, 2003.

——. *Global Environment Outlook Update 2006*. Nairobi: UNEP, 2006.

——. "Iraqi Marshlands: On the road to recovery." At www.unep.org/Documents .Multilingual/Default.asp?DocumentID=449&ArticleID=4902&l=en (accessed December 26, 2006).

——. *The Mesopotamian Marshlands: Demise of an Ecosystem*. Nairobi: UNEP, 2001.

——. *Post-conflict Environmental Assessment—Albania*. Nairobi: UNEP, 2000.

United Nations Environment Programme, Regional Office for West Asia. *A Rapid Assessment of the Iraq-Kuwait Conflict on Terrestrial Ecosystems.* Bahrain: UNEP, 1991.

United Nations Environment Programme and United Nations Centre for Human Settlements (Habitat). *The Kosovo Conflict: Consequences for the Environment and Human Settlements.* New York: UNEP and Habitat, 1999.

United Nations Food and Agriculture Organization. *The State of Food Insecurity in the World 2003.* Rome: FAO, 2003.

United Nations High Commissioner for Human Rights. *Access to Justice for Victims of Sexual Violence,* July 29, 2005. At www.ohchr.org/english/countries/docs/darfur 29july05_En.pdf (accessed December 26, 2006).

———. *Colombia: UNHCR's Protection and Assistance Programme for IDPs and Refugees.* New York: UNHCR, 2004.

———. *International Protection Considerations Regarding Colombian Asylum-Seekers and Refugees.* Geneva: UNHCR, 2005.

———. *State of the World's Refugees 2006.* New York: UNHCR, 2006.

United Nations High Commissioner for Human Rights, Engineering and Environmental Sciences Section. *Refugee Operations and Environmental Management.* At www.unhcr.org/protect/PROTECTION/3b03b2754.pdf (accessed December 27, 2006).

United Nations High Commissioner for Human Rights in cooperation with the United Nations Mission in the Sudan. *Deepening Crisis in Darfur Two Months after the Darfur Peace Agreement: An Assessment.* New York: UNHCR, 2006.

United Nations Independent Inquiry Committee into the United Nations Oil-for-Food Programme. *The Management of the United Nations Oil-for-Food Programme, Volume I Report of the Committee.* New York: Independent Inquiry Committee, 2005. At www.iic-offp.org (accessed September 17, 2006).

United Nations Office for the Coordination of Humanitarian Affairs. *Guiding Principles on Internal Displacement,* 2nd ed. New York: United Nations, 2004.

United Nations and World Bank. *Joint Iraq Needs Assessment.* New York: United Nations and World Bank, 2003.

UNICEF, *State of the World's Children 2005: Children under Threat.* New York: UNICEF, 2004.

U.S. Commission on International Religious Freedom. *Asylum Seekers in Expedited Removal: A Study Authorized by Section 605 of the International Religious Freedom Act of 1998.* Washington, D.C.: United States Commission on International Religious Freedom, 2005.

U.S. Congress. Joint Hearings Before the House Select Committee to Investigate Covert Arms Transactions with Iran and the Senate Select Committee on Secret Military Assistance to Iran and the Nicaraguan Opposition. *Iran-Contra Investigation.* 100th Cong., 1st Sess. (1987).

U.S. Department of State. *Erasing History: Ethnic Cleansing in Kosovo, May 1999.* At www.state.gov/www/regions/eur/rpt_9905_ethnic_ksvo_2.html (accessed December 8, 2006).

———. *Future of Iraq Project Briefing,* November 1, 2002 (Declassified), 6. At www.gwu.edu/~nsarchiv/NSAEBB/NSAEBB163/iraq-state-02.pdf (accessed December 26, 2006).

——. Office of the Coordinator for Counterterrorism. *Country Reports on Terrorism 2005*. Washington, D.C.: Department of State, 2006.

U.S. Government Accountability Office. *Community Investment: Los Angeles's Use of a Community Development Block Grant Exemption*. Washington, D.C.: GAO, 2002.

——. *Critical Infrastructure Protection: Department of Homeland Security Faces Challenges in Fulfilling Cybersecurity Responsibilities*. Washington, D.C.: GAO, 2005.

——. *Post-traumatic Stress Disorder: DOD Needs to Identify the Factors Its Providers Use to Make Mental Health Evaluation Referrals for Servicemembers*. Washington, D.C.: GAO, 2006.

——. *September 11: Overview of Federal Disaster Assistance to the New York City Area*. Washington, D.C.: GAO, 2003.

——. *United Nations Oil for Food Program Audits*. Washington, D.C.: GAO, 2005.

——. *Rebuilding Iraq: Actions Needed to Improve Use of Private Security Providers*. Washington, D.C.: GAO, 2005.

——. *Recent Estimates of Fiscal Impact of 2001 Terrorist Attack on New York*. Washington, D.C.: GAO, 2005.

——. *Review of Studies of the Economic Impact of the September 11, 2001, Terrorist Attacks on the World Trade Center*. Washington, D.C.: GAO, 2002.

——. *September 11: Health Effects in the Aftermath of the World Trade Center Attack*. Washington, D.C.: GAO, 2004.

——. *September 11: Monitoring of World Trade Center Health Effects Had Progressed, but Not for Federal Responders*. Washington, D.C.: GAO, 2005.

U.S. House of Representatives. Hearing before the Subcommittee on Immigration, Refugees, and International Law of the Committee on the Judiciary. *Central American Asylum-Seekers*. 101st Cong., 1st Sess. (1989).

U.S. Senate. Committee on Health, Education, Labor, and Pensions. *Children of September 11: The Need for Mental Health Services*. 107th Cong., 2nd Sess. (2002).

——. Committee on the Judiciary. *U.S. Immigration Law and Policy: 1952–1986*. 100th Cong., 1st Sess. (1987).

——. Hearing Before the Subcommittee on Immigration and Refugee Affairs of the Committee on the Judiciary. *Central American Migration to the United States*. 101st Cong., 1st Sess. (1989).

——. Intelligence Committee. "Postwar Findings About Iraq's WMD Programs and Links to Terrorism and How They Compare with Prewar Assessments." At intelligence .senate.gov/phaseiiaccuracy.pdf (accessed September 16, 2006).

Vargas, Claudia María. "Cultural Mediation for Refugee Children: A Comparative Derived Model." *Journal of Refugee Studies* 12, no. 3 (1999): 284–306.

——. "Women in Central America." In Nelly P. Stromquist, ed. *Women in the Third World: An Encyclopedia of Contemporary Issues*. New York, Garland, 1998.

Vargas, Claudia María, Deborah O'Rourke, and Mahshid Esfandiari. "Complementary Therapies for Treating Survivors of Torture." *Refuge* 22, no. 1 (2004): 129–137.

——. "A Triangle of Hope for Survivors: Integrating Psychotherapy and Bodywork for Chronic Pain and Cultural Loss." *Rehabilitation Review* 24, no. 10 (2004): 18–21.

Vellinga, Menno, ed. *Social Democracy in Latin America: Prospects for Change*. Boulder, CO: Westview, 1993.

Villiers, Janice D. "Closed Borders, Closed Ports: The Plight of Haitians Seeking Political Asylum in the United States." *Brooklyn Law Review* 60 (Fall 1994): 841–901.

von Clausewitz, Carl. *On War*. Ed. and trans. Michael Howard and Peter Paret. New York: Alfred A. Knopf, 1976, 1993.

Walsh, Lawrence E. *Iran-Contra: The Final Report of the Independent Counsel*. New York: Random House, 1993.

Weine, Stevan M., Dolores Vojvoda, Daniel Becker, Thomas H. McGlashan, Emir Hodzic, Dori Laub, Leslie Hyman, Marie Sawyer, and Steven Lazrove. "PTSD Symptoms in Bosnian Refugees 1 Year after Resettlement in the United States." *American Journal of Psychiatry* 155, no. 4 (1998): 562–564.

Westing, Arthur H. "Environmental Warfare." *Environmental Law* 15 (Summer 1985): 645–666.

Wilkins, David E. *American Indian Politics and the American Political System*. Lanham, MD: Rowman & Littlefield, 2002.

Winer, Jonathan M., and Trifin J. Roule. "Follow the Money: The Finance of Illicit Resource Extraction." In Bannon and Collier, eds., *Natural Resources and Violent Conflict: Options and Actions*.

Wing, Adrien Katherine, and Mark Richard Johnson. "The Promise of a Post-genocide Constitution: Healing Rwandan Spirit Injuries." *Michigan Journal of Race & Law* 7 (Spring 200): 247–315.

Winter, Roger. *Terms of Refuge: The Indochinese Exodus and the International Response*. New York: Zed, 1998.

Woodward, Bob. *State of Denial: Bush at War, Part III*. New York: Simon & Schuster, 2006.

World Bank. *Attacking Poverty: World Development Report 2000/2001*. Washington, D.C.: World Bank, 2001.

———. *Breaking the Conflict Trap: Civil War and Development Policy*. Washington, D.C.: World Bank and Oxford University Press, 2003.

———. *The Economic Development of Iraq: Report of a Mission Organized by the International Bank for Reconstruction and Development at the Request of the Government of Iraq*. Washington, D.C.: World Bank, 1952.

———. *Sustainable Development in a Dynamic World: World Development Report 2003*. Washington, D.C.: World Bank, 2003.

———. *World Development Report 1997: The State in a Changing World*. Washington, D.C.: World Bank, 1997.

———. *World Development Report 2006: Equity and Development*. New York: Oxford University Press, 2005.

World Bank and United Nations. *United Nations/World Bank Joint Iraq Needs Assessment*. Washington, D.C., and New York: UN and World Bank, 2003.

World Commission on Environment and Development. *Our Common Future*. New York: Oxford University Press, 1987.

World Health Organization. *Working Together for Health: The World Health Report 2006*. Geneva: WHO, 2006.

Yehuda, Rachel, ed. *Treating Trauma Survivors with PTSD*. Arlington, VA: American Psychiatric Publishing, 2002.

Zlotnick, Caron, Mark Zimmerman, Barbara A. Wolfsdorf, and Jill I. Mattia. "Gender Differences in Patients with Posttraumatic Stress Disorder in a General Psychiatric Practice," *American Journal of Psychiatry* 158, no. 11 (2001): 1923–1925.

CASES CITED

ACLU v. Ashcroft, 334 F. Supp. 2d 471 (SDNY 2004).

American Baptist Churches v. Thornburgh, 760 F.Supp. 796 (NDCA 1991).

Benslimane v. Gonzales, 430 F.3d 828 (7th Cir. 2005)

Brown v. Board of Education of Topeka, Kansas, 347 U.S. 483 (1954).

Cetacean Community v. Bush, 386 F.3d 1169 (9th Cir. 2004).

Charkaouri v. Canada (Citizenship and Immigration), 2007 SCC 9 (2007).

Doe v. Gonzales, 386 F. Supp. 2d 66 (DCT 2005)

Doe I v. Gonzales, 449 F.3d 415 (2nd Cir. 2006).

Environmental Defense Fund v. EPA, 489 F.2d 1247 (D.C. Cir. 1973).

Ex Parte Endo, 323 U.S. 283 (1944).

Ex Parte Quirin, 317 U.S. 1 (1942).

Fleming v. Mohawk Wrecking & Lumber, 441 U.S. 111 (1947).

Gailius v. Immigration and Naturalization Service, 147 F.3d 34 (1st Cir. 1998).

Hamdan v. Rumsfeld, 165 L. Ed. 2d 723 (2006).

Hepting v. AT&T Corporation, No C-06-672 VRW ORDER, July 20, 2006,

Hirabayashi v. United States, 320 U.S. 81 (1943)

Hirabayashi v. United States, 828 F.2d 591 (9th Cir. 1987).

In re Agent Orange Product Liability Litigation, 2005 U.S. Dist. LEXIS 3644 (SDNY 2005).

In re All Matters Submitted to the Foreign Intelligence Surveillance Court, 218 F. Supp. 2d 611 (Foreign Intell. Surveillance Ct. 2002).

In re Sealed Case No. 02-001, 310 F.3d 717 (Foreign Intell. Surveillance Ct. Rev. 2002).

In the matter of Jaballah, 2003 A.C.W.S.J. LEXIS 4031 (Federal Court Trial Division, Toronto 2003).

Korematsu v. United States, 323 U.S. 214 (1944).

Korematsu v. United States, 584 F. Supp. 1406 (NDCA 1984).

Natural Resources Defense Council v. Evans, 364 F. Supp. 2d 1083 (NDCA 2003).

Natural Resources Defense Council v. National Marine Fisheries Service, 409 F. Supp. 2d 379 (SDNY 2006).

Olin Corporation v. Insurance Company of North Carolina, 966 F.2d 718, 720 (2nd Cir. 1992).

Osorio v. Immigration and Naturalization Service, 18 F.3d 1017 (2nd Cir. 1994).

Prosecutor v. Radislav Krstic, Case No. IT-98-33-T. At www.un.org/icty/Supplement/supp27-e/krstic.htm (accessed September 4, 2006).

Prosecutor v. Kunarac, et al, IT-96-23-T& IT-96-23/1-T, 22. At www.un.org/icty/kunarac/trialc2/judgement/kun-tj010222e.pdf (accessed September 10, 2006). Affm'd by the Appeals Chamber, *Prosecutor v. Kunarac, et al.*, 12 June 2002. At www.un.org/icty/kunarac/appeal/judgement/kun-aj020612e.pdf (accessed September 10, 2006).

Qun Wang v. Attorney General, 423 F.3d 260, 270 (3rd Cir. 2005).

United States v. Allied Oil Corp., 341 U.S. 1, (1951).

United States v. Olin Corporation, Civil Action No. CV80-PT-5300-NE, Consent Decree, May 31, 1983.

United States v. Olin Corporation, 606 F. Supp. 1301 (NDAL 1985).

United States v Reynolds, 345 US 1 (1953).

United States v. United Mineworkers, 330 U.S. 258, 304 (1947).

United States Grain Corporation v. Phillips, 261 U.S. 106 (1923).

Winters v. Legal Services Society, File No. 1999 Can. Sup. Ct. LEXIS 57, (1999).

Woods v. Cloyd W. Miller, 333 U.S. 138 (1948).

Index

About the Authors

Phillip J. Cooper is professor of public administration at the Mark O. Hatfield School of Government at Portland State University. He received his PhD from the Maxwell School of Citizenship and Public Affairs of Syracuse University. Before coming to Oregon, he was the Gund Professor of Liberal Arts in the Department of Political Science at the University of Vermont. He is a fellow of the National Academy of Public Administration and was the first recipient of the Charles Levine Award for Excellence in Public Administration Scholarship, Teaching, and Public Service, given by the National Association of Schools of Public Affairs and Administration and the American Society for Public Administration. He is the author of numerous books and articles on sustainable development, public administration, administrative law, constitutional law, the Supreme Court, refugee issues, and law and public policy. His books include, among others, *Implementing Sustainable Development: From Global Policy to Local Action* (coauthor), *By Order of the President: The Use and Abuse of Executive Direct Action, Governing By Contract, Battles on the Bench, Implementing Sustainable Development: Experiences in Sustainable Development Administration* (coeditor), *Hard Judicial Choices*, and *Public Law and Public Administration*, now in its fourth edition.

Claudia María Vargas is associate professor of pediatrics at the Oregon Health & Science University and associate professor of public administration at the Mark O. Hatfield School of Government at Portland State University. Before coming to Portland, she was director of intercultural programs at the Vermont Interdisciplinary Leadership Education for Health Professionals Program and research assistant professor of pediatrics at the University of Vermont College of Medicine. Professor Vargas earned her doctorate from the University of Southern California. She has taught internationally in Spain and Latin America, including field experience in comparative health administration. Her work has emphasized interdisciplinary and multi-disciplinary approaches. She is the author of numerous books and articles on sustainable development, refugee service delivery, women, disability, and health, and complementary therapies for survivors of torture. Her publications include *Implementing Sustainable Development: From Global Policy to Local Action* (coauthor), *Caring for Children with Neurodevelopmental Disabilities and their Families: An Innovative Approach to Interdisciplinary Practice* (coeditor), *Implementing Sustainable Development Administration: Experiences in Sustainable Development Administration* (coeditor), *Bridging Solitudes: Partnership Challenges in Canadian Refugee Service Delivery* (editor), "Community Development and Micro-Enterprises: Fostering Sustainable Development," "Sustainable Development Education: Averting or Mitigating Cultural Collision," and "Women in Sustainable Development: Empowerment through Partnerships for Healthy Living."

The authors have worked together on sustainable development research for many years, serving as consultants to the United Nations, the World Bank, and a number of countries. They have facilitated international programs on sustainable development implementation, or were lead presenters for conferences involving participants from many countries.